Reflections

*The Workers, the Gospel and
the Nameless House Sect*

Compiled by:
Daurelle Chapman

RESEARCH AND INFORMATION SERVICES
BEND, OREGON
1993

Research and Information Services
1972 Northeast Third Street, #130
Bend, Oregon 97701
U.S.A.

Published in the United States by
Research and Information Services

Library of Congress Catalog Card Number: 93-87206

ISBN 0-9639419-1-7

Printed in the United States of America by
BookCrafters
Chelsea, Michigan

Table of Contents

Table of Contents

Introduction

Dear Reader,

The experiences contained herein are real and have happened to real people. Although there are many hundreds, perhaps many thousands, who could tell of similar experiences with this group which calls itself "The Truth," this first volume contains just 57 personal accounts from around the world, plus the correspondence of ex-"friends" with workers or "friends."

As you study their writings, try to understand their pain as well as their joy. Some of you will identify with their experiences; some will not. Not everyone has left the group for the same reasons. Some are now in churches, and some now have a relationship with God outside of organized religions. A few don't want to have anything to do with religion or God. Some have felt willing to include their names. Some are not able to do this yet—either because of fear of harassment or out of the very real danger that by speaking up, they will be shunned by family and friends who are still in the group. Only one who has left a cult-like group can understand the trauma which must be overcome in order to lead a life of freedom—free to think for themselves without feelings of condemnation. Most come from extended families who have been a part of this fellowship for generations; thus there is the real threat of the break-up of families when one gathers the courage to be open about their new-found freedom.

Reflections

Here are a few thoughts from the heart:

- Rejection hurts. All of us grieve over lost friends and close relationships. This means we are sometimes angry, and often incredibly sad. We pray that we will not become bitter.
- Forgiveness cleanses. May we have the grace of God to forgive as we have been forgiven.
- Love heals. Some of us have now had a first (recognizable) taste of God's unconditional love—unfettered by man's traditions. May we extend that love to others.
- Patience waits. We have been through such trials. We need patience to wait for the return of emotional strength and clear thinking skills. It takes courage to resist compromising our determination to stand for truth.

We are from many walks of life, but we share a heritage common to those who have come out of an exclusive religious group. We have often felt very alone in our struggles, because we have been conditioned to trust no "outsider." We have been fearful of many things, yet we have pressed on in our desire to know truth. We open our lives on the following pages in a desire to encourage any others who may be struggling with similar issues.

If you are still attending meetings, please understand that what we have shared is not meant to offend. There are many reasons why we have written, not the least one of which is love for others. You may accuse us of anger, unwillingness, or any number of negative characteristics, but please don't make the mistake of judging everyone the same, and look for the love alongside the anger; the willingness to submit to God next to what you may perceive as unwillingness.

I'm glad that God, in His unconditional love, looks upon each one of us as unique individuals and offers the gift of His righteousness to us all. *"For God so loved the world that He gave His only begotten Son that whosoever believeth in Him should not perish, but have everlasting life."* John 3:16.

Whether you are associated with this "fellowship," or know some who are or have been, our wish is to encourage you to become more knowledgeable about this little-known sect. If you are searching for answers from within the group, we hope that you will keep seeking real truth, and not readily accept their claim to be the "Truth," without allowing yourself to think clearly as you carefully examine the claims that are made.

Daurelle Chapman

Chapter One

The Two-by-Twos

This book contains individual accounts of experiences related to a little-known, world-wide religious group. For the benefit of those outside this sect who may be unfamiliar with this group's terminology and doctrine, this first chapter describes terms and beliefs you will encounter throughout the remainder of the book.

The members of this group claim no name, but among themselves refer to their group as the "Truth," or the "Friends" (not to be confused with the Quakers). Others have called them by various names such as the "Two-by-Twos," and the "Way," (not to be confused with The Way, International—a different group). Their ministers have officially registered the group with various government agencies under the names of "the Christian Conventions" in the U.S.A., "the United Christian Conventions of Australia" in Australia, "The Testimony of Jesus" in the United Kingdom, "The United Christian Conventions of New Zealand" in New Zealand, and various other names in other countries. They are sometimes confused with the "Cooneyites" with whom they once were united, though the Cooneyites are now the smaller of the two sects.

The members usually refer to themselves as the "friends," or the "saints." Their ministers are referred to as "workers." They sometimes use the terms "spiritual Israel" or the "Kingdom" to refer to those who follow their belief system. They use the King James Bible exclusively in English speaking countries and use only their own compilation of hymns, entitled *Hymns Old and New,* in their gatherings.

The group opposes all church buildings, viewing any such structure as conclusive evidence of a false church. *Friends* are assigned to Sunday, Wednesday, and Union fellowship "meetings," which are always held in designated homes. Visitors may attend "Gospel Meetings" or "Services" held in rented halls or other convenient buildings. "Conventions" are large, annual, regional gatherings and are usually held in rural areas in buildings specially constructed and maintained for this purpose.

Their services consist of: (1) Sunday and midweek: hymn singing (acapella), prayers, testimonies; (2) Gospel Meetings: hymns (often with piano accompaniment), prayer and preaching by the *workers;* (3) "Union Meetings:" larger version of #1 usually held once a month; (4) "Convention:" extended preaching sessions, testimony, eat and sleeping over several days; and (5) "Special Meeting:" a one day version of *Conventions.*

Communion is served weekly at Sunday morning *meetings* and reserved for those baptized into their group by the *workers.* Baptism is by complete immersion. The member must conform to standards set by the *workers* in their "field" (local area) before baptism will be granted.

The *workers* state that they believe and follow the teachings of the New Testament and refuse to publish any statement of belief. The importance of a celibate, unsalaried, homeless, itinerant ministry and *meetings* in the home are the fundamental teachings which are stressed. This appears to be the sum of the "gospel message" which they proclaim.

The following represent some areas of doctrine in which this group differs from most Christian beliefs:

The *workers* teach that salvation can only be acquired through hearing and "professing" through one of their *workers*.

They do not believe that Jesus and the Father are one and the same God. The *workers* teach that Jesus was a god-like human on whom the "Christ Spirit" settled, and who gave the world a pattern of perfect ministry. Jesus is sometimes referred to as "divine," "god the son," or "a god"—though they do not mean by this that Jesus is in any sense God, in the way the Father is called God.

It has been preached that the "Word made flesh" of John 1:1, 14 refers to the *workers* themselves.

They have taught, and most continue to assert, that the group is a direct, historical continuation of the "New Testament Church," having no earthly founder.

Godhood is not ascribed to the Holy Spirit. It is believed that "the Spirit" is an attitude, emotional feeling, or force originating from God.

The propitiatory sacrifice of Jesus on the cross is not enough to produce salvation, according to the *workers*. Instead they hold that one must continue faithfully in their belief system through self effort, self denial, and unquestioning submission and obedience to their "shepherds" until death.

It is believed that Jesus died to save only those who follow their ministers, and that His "pattern life" and "pattern ministry" were the primary goal of His earthly sojourn.

They claim to have preached in every country of the world. Membership is estimated to number up to 600,000 worldwide. In 1987-88, Canada listed

226 *workers* and the U.S.A. listed 845 (of which 63% were female, 37% male).

They claim no organization and no headquarters. However, this church is run by a group of senior "Head Workers" (known also as "Overseers"). There are various geographic areas each of which is controlled by a male *Head worker* who assigns *fields* to the *workers* under his authority. "Elders," who have *meetings* in their homes, are appointed by the *workers*. *Workers* and *Head workers* hold regional, national and international "Workers Meetings."

For further information regarding the group, consult the Source List in the back of this book.

Chapter Two

Howard and Elsie Barnard:
The Truth Shall Set You Free

We came out of the so-called Truth in March 1992. We are glad that by the Holy Spirit's guidance we were delivered from the *Secret Sect* cult. We are happy to be worshipping with fellow believers in the Mennonite Church here in Aberdeen.

Wayne Harris told Howard one time after he had quit taking part in mtgs., that he needed to get back in and take part and take the emblems for strength. We have never read that we take them for strength. We should do this in remembrance of what Christ did for us on the cross, died and rose again in His resurrection.

Then in February 1992 Rosetha Newman prayed before taking emblems that those who needed them should partake and those that didn't need them shouldn't partake. Here too, we don't partake for our need.

Rosetha Newman and Bonnie Dirks visited us at the time we quit going to mtgs. They suggested that Howard could go back to the Mennonite Church and I should come to meetings. We chose to go together to worship and praise our Lord and Saviour and God our Father. For I promised Howard at the time of our engagement that I always wanted to go where he went as Ruth promised Naomi in Ruth 1:16 "for whither thou goest, I will go; and where thou lodgest I will lodge: thy people shall be my people, and thy God my God:" We wanted to stay united.

We learned more about the Secret Sect since reading the books and appreciate them. Now the Truth of God has set us free.

Our Love in Christ, because of His Grace.

Address:
Howard and Elsie Barnard
1540 S. 2700 W.
Aberdeen, ID 83210

Chapter Three

Katherine J. Bates
"I Will Restore to You the Years that the Locust Hath Eaten" ----Joel 2:25.

It was 1960 when my parents first started taking us to church. At least that's the first I can remember. I remember hearing a preacher talk about one being left and the other being taken, and it made me start to wonder if I would be left. One day when I was playing in my room, I heard my mother scream, "Come quick." I ran to the living room to find the TV playing and my sister gone. In the kitchen the pork chops were frying and my father was gone. I took off in a dead-heated run to the backyard to find a sheet half hanging and my mother gone. I dropped to my knees and began to cry begging Jesus not to leave me behind. All at once I felt a hand on my shoulder. I knew at once it was Jesus. He had come to take me with him. As I looked up I saw my Mother wondering why I was crying. That began my search for Religion.

We attended the Nazarene church for many years and I became very familiar with all their do's and don'ts. When I was 18 I finally gave my heart to Jesus. Like many teens I was in and out of trouble. Dating was a new experience for me, but my biggest problem was believing that everyone was my best friend. At 21 I became pregnant with my daughter, who I kept. She is a healthy 22 year old today. When this pregnancy occurred, I cried out to God to forgive me and help me to live a better life and be the best parent I could be. I later met and led a young man to the Lord. We were later married and had two sons, Enoch now 20, and Elijah now 18. As the marriage progressed it became quite evident that John was not taking the marriage or our religion as seriously as myself. He became very upset at even the mention of tithing or going to weekly prayer meetings. We began to argue a lot, mostly about religion. He said once that had I not led him to the Lord then he would not be bothered by all this and from that day on he became very abusive. Even though the marriage continued, it became unbearable. The abuse was more and more frequent. I was at the point I could not go on. I filed for divorce.

All alone and feeling like a failure, I retreated into myself. Starting over I felt that a new church and friends was the place to begin. Searching for a church that I felt was scriptural was easier said than done. I finally asked my Mom where I should attend. She suggested the Church of Christ. That was where she and my father were attending. I had a hard time accepting all the beliefs of this church, but I read my Bible daily and attended on a regular basis. This is where I met my second husband, Bob. Everything seemed fine until we decided to marry. Our marriage would not be accepted because I had been divorced. After 5 years of dating, we married and were soon kicked out of the church.

In my search for a new church and hungry to be in fellowship, I was invited to a Gospel meeting by an old friend of mine from high school. The first few meetings I attended all alone. The women workers were very nice and always wanted me to stay after and talk. One of the women workers told my friend after I left that I would be back. After a while Bob's curiosity got the best of him and he agreed to attend a Sunday afternoon meeting held at my friend's house. We attended, and Bob seemed impressed. Bob's days off from work rotated every week. One week he would be off Monday-Tuesday, the next week Tuesday-Wednesday. After every Gospel meeting the next meetings would be scheduled on Bob's days off. So we began to attend twice a week plus Sunday morning. I was still not sure what these people were all about, when one evening the workers opened the meeting for people who wanted to profess. Bob stood up and as he did he pulled me up with him. After we returned home I sat in the laundry room and cried my heart out. Bob could not understand my tears. I told him I did not want to look or dress like that; that could not be what religion was all about. He reassured me it would be all right and that the workers would give me plenty of time to change. It was only a matter of weeks before I was expected to put my hair up, and that was only the beginning.

Soon after, the workers would stop by unexpected just for a little visit. Once I was cleaning windows and I was dressed in a pair of sweat pants. The younger worker explained that anything I could do in a pair of pants; I could do in a skirt. She also said she jogged in a skirt. So in my embarrassment, I vowed, to the workers, never to wear pants again. However I would sneak around and wear them when I was cleaning house or working in the flower bed, but I would spend so much time running to see if the workers were coming into the drive I could not get anything done. I soon packed my pants away and became the obedient little professing wife.

Soon convention time came and I was working at preps when a sister worker picked up my hand and exclaimed that my wedding ring had a beautiful diamond, but in Truth we did not believe in dia-monds. Afterwards at home my husband said maybe I should let him take it off, after all it was just a ring, and we didn't want anything to stand in our way of being good professing people.

That year after convention we had brother work-ers in our field. We were sure it would be a relief not to have sister workers breathing down our backs. The brother workers moved right in and made themselves at home. They stayed in our home a lot, and it became home base for them. Once when they were talking after dinner, the subject of TV came up. I said ours had not been on in a very long time. The brother worker said maybe we should move it to the basement, that would relieve the temptation. Temptation was not the problem.

Sports became the next topic of conversation, only because my boys were very good baseball players. It was explained that people in Truth did not play in sports—not because the games them-selves were bad—but because of the lack of good sportsmanship. Our daughter was a cheerleader. We felt no need to even ask about this. We already knew the answer would be no. The children felt that this should not pertain to them because, at this time, none of them professed.

When we asked about my daughter being able to wear slacks to school, we were immediately told "NO." When we explained that she was the only professing girl not only in her school but for 35 miles in any given direction, the answer was still "NO." Poor Laura went from being cheerleader, popular, stylish dresser, to a bun wearing, dress wearing, outcast. The workers did not seem to un-derstand. Once a worker showed up just as Laura came home from school wearing a pair of bib-over-alls and he immediately told her she could make a better impression if she dressed like a girl, not a boy, and if she did, she would be winning all her friends to the Truth.

Christmas was soon coming, and the children had always celebrated this season with my Mother on Christmas Eve and with their Father and his family on Christmas day. It was such a joyful family-filled time for all of us. We were quickly told that no holidays were celebrated; that they were all pagan holidays designed by non-Christians. The children were beginning to tire of all the rules. But with their little chins held high, they moved forward. Once we were with workers during special meeting time and we were asked how the Christmas season was affecting the children. I explained they were doing fine. I asked how it affected the workers as children. Much to my surprise I found that every worker present had celebrated Christmas as a professing child. Not a big show, but with the giving of gifts. I was furious. From this day on, we celebrated Christmas with our children; not a big show, but with the giving of gifts.

A young brother worker, at the age of 19, became good friends with my daughter. Not only did he live in my home but meetings were being held in our area—so they had plenty of time together. This relationship was nothing more than a brotherly, sisterly friendship. He told my daughter that he thought she was pretty. My daughter made the mistake of telling this to another girl who lived on the convention grounds, and before we knew it this young boy was being shipped off to another state. When we asked what was going on, we were told he had become too familiar with my daughter. We were also told that he had also become familiar with the young girl that lived on the convention grounds; he had tried to kiss her.

The following summer my daughter professed. She was now 14. She had gone to preps at a nearby town, and during convention she took this most important step. The next day a sister worker approached her about being baptized. Laura said she felt she was ready and the sister worker agreed. The day before the baptism, my daughter was helping in the kitchen when a few girls who bunked in her dorm announced that she should not be baptized because they had searched her suitcase and found mascara. Humiliated she fled. Later, though the incident was never mentioned, she was baptized. I was soon told by the mother of these girls that she (this mother) had made sure no one could come to preps or convention unless accompanied by a parent, in the years to come. I could not understand why such a fuss was being made over a girl who was the only girl within 35 miles of any other professing children, who had just professed herself and was as good as gold all during preps and convention. Didn't they want these children to become friends and have fellowship?

No, the answer was jealousy. I was informed by the mother of these girls that because my daughter was so beautiful, that they were afraid that she might get first pick at any eligible young professing man. After all, the number of young professing boys was very slim. The possibility existed that her daughter would be left without. This had to be the most stupid excuse I had ever heard. They would try to keep my daughter from being baptized and attending convention alone because they might be left an old maid? Where were their priorities? Just because they thought she was too beautiful and might marry inside.

Shortly after this incident a professing woman and I became friends, we would shop and spend hours together. It was such a relief just to have a friend. Her 3 daughters became good friends with my daughter, and we did everything together. One day while shopping the girls were in the dressing room when my daughter exited with a large red mark on her face. When I asked what had happened, she said one of the girls had slapped her. When I confronted the girls they said they were sick of my daughter always getting new clothes and being the envy of everyone. I then confronted the mother of the girls and her reply was "everyone feels this way." By this time I was the most confused person in the world. I could not understand, if these people were in the only true church, why they were acting like this. Complaining to the workers did no good. The brother workers could not be bothered with such silly things.

About this time Laura began dating a professing boy. Because he lived so far away it only seemed logical, on the nights they would have a date, that she stay all night at his house. When word of this got out, in no time it was all over the field. His parents were so afraid of what people thought. During Special meeting time our two families met at a restaurant so we could travel together. Their son was allowed to ride in our car until we were a mile outside of town, then he had to ride the rest of the way in with his parents. They wanted it to look as if we had arrived together only by chance.

The following year we were blessed with sister workers in our field. However, one sister worker, named Jeanette Ford, did not like me and left little doubt about how she felt. A short time later she began to rebuke me for my testimony. Every meeting she was in where I spoke she would find fault. It seemed every Monday morning we were being paid a visit by the sister workers about my testimony not being acceptable. One testimony that stands out in my mind, was where I used the scripture Isaiah 47:2-3; *"Take the millstones, and grind meal: uncover thy locks, make bare the leg, uncover the thigh, pass over the rivers. Thy nakedness shall be seen: I will take vengeance, and will not meet thee as a man."* I continued to expound in my testimony that we may hide things from our friends and family, but there would come a day when we would stand naked before the Lord, hiding nothing and being judged. I was rebuked for using the word naked in mixed company.

Being in the Truth, our friends in the Anderson area were few, so doing things together seemed very logical. One Sunday, one of the friends was having a birthday dinner for his mother. He had invited us to stop by for cake that afternoon. When I arrived the sister workers were there, and everyone was sitting around talking. The eldest sister worker gave me a look of disgust. I could not figure out what I had done, but the following Monday when she arrived at my house for a visit, she informed me that families were to fellowship together and that this family was not mine and I should not be including myself. It was not for me to take upon myself to be included in everyone's affairs. When I told her that I had been invited, she explained that I was not wanted there and that was that. I always wondered who didn't want me there. Years later, I found out this sister worker had a "crush" on the man who had invited me and she was very jealous of our friendship.

Bob worked evenings and he began to worry about me driving so far at night alone with the children to meetings. Bob had mentioned this to a friend who also attended meetings. Our friend offered to let me and the children ride to meetings with him. After all, we lived in the same town and went to the same meetings; killing two birds with one stone, so to speak. Soon I was confronted by a sister worker who said someone who loved me and only cared about me had mentioned that they did not think it appropriate for me, a married woman, to be alone in a car with a single man. What would people think?

The workers soon approached us about being baptized. I had been baptized at age 18 in the Nazarene church, and baptized five times in the Church of Christ. Because I could not conform to their beliefs, they continued to baptize me, telling me each time that my problem was that I was being baptized, but not truly believing that the baptism would change me. When I explained to the workers that I saw no need to be baptized again, they told me that no other baptism was scriptural because it had not been done by workers, the true servants of God.

By this time I was so worn down that I questioned what this religion was all about. It took us an hour and thirty minutes to drive to Union meetings. It took us 35 minutes to drive to our regular Sunday meeting. There were no children except mine who attended any of these meetings. If we had been allowed to drive only 25 minutes to the south, not only were there lots of children my children's ages, but it was closer for us. When we asked permission to change our meeting, we were told that meetings were not about pleasing ourselves, but pleasing God. We were to make ourselves patterns after the workers lives. Their entire lives were sacrificed and so should ours be. The workers would never have children, so they could never understand why I was so caught up in worrying if my children could attend a meeting so they could be with friends their own age. They pointed out how the workers traveled great lengths to come to Special meetings, and I was worried about driving 35 minutes to a Sunday morning meeting. Their advice to me was to search within, and find the real problem.

After this conversation, it seemed everything I did or said, I was being rebuked for. Everything from the length of my dresses to the length of my testimony. I was told at convention by two sister workers that my dresses were following the traditions of the world. I told them I wore my skirts this length because I worked in a barber shop and bending and stooping all day long, I felt this length was more modest. They insisted they were too long and I must keep all my hems uniform, a hymn book length from the floor.

Also, all testimonies were from God and should only be 2 minutes long, and 1 minute for prayer. With this timing no meeting should go over the intended hour. I wasn't an elder and didn't feel it should have anything to do with me if the meeting ran over. But for some reason I was being blamed for that too.

I continued to ask questions about scripture and was continually told to check my attitude. I was so sick of all that Truth had to offer I began to contemplate leaving.

My children had complained to the place where my oldest son had left home at 14, to go live with his dad because he couldn't stand it any more. When we attended the court proceedings for the removal of my son from my home to his fathers, the judge asked Enoch why he wanted to leave. He explained to the judge that the church was driving him crazy and we no longer had a home, but a dictatorship by the workers. He said we were not a family anymore; that the Truth had ruined that. When the judge questioned me, his first question was: "What was the name of this church?" I said it had no name. He asked me where it was located. I told him we met in homes. He asked me just what we believed. I could not tell him, because I did not know myself. After a long pause, the judge said he would not only grant my oldest son to live with his dad, but if my youngest son wanted to go, he would grant this. My youngest son stayed with me but later tried to commit suicide. Leaving me was not what he wanted, it was just to be rid of this church.

We were told by a doctor that counseling might help. At the first meeting with this psychiatrist, most of his questions were directed at me. He asked many questions about this religion, and why it would be so important to me that I would stand by and watch my children suffer. He stared at me, waiting for an answer. I could find no words to explain. I finally said something about it being the only true way. He said that he was a Christian and he would never think of subjecting his family to the things I had asked my family to suffer. Later I read the report that this psychiatrist had sent to our family doctor. In it he suggested that the **MOTHER** needed psychiatric help. When I told the workers of this, they explained that the world's way was a psychiatrist, but Truth's way was God.

My daughter had a nervous breakdown between her junior and senior year. The pressures of the church and all that was going on in our family life was just too much to bear. Again we saw a psychiatrist, this time a woman. I thought she would better understand me and my situation. Her questions were much the same as the male psychiatrist we had seen the previous year. Once during a visit she asked me why I wanted to look like this. I tried to explain from the depths of my heart how I felt. She stared at me with a pointless look and said; "Have you ever considered changing churches?"

The year before this my dad had died and a brother worker told me not to worry; my dad was where he belonged. He had no right to the throne room of heaven; only those who professed in the true way had access to heaven. A real comfort! My whole world was crashing down around me. Soon I felt *the only way out was to leave.*

One day I stopped at a Christian bookstore hoping to find something encouraging to read. I was drawn to a shelf about cults. After reading only a short while, I was convinced I was involved with a cult. Continuing my research only led me to believe more and more that this was a cult. Shutting us off from the outside world by not letting us vote, or read newspapers, no TV's, no radios, or anything that would connect us to the outside world; and not being involved with our families if they were not members of the Truth. We were totally shut off. This was a cult! I knew it, and if it was the last thing I did I would rid myself and my family of this terrible association.

I began to try to talk to Bob about how I felt but he did not want to hear anything about it. He would only say this is the true way and I don't know anything that even comes as close as Truth. One Sunday morning Bob and I were on our way to meeting when I decided and announced that I was not going to meeting, so would he please drop me off at McDonalds so I could drink coffee until he returned after meeting to pick me up. He did not drop me off but continued to drive around while I told him how I felt. He suggested I call a meeting with the workers and tell them my feelings.

I called this meeting and soon two sister workers and two brother workers showed up. I asked why I had to wear my hair up, because I could find no scripture that said I had to. They used the scripture; 1 Corinthians 11:15 *"But if a woman have long hair, it is a glory to her: for her hair is given her for a covering."* I asked where it said I must wear it up and was told it showed discipline. Being more like the workers. I then asked about wearing dresses. The scripture was 1 Timothy 2:9; *"in like manner also, that women adorn themselves in modest apparel, with shamefacedness and sobriety; not with broided hair, or gold, or pearls, or costly array."* I then asked why did professing women braid their hair? I was told that the problem was ME and nothing else. When I asked whether the Truth believed in the Trinity, I was told the word Trinity was found nowhere in the Bible. When I asked if they believed that Jesus, God, and the Holy Spirit, are three in one, the workers used double talk to try to confuse me and skirt the issue. I asked another professing couple to be present as my witnesses of what was said. I wanted someone to hear both sides. The other couple had professed for seven years and had some problems with "things" going on but had never even considered leaving. They only agreed to sit in on this meeting because of my fear of being alone with the workers and because they had some questions too. After a short while one of the sister workers screamed at me and a brother worker agreed with her that the problem was ME. An hour had soon passed and nothing was being solved except I was blamed for everything that had ever gone wrong in the Truth. The wife of the couple finally spoke up in my defense and asked how this could be Kathy's problem, when she felt the same way. Soon the husband spoke up and stated that he had no opinion and had only agreed to sit in on the meeting as a friend to me, but that after he saw how I was being treated by the workers and their apparent hatred for me, he had decided that maybe my questions were valid. This couple never attended another meeting after that day.

At this point the head brother worker stated that he still felt the problem was me and that with this kind of attitude, the best thing he could do was to take my testimony from me. With attitudes like the ones I had portrayed that day, it was the only thing that did make sense. He said the questions that I had asked showed him that maybe Truth was not for me. I told the workers I had been treated better by the people from the Church of Christ, and Jeanette Ford said, "Then why don't you go back there?"

So I rose to my feet and said "without a testimony, I cannot take part, so I am of no threat to you now." I told them I would not be attending any more meetings, and with that I left the house.

After all this you would think my problems were over. But in reality they had only just begun. My husband was very angry, not at the workers but at me for not settling anything. Little did he know how hard I had tried. I told him I was leaving Truth. He explained to me he loved this way and saw no reason to leave and if I chose to leave I would be on my own. I left Truth, never to return. The workers told me that if my husband followed me and left, *then his blood would be on my salvation*. The workers encouraged him to continue on in meetings. They told him when and where a meeting was being held by leaving notes on the door addressed to him. He would have messages left on the answering machine with only an invitation for him and no one else in the family. The mail he would receive from the workers would be addressed only to him without any mention of other family members. He was told by a sister worker that because I had left the Truth we were now unequally yoked, and that he would have scriptural grounds to remarry, should he divorce me. They continued to correspond with him through letters, encouraging him to come to meetings and reassuring him that he had done nothing wrong; it was all me. My whole world was crumbling down around me.

For two years we lived in the same house, never so much as speaking. I was living my own life and he was living his. None of us were attending meetings or going to church anywhere. My whole life was falling apart. I turned away from God and blamed Him for everything. I swore I would never go to church again. I became very bitter about everything that had happened.

About this time my cousin from California came for a visit. He wanted me to go to church with him in Indianapolis and meet his old pastor who had come to Indiana to start a church. The last thing I wanted was to go to church. He was so excited and continued to tell me all the great things that God had done in his life. He was so full of joy and wonderful stories of God's grace. I argued with him that all God had done was make a mess of my life. Finally one night I broke down and told him the whole story. After I had finished he asked me to please come to church with him just one time.

I agreed, and on Sunday the first sermon I heard was about all of God's children. He told how we were all unique; none of us the same. We were not expected to think alike, look alike, dress alike, act alike. We were all individuals, and God loved us just the way we were. The following Sunday I attended again to hear another message about how God wanted us to come to him just the way we were; that he did not expect perfection or someone else telling us how to act or how to be religious. God wanted us for who we are, sinners. That so touched my heart that at that very moment I asked God to forgive me and to help me to fix the mess my life had become.

The following Monday I visited the pastor's office. I told him what a mess my life had become. His advice to me was to go home, accept all blame, ask Bob to forgive me and let my life shine JESUS. What a tall order! But I was determined to let God finish this work he had begun in me when I was 18, if it was the last thing I would do. Soon my youngest son, who was now 16, became interested and started attending. He was soon saved and later was baptized. My husband saw the joy that Truth had never offered and he too wanted it. He later realized that after 20 years in the Church of Christ and 5 years in the Truth that he was not even a Christian. He had never truly given his heart to Jesus. After this glorious day when he gave his life to Jesus our lives began to heal from all the wounds the Truth had inflicted. We began to counsel with our pastor and soon our friends and family were invited to our remarriage and new lives as Christians. My oldest son, Enoch gave me away, and my daughter Laura was my maid of honor. My youngest son, Elijah, was Bob's best man. The wedding was beautiful and our marriage was saved through our willingness to be obedient to Christ. About 5 months later, Laura was saved, she was 19 years old. Enoch has attended but has never made a commitment.

This story is, by far, not the only one of its kind. However any story that has heartache and despair should not go untold. People need to heal from wounds inflicted by churches like the Truth, and the best way is to tell that story over and over. We need to be reassured that we are not crazy or have an **ATTITUDE** problem. We need to know that we are loved by friends and that it is O.K. to disagree. God wants us for who we are, not some robot made by a religious system. Jesus came to save the sinner, not the righteous. Praise be to God for people like Cherie Kropp, Doug Parker, and David Stone, and most of all Threshing Floor Ministries who print and distribute literature, and the many more who take stands to walk away when it's not the popular thing to do; to be an outcast for Jesus. When all the odds seem to be against us we stand united with Christ. And last, but not least, for questioning minds who will not stop studying and looking for answers. Praise be to God that He sent His only begotten Son, that whosoever believes shall not perish but have everlasting life.

Address:
Katherine J. Bates
414 W. 8th Street
Anderson, IN 46016

Chapter Four

John and Karen Boe

Grace and peace to you from God our Father and the Lord Jesus Christ, who gave himself for our sins to rescue us from the 2x2 cult and the present evil age, according to the will of our God and Father, to whom be all glory forever and ever. Amen!

Each time I read the apostle Paul's epistle to the Galatians I am struck by the timely message it has and how it seems to be talking specifically to those in the 2x2 fellowship. I continue to be astonished that I so quickly deserted the one true faith in October of 1984, and made a fool of myself for 6-1/2 years in that foreign fellowship. I continue to struggle with much denial, anger, guilt, frustration, hate and the like. But mostly fear. Fear: because my daughter, KK Boe, is still in the fellowship. Guilt: because I was so instrumental in her getting into this thing in the first place. No, I'm not totally discouraged. I have a strong faith and I trust the Lord to rescue KK in a manner just as miraculous as he used for my wife and me in April 1991. I want to "name it, and claim it," but instead, I pray to remain faithful and patient until He is finished using KK in a job right where she is.

During the entire period I was with the 2x2s I never ceased asked questions. I never got answers from anyone. It was always an admonition to go to yet another meeting where everything would then be ok. I turned to my computer in an effort to "talk" to someone. I wrote volumes. I even made progress on a book describing my experiences, and the doctrines of the 2x2s. Then I was given the book *Has the Truth Set You Free* by the Luxons. They said all I wanted to say—and more; but with a loving spirit. Instead, my book was full of hatred, frustration, and anger. After I read their book I put mine down and have never gone back to it.

Another reason I have not been very vocal about this very subject I want to talk about, is because of where KK is yet today. I want to say as little as possible so as to not furnish those in the 2x2 fellowship ammunition with which to distort, gloat and use against me. They do that so well.

Following is a letter to a former worker, Greg Lee, with whom I correspond at least once a month. At times his questions and obstinance overwhelm me. (eg: he can't see the difference between the Son of God, and God the Son.) My letter to him describes some issue mentioned above. I often have dreams, with delusions of grandeur, where I preach to the 2x2s at convention and straighten them all out with my brilliant logic, oratorical skills and quoting the Bible—but then I wake up.

My wife and I are very active in a program called "Evangelism explosion," which was developed by D. James Kennedy of Fort Lauderdale, Florida. It has given us the tools with which to explain where we are spiritually, as well as witness to others and proselytize. We are very solidly in the "Christian Camp" today and wish you all the same. I would appreciate hearing from any of you ex 2x2s. I trust you will understand my reluctance in lieu of KK's vulnerable position.

May 6, 1993

Letter to Mr. Greg Lee

Dear Greg,

Most everyone in the fellowship has a pretty good idea what is going on in the world with anyone else in the fellowship—if they want to ask. There is a tremendous network of correspondence and telephoning. Their motive is not intended to be injurious, but most often the result is not positive or uplifting. That contradicts what we were told when we were shown letters from friends and workers all over the world.

We are very apprehensive about discussing things of a spiritual nature with former friends still in the fellowship. We have seen too often how facts and information is repeated out of context, then distorted, and generally used as a tool to ridicule instead of uplift. People who ask questions about KK quite frequently already have the answers. They often know more about her than we, and yet they ask questions knowing our relationship is strained, and they gloat in that fact with self-righteous piety and a superior attitude.

Doesn't that sound familiar? "Proud of their humility!" Pharisaical.

KK is living in Cody, Wyoming and working for the USFS 8 to 9 months of each year. Without her formal degree in forestry yet, she is unable to get the full time job she wants. She will not accept help from anyone (including Mom and Dad) to go back to college and finish her work there. She is a rugged individualist and stubborn to a point, just like most all the friends. She has bought her own 4 wheel drive pick em up truck which looks like it went through WWII. Her physical health has improved 100% since leaving the work. However, whenever she is back in the environment of the friends, and especially certain workers, her health deteriorates alarmingly and very rapidly. It relates to a psychological dependency which the friends have developed within their own group. Their relationships are not founded on love nor on a grateful heart for what Christ has done for them, but rather on a sick assumption that there is nothing available as an alternative. They believe they must do and be better and worthy in order to merit going to heaven. They dismiss Romans 6:23 as being too easy, simple and impossible. They can't grasp an unconditional love which would give such a free gift. They label it as "easy believism."

Indeed, one of the first questions friends in the fellowship want to ask us is, "Where are you going to church?" Certainly not out of true concern, but out of arrogance. If they knew, then they could put a label on it and ridicule and mock it. They have ready answers for any denomination or church they have ever heard of. If it is Baptist: oh ya, once saved, always saved; if it is the Roman Catholic: oh ya, the pope and praying to Mary; if it is the Assembly of God: oh ya, like Jimmy & Tammy Faye Baker or Jimmy Swaggert; if it is the Episcopal, Lutheran, or Presbyterian: oh ya, with all the homosexual problems in the clergy; ...ad infinitum.

What they are really saying is, "Where would you have me go if I were to leave the fellowship?" *That is a very good question!* However, it does *not* have an easy answer. We have found it very difficult...yes, impossible to find a perfect fellowship. Yes, if we find one that claims to be "God's perfect way" (like the 2x2s claim) we will run in the opposite direction away from it. This is not to say that there is no Christian Church, for there is and always has been, and always will be a fellowship of true believers. Maybe not united in a formal unit and identifiable as we would make it, but yet His church. This paradox results in people like Wm. Irvine, Cooney, William Lewis, Taylor Wood, Garret Hughes, etc. Sincere about reform and cleansing the local churches but wrong about how to go about it without ending up in heresy themselves.

Has the motive of the founding fathers of the 2x2 fellowship been love and gratitude for the free gift of salvation which Jesus offers to each? If it was, it is gone now. The testimonies of the friends attest to that fact. What do they glory in? What do they give thanks for? Answer: *"The day the workers came into their lives!"* Not the day Jesus rose from the dead as the first fruit of them that sleep. Not the day they acknowledged Jesus as their Savior, Lord and King. Not the day the Lord saved them. How many times have you heard someone stand up and cry about how happy they are for not being in this or that denomination any more? Talk about a self serving love. How can God honor that? Christianity is first of all a living personal relationship with Jesus. Second, we do not have to wait and see, wonder if, guess, or hope to get to heaven when we die. 1 John 5:13 says that the Bible was written so that we might know right now, and not wait to find out if we are going to heaven. What glue would hold people in the 2x2 fellowship if they taught that? They instead are bound by the need to "be more worthy and living in His will."

KK was home for a week during Christmas time with a boy friend, Harold Musser, 16 years her senior. We were with them in Cody over the Easter week end. They both say anything more than friendship is out of the question because his exwife is still living. Meanwhile life is complicated for them as they struggle for answers in many areas other than that. He is an advocate of tolerance.

However, tolerance is not the answer. That is what the deceiver would have you believe in order to put you in neutral.

My prayers usually ask for things in my time frame rather than in His. This includes KK and you getting out of the fellowship. Not necessarily just coming home to our home in Bismarck, but home to the freedom and the real truth that will set you free. I can appreciate your wanting to see something better before you "jump." If you see yourself as hanging on to a floating log way out in the middle of the ocean with no other escape, rescue, or alternative in sight, then you are indeed to be pitied. For that log will sink too.

We are in good health mentally, financially, physically, and most importantly—spiritually.

None of us need the diatribe you and I heard two years ago at that "extra" meeting in Hunter, or the shame perpetrated at the Jamestown special meeting the same year. How you and the Burchills can forget that garbage is beyond my comprehension. I say I forgive them, but I still feel anger, so God has a lot of work to do with me yet. (I rationalize it as righteous indignation.)

Do you have a phone #? I still get in GFK every other month. I do not always remain over nite (RON) there. Thanks for your letter.

Love, John

Note from John T. Boe:

There is so very much I would like to say and share with all of you who have been through the same fire as I in the 2x2 cult. I trust that someday we will all meet in heaven and be able to discuss and understand the whole purpose of our journey. He is faithful and just and will hear and answer our prayers. "Believe in the Lord Jesus, and you will be saved—you and your household." Acts 16:31.

Sole Deo Gloria.

Address:
John & Karen Boe
3139 Winnipeg Drive
Bismarck, ND 53501

Chapter Five

Ian Carlson

I was born in Dublin in 1932, the youngest of three boys. Dublin is the largest city in Ireland with a population of about one million, but at the time I was born, the population was around 450,000 the vast majority of whom were Catholics. Of the small Protestant population about 65% would be Church of Ireland (a branch of the Anglican Church), 18% Methodist and the balance made up of Presbyterian, Baptist, Brethren, etc.

My father and his sister had become disillusioned with the Methodist church while in their late teens, and some years later they came in contact with the workers and both "professed" without any real understanding of the workers' doctrine. My father left the group when he realised that the workers considered all other churches to be false. His sister, my aunt, continued in the meetings.

My aunt's profession and baptism are rather interesting as they throw some light on Edward Cooney's outlook and beliefs. The Open Brethren had built a very large hall in Dublin called "Merrion Hall," which could seat about 3,000 people, and it was at a meeting there that my aunt "made her choice". Before she was baptised by the Brethren however, she heard about the workers and attended Avoca Convention, which is about 40 miles south of Dublin. Mr. Cooney spoke, and at the end of his address he asked if there were any who wanted to be baptised, and my aunt stood up. After the meeting Edward Cooney spoke to those who wished to be baptised, and asked my aunt where she had heard the gospel. She told him Merrion Hall, and he would certainly have known that she hadn't professed through any worker, but he raised no objection and just asked Eadie Weir, one of the Dublin friends, to help her get ready. It is hard to imagine any of the present-day workers displaying such a tolerant attitude, but it shows that Edward Cooney never believed that one could only be saved through the workers.

Religious instruction is part of the school curriculum in the Irish Republic, so I received a certain amount of orthodox teaching. Most schools in Ireland are run by the churches, though funded by the Government, and Mount Jerome, the first school I attended, was run by the Church of Ireland. When I was about seven, we were sent to a Methodist school, and finally I attended Wesley College, a Methodist secondary school.

Until I was about eight, my mother and father never attended any church, though as children we were sent to the Church of Ireland Sunday School on Sunday morning and usually attended Children's Service on Sunday afternoon. My aunt then invited my mother to the meetings and my mother professed through Hugh Breen and Joshua Gamble. My brothers and I were told we could please ourselves about whether we went to Sunday School or not, and we decided to stop. We quite enjoyed Sunday School and Children's Service, but as we were now required to attend the meetings as well, our decision was hardly surprising.

Until I was about 16 my father did not attend any place of worship on a regular basis, but he and I would sometimes go to either Merrion Hall (Open Brethren) or to an Interdenominational Service at the YMCA. I enjoyed being with my father and con-

sidered either Merrion Hall or the YMCA a considerable improvement on the meetings.

Coming from a divided home we were never really accepted as being children of the friends. On
the other hand we were not allowed to take part in
what the workers considered to be worldly pleasure, and consequently, like most children from
divided homes we tended to get the worst of both
worlds. Life at any rate became rather dreary, but
whether this was due to my mother's involvement
with the meetings, or the effects of World War Two
is hard to say, as a lot of changes in our lifestyle
occurred about the same time.

Neither of my brothers professed, but when I
was 16 my father professed again and continued in
the meetings until his death. He never really accepted the idea that only those who professed
through the workers were saved, and was aware of
many of the group's shortcomings. He adopted the
view however, that there were faults in all groups,
and that there was little to be gained by changing
to another church.

I professed through Willy Driver when I was
eighteen. Willy was home from Africa at the time
and did not have a companion. At the time I did
not realise how unorthodox many of the workers'
ideas were. In fact it is only since leaving the group
that I have come to see the real message the workers were and are preaching. I had always assumed
that the workers believed in the Trinity, as they
baptise in the name of the Father, Son and Holy
Ghost, but their teaching on the subject seems dis-
tinctly hazy. While the Bible makes mention of the
Holy Ghost or Holy Spirit many, many times, the
workers never speak about Him. If they mention the
word spirit at all, it is usually to warn against having a hard spirit or a bad spirit, by which they

usually mean expressing an opinion which differs from their own. Friends who question the doctrine or authority of the workers are often charged with having a "Bad Spirit." The workers in fact seem to use the charge "Having a Bad Spirit," in much the same way as communist dictators use the charge "Crimes Against the State."

A couple of months after I professed I attended my first convention. During the war no conventions were held in Ireland, so as I had not attended any as a child, that first convention left a very clear impression on my mind, and it is interesting to look back and notice the changes which have taken place over the years. In Ireland at that time, baptisms were usually carried out at convention, generally while one of the meetings was in progress, so they tended to be very private affairs with usually only the workers and those about to be baptised, present. On Sunday morning the bread and wine would be passed around the convention, several cups being used, and from time to time these would be refilled from jugs. This was also the custom in New Zealand when I arrived here, and in fact continued until about 1980. No public address system was used in Irish conventions and during periods of heavy rain hymns were usually sung, as it was impossible to speak above the noise of rain on canvas.

In addition to the minor changes however, there is one very important change which has taken place. There was not nearly the same amount of travel on the part of the workers, so workers at a convention tended to be few and mainly local. Consequently, about fifty per cent of the time was left for the friends to speak, and many people in Ireland would speak for ten or twenty minutes, and some very helpful thoughts would be expressed. The convention was very much a partnership between the friends and the workers. Now the contribution from the friends has become a farce with much emphasis being placed on brevity, and on getting the maximum number to speak. In fact, if one listens at convention to what are called testimonies, one soon realises that little of what is said can be classified as "testimony," in any normal sense of that word.

When I professed, most of the older female friends wore black stockings and the workers still preached against silk and nylon ones. The history of the "Black Stocking Mentality" is quite interesting. When William Irvine left the Faith Mission and formed the "Meetings," he copied most of the Faith Mission's ideas and as the female "pilgrims" in the Faith Mission wore black stockings, he insisted the female "workers" do likewise. The female workers in turn did their best to impose the same standard of dress on the friends, so despite the fact that the doctrine had no scriptural grounds whatever, it was still being preached in the fifties as being the only acceptable mode of dress for female Christians. It would have been interesting to see what would have happened had the friends adhered to the doctrine for a few more years when black stockings became highly fashionable.

When I was about twenty we had the meeting in our home, and I was conscious that it caused my parents a surprising amount of stress. I know that my mother always felt on edge when a worker was present, particularly a sister worker. This is hardly surprising as several of the older sister workers in Ireland had a special kind of ministry: faultfinding---and I can think of some that made it a full-time ministry.

Faultfinding was not of course confined to the workers. From time to time the friends in Dublin would organise a picnic or game of soccer, but almost invariably someone would complain to the workers about some misconduct, real or imagined, and the activity would be stopped. The Irish have a reputation for being "priest-ridden," so perhaps it is not surprising if the Irish friends seemed to be "worker-ridden."

I worked near Glasgow for a couple of years, and it is noticeable that the workers seemed to have made little impact in that area of Scotland. This seems strange considering the fact that William Irvine was from that locality. I also spent a year in England near Birmingham where the friends were even more thinly scattered. Oddly enough, although I had little contact with friends or workers in England, I felt very close to God and I believe I grew more spiritually during that time, than during any similar period while in the meetings.

I emigrated to New Zealand in June 1960, and found conditions here as far as the workers and friends were concerned very similar to those prevailing in Ireland. This was hardly surprising as the head worker at that time was Willie Hughes, an Irishman. In 1962 I moved to Auckland where I met my wife Valerie, who is a New Zealander, and we were married in 1964. We had four children, three boys and a girl, and we now have one grandchild, a girl.

My doubts regarding the doctrine preached by the workers go back a large number of years. Like my father I did not believe that the workers and friends were the only ones right, but this did not seem all that important. I now see, however, that the authority of the workers would have collapsed were it not for this myth, and that the workers had a vested interest in preaching "salvation by membership." At any rate, about eleven years ago a Brethren missionary moved into the house behind ours, and I was surprised to see how often spiritual matters came up in their conversation, quite naturally. I realised that the friends rarely speak of spiritual things when they come together, nor do the workers when they visit. I remember, in fact, one time when I was in the hospital, two brother workers came to visit me. And the man in the next bed, overhearing our conversation, presumed they were from my work. "Out of the abundance of the heart the mouth speaketh" and if spiritual things are really important to the workers and friends, one would expect it to show up in their conversation.

About this time I started to visit other churches, and also read Christian books. I found reading Christian books particularly helpful, and was conscious once again of spiritual growth.

I had been becoming more and more disillusioned with the meetings, but decided to put off a decision until I had revisited Ireland. I had hopes that maybe things would be better over there, and I think it is fair to say they were, but only slightly. While I was there, however, I obtained a copy of *The Church Without a Name*, which impressed me greatly. The book made me realise how wide my area of disagreement with the workers really was, as there was nothing in the book which had not already occurred to me, but usually only one thing irritated me at a time. When I realised how the workers had deliberately concealed the history of the group, and made a great mystery of how the group started when in fact no mystery existed, I lost what little confidence I had in them. Jesus said "I am the Truth," and it is ironic that those who claim to be His only true preachers, have gone to such pains to conceal that truth about how the group started.

My daughter and her husband left the meetings in September 1992 and my wife and I left about three weeks later. Since then we have visited various churches and found several where we felt we could have settled. We finally decided on the local Baptist church where we were made very welcome without being pressured, and where there is a strong emphasis on prayer. My daughter and her husband settled in another Baptist church nearby.

Since then four more friends have left the meetings together with three children and are attending the same two baptist churches (four in one church, four in the other). We have formed our own support group and are in touch with many ex-members both here and overseas. My wife and I have no regrets whatever for the step we have taken and have an assurance of salvation that we never possessed while members of the group. Our decision to leave would have been much more difficult had more of our relatives been in the meetings, and in that respect we were very fortunate.

Our hope and prayer is that more of the friends and workers will be willing to take the same step as we have done, and put their faith in Christ, rather than in a group or system.

Address:
Ian Carlson
19, Laurence St.
Hamilton, New Zealand

Chapter Six

Daurelle Chapman

This is my story. It is not written for any purpose but to tell my story. I do not expect it is the experience of anyone else. It is good for me to look back over my life and see a little of the broader picture of God's dealings with my life.

I grew up in Ohio, a child in a God-fearing home. We went to church together, sang hymns together, and talked of God together. As a teenager I was involved with a small group of friends at our high school who studied the Bible and shared times of fellowship and prayer. It was a unique time in my life—being a teenager in the early 1970's brought many feelings of companionship with others seeking a "spiritual awakening." I did seek God early in my life, and although I can't point to the specific time and place, I asked God at a young age to come into my life and be master of my life. I was born again. I trusted in Him to lead based on the promises in the Bible.

I moved to Oregon in January 1977. I turned 21 that year and looked forward to what God would have for me in this new place where we knew no one. I went to California for a few months of further schooling that summer. While I was there, I received letters from my folks about some very nice Christian people they had met in Bend. They described the way they met in homes and the way their ministers went out, etc. When I returned to Bend, I attended some "Gospel meetings." I was not attracted by the preaching, but the love of the people drew me in—I had not yet made friends in the area and so was glad of the warmth of the "friends."

The summer of 1978 I stood to my feet in meeting to "profess." I was aware immediately afterwards that my intentions were not understood. People came up to me and congratulated me. Some were slightly choked up—I could see that they believed I had just become a Christian. I was a little embarrassed, but didn't feel I could kindly set the record straight without embarrassing and/or disappointing them. The message I responded to was to "...show by standing that I wanted to follow Jesus in *this* way." In my mind it meant only that—I wanted to follow Jesus in this way, that is, *this* church as opposed to some other church/method of worship. I believed I was born again and had met another group of believers to fellowship with. I had never felt that the denomination I attended mattered so much as my salvation. (Salvation was not the same in my mind as any particular "way" or form or manner of worship.) My professing to me was akin to joining a church (not in the sense of joining the body of Christ, but simply declaring I wanted to be attached to this particular part of the Body/church).

Time passed, however, without openly dealing with this difference. I enjoyed the people so much, I thought it didn't have to be an issue.

That winter I met my future husband. Any differences in spiritual understanding were laid aside in the busy days of being young and in love. The following spring we were married. We have enjoyed now 12 years of a happy marriage and have been blessed with three fine children.

Sitting in meeting those many years, I was always uncomfortable with references to this being the "only" true church, or Christ's "only" true Body, because I knew differently from my own experience. As the years passed, I came to understand just what was meant by the terminology used by the "friends" ("outsiders," "the Truth," "the Way," "professing," "the friends," "the servants," etc.) I valued the commitment I saw in my husband to live for God. There was nothing shallow in his dedication to serve God, nor in many others I came to know.

Finally, in the winter of 1989/1990, I began to see clearly that to truly be a "professing" person, more of a commitment to this "way" was required. I acknowledged to myself that I had let friendships with the people take the place of searching the Scriptures on important issues. John Sterling was in our field. I was attracted by his talk of the *spirit*. When I think of his influence I always think of the word "mystical." I began to allow that perhaps my past experience and knowledge of God was only leading me to this "Way." There was time last summer when perhaps I truly was a professing person. I remember clearly being hungry to *hear* anything and everything I could from the workers. I had a love for the workers, the meetings, and the fellowship of the people. I knew what it was to be willing for whatever God would require of me and felt He was working growth into my life.

However, at the same time, I was very clearly aware in my heart that to be "professing" I had to put my faith in this *ministry*. I could not continue without searching out the reason for this. I asked several workers what the object of my faith was to be, because deep inside I felt the belief among the friends included more than just faith in Jesus. Their answer was "Our faith is in Jesus, of course!" usually said with a puzzled or shocked expression. Obviously, faith in Jesus meant one thing to me and another to them.

From last summer until now was to be the most troubling time of my life. I cried to God daily for resolution to the struggle within me to understand **REAL TRUTH.** I needed to know the **TRUE GOSPEL.** My every waking moment was consumed with desperation——I could not even put my finger on the questions that divided me from the friends sometimes, but I was conscious of a tremendous battle raging. There were many times, especially early on, when my faith even in God's existence was severely shaken. Even so, there was always a thread of faith that would not break. There was, even in the darkest times I knew, an underlying knowledge that God would see me through. I looked forward to having a faith "more precious than gold," because I knew I was in the fire that would produce it.

This may seem melodramatic to those who have known me these past months. Probably all that showed to others was my weight gain because of the stress! But I didn't want to bring anyone else into the pain that I was experiencing. I knew of no one who could fully understand my struggles but God Himself. I was so comforted by God's presence, by His promises to see me through this, and by the knowledge that He alone knew all about me and my struggles. I committed it all to Him constantly and prayed earnestly for *His* resolution.

There are many feelings and thought processes that I have known and gone through these last months. I do not claim to have "arrived." But I feel as if major strides have been made in my own "race for the mark of the high calling." God is faithful! He is faithful! God answered two specific prayers of mine in His time. First, I prayed earnestly that, if there was a person with true faith on this earth outside of this "way," He would bring them into my life. (There was too much distance in time and space from my old "brethren" in Ohio.) Each step of His leading seems to have allowed time for personal questioning between God and me without others' opinions before the next step. But in His time, God brought into my life two women whose testimonies speak loudly to me of Him. They are two new neighbors here in Beaverton. Secondly, and most importantly, I begged God for an answer to "What is sound doctrine?" It was not enough for me to just have an idea of what was being preached by the workers any longer. I needed to *know* what they as a body believed to be the doctrine/teaching of salvation. And then I needed to compare that to the scripture and what I had believed from a child, and ultimately come down off the "fence" between the two and know where I put my trust. The answer to part of this came in the book *Has the Truth Set You Free* by Gene and Grace Luxon. Finally, someone had put down what the doctrine of the Friends is, in an organized fashion. And then they put alongside that the doctrine of most Christians in the world today (the beliefs I had put my trust in as a young person). Finally I understood the questions! And with the right questions came some understanding. I trust God for more understanding as I now continue to seek Him and yield to His Word, which is truly a "light" in this dark world.

I don't know what the future will bring as far as relationships with the friends, because many will feel I've "lost out." Or perhaps they will feel I never was "in." They probably will not be able to understand my confidence unless they go through the same examination of their faith, and I don't know that they will think it necessary. One professing friend told me that no matter what she would still be my friend. Well, that's a nice thought, but it is not enough for me. Friends are nice, but fellowship is what the soul craves. I have enjoyed a fellowship with my heavenly Father these last months that I treasure above all else. I know He will continue to guide me. There is such a song in my heart for the One who died for such a sinner as I—He alone is worthy of all praise and adoration!

I have learned many things these past months:

"Feeling satisfied" is not enough.

Knowledge of God is critically important.

Confusion is not always of Satan.

Doubt is not always bad.

God is faithful.

God is faithful.

God is faithful.

God is LOVE.

February 20, 1991

Address:
Daurelle Chapman
152 Barker Rd.
Oregon City, OR 97045

Following is a letter dated April 27, 1991 and addressed "To the Friends who know me"

There is much I would like to say to you all, but I don't know how much you would take from me.

I am a Christian. Jesus is my Lord and Saviour. He said that any who believe in Him would have eternal life—be born again. The Bible makes that plain over and over again. "Believing" means to trust, and entrust or commit ourselves to Him. It is a total yielding of ourselves to Him. The Bible says we can know we have eternal life, not just *hope* we have new life.

The Bible doesn't say to be right with God we have to follow any particular "way" or "type" or "denomination" of church. We are instructed to follow Jesus' commands. Jesus did not command that the ministers in His Church go out as our workers do. Salaries for ministers were not forbidden. Marriage for ministers was apparently the norm and not the exception. Homes were not forbidden. The Bible says when we are born again, we are born into the church—Christ's Body—the family of God. It does not limit His family to any one method of organization.

Most of you will feel I am totally wrong in believing as I do, but I challenge you to examine the scripture on the doctrine of salvation. I challenge you to prove that the denomination of the "Friends" is anything more than another denomination. Some have accused me of not being "childlike" in spirit. To that I would like only to say that one characteristic of children is that they ask until they receive an answer they understand. Questions bring answers. And answers build our faith.

My faith has been deepened as I dealt with questions such as:

- Who or what is the object of my faith?
- Who is Jesus? (the son of God, the Creator, Almighty God, equal with God, God Himself come in the flesh.)

- Is the "way" of salvation a system/method, or a person?
- Does Jesus, the person, equal a system/method?
- Does my obedience make me righteous before God?
- What do I depend on for my salvation?
- What is the "gospel?"

One question seems to follow the other—I have several pages of just questions that have come to my mind over the last months.

I do not seek to hurt anyone's faith in God. I have felt as I have examined my own faith that if my faith could not stand up to real questions, then I didn't have much. God is faithful to answer. I remember times when I could not say that I knew anything at all except that I did love God. I wondered at times if that was all I could ever know for sure.

I could go on and on. I do love to talk about the Lord Jesus and what He means to me. That is why I am writing this..it has become very difficult for me to share from my heart in meeting as I have faced up finally to the fact that this church teaches that to follow Jesus means to follow their ministers only, and that their ministers alone can offer the true gospel to the world. I find I have to watch my words when giving my testimony, lest someone think I am trying to "attack" them, when I only want to speak of my confidence in Jesus and what He means to me, regardless of my local church affiliation.

There is much more I could say—I wonder if anyone wants to hear it. I have determined that I will not hold back my true testimony any longer when I have opportunity to share it. I certainly don't have all the answers, but the relationship I have with God is very real, and I trust He will continue to guide me.

I do enjoy your friendship! I would like to enjoy your fellowship as your sister in the Lord. I will not be at meeting all the time now, and when I am I don't expect I will share, but I do welcome any contact from any who are willing to talk about their faith.

Love,
Daurelle

Letter to Workers in our field.

May 1, 1991

Enclosed is the letter I am sending to some of the Friends I am acquainted with and who might wonder what is going on with me. Maybe you will sense the progression in my thoughts and attitudes since we last visited.

I am frustrated with people (I'm not saying you) who have no clear idea of what they believe and why. I am frustrated with all of the fears that I perceive among the friends. Fear of "losing out," fear of being "found out," fear of "having the wrong spirit," fear of being seen in a condition that doesn't look "professing," fear of questioning, fear of knowledge that might not reinforce what they've been taught, and on and on and on. I am frustrated with the judgmental attitudes I see among the same people. I am frustrated with a system that seeks to hide problems among its people rather than be open and honest. I am frustrated by what I see as a lack of moral conscience among some regarding sin, and a ministry that does not seem willing or able to address the issue of sin and our true state before a holy God.

I am not speaking about you personally on any specific issue—I'm speaking about my impressions over the years and now as I have heard first-hand accounts from various people who have been hurt by the fellowship.

I was disappointed in our visit, only because of my lack. I am not very good at keeping to the point (as you may have noticed). That doesn't mean I don't know the value of keeping to the central issue, it just means I'm not very comfortable in a "confrontation;" and if it seems like that's where we're headed, then I tend to back off. It's hard for me to accept that others I esteem in some way are not in agreement with me. I like to draw people together, not divide them.

You tell me if I believe something, just "go with it." I would like to respond that that's easy for you to say! I am "going with it," in the sense of pursuing my relationship with the Lord. However, can you put yourself in my place—trying to "get on" with my life, while my husband and children are being taught in subtle and sometimes not so subtle ways that I am an outsider/lost/not a part of God's family/"false"/or at the very least sincerely wrong but no less "lost." The doctrine the workers teach by what they preach (and often by what they neglect to preach) seeks to divide my home, and I have a hard time not resenting that. This is an area where I am learning many lessons these days—mainly having to do with understanding what "believe" means...learning what it means to trust God and to entrust my all to Him. That includes my family.

Regarding my opinion of the fellowship as a cult or whatever...I was thinking the other day that at the very least it seems like the Friends are a part of the True Body of Christ that is guilty of causing division in that Body because of thinking they are the only ones that keep Jesus' commandments. (I think this might be the case with those who truly do understand who God is, and what he did for them—the true gospel.) At the worst, it seems to me that the fellowship is a type of cult in those areas where there are people who are discouraged from questioning, and where the "way" is presented as a part of the good news of salvation. There seems to be a difference depending on what message has been preached or understood from the workers in any given field, etc.

I keep thinking about your opinion that percentage-wise there are far more people who are more committed in this church than in the other churches. I would like to know how you judge that. What is it you see in peoples' lives to make you feel that way? I would appreciate an answer on this.

And I wonder how you are doing these days. I have always liked you and respected your love for God. What are your thoughts on all this?

I hear that workers are advising people to "burn the books." They are considered poison. Why are people afraid??? Someone very dear to me wrote that she "loved me, but not enough to let you change my love of the truth, and let some modern, new, idea change me from my love of the Truth as we know it..." That was a shock to me. I don't think people realize that there has been saving faith in Jesus Christ as Lord long before this church ever started. I don't think the Friends realize what true Christians in this world believe. There are so many similarities between the Friends' Church and other churches that have sprung up throughout history

(and particularly around the same time this fellowship started), each claiming to have a true
revelation from God as to how we should obey
God.

Someone here said they thought God was
"weeding out" His Church. The response given was
that maybe God was "drawing out" his Church. I'm
not saying that's the case, but I did think that was
food for thought.

Our doctrine should be stated plainly. People
shouldn't have to sit in meetings for years to understand what is being preached. There are several
words I would like to see defined by the workers—
words like "truth," "believe," "righteousness,"
"way," and "gospel." Howard has given straightfor-
ward definitions for a few, and implied definitions
for others. These are basic to our understanding of
the same "gospel." Would you write me back with
your thoughts on these? Is it true that workers are
advised not to put things in writing regarding doctrine? I have a hard time believing that. Would you
please take a little time for me and write to me?
Some feel that since I've sat in meetings over all
these years, I should understand what the message
is. But I am saying that it is usually anything but
clear, and I am not alone in feeling this way. Perhaps you feel that God hasn't revealed the message
to me yet. Well, isn't there a clear gospel message
that can be stated, regardless of anyone accepting
it?

A couple of other questions for you—could you
write down your concept of who Jesus is as related
to the Father, and the Holy Spirit? You say that you
believe that Jesus is God. Well, what do you mean
by that? Do you believe that Jesus was God come
in human flesh? Do you believe that Jesus is equal

with God the Father? Would you mind giving an answer on that too?

Also, what does it mean when people say others have a "bad spirit?" Do they mean they don't have the Holy Spirit? Do you believe the Holy Spirit comes and goes from our lives? Why do the Friends refer to the Holy Spirit as an "it" when the scripture uses the personal pronoun "him" in reference to the Spirit?

So what do you think? The only thing about letters is that there's no immediate feedback. That's probably good for me, because it helps me keep on track with my thoughts. I am not asking for any confidential type of help. I feel it's very important to keep everything open these days. I hope you recognize that I am not perfect. I have faults and failures—I like that button that says P.B.P.G.I.N.F. W.M.Y. (Please Be Patient, God Is Not Finished With Me Yet.) I don't expect you to be perfect or have all the final answers either. But there is a basic message of salvation—there is truth to be found! Right??

I don't expect you to write me a book (ha!). But I think it's fair to ask for answers on these type of questions and get them at least in a condensed way. It seems fair to ask a "reason for the hope that lies within you."

Thanks for your time and efforts that come my way. I look forward to hearing from you soon.

In Love,

Daurelle Chapman

Chapter Seven

Ken and Shiela Coolidge

We wanted to write to our Friends to let you all know where we are on our journey as a family. These last couple of years we have experienced the full range of gain and loss that this life offers. We are glad for every experience that gives us insight into our own feelings, beliefs and ideals. Know that everyone of us walk our own path and as such we all are responsible for our own salvation. We, like others, have been frustrated in the past with choices others have made based on what we believe. Shiela and I believe that we have released that outlook from having dominion over our future relationships. We have had the privilege of having meeting in our home for several years and having loving relationships with all in the meeting. We value the fellowship of all who call upon God.

We have enjoyed fellowship with many from all parts of the country. We have more recently enjoyed fellowship with others who are not part of the "truth." We have been taught that there can be no fellowship with anyone outside of our group. So you would understand that this has been one of our conflicts. Jesus promised that the Holy Ghost would reveal His will to all that call upon His name. Thought of the struggle that Paul would have had, with those that he had been in fellowship with as a pharisee, when his revelation of Jesus was known. Paul suffered for the Truth from those who had missed the point that God is not worshipped through some method or set of rules, but, through

accepting the Gift of Salvation. We don't earn salvation with our very best. It is a freely given gift
from God. We cannot by some form or method enter into the Kingdom of God. We know that God is
not worshipped in buildings made with hands even
homes made with hands, but He is worshipped in
the hearts of His people and there will be evidence
of this in their walk in the world. If we love God
then we are walking in the light He has given us.

We have been led to believe that this fellowship
has no founding fathers but can be traced all the
way back to Jesus. When you make a fearless
search of our history you will not be able to go further back than late 1800 early 1900's and to a man
by the name of William Irvine and fellow preacher
by the name of Edward Cooney. We weren't bothered by having a founder so much as being
deceived that we didn't. So what's the point. Can
we now honestly say that salvation can only come
through the workers and all others are false preachers? If we do say this, how did William Irvine
receive his salvation? His revelation came and was
nurtured through an organization known as Faith
Missions, which we understand still exists and is
still sending out workers 2x2 but who do not believe that a particular affiliation is as important as
the relationship that we have with God. If you
doubt what I am telling you then review the songs
and the workers who wrote them. Do you find any
workers who wrote songs prior to 1900? It is a little ironic that some of the songs are by well known
preachers and Catholic monks. "When I Survey,"
was written by Isaac Watts (1674-1748) a well
known English preacher. "Jesus The Very Thought
of Thee," was written by Bernard of Clairvaux
(1091-1150), a Catholic monk. Fanny Crosby wrote
thousands of hymns, including, "Tell Me The Story

of Jesus," one of our all-time favorites. She also preached the gospel in the Bowery in New York City, was blind and lived until her mid 90's. A second thing you can do, is do a search of who professed through what worker and once again you'll get stuck around 1900 and won't be able to go any further.

So where else does this little revelation take you? If you have done your homework, and have got the founding father issue under your belt, then where does, "we are the only true way," statement put you. We can't be the only way when our "roots" are the same as those we have belittled. We are thankful for those who brought an awareness of God's will and salvation to us. How do you deal with the dishonesty? We need to let all accept responsibility for their own actions. It is their service and reward, or the lack thereof. What we would seek to encourage is an honest and sincere evaluation of your own relationship with God, the Son; God, the Father; and God, the Holy Ghost. When this has been your portion, then you will be amazed at what doors will open and what joy you will find. You will not have hang-ups with whether those you are relating to have found God through workers or through some other means. The false barriers that have been created between you and others will disappear and you will find yourself reaching out to a hurting and perishing world rather than withdrawing and criticizing them in their need.

I love that story of the Good Samaritan and all the little lessons that the story has had for me. First, that the man was a stranger and hurt and no one to care for him. He was dying from lack of care. Two very religious people went out of their way to side step this man and his need. Have thought they could have been too busy going to the Synagogue for their religious observances and really missed what God's will was for them. They didn't realize helping the stranger was more important than appearing righteous before each other. At that point in time, the Pharisee thought he was in the Truth of God. Have you ever felt guilty that you have missed meeting because you were helping someone in need? I have come to accept that as I am involved with life's challenges, that God has some illustrations to help me cope without fear, shame, or guilt. This only involves my conscience and not what anyone else feels is right for me. Likewise, I do not have the right to tell anyone what is right for them for they are only responsible to God for their own personal actions. I'll say that this has been a real hang-up for me in trying to serve God and has prevented me from growing.

The second story that I have appreciated is the story of the prodigal son. I have always enjoyed how the son was received and honored when he returned home, but these last few years I have appreciated the father's attitude when the son chose to leave home. We notice that the father never shamed the son for leaving and let him know that he loved him despite wanting to leave home with his inheritance. His welcome home was like a new birth and the joy of a parent receiving that son who could have been dead. The second part of the story that has been speaking to me is that of the son that remained home and his reactions. To me, outwardly he was doing all the right things, but inwardly he was rotting away with resentment. He was doing all the right things without the benefit of joy. I would like to think our Father was not making idle promises when He speaks of fullness of joy.

Recently, I asked: "What is the Truth?" I have asked several people, but all professing. Their answer was: a ministry of workers going out 2x2 and meeting in the home.

These answers are obviously wrong when we check the Scripture. Jesus said, "I am the Way, the Truth and the Life: no man cometh unto the Father, but by me." Love the statement that we sense Truth more than we think it. We know it more than we understand it. We can see it more than we can explain it. We know all of the words Jesus said were Truth. But we know that is not all of it, because it says there are not enough books to contain it all. No one has exclusive rights to God's Truth. The Truth comes to those who are searching for it and is free to those who sincerely love it. The Truth cannot be bought, sold, bartered, or traded. There is nothing secret about Truth, it will find us where we are and the hallmark of those who have discovered the Truth is their eagerness to share it. Lies cannot stand the test of time. Never compromise your right to know Truth. It won't betray or disappoint you. Actions demonstrate the Truth.

The TRUTH is NOT:

- Workers going out 2x2
- Meetings in the home
- Conventions

The TRUTH is:

- JESUS
- In us when we use His life of service as an example
- In us when we are motivated by Love

Shiela and I have enjoyed a new love and freedom that we were missing for 22 years. This new love is with the absence of fear. Some say they can't coexist. This love and freedom has come at a cost, but it has been worth it. When you can work past the guilt and shame that others try to put on your walk, then you will truly know of the Truth setting you free. We know that the Truth needs no defense and can stand the test of time. Lies do not stand the test and are constantly being defended. We have found that some may distance themselves from you as you turn loose of fear and start reacting in love. On the other hand some will draw nearer and you will share a sweeter fellowship. We will continue to love all no matter how they react to our joy and love. If you have questions call us and we will be open and honest with you as we have always tried to be. Don't rely on someone else's opinion—do a search yourself. The words from Ecclesiastes were real to me as I was finishing this letter. A time to be silent, a time to speak. I have probably remained silent for too long and when writing said too much, but I trust God's leading.

Love, in Christ.

June 20, 1993

Address:
Ken & Shiela Coolidge
13023 SE Hobe Hills Dr.
Hobe Sound, Fl 33455

Chapter Eight

Michelle Coy

I was going into the fourth grade when my family joined the 2x2's. We simultaneously moved out to the country, to a place called Flannigan Creek on Moscow Mountain, just out of Viola, Idaho. We moved out there, because my newly professing Aunt, Uncle and cousins lived there, along with many other 2x2's.

I was quiet and shy, with a great imagination. I learned to wear dresses, grow out my hair and be separate from the "world." My friends became those from professing families (including my cousins), and I began to feel farther and farther away from school mates and previous friends I had made outside of gospel meetings. I didn't know how to explain to them why I wore dresses now and why I felt uncomfortable with competitive sports.

After an hour long bus ride home each night, I looked forward to greeting my dog and wandering with him in the woods or down to a nearby creek, which served as a swimming hole, a frog catching pond, as well as attempted ice skating in the winter.

It was during this time that I imagined living some time in the past—where dresses and long, braided hair was the norm, and when learning skills like sewing were practical. It was the same way at conventions. I imagined I had escaped into a secret world. And so it was, so secret. I couldn't even explain my "weird religion" to my best friend, whose family was, and still are strong Christians.

I professed when my peers did and I listened attentively at gospel meetings, special meetings, and conventions. I took part regularly Wednesday's and Sunday's. I remember praying several times, wishing I could really, truly feel God in my life—but was always left with a black void. I concluded that I must not be praying right.

We were told to pray for others. That God wasn't to be bothered with our every day thoughts or needs. That God wasn't a "Santa Claus," as so many "worldly Christians" believed, as they prayed even for financial security! We were told to not pray for earthly things, but for the right spirit. We were to put "every thought into submission." I can remember riding home on the school bus and struggling with every thought, thinking God would punish me if I thought "wrong."

As the years passed, things began to change and soon my older sister graduated from high school and married outside "the truth." We found ourselves moving back into town and leaving the 2x2's altogether. My mother was seeing an outside counselor who advised her to leave the high stress of an extremely legalistic lifestyle.

I slowly eased myself into the "world" again. First, trimming my hair, wearing shorts, then makeup, etc. My junior year of high school we moved to Lewiston, Idaho, where I had to make new friends, I picked odd companions. And it was tough, because I was so shy.

In the years to come I experienced what a lot of young ex2x2's experience. **REBELLION!!** I smoked, drank, did all that I could, and many things I am not proud of.

Many years later I returned to meetings, (my parents had also), and re-professed, hoping to heal a troubled relationship with my family. During this time I was living on the Oregon coast in a program called Job Corps. It was there that I was diagnosed with a mental illness, as I suffered great depression and anxiety.

I attended college soon after, and met the man I was to marry. We sought out a Christian pastor, who required couple counseling before the wedding. It was then that we described gospel meetings to him, telling him it "had no name." The pastor talked to a friend who had seen the book, *The Church Without a Name*, and the next week he gave it to us, telling us that what we were involved in was, in fact, a cult, and that we needed to "get out."

The anxiety was strange, I had physical symptoms as I prepared to accept that what I had been taught was **TRUTH** was actually a **LIE**.

It has been three years. We are now Christians, as is my entire family. (Praise God!) And now I pray for all the petty little things I can. And God answers every prayer.

Love, in Him.

Address:
Michelle Coy
619 6th St.
Lewsiton, ID 83501

Chapter Nine

Dan Curtin
Truth vs. "truth"

My wife and I have been on the inside of this fellowship called by some the 2x2s, but known to those professing as "the truth," "the way," "the testimony," or "this way of truth and righteousness." Having been born again by the word of God prior to joining this group thirteen years ago, I was certain that, just like me, these people meant that the "Way" is Jesus; that the "Truth" is Jesus. Only a few years ago it dawned on me that they do not mean that by their usage, but instead, they mean their group as "the way," etc. That was very hard to deal with, and I felt I'd better look a little further into what this group really is all about. Enter *The Secret Sect*, by Doug & Helen Parker. That filled me in on the facts of the group's origin, power struggles, and formation of its mythology. I became angry as I read this well documented account. Angry because I don't like being ripped off— especially in God's name

Enter *The Church Without a Name*, by David Stone. This is the true story of one family's victory in Jesus over this "secret sect." And within the pages of this book there is healing for those whose spirits have been bruised by this system. The healing is really in Jesus Christ. The book leads us to Him as it exalts His amazing grace.

So, what now? That's easy—at least on the surface. We, my wife and I, are getting out. In spirit we are out right now. We are in the process of preparing our "going public" statement. We have stopped going to meetings, except Sunday mornings, and we no longer do the social scene with the friends (those group reinforcement sessions). The shunning has begun, by "friends" and workers alike. It was right on schedule as David Stone said it would be.

Perhaps some reflection on a number of events will help others understand why we reached the decision to get out of this group. From here on I'll refer to it as a "cult," because we are now satisfied that it is just that—not a crazy "people's temple" type cult, but spiritually just as deadly.

Several years ago when we realized what we were involved in we thought, "Well, let's turn the church around by our testimony." Whoa! Mistake number one. We really learned the meaning of the old folk saying: "Never try to teach a pig to sing. You'll only frustrate yourself and annoy the pig." How appropriate! Those who have tried to turn this cult into something better will know what I mean. Jesus let us stumble a bit, trying to do it our way— and we accept that, and now we are doing it His way with an incredible out-pouring of love from sources never dreamed of.

After our failed efforts, having our testimony distorted by those who view life according to William Irvine's gospel, and being on the "suspect list" of workers and elders, I recalled an old Roger Miller song of the late 1960's, "Don't Roller Skate In A Buffalo Herd." It was a tough lesson to learn, but we are wiser for it—and free in spite of them. Enough banter: on with the events I should have started three paragraphs back.

Two weeks ago the 23 year old son of a young professing couple killed himself. No one, not even his parents, seemed to know what monsters he was battling.

The young man came to his parents home on a Sunday morning and told his dad he wanted to talk with him. Dad said "not now, you know we have to go to meeting. If you care to talk, wait here until we get back."

While waiting, the son got out dad's 22 calibre pistol and waited until he heard the car pull into the driveway as the family came home from meeting. He went into his brother's bed room and shot himself in the head. The younger teenage brother found him.

We went to visitation. And it was the coldest experience of our professing years. The "friends" could he heard saying all manner of terrible things about the young man and his "worldly" girl friend. There was a lot of head shaking and tongue clucking—very noticeable throughout the group. People refused to acknowledge me and my wife. They can't bring themselves to accept her appearance. You see she has a very short hair style. She had brain surgery ten months ago, and that required the medical staff to shave her head. Her hair is growing back (and really looks neat now). But as you know women's hair, to these people, is a measure of their salvation.

My mother-in-law, a true blue "friend" all her life, was rebuked because she wore a red dress. And so passed our visit to the funeral home. We spoke with the parents of the deceased, and reminded them that the group may not offer healing or understanding during this "every parent's worse nightmare," but Jesus will. We then left.

At the funeral the following day the workers both kept true to form using a lot of repetition to drive their message home. The message that day was essentially "You have to stay in the true way; keep pressing on, or this could happen to you." This revealed to me how crude, callous, ignorant and devoid of compassion this "ministry" really is.

During the funeral service the young girl who was the girl friend of the deceased stood up and interrupted the brother worker who was ragging on about the need to keep "true and faithful to the way." She said: "This is wrong, this is wrong. Doug didn't have anything to do with you people or your church. Why do you have to say these things? Why can't you say a few words about his struggle? Why can't you say what a kind and loving person he was?" I don't think the people will soon forget that scene, but I know they will twist it too.

New scene. November of 1989. I took my wife to the emergency room with an unbearable headache. After several hours of tests she was put into intensive care, and we were told she had an arterial-veinous malformation in the right front quadrant of her brain. This AVM could rupture and cause death, or leak and cause paralysis. Surgery was required to remove it, and yes, there was a chance of death or paralysis from the surgery also.

If you are in love with your spouse, just imagine the fear, pain, panic at this moment when you suddenly find yourself talking about "what if I die in surgery," "what if I'm paralyzed from it?" I have never in my life felt such pain in my heart, not during Viet Nam, or at any other time. After a lot of tears and banging on Heaven's door, the day arrived for surgery. My wife was incredible. As the orderly was pushing the gurney into surgery my wife kissed me and said "Jesus said he would never leave us, I'm not afraid."

For several days before surgery I spent a lot of time on my knees—and I could not bring myself to sleep in our bed so I slept in a chair in the intensive care room where my wife was hooked up to a variety of bio-medical machinery. The nursing staff were magnificent around the clock! Of course family and "friends" came to visit. There was the anticipated head shaking, and my wife's sisters cried a lot—by then I was cried out.

One day the workers came. They just stood in the room and said nothing. Then on the day of surgery (which took 10 hours) they came again. They said nothing to me, but seemed to enjoy visiting with my wife's parents—dad's an elder in the church. Other of the friends came to briefly say "we'll be thinking of you."

But Christians came too! Boy did they come! From my office, from my wife's office, all day long they were dropping in. And everyone spoke of Jesus, of prayer, and they hugged me, and they reminded me that a great network of prayer was going up for my wife, for the surgeon, for everyone! And I appreciated that. Jesus responded days before. I know he sent angels to guard my wife in that intensive care room, and I know they were in surgery also. (I believe it is in Hebrews where the writer says of angels that they are "...ministering spirits. Sent to minister to those who are heirs of salvation"). It's true, we experienced it by the Grace of God. I know they were there. I could feel it. And I was very calm from that point on.

God gave me back my wife. No paralysis either! Even through our joy I could not help asking "where was the ministry of the workers?" Answer: there is none. One cannot impart what one does not have, and where there is no love there is no God. Our evangelical, Catholic, Lutheran, etc. friends ministered God's love!

Before I brought her home from the hospital, I went out and bought a very nice NEC, flat screen T.V. so she would have something to entertain her during her recovery period at home. When my mother-in-law saw it she nearly freaked out! She said to my wife when I was not there, "I thought he had a better understanding of salvation than that." Can you believe it?!? I'm not kidding, this really happened!

After a ten week convalescence, my wife was pretty much back to normal—except for a boot camp-looking hair style, and a scar from the 50 stitches that were used to put her skull back together, so for a few weeks she wore a wig. Well, one night we were invited to supper with our elder and his wife. Workers would be there for what I call their obligatory special meeting visit. We went, and endured an evening of idle chatter, which reminded me to ask myself again: "where is the ministry?" The next day one of my wife's sister's called with the grapevine update. One of the brother workers who was at supper with us asked my sister-in-law if my wife was still professing. He said he couldn't tell because she "looked like some kind of Hollywood actress with her hair the way it was"—and he meant it! How pathetic. Here my wife wore a wig so as not to offend the workers, and that was their response. Now she does not wear the wig, and they are offended because her hair isn't kosher! The pharisees of the first century would he proud of these folks.

Going back a few years to another event. Our oldest son (now 23) professed at age 13. He played the role for several years, and gave really neat testimonies at meetings. About his sophomore year of high school he decided to quit professing. No one, not a worker, not an elder even asked why. None of them came to visit, or even called. By his senior year he had some real emotional problems that landed him in the hospital for several weeks. Again, no one came to see him except "outsider" friends from school and their parents. He came through it well, and is successfully serving in the U.S. Air Force at this time. Where was the ministry? Not with the "lost sheep," I can assure you.

Another event. 'There is a "dirty old man" in our Sunday meeting. He's one who really plays the game, complete with tears splattering over the pages of his bible at every Sunday meeting. He has a history of "touching" women—any and all. About a year ago he was brought into court on a charge of sexually molesting his 12 year old granddaughter. He got headlines in the local newspaper, and immediately began damage control efforts by saying he was "set up" by a vengeful daughter-in-law. Not true. The social worker at school called the police as is the way it so frequently is discovered through a child's sharing the horror with her peers—who tell the teacher. Her mom got a call from the police, and that's how she learned of it. The old man (late 70's) now has the story out that he has been cleared by the court. And the friends buy that. Workers still favor his home. He was never disciplined in the church. He still is in full participation. We called the D.A.'s office to check on the status of the case. The judge stayed sentence for two years while this man gets professional help.

He cannot see the grandchildren without supervision. If he violates any of the court order he will go to jail immediately. I've asked a certain elder why, if this is the real church just like in the first century, there is no leadership, and no discipline. Why are things just ignored. He could not answer. I asked him where the ministry is, and again he could not answer. My father-in-law attempted to give me an answer by saying "you know, the tares will be among the wheat until the harvest." I said "tell that to the abused child and her mother."

We also have a new family in the church in the town next to us. The father in that family has been having an incestuous relationship with his teenage daughter. When it was discovered, they moved here, and people are simply ignoring/denying it even though our Department of Health and Social Services is involved. And my wife is shunned because of her hair? My mother-in-law is rebuked for the color of her dress?

And these events are really nothing compared to the heresy that the workers preach from the platform. For example I heard a sister worker say "Jesus drank of the cup of suffering and death, and we all must drink of that same cup." I heard an older brother worker say "Jesus will save us if we are willing for the conditions; if we are willing to make the sacrifice to be worthy of salvation." I have also heard workers say that there is salvation only through hearing the gospel from the workers. Their "gospel" is *not* the Gospel of Jesus Christ. I know that now. It has taken 13 years to discover that, but now that we know, we must leave—there is no other choice. I hope anyone who reads this will understand. This is just a little of what we have been struggling with. The worst part, for me, has been trying to deal with the deception that can be traced to George Walker and his seizing control of the group back around 1914. Have you ever noticed how the older generation speaks with a hushed reverence when they mention George's name? My wife grew up in a household out East where George frequently was a guest. I think part of her "fear" of leaving relates to the constant exposure in her childhood to this wolf in sheep's clothing.

But these examples are only a glimpse into what are the standard, everyday responses of the 2x2 church to the legitimate concerns of those searching for the TRUTH.

August 7, 1990

Address:
Dan Curtin
1032 W. Cecil St.
Neenah, WI 54956

Chapter Ten

Bob N. Daniel
My Odyssey

PROLOGUE

I find that I am torn between two very emotional feelings as I prepare this paper. On the one hand I have great concern that all of the negativism represented by this life changing experience could or will be multiplied as readers react in unbelief, and/or disgust and aggravation because I am messing with the "cocoon" of comfort they have built around their lives in the "fellowship." From my perspective, and it is somewhat overwhelming at times, I REALLY WOULD LIKE TO HAVE THE "PEACE OF IGNORANCE," which could be so comforting when I confront the alternative struggle of telling the truth to people who, mostly, don't want to hear it.

On the other hand, I am NOT ignorant of my experiences. For thirteen years I was victimized by a false gospel, preached by a "ministry" system built on cunning and deceit, and unwilling to reduce their doctrine to writing—falsely insisting that "only the Bible is our doctrine." Great and extraordinary effort over almost 100 years, by many hundreds of men and women who have made up this ministry, has intentionally and (in cases of the inexcusable ignorance of some) unintentionally twisted God's Holy Word, teaching an EXCLUSIVE doctrine, redefining terminology, while abusing thousands, even hundreds of thousands of God fearing people who obediently sit under their ministry!!

I REALLY DON'T FEEL THAT I HAVE ANY CHOICE. If my life is to have any meaning at all, I MUST DO WHAT I MUST DO to join a significant number of ex-2x2s who insist that the TRUTH be presented in as many formats as may be reasonable, so that ANY who may inquire will be challenged to look and see!

Although perhaps absurdly miniscule when my puny efforts are compared, I noted recently when reading about Martin Luther, how, when he was summoned by the Pope to appear at a hearing before his legate, he "refused to recant his views unless they were refuted by means of Biblical argument." At the Diet of Worms in 1521, Luther's famous response was; "Here I stand; I cannot do otherwise; God help me. Amen."

THAT IS EXACTLY MY RESPONSE. And 472 years later, the problem is still the same. Read on.

FREEDOM

It has now been exactly 3 years (to the day), since we were FINALLY told the full truth about numerous troubling doctrinal questions I had been asking about for many years related to the 2x2 fellowship. Everett Swanson, a very respected senior worker, visited us at the request of the local elder, Bob Pfister. Because of my insistence, Everett admitted as factual, much of what is believed (even though seldom taught), by the Christian Convention Church ministry. This church is registered with the U.S. government by this name, although very few of the members know about this registration. The group is more commonly called the "2x2s" or "Cooneyites" by outsiders, but a whole host of other names, including "the truth," "the fellowship," and several other favorites, by the members. All of this from a group who claim no name and also falsely claim no earthly founder.

My wife Joan and I were a part of this sect for approximately 13 years. We had Wednesday night meeting in our home for almost 8 years, and I was in charge of the Sunday morning meeting in the absence of our elder. The workers said that we should be like children, and I, like most children, was continually and I thought lovingly, asking questions. As you will see, I trusted these supposed "men and women of God" as best I could. I enjoyed the dialogue! They didn't!

NEVER, in our 13 year association did we EVER QUESTION the sincerity or Christianity of the workers or the friends. I just KNEW there was gonna' be good and accurate answers that would be forthcoming one of these days, if I could just get my questions worded correctly so that they could understand from where I was coming. Oh, for sure, we found out early on that some of the friends and workers believed that this was the ONLY WAY, but usually we considered the source. Usually these "radical pronouncements" came from folks we felt, based upon what we observed about them, were very loving, but Biblically ignorant people. On many occasions, based upon the promises in God's Word, we debated our own PRIOR salvation with them, as well as the possible salvation of some of our loved ones of whom we were intimately acquainted. We THOUGHT that our arguments were compelling, since we had God's Word to back us up. Alas, not so!

We were definitely at fault when we failed to properly reckon with this problem 4 or 5 years after becoming involved, when we became aware that we were expected to be baptized AGAIN. Our very troubling meeting with worker Harold Bennett at that time SHOULD have told us all we needed to know. More on this follows. Suffice to say, as you will see, these questions finally caused the "big guns" to be brought in to pronounce judgment on both of us.

We seldom ever had reason to miss meeting unless for sickness or being out of town. All who knew us would know how "hearty" we were. Now, as a result of being falsely judged, I have not attended a meeting since that "glorious" morning in our home on this date 3 years ago. At that time, after giving our testimonies related to our salvation many years earlier, Mr. Swanson had the audacity to tell us *"you are not now saved, nor have you ever been."* Indeed, the Truth (big "T:" God's Word), and "the truth" (little "t:" the 2x2s), have both SET US FREE! And we are very thankful.

GROWING UP

Joan and I were both born in 1934 in Cincinnati, Ohio to church going parents who were very simple people, not far removed from the farms of Kentucky.

Although attending different church locations, we were in the same (very fundamental) denomination, and we did not become acquainted with each other until age 15 or 16. Our earliest memories, and indeed our whole life, centered around church. Each week, virtually until we were married at age 19, we attended services on Wednesday night, Saturday night, Sunday mornings and Sunday nights. And if there was a revival, of which there seemed to be many, we could be in church every night of the week.

I can recall a definite date, September 27, 1952, at age 18 after returning from 4 months out west, away from home, when I made a very strong commitment to serve the Lord. I wasn't in church. I was in downtown Cincinnati, on Vine between 5th and 6th streets. However, as a youngster, many times I went forward at "altar calls" and earnestly prayed and cried as I continually asked Jesus for forgiveness and to come into my heart. I believe that with a certainty, now that I more fully understand God's Word wherein "He is faithful and just to forgive me of my sin and to cleanse me of all unrighteousness." I was BORN AGAIN at a very young age, perhaps as young as 6 or 7.

Probably most of us can recall incidents or people in our lives that have much significance. My great aunt, Miss Flossie Calhoun, was just such a person who provided many incidents that have been a beacon for my life. She had been a school teacher, but had gone completely blind from cataracts before she was 40. I must have been a favorite among many nephews and nieces, and she played a HUGE role in my formative years. She refused the little government assistance available back then (1930's), and made her living sewing aprons and selling them, as well as other "stuff" she could carry with her, going from house to house. As a lad I would often accompany her. I stayed at her place a lot, and I have "zillions" of memories of lying in bed listening to the many Bible stories she was so adept at telling. I would go with her on her rounds to her customers, which at times required us to ride a streetcar. Many times, and it didn't matter how many people were around, she would close her eyes and rather loudly exclaim "Thank you Jesus," or "Praise you Jesus," or some such prayer, spoken aloud, even on a crowded streetcar. As I got into my teens I'll admit it became embarrassing to be with her at times, but I really loved this dear lady. After more than 40 years of reflection, I believe her to be the best, most righteous person I have ever known. I knew that she was ALWAYS praying for me, even long after I had married and had a family of my own. AND, JUST WHAT MIGHT THIS HAVE BEEN "WORTH" TO ME OVER THE YEARS? INCALCULABLE!!!

MARRIED LIFE AND A FAMILY

The church in which we grew up was Pentecostal. It was VERY INTERESTING to learn, after marriage, that both Joan and I did not agree with some of their teachings and practices. So, mostly as a result of moving from Cincinnati to Detroit to join a new life insurance company, we decided to look around at other churches. We had never even been inside another church other than the one in which we were raised. With 3 children now, we had even more reason to be careful.

We were absolutely delighted to find so many committed Christians, whose love of the Lord was obviously the center of their lives, in a large Baptist church we attended for 3 years. We then moved back to Ohio, but to the Columbus area this time. We again attended a Baptist church for the first few years. We did not know until later that there were so many DIFFERENT Baptists, and that their doctrine varied considerably, depending upon with which "association" each local body of believers was affiliated. When we found that our church was a member of an association which included the National Council of Churches organization, and that this group regularly donated funds to the "Black Panther" terrorists, we resigned (in spite of the pastor telling us that our exit wasn't Biblical, and perhaps was even "sinful") and became affiliated with the Grace Brethren Church. I find it very difficult to accept denominations. I am a Christian ("the disciples were first called Christians in Antioch." Acts 11:26). We only cared whether the Bible was being preached. Although we later became very "unenamored" with much of the politics of large church organizations such as at Grace (which grew from about 300 to more than 3000 in the 7 years we were there), we both, especially Joan, learned a great deal about correct doctrine through an intensive ministry which included many opportunities for growth in Bible study type sessions. We even had a high school group of 20-30 kids meet in our home once each week for Bible study for approximately 7 years. We remained a part of the Brethren church until we moved to Oregon in January, 1977.

Both of us, but Joan in particular, wondered why it was necessary to attend an organized church. I tried to "go along" with her wishes of NOT attending a church, especially after not being that impressed with the several that we visited here in Bend. So, we started reading the Bible daily, and read it entirely through in the first 4 months of living in Oregon. We both bear witness that this was the most precious time of our lives, as we literally wept through familiar and not so familiar passages, realizing that new understanding was abundant.

OUR ODYSSEY

Not long after the events just described, during the completion of the construction of our second home in Bend, I overheard a conversation between 2 of 3 brothers who were the mason contractors. One asked the other; "are you going to gospel meeting tonight?" With my interest aroused, I then asked the older brother about what church they attended. He acted embarrassed, noted that his church had no name, and after a few remarks quickly dropped the subject. Of course, this really piqued my interest.

I remember noticing their wives occasionally dropping by the job site. They were very attractive with very long hair, always worn loose, hanging considerably below their waists. When Joan was younger this style was my preference. I mentioned all of this to Joan and this made her very curious! Since it was mostly at her insistence that we were not attending church services, as crazy as it seemed to me then and now, after hearing my report, she really wanted to check it out further.

I brought up the matter of his church to the older brother on several occasions thereafter, and was really dumbfounded that he didn't seem to want to talk about it, usually seemed embarrassed, or almost ashamed. Finally, after moving into the house in May of 1977, Joan "cornered" the older brother when he dropped by to finish something. She said, "Ted, Bob has the idea that you don't want us to go to your church." Now, he was even more embarrassed. With a red face he tried to explain that they don't believe that they should act upon "casual comments," but since we were obviously sincere, he would call their workers and have them give us a visit. They were at our home within the hour!! We were invited to one of their gospel meetings a few days later, and this little lady who didn't want to go to "church services," couldn't wait to attend.

For years the friends would have a good laugh about my "attitude" problem those first couple of meetings. I have always derided proud or vain acting folk. But, here I was, driving my Cadillac up to this run-down Grange hall in the tiny town of Terrebonne, Oregon. Going inside, I was "invited" to sit on an old, hard, wooden bench, which sure was different from my accustomed padded pew. We sat around the only "pot-bellied" stove I'd ever seen at that time, and I remember thinking that this place was at least a hundred years old when Abraham Lincoln was president!! Then I heard just about the worst singing I had ever heard, and listened to the two ministers speak, and I absolutely had no idea what either one of them meant by what they were saying. Both are now out of "the work;" the first leaving almost immediately and the other a couple of years later. I listened very attentively. I knew something about God's Word. But they just weren't making sense, and I don't mean that they were not just making "spiritual sense." Even their casual conversation didn't communicate. It seemed that the only explanation was that they may have been nervous.

After this meeting, I spoke to Joan, noting that they were just about the most friendly people I'd ever met, but I really felt sorry for them. This was REALLY BAD, I WOULDN'T BE COMING BACK!! WRONG!!

The next week we returned with our oldest daughter. Everything was just as "bad," and this time, both Daurelle and I stated that we wouldn't be coming back. WRONG AGAIN!!

After this we were invited to a picnic at the home of the grandparents of Ted, the man who first invited us. Again, these seemed the most "loving" group of folks we had ever encountered and I have always thought of this day as THE DAY when I was "won over," yet there was NOTHING said about Jesus, their teachings or doctrine. We felt that we had met a bunch of folks who really did want to be our friends. Although their worship seemed very simple, even somewhat primitive, we immediately accepted them as true born again believers and thought they accepted us the same way. The differences we observed even seemed refreshing. We assumed by what we did understand of the messages we heard preached, and our understanding of the conversations between us, that the workers and friends knew the same Father, Son, and Holy Spirit we had known most all of our lives. We began to go to the home meetings, and, beginning with the FIRST ONE, we partook of the emblems, not having the slightest inclination that we were not supposed to do this. Early on, we even began participating in the "testimony" part of the meetings. No one ever said a word to us, either pro or con, about our NOT participating—which we later found that we shouldn't be doing. And it wasn't too long until I stood to my feet in a Sunday morning meeting. I clearly recall nervously stating: "I am going to stop trying to prove all of you people wrong; I just want to prove that God's Word is right!"

In retrospect I am so happy that even then, in my view, God was guarding what and how I stated my commitments. The reaction from the folks in our meeting was very positive to this statement. When the senior worker, Lloyd Njos, asked in gospel meeting: "Is there any here who wants to follow Christ in this manner and in this way?," Joan and I both stood to our feet—"professing," as the term is used. To us, this was no different from our joining other church families when we moved to a new city. We had no reason to think otherwise. Now to be certain there is no misunderstanding, and we have discussed this many times since, if Lloyd had phrased his question in the manner we have heard consistently since, we could NOT have "professed!" He asked us if we wanted to "follow Christ in this way," a "way" which seemed to have attractive characteristics. He did NOT ask if we wanted to RECEIVE Christ—as we most certainly had already received Him more than 25 years earlier. And, by this time, we had testified about the fact of our salvation CONSTANTLY to many, many, of the friends and workers. This information is certainly not new to them. Nothing in Lloyd's words caused us to think that we were being invited into a group which taught an exclusive doctrine regarding salvation! And I now believe this lack of candor to be intentional.

That summer we were invited to attend convention in Saginaw, Oregon. I clearly remember the one day we attended. I took copious notes of what was said from the podium, and there were some statements made that I knew contained serious error, which I immediately brought up to others. These folks made me feel as though I shouldn't be concerned. And since the speakers were obviously so very pious and even emotionally moved by what they said, I pretty much decided that I probably was over-reacting, and I would soon get better understanding.

Then at lunch, while waiting in line, Christine Durflinger, Ted's grandmother, introduced us to another couple with this statement: "Bob and Joan, I'd like you to meet Mel and Myra Anderson. Mel and Myra, Bob and Joan JUST HEARD THE GOSPEL TODAY FOR THE FIRST TIME." This statement struck both Joan and I like a brick! We talked about this between ourselves and, not wanting to hurt Christine's feelings, we again fell for what was to become an all too familiar pattern of finding a way to excuse the error of so many for so long because they were "such sincere, beautiful people"—she just didn't understand. And, for sure, we couldn't help them if we left.

We continually sought opportunities to talk with workers about what is believed. Once, after driving several hundred miles to have an inspiring talk with worker David Jennings, I remarked to Joan about how wonderful it would be if our grandchildren might end up in the work. Joan even speculated about whether we should offer our own lives to this ministry. The worker in our field, Lloyd Njos, had a good laugh at that. And we wondered why.

If "feelings" had anything to do with correct belief and/or doctrine (they most assuredly don't!!), then at that time we were certainly the most sure as anyone could possibly be that we KNEW we had found, as I used to say, "the best EXPRESSION of God's church on the earth." And this is the phrase I most often used in my "debates" with any and all who were willing to talk with me. I know many will remember this oft used phrase, which was always followed by; "And if I find a better way, I'll join it!" Time after time, I used these statements as I related incidences about other Christian friends and relatives who had never heard of this fellowship. I was so incredulous about what we had "found," at about this time I began calling the group the "SS" (for Secret Service), not knowing anything about the book with a similar name, *The Secret Sect*, which has "explosively" exposed the cover-up of the origination of this church.

We so trusted the friends and the workers, the last thing we could have imagined was that their version of the gospel was different from the clear teachings of scripture about which we already had some familiarity. The FACT that we sat through 13 YEARS of this ministry without recognizing that there was heresy taught, is ample proof to a reasonable reader that these objectionable doctrines ARE NOT brought out in their "sermons" in a manner that a trusting soul would recognize. Now that we are learning of the degree of dysfunctional ministers, members, and teachings, we are frightened and filled with dread as we consider the possibility that our grandchildren could become victims of, and participants in, this cultic ministry.

We attended at least parts of every convention at Saginaw for 13 years, and even went to other conventions, especially Chelan, Washington—where I so enjoyed the messages of one Everett Swanson. In the early years, Joan commented a couple of times on the conventions as "sitting in heavenly places." Now, as much as I was interested and even intrigued, I certainly never reached that level of "comfort." This oft repeated phrase, recited by others, made me VERY uncomfortable. My vision of what Heaven was going to be like was certainly far beyond this, and over the years I resented the workers attempts at "selling" me on this being "IT!" Many of the messages were preached by some very talented speakers who had considerable charisma. There were some great sounding thoughts and we assumed them to be scriptural. Yes, there were times when we didn't understand some of the phrases and remarks, but we tried very hard to fit in.

I was thrilled when Wednesday night meeting was placed in our home not long after Joan and I were baptized, and we enjoyed this "honor" for approximately 8 years, right up until the day of their "pronouncement of judgment." But conventions gradually lost their appeal, as we heard almost the same things over and over. We were disappointed when our questions were not answered, but we again hoped that they would be answered if we were just patient enough.

So, we settled in, going to home meetings, gospel meetings, and "sings," and enjoyed being invited to various folks homes for dinner and fellowship, and inviting them over to our home. Often Joan and I would comment after one of these sessions at how unwilling most seemed about discussing spiritual matters. That is not to say that I would let it remain as they wished. I was certainly willing to be a bit pushy if needed, to find out what was thought about scriptural matters, but I ALWAYS felt that they accepted my friendly "proddings" in the loving "spirit" in which they were given. I certainly DID NOT know that I must have been engendering a lot of suspicion, which today, is really "grist for their mill!" Some "backtracking" might help here.

Four to five years after "professing," we found that there was some talk (gossip?) about our never having been baptized. Both of us had talked with the workers about this matter, and had been assured that this was not important, that if and when we needed to take this step, we would know. Since we had both been baptized TWICE, it seemed ludicrous to consider that this should be considered again. I wasn't as adamant as Joan. To me, if they wanted me to do this, fine. I felt like I wanted to be a part of the group. I even remember thinking and stating that if they wanted me to stand on my head, that's o.k.! But, not Joan!! We met with former French professor, now worker, Harold Bennett. After a lot of tears on Joan's part and a lot of loud words on mine, he informed us that we had to renounce our prior baptisms to become a part of this, THE ONLY TRUE WAY.

Now, why didn't we VOTE WITH OUR FEET THEN?? Looking back, with my "20/20" hindsight, I can now hardly believe that we continued after this. I can only say, that by this time we were so enmeshed with the group, with two daughters marrying professing boys and already presenting us with grandchildren, with our whole life centered around the fellowship, we never really even considered walking away. We just never dreamed that the answers to our questions that would eventually be forthcoming due to our demanding same, would represent the heresy that these workers surely teach. Also, we were assured by the "friends" that they did not judge our salvation. With that in mind, Joan decided she should be baptized with me, since she loved these people and wanted to identify with them. She was told that she would understand better after baptism. So she became patient and willing for what God might teach her. How blind and trusting we were!

More years fly by, and by late summer of 1989, we now have seven beautiful grandchildren. My family now makes quite a flurry when they all arrive at gospel meeting, with all of the children racing to sit by grandpa and grandma. We were very happy. Professionally, both my sons-in-law, Mike and Dale, as well as my son Kevin, all worked with and for me.

And then, IT HAPPENED!

I was on a business trip to Ohio when I made a routine call to my office. My secretary, Judy Renner (who, though Baptist, I always accepted as a sister in the Lord), advised that "this office is in an uproar!" She said that Dale had a client prospect come in for an interview, and during the course of the interview the client asked Dale if he believed that Jesus was God. Dale responded, "of course not, He's the Son of God." The man then carefully restated his question, to which Dale answered with a firm "no." The man immediately got up and left!

This caused quite a stir, since Kevin and Judy most assuredly asserted that Jesus WAS God, while Dale and Mike denied this with statements like; "how could He pray to Himself," and, "how could He sit on His own right hand in Heaven," etc.? Here were two young men who, up to this time, were really competitors. But, oh my, did this galvanize them and bring them together for the common cause.

Over the phone, I immediately responded with Genesis 1, where we are told that GOD created the heavens and the earth. Then in John 1 and Colossians 1 we are told that JESUS created all that is. It seemed clear to me, since there is assuredly only ONE GOD, that the Bible was telling us that the CREATOR GOD and the CREATOR JESUS were one and the same GOD—EVEN IF OUR FINITE MINDS CAN'T COMPREHEND IT. When I hung up I thought: "well now, this is no big problem. They just don't understand." By this time in our sojourn among the friends, I was fully aware that the big majority DID NOT know what or why they believed. With a few notable exceptions, they were (and are) mostly, very lazy scripturally—preferring that all questions be settled by a worker, even when the Bible is clear. So as I drove across the country, I dug into the Scriptures. By the time I arrived in Bend I had found 27 references which clearly taught that JESUS was GOD. I was anxious to "lay this on them." I JUST KNEW THAT THEY WOULD UNDERSTAND! WRONG AGAIN!!

I spent the next 8-9 months, pretty much constantly (I even retired to pursue this!!!), in conference after conference with friends, elders, and workers. At one time we had several of the friends visit our home, and this matter came up for discussion. My son-in-law's mother, a loving, sweet lady if ever there was one, was there. When I noted the clear and unmistakable reference to Jesus being God in John 1 ("In the beginning was the WORD, and the WORD was with God, and the WORD WAS GOD..."), she exclaimed "Oh, I didn't know that 'the Word' in that verse was a reference to Jesus!" We were, and still are, dumbfounded by this lack of knowledge which we have since found to be so very typical!!!

Later, in August during convention, on two separate days after lunch, a group of us were sitting in a circle chatting. One of the ladies who was at our home (noted above) asked me in the presence of the other 16-18 folks "if we could talk about THAT subject we had discussed at our home."

I said "of course, be glad to," not giving a thought to whether or not this was considered "my place."

I began this "session" by telling all that were there that I had a question which I needed to ask each of them. I assured them that it was not a trick question of any kind. My question, asked individually to each of them going around the circle was: "Is Jesus God?"

Every person there answered "no" to this very crucial question. I WAS IN SHOCK!! So I tried to show that God's precious Word taught this truth throughout the book. Apparently I failed to convince anyone. I KNEW THEN AND THERE THAT WE WERE IN TROUBLE!! But, even though I was kinda' reeling from all of this, probably because so many of the workers seemed so kind as we probed our differences over the next several months, we still had never considered that we might one day leave. Surely truth would win out!! AGAIN, WRONG!!

We have MANY letters from numerous workers, elders, and friends, who take about every position one could take, while we attempted to reason with them. The subject of who Jesus is, though, was just the tip of the iceberg.

When Everett Swanson came to our home with first year worker Steve Watts, again we were still desperately hoping that reason would prevail. It was only then that we learned that they not only didn't believe the Biblical account of who Jesus was, but what we had suspected and dreaded since hearing it mentioned by a few, was stated loud and clear as Everett reaffirmed their teachings.

He stated that IT WAS A REQUIREMENT THAT: **1.** EVE-RYONE MUST HEAR THE GOSPEL FROM A WORKER TO BE SAVED; **2.** ONE MUST BELIEVE IN THIS PARTICULAR MINIS-TRY, ONLY, TO BE SAVED; and **3.** YOU MUST MEET IN HOMES TO BE SAVED.

It doesn't matter that none of this can be backed by ANY commands in God's Holy Word. Indeed, they "interpret" Scripture, by twisting it to back up their heretical teachings. So it was at about this point that Everett made his grand "pronouncement of judgment" upon both of us, noted earlier.

And to think, I used to drive hundreds of miles just to hear this man speak. He was VERY convinc-ing in these messages, but he NEVER, while I was in attendance at least, preached any message that made me suspicious of him. And this is the case with most all of the workers. They are aware that the "real doctrine" which they are bound to uphold would offend many of the flock they are supposed to lead. And for certain, it WOULD offend many or most of those whom they are trying to proselytize.

I was devastated. I was hurt. I was angry. I never went back. BUT GOD IS GOOD!! GOD IS FAITHFUL!! We enjoyed being at home again, just the two of us together, having our own Bible studies, not unlike our experience of 13 years earlier when we first moved to Bend. We felt a need to send out a letter to a number of folks we thought of as close friends. We had not yet heard of an "exit letter," as we now know to be a rather common practice of sending an explanation by those who leave. In our three and one-half page letter which was sent out to 40 fami-lies and 40 workers, we poured out our hearts, trying to explain what had happened. Anyone who hasn't seen this document is welcome to read it, and make their own judgments as to our love or lack of same which is expressed. We only told the provable truth.

You would have to read and compare the few responses to our letter to believe what was sent to us. Some are quite vicious. One elderly lady told a friend of ours: "I hope he burns in hell"—referring to me. A brother worker, Lowell Stidolph, ANGRILY told us four times in his response to "...go back to that family into which you were born so long ago...," "God doesn't have any orphans", etc. And I've had enough of this kind of stuff to last a lifetime. BUT I WILL CONTINUE TELLING THE TRUTH!

Almost immediately after we stopped going to meetings, our good friends, Charles and Janice Gibbs visited us. They had attended meetings the past few years, although, unlike us, they were very wary and suspicious. I believe it safe to say that they WANTED to believe that this group was "for real" as much as we did. In spite of our assurances then that not ALL believed this was the only way, they wouldn't "buy" our story. Anyway, they gave us a packet of information which they had received from CRI (Christian Research Institute) about this group. To put it mildly, we were really surprised at the existence of this kind of data. We immediately sent away for a lot of the suggested material. THE WORK THAT WE ARE COMPELLED TO DO SOON BECAME EVIDENT!!

It would be a misrepresentation for me to suggest that during our "fellowship" with the friends, we have been victim, as others surely have, of many or all of the very negative experiences noted in several books and abundant letters now crisscrossing this country and indeed the entire world.

Mostly, we were treated wonderfully, by workers and friends alike WHILE WE WERE IN THE GROUP. For years we had been made aware that in Oregon we had a loving, caring, group of churches. Always, the credit for this, in my hearing at least, was because of Howard Mooney. To his credit, he seemed a very loving man, and this attribute was supposedly reflected by the people. But, SINCE OUR EXIT, all doubts have disappeared about the validity of these writings by ex-members which detail the terrible and even tragic episodes in the lives of so many who are now publishing details of their past. To use John Sterling's words, "They're not villains, Bob, they're victims," when he referred to some who had "lost out."

And now, so are we their victims, although we most assuredly have not lost out. This is apparently one of those infamous groups who "shoot the messenger," instead of correcting the problem. Because I had the audacity and the tenacity to keep asking some very disturbing questions, and (Biblical) answers were not given, it is evident that there is a 'campaign' existent to make US the guilty parties, rather than ever admit that the workers heretical teachings are what has caused this division. In addition to some very UNLOVING opinions expressed as a result of our memos of the past, I have recently been made quite aware of just how unkind, unjust, and unbiblical some of the "friends" can be.

Since typing the first part of this letter, I received a call from a man in Arizona who responded to some of the literature we sent. He was unwilling to tell me all of the supposed "dirt" he said was going around about me, but wanted me to know that the "workers" had recently had some meetings with my SISTER, who had told them all that they needed to know, and satisfied them that I really was some dangerous "weirdo!" Now, I have four sisters; two in Cincinnati, one in Houston, and one in Atlanta. None of these sisters know of, nor have ever had a conversation with any of these folks about their brother.

Then, in another state, the brother of a worker advised me that some of the "friends" in the Redmond church here in central Oregon had been making "very disparaging remarks" about me, telling, among other things, what a troublemaker I was, and how thankful they were that I had been removed from their midst.

Also, another former member has advised that the friends are making comments about my attempting to get a "following."

Add to this a personal confrontation by a professing man at the funeral of my son-in-law's dad recently, when he inquired of me: "Bob, how ya' doin'? Are you ready to meet the Lord?"

My response was a very positive "You bet I am...I'm anxious for Him to split the skies! TODAY!!!"

His only response was a very blunt "NO YOU'RE NOT!!!!" And he then walked away, leaving me "speechless," as hard as that might be for some to understand. I GUESS HE TOLD ME!!

AND, BEFORE THE LORD, I HAVE NEVER DONE ANYTHING TO THESE PEOPLE BUT LOVE THEM.

Howard Mooney became my friend. He was often in our home. On several occasions over the years I have heard him state that "one of the reasons we know that this way is true is because it works." And, indeed, this entire organization IS kinda' "wondrous to behold" from the perspective of the smooth operation of their conventions; the role of the workers and their ability to "wrest" from the flock the respect and honor attributed to them;

their unwillingness to ever put ANY doctrine in writing, which disallows the normal challenges which another could offer regarding their beliefs, etc, etc., etc. IT IS BRILLIANT. BUT BECAUSE IT WORKS HAS NOTHING TO DO WITH IT BEING "RIGHT!"

ARE THE CATHOLICS OR THE MORMONS OR THE JEHOVAH'S WITNESSES AND MANY OTHER PROMINENT FALSE RELIGIONS AND CULTS "RIGHT" JUST BECAUSE "IT WORKS?" Because 'it works' is indeed **NOT** the criterion. GOD'S WORD IS THE CRITERION!!

HOW BIG IS GOD?

Man cannot comprehend the God of this universe, who is so big, so magnificent, so awesome, as to make ridiculous a comparison of the size of an ant vs. the size of the entire solar system, to the puniness of man *versus* how "big" is his God.

The Scriptures clearly teach us that EVERYTHING that IS was spoken into existence by our God and Savior Jesus Christ. (John 1:3, Colossians 1:16, etc.) Just how significant is this? Recently I have read estimates of galaxies containing more than 100 BILLION stars, and there are more than 100 billion GALAXIES of stars!! We are even told that there are as many stars as there are grains of sand, and that God has named EACH STAR!!

And the ONE and ONLY God that made it all, looked down through time and saw that the one creation He had made with which He could have fellowship was totally and desperately wicked and depraved. Because God gave man free will, man had the ability to choose between good and evil. He could choose to love God and believe His Word, or reject both Him and His Word. Yet, regardless of our willingness to sin, He still loved us so much that He was willing to pay the ONLY PRICE THAT COULD EVER BE PAID, by descending to this puny earth, manifested in the likeness of a man, as

Jesus Christ, and dying in our place, so that we wouldn't have to suffer ETERNAL DEATH. Although the finite mind of man cannot comprehend this mystery, and God chooses to describe it as the sacrifice of His Son, His Word states that GOD, in His manifestation as a man, died for ALL of our sins; past, present, and future. And this occurred almost 2000 years before we were ever born and able to commit those sins. That makes them ALL paid for, doesn't it? PRAISE THE LORD!!

THE YEARS OF THE LOCUST

I will admit to feelings of frustration and anger, at times, when I think about the possibility of 13 wasted years. But, thank God for His Word, wherein I find comfort. In Joel 2:25 God promised to "...restore the years that the locusts have eaten." If He was willing to do this for His people in that day, I know that He wants something good to come from our misguided "wanderings", and can make "something beautiful" out of the "rags" of our lives in this day.

So, I KNOW this, and this is my testimony; if I had been the ONLY man on the earth, JESUS CHRIST, the Creator GOD of the universe, WOULD HAVE DIED FOR ME!!!

May God our Savior's NAMES (all of them) be praised forever!

AMEN

Respectfully submitted, with permission to reproduce either ALL of this document in it's entirety—or NONE of it, so as to help eliminate any misrepresentation due to comments being taken out of context.

Address:
Bob N. Daniel
17450 Skyliners Road
Bend, Oregon 97701

Chapter Eleven

Joan Daniel

At the age of 13, I returned with my family to our home in northern Kentucky, after living a year in Bend, Oregon. A minister came to our church for a revival. His sermons were mostly Scripture; powerful and clear. I realized I was a sinner and needed to believe on Jesus Christ as my Saviour. I was baptized two weeks later. It was a very meaningful experience for me and since that time, I have never ceased to have the desire to follow Jesus.

I never questioned the Word of God, but it took me about seven years before I started questioning what people taught me. As a young adult, I encountered teachings I thought were contrary to the Bible, but because of family, I didn't make waves. Also a certain amount of fear was instilled in me to not speak or act against those teachings of the church in which I was raised. I believed they were the only true Christians; the only right way. They were my authority.

We then moved to Michigan and visited a North American Baptist church. I was so surprised to find true believers in a different denomination. They accepted us as fellow Christians, and our earlier baptisms, but I did have difficulty understanding their doctrine of Eternal Security. I was still under the bondage of thinking that if I died with unconfessed sin in my life, I would be lost; good works and rules to be obeyed were necessary to salvation.

Years later when we moved to Ohio, I found the Grace Brethren church also believed in Eternal Security. By then I thought I understood it, and only had a few reservations. This church required us to be baptized again. I rebelled, but not for long. Here were these neat people who taught a lot of right things and stressed how important it was to know the Scriptures. It was impressive to hear their explanations based on Greek and Hebrew. How dare I NOT agree with them on baptism! My lack of confidence, and thinking that I needed to submit to their authority, caused me to "cave in" to the pressure to be baptized a second time so that I could belong.

I was a teachable person. The fact that I could not trust the Holy Spirit to teach me from the Scriptures without a minister's guidance was directly or indirectly planted in my mind. After all, I didn't know Hebrew or Greek; I hadn't gone to seminary! However, questioning was considered good. I'm glad for that!

Some questions we had coming into the 2x2s and brief comments:

Their claimed apostolic ministry:
I could never put the workers on a level with the New Testament Apostles. To me they were no different from ministers in other churches.

Women workers:
I wrestled with this. I had been taught that women shouldn't exercise authority over men and I couldn't find in the Bible where women preached. I tried hard to rationalize this one.

Their exclusiveness:
This did not compute with me. I knew too many people who loved God and I believed they were Christians.

Continuing revelation:
I knew this was wrong. I thought surely only a few had this misguided notion.

Their meaning of salvation:
I asked Howard Mooney about this and he told me
to make a study of what we are saved from. I still
have the study. It didn't help my confusion as to
what being saved meant to them. John Sterling,
shortly before we left, leveled with me, saying "that
is an ambiguous term; salvation is a progressive
thing; we don't know if we are saved until we die."

The celibacy issue:
We often asked about this and were assured by
some workers that if they wanted to marry, they felt
free to do so. That, in order to marry, they were
required to leave the work was not mentioned. It
soon became obvious this was a rule.

The history:
We were given Dr. Jaenen's notes to support their
claimed lineage back to the early church. Not
knowing much about history, this impressed me. I
wasn't told he was a 2x2.

Women's appearance:
I was given workers' notes about this, and I pointed
out to the worker that gave me the notes the emphasis should be on the meek and quiet spirit, not
on outward appearance. However, I was willing to
bow to these rules.

After a long period of questioning and not receiving satisfactory answers, I became embarrassed
when Bob would ask the same questions over and
over. I wanted so much for the workers to be right.
I enjoyed being with these people. Our daughters
had married such wonderful young men. We were
enjoying being grandparents. We didn't stop to notice how our world had shrunk—we were enjoying
our new life. I decided it would be best to just stop
asking the workers and wait for God to give us the
answers. Once, I thought we had gotten some an-

swers in a convention, but they didn't hold up to careful study. I was still maintaining my pattern of looking to ministers for answers—only now I was losing my freedom to question.

About the time of our discovery that the "friends" didn't believe that Jesus is God, I woke up to the fact that I was following a "way" and not THE WAY: JESUS CHRIST. I saw how I was obeying men (workers) rather than God. I remember the day this became clear to me and I prayed one of the most meaningful prayers of my life. I confessed my error and asked God to lead me into all Truth, recognizing that His Word is Truth. In gospel meetings, I began noticing how much the workers talked about the ministry. Speaking in meetings became harder for me. Previously, I had been inhibited at times in saying what I got from Scripture, often coming out with phrases that went along with what others spoke. I did not want to cause any problem by saying something "different." I wanted to "fit in." I remember once when I felt I had compromised—I always cringed when I heard anyone talk about "false churches" or "false prophets," but this night I used those terms. Of course, I rationalized that there really are a lot of false churches and prophets out there, but I knew deep down in my heart that the "friends" thought I was speaking of ALL churches and preachers outside of "this way."

I began to feel guilty as I remembered conversations I had had with the friends which probably left them feeling good about me, but me feeling uncomfortable. Once I stated to one of the friends how much I appreciated the patience the friends had shown us and what a burden we must have been with all of our questioning. She said that there had been times when she thought we never were going to understand. (This was after our baptism.) I won-

dered what she was talking about, but pride kept
me from asking. Then another time I spoke with
Harold Bennett and told him how glad I was that
he had been so honest with us. I was glad to have
the problem of baptism behind us. (I still didn't
think it should have been required, but I was told I
should be patient; that one day I would understand.)

In the months just before feeling forced to stop
being a part of this fellowship, I remember twice
having something I enjoyed from the Scripture, only
to hear the opposite spoken by an elder's wife.
Both times I just didn't speak, but it troubled me. A
couple of times, I told John Sterling (worker) that I
disagreed with him and he thanked me for telling
him. A year or so prior to this, he had mentioned
to us how he dealt with an "outsider" who disagreed with him. He said he just went along with
him when he visited him, but then when he got
him in the gospel meeting he "let him have it."
(The man he was talking about was quite outspoken
in his defense of the Scriptures. As much as he
liked the people, he would not back down when
confronted by error.) It became evident that John
was "handling" us in much the same way.

John told us a year or two prior to our leaving
that there was a founder around the turn of the century. This confirmed to us that this was no more
than another denomination. Other churches have
beginnings other than continuation from the time of
the early Church and we knew there are not apostles today. The only troubling part of this disclosure
was the prior deception. Later we were surprised to
find some people had left because of hearing about
the history. I made the statement in a meeting with
John, our two daughters and their husbands that it
seemed people were founded on the "church" in-

stead of on Jesus Christ and that if we are founded
on Jesus Christ we can't be shaken in our faith (or
words to that effect). I little realized that many are
founded on the "system" of ministry and church in
the home, rather than upon the rock of God's
Word. It finally was apparent to me that the "system" or "way" is represented as central to a
person's salvation. That is why so many of the
workers' talks are on the ministry and way of doing
things. At the time of our leaving, I remember one
professing lady, who had come from another
church, talked with me about this and she remarked
that she was sick and tired of hearing about the
ministry and wondered when they were going to
preach the Gospel.

When Bob renewed his questioning, I was praying furiously for God to not let us be deceived.
When Everett Swanson told us that "you are not
now saved; nor have you ever been" and said we
had to renounce our former religious experience, I
was so glad he had been honest with us. The effect
of Everett's words, and the knowledge that our
elder had told Bob he could not fellowship with
those having differing beliefs, sent us into a state of
limbo. Now what? Bob was hurt and reacted much
as he did when his Dad died years ago. I felt rather
numb, but "strangely" joyful. I believed that God
had answered my prayer.

One of the first things we did was to sit down
and read about Salvation. As we read the Word, we
rejoiced in the FACT that we were indeed saved. We
cried a lot of happy tears as we read the Bible and
saw the faithfulness of God. Bob was ready to go to
another church much more quickly than I. I needed
some time in the Word without outside influence.
So we began a time of reading together and talking
with one another.

After we stopped going to meetings, Janice and Charlie Gibbs, our good friends who had been coming to gospel meetings and who we believed to be Christians, gave us the CRI material and we wrote Threshing Floor. We first read *The Church Without A Name,* and identified with most of it. Later we sent away for *The Secret Sect.* In a visit with John Sterling when he came back to the field (Everett left shortly after his visit with us), we asked him about the history. He confirmed what we had read in *The Secret Sect,* except he left out Edward Cooney. I asked him about Cooney and he acknowledged that he was part of the early group.

John came to visit with us and tried to get us to come back to gospel meetings. In one visit he had with us and our daughter, Daurelle, he was agreeing with most of our remarks regarding other people being Christians outside of this fellowship. He told us about a young man he knew years ago whose Christianity he didn't question. Daurelle asked him why he didn't preach what he believed and let people know that there are Christians outside of this "way."

He said, "Oh, I couldn't do that."

Tears came as I said to him, "John, that is so sad, you can't preach what you believe."

Of course, since then we have talked with many workers and have found that often when we disagree with them, they will restate things in such a way to make you think they are agreeing with you. I never observed deception more clearly than in our experiences with these people. Often we came away from talking with a worker thinking that we had our question answered only to realize he had not answered us at all. It makes you feel like you are on a mental yo-yo.

The Gibbs, our son, my sister and her husband, and Bob's secretary and her husband offered to have a Bible study with us. We studied the book of John and the joy of the Lord filled us. We were surprised at how often we wept as we read the Word of God. His Word was a balm to our souls. He is faithful! The harsh letters and remarks of workers and "friends" did not take away our joy. We had to deal with anger and the frustration of the shunning. When you love someone you want to reach out to them and hope for love in return. Unrequited love is difficult to handle. But the love of God and the love shown us by Christians outside of the "friends" helped immeasurably.

I believe my lack of confidence in searching the Scriptures has contributed to my being deceived by the 2x2s. I know we were very cleverly deceived, but I must share the blame for allowing myself to become a victim of this deception.

At last, I saw the need to revise my thinking. I needed to rely solely on the Word of God. It was very hard for me to leave my daughters, sons-in-law and grandchildren and stand for what I honestly believe. But the relief of not having to rationalize or bend my thinking is freedom. People MUST be free to study God's Word, and live according to His Word without anwering to man. Being able to do this with an honest heart is a precious freedom to me. I must not be lazy and let someone else work out my salvation for me, but put my trust in God as He is revealed in His Word—not in what men say about His Word. God's Word must be my authority.

We have had to search the Scriptures more diligently than ever before in our lives, to find out what we believe and why we believe. The result has been a deepening of our faith in God, an assurance of our salvation, and a continual joy as we fellowship in His Word. There have been rough spots. Bob and I have had our differences, and I've come to appreciate the differences between people. As we interact with one another we can have our faith fine-tuned. We take the Word of God as our sole authority and test all doctrines by that plumb line. We don't want to follow men; we want to follow our Lord and Saviour Jesus Christ, as He is revealed in the Holy Scriptures. We are not perfect. We do not know everything, and are not "authorities" with regard to the teachings of Scripture. If you read anything we might send out and do not agree, please feel free to let us know. We want to grow in the grace and knowledge of our Lord.

We are enjoying the freedom of not answering to man for our appearance, or what we do with our time, or what we believe. The "bondage" of our Creator and Lord is glorious freedom. To walk in the light of His Word is freedom. To know the Truth has indeed made us free! The wonderful grace of Jesus has set us free! The joy of the Lord fills our hearts.

1 Peter 1:7:9 *"That the trial of your faith, being much more precious than of gold that perisheth, though it be tried with fire, might be found unto praise and honour and glory at the appearing of Jesus Christ: Whom having not seen, ye love; in whom, though now ye see him not, yet believing, ye rejoice with joy unspeakable and full of glory: Receiving the end of your faith, even the salvation of your souls."*

Chapter Twelve

Linda Dingeldine

I have come through the fire,

I have left the church that a very dear friend introduced me to,

I will ever be thankful to her for getting me to a church.

I am thankful they encouraged all to study the Bible.

I am thankful it is there for some people like me who need it at a time in their lives.

I am thankful my friendship with my dear friend came through the fire.

I have learned what great joy it is to have freedom in my love for the Lord.

I have learned that the "workers" are human also, and are subject to error.

I have learned that it doesn't matter where you worship, just that you worship the Lord.

I have learned forgiveness of a "worker" telling me I was never one of God's children.

I have learned that a bun is not a salvation issue.

I have learned God can reach you on a dusty road where there is not a "worker," just God!

I have learned that, no matter what body of people you worship with on Sunday, we all have flaws. Only Jesus is perfect, and only the Lord is to be worshipped, not the "workers".

The following verses have helped me put things in perspective. They are from the New International Version.

- Ephesians 5:17 *Therefore do not be foolish, but understand what the Lord's will is.*
- Romans 12:2 *Do not conform any longer to the pattern of this world, but be transformed by the renewing of your mind. Then you will be able to test and approve what God's will is—His good, pleasing and perfect will.*
- John 6:39 *And this is the will of Him who sent Me, that I shall lose none of all that He has given me, but raise them up at the last day.*
- John 6:40 *For My Father's will is that everyone who looks to the Son and believes in Him shall have eternal life, and I will raise him up at the last day.*
- 1Thessalonians 5:16 *Be joyful always;*
- 1Thessalonians 5:17 *Pray continually;*
- 1Thessalonians 5:18 *Give thanks in all circumstances, for this is God's will for you in Christ Jesus.*

Yes I am thankful for all the experiences that I have had. I am thankful that I attended the fellowship of the 2x2s, truth, or whatever name that you know them by. For that is where I heard the word of God spoken and that's where I made my choice to give my heart to the Lord Jesus Christ.

I am thankful I came away and am around people who have great joy in the Lord, and are not heavy-hearted. I am in a place where it is not important what I look like, but that I love the Lord.

I still have a friend that is still with the "way" and I know she loves the Lord and is a Christian. She chooses to meet where she meets and I will meet where I meet. I know God can reach anyone

He wants to, and it doesn't matter if it is on a dusty road with no "worker," "pastor," "priest" or "other Christian." He can reach you in the "way" or in the church you are attending today or in a prison such as that in which Paul preached. You can worship anywhere, whether this place or that, here in the country where we have all the freedoms we have, or in a country where they have tried to suppress the Word of God, even in a prison of war camp where you carry God in your heart where you go.

I pray God will reach those who hear His Word no matter where or whom they hear it from and that they find as much joy as I have found in His love.

Peace and Joy of God to you.

August 2, 1993

Address:
Linda Dingeldine
4117 Woods Rd. E.
Port Orchard, WA 98366

Chapter Thirteen

Noel and Christie Dolven
The Testimony of Someone Raised in the "Truth"

Personal experience: I'll quote bits of letters I've written to friends after leaving the "truth."

I grew up in "the truth." I spent *years* in the "truth" feeling worthless, dejected, unaccepted, rejected, depressed, oppressed, repressed, distressed, discouraged, hopeless, helpless, unhappy, and struggling to have the fruit of joy. I spent *years* in unrest and struggling for peace. I spent *years* sacrificing—I'd heard that "the more we sacrifice, the more joy we have." I spent *years* uncertain every moment of my soul's salvation; taking comfort in my devotion to reading, praying, going to meetings, taking part, modest appearance, being spiritually-minded—only to find out that I based my soul's salvation on the wrong things. I was taking comfort in the fact that I'd found what is called "the truth" because of its structure (homeless ministry and home churches). I trusted in "the way" because it was "from the beginning" and "unchanging" and "scriptural" and that there was "unity" and "love" between the friends. I felt sorry for all the poor deceived people in "false churches" and "worldly religions" with their "false peace" and "false joy." I loved the people in the "truth" and always felt a strong bond to them (even though I never felt inside that I quite measured up to their standards). No matter how hard I tried, I felt I was missing something.

Other people claimed to have joy and love and peace. I was restless and angry with my family much of the time, I felt trapped as a wife, mother, and in a life-style that I believed to be right, but which I resented. I didn't openly confess, even to myself, these feelings until just before I quit professing. The harder I tried to be what I should be, the worse my lacks (and especially, my anger) became. I began to listen intently in meeting to find out what I was doing wrong, what I wasn't willing for, what the illusive "key" was. I read self-help books, psychology books, positive-thinking books gleaning bits and pieces that helped but never cured me. It was like treating the symptoms but never discovering the cause of the problem. Positive thinking books led very subtly and with deceptive use of scripture and "scientific" terminology into the occult, meditation, self-hypnosis, etc. The power there was very scary. Finally I figuratively beat on God's chest and said "Keep me from Satan and self-deception! Give me love, and peace and joy 'ere I die!'"

And then one day, I was at the library and I found *Beyond Ourselves*, by Catherine Marshall. I realized as I read it that my view of God was awful and, suddenly, I realized that I wasn't born-again. That was it! That was the cure! Now, how to be born again? That became my new quest. I listened even more intently in meeting, read my Bible with even more diligence, subtly asked the workers their opinion but couldn't seem to find the answer. In meeting, I heard only that we were supposed to be born again, but not how. When I asked the workers, I got a put-down—"You mean you've been to meetings all these years and don't know?" It was agony. Why did God have to make it so hard? Finally I decided to read God's infallible Word from

Matthew to Revelation: *1)* pretending I'd never heard of "the truth" before; *2)* reading on a literal level, not spiritualizing or adding "understoods" to passages; and *3)* keeping a notebook of topics and questions under which I would write verses that applied to those topics. I promised myself that I would be completely objective and I prayed for God's protection from Satan and self-deception.

I was astounded at what I found. Everything I had been taught was diametrically opposed to what I found that the Scriptures taught. To make sure I wasn't mistaken, I listened attentively in meetings and went over convention notes. I was sure that, since I'd learned most things by osmosis, I must have learned them wrong. I was scared to death to go to Hell and also felt the weight of responsibility for my family if I should lead them astray. I began to pray for a revival among the workers. I found out **HOW** to be born again.

I began to discuss my finding with my sister and a trusted friend. The trusted friend immediately "told on me" to the workers, who were immediately over to visit with very short notice. People in meeting began to notice the change in my testimonies and began to be uncomfortable around me—I was "different," I had **JOY**. My husband was taken aside and questioned as to "what has happened to your wife?" He was innocently unaware, as I hadn't shared with him. Our marital relationship improved drastically. I was no longer restless or feeling trapped, or angry, or like I was missing something. I had the assurance that I was going to Heaven and that gave me peace. I learned that salvation wasn't something I could earn, it was a gift through faith in Jesus Christ—that He had lived a perfect life in my place and took the punishment that I deserved in my place. I learned that God is *too* interested in my natural life, not just my "spiritual" life; that He did *too* want a personal relationship with us. (I had been taught the opposite.)

I was born again before I found out that "the way" DOES have a beginning, DOES have a man for a founder, it HAS had many changes in doctrine and structure since it was founded in 1897, it IS scripturally unsound in many areas, the love it claims is conditional even among the friends (and more so towards those who leave), and that the unity is superficial and based only on appearances. When I learned these things, I felt free to share with my husband.

It was over a year after I was born again, that we decided to leave the "truth." It was a wrenching decision—we loved the people with all our heart, we had no "outsider" friends, we knew our whole structure of life would change, and we knew we would be ostracized. Also, at the ages of 3 and 5, our children were too young to understand why they couldn't see their friends again. I've already related the painful rejection by the friends when we did leave, and the stories that circulated.

However, if we had it to do over we'd do it again. Our lives are so much more whole, full, content. Our children are enjoying a normal and happy childhood, without fear and guilt over every tiny little thing. I'm free of depression. My only sorrow, and it is great, is that we have lost our friends in the "truth." They are too fearful and suspicious of us to chance disobeying what they've been taught, and maintaining a friendship with us.

I forgot to relate a few things. When we left, a close friend had a baby about 2 weeks later. I called to congratulate her and asked when would be a good time to come see the baby and bring a gift. She was too fearful of me to allow me to come or to receive the gift.

Another incident: When my son was 4, he went to an eye doctor who used Disney and Sesame characters to help with the exam. My son had never watched TV and didn't know who or what they were. The Doctor was incredulous when he wanted to know if it was OK to like them. I didn't know what to say for sure, but couldn't see any harm in liking them. Another instance of an abnormal childhood.

Address:
Noel and Christie Dolven
E. 7412 9th
Spokane, WA 99212-0181

Chapter Fourteen

Kay Arvig Downs

The following is a letter Kay wrote to Forward Press, Spring 1991 issue, along with quotes from some personal letters received from her and reprinted with her permission.

Kay went to be with the Lord July 30, 1993 at the age of 81. She is greatly missed.

Dear Ones,

Here we are—several different ones, none conscious of the other doing the same, having felt called out to do or say what we could to reveal the error in the Christian Convention church group, each of us having been believers in it for a time. But it seems that at the present time I'm the oldest of us, and Doug Parker was the second. (I'm speaking of the ones I know who wrote about it.)

As a result of you telling me that my letters seem to "Ooze a spirit of Joy in the Lord" I just got the idea that maybe it would be good for me to express my point of view as the oldest of us, a very encouraging outlook. I remember how it was with me when I was active in the same way you are today (40 and 50 years ago). It was a very depressing and trying time in my life, and at that time I couldn't have written in the same happy way I do now. But at that time I did have older friends, "exes" from that sect, who encouraged me as you say I do with you. They are all on the other side now, in that "City of Zion."

Let me give you a quick summary of how I happened to be interested in what is so vitally important to the group of us now. In my earlier adult life I suffered the trauma of losing (by death) our first-born son at two months of age, and later my husband, Ted Arvig, who had spent six years as a worker. That sorrow caused me to seek the Lord in a more serious way than many of my friends did, they being almost exclusively "in" that belief. Ted was quite ill, too, much of his last 20 years (eventually dying of bleeding ulcers).

Our second son, Ted Junior, is now 43, living in San Antonio, Texas, and while he is a born-again Christian and really practicing the life of such a believer, he finds himself influenced to this day by some of the things our little family went through in the 1950's and '60's.

My husband, Ted had been a companion of Ron Campbell as a worker, mostly in Idaho, in the 1930's. When we first saw a remarkable lack of love and respect of truth about many matters, we thought of course that the workers who were a little older, or a little more intelligent and high up in authority would quickly straighten things out to be what they should be in the "only right church" of this, our day. When one after another of these leaders failed us, we began putting two and two together, remembering how these workers spoke in a derogatory or scornful way about certain other ex-workers who had disappeared from the scene. And this included Ron Campbell, Glenn Smith, Matt Wilson, Alfred McGowan, Ed Kerr, August Gustafson, etc. All of whom we contacted in a close personal way later.

It happened that Ron Campbell had retired to his old farm in South Australia to be with his two sisters, and Ted still had his address there, even though there had been no contact for so long. I was the letter writer for both of us, so we wrote and sure enough Ron answered. He was overjoyed to find someone here in America who did not fully condemn him, as had been done by the head workers of those states where Ron was a worker. Ron was our dear friend until he died 20 years or so after that. He came to America and used our home as his headquarters while he attempted to right matters once more, by telling the real truth to all members of the sect who would hear him. After many months of this, and thankfully with the cooperation and help of Will Sweetland and Dr. Rittenhouse who had been closely associated with Jack Carroll's ministry in the western states, but were by then as much "out of the way" as we were. To his great dismay he saw once more that it was impossible to straighten out the problem and really help put the converts "back on course" with the true Christ as Head.

In the meantime, Ron and friends somehow found addresses of others who had been treated the same way (excommunicated) all over the world. I began writing to some of them and in turn they would pass my letters on to others who responded. That was how we had those mentioned above in our home, including Irvine Weir, Ed Cooney and others I fail to recall right now; also Doug Parker, his parents and wife (as well as Patricia Roberts, author of The Life and Ministry of Edward Cooney).

And so, you dear ones, who follow the same endeavor today can now think of me as one still living and still active who can look back over the 35-45 years since I first felt the call to expose the error, as you are now experiencing it. I have told several of you how I still see little change in any of those people excepting the few who were personally called out by God, and I see no credit due us for what we wrote, said or did! But these are different times, it is nearer the end time, and so it just might be that what I can contribute at this later period would be of some help to you via God's guidance.

The main kind of help to you that I have in mind is to lift your spirits if you get "down" and discouraged in any way. For today I am as secure in faith in our triune God and as truly happy, contented as anyone on earth that I know of. God has been so good in every way. I see that more and more all the time. I mean that now I see where it was necessary for me to have suffered many things in those days mentioned, that are not bearing good fruit, true dividends. OH! They are so well worth everything in my past! I see so much to be delighted about in the Lord today that each morning as I view the situation I say to myself, "Ah! All this and heaven, too!" The fact I'm telling you about this is that most of my Christian associates remark often about getting vibrations of joy from what I say or write. God forbid that I should say that boastfully. I only say so to you to encourage you that your endeavor will no doubt turn out to be the same. Remember Isaiah 60:22 "In its time I will do this swiftly."

Kay Downs

From Letter of March 27, 1993:

With each of you couples or singles who have recently "come out from among them," I'm so delightfully amazed over how "right on" your present understanding is, of the doctrine of Christ according to the Bible as I see it. You just seem to hit the nail right on the head exactly, as I see it.

You speak several times of that mark of joy. It's as much a mark of healthy vital signs spiritually as blood pressure is.

In 2 Thessalonians 1:3 I specially like the way it's said in the NIV, "I thank God for you because your faith is growing in Christ as well as is your love for others."

Chapter Fifteen

Don Ford
A Letter to the Friends

During the past year, I have written this letter to you many times in my head, but this is the first time I have written it on paper. Most of you have known me for over 25 years. The love that I have for all of you has not grown old or cold. For years we shared the same purpose: to love and serve God, wanting His will fulfilled in our lives. That hasn't changed. In the past year I have read my Bible and prayed more than at any other time in my life. I have learned so much, see much more clearly, and I feel a great peace. So many good things have taken place in the past year, as well as some not so good.

There has been so much misunderstanding, but I expected this. I have nothing but love and compassion for the friends and workers. I have not spoken against them, and do not intend to do so. I know I am not qualified, nor is it my place to criticize, judge or condemn. I have far too many faults to be pointing my finger at others. I have a love for all of humanity, even those who are not Christians.

Some have probably speculated, or heard rumors, as to why I discontinued going to meeting. Over the years in this fellowship, there were many things I didn't understand, but we were taught not to question. Those who questioned seemed to be regarded with disapproval. I never understood why because the Bible doesn't say it's wrong to question. How are you going to: "Prove all things"

(1 Thessalonians 5:21) and "be ready always to give an answer to every man that asketh you a reason of the hope that is in you with meekness and fear" (1 Peter 3:15), if you don't ask questions?

The authority that speaks for God is the Scriptures. Even though it is often stated that the fellowship is guided solely by the New Testament teachings, no one knows the Scriptural reason for some beliefs or practices. This is sad. Last year, a brother worker gave me as the reason I should believe something: "Don, you just have to believe the workers." Without a Scriptural reason, to "just believe the workers" is to have faith in the words of men. The Bible tells us to "Have faith in GOD," not men, and God's word is found in the Bible.

We have often been told that this fellowship goes back to the Garden of Eden or to the time when Jesus sent the 12 and 70. So, I was very surprised and disappointed to learn that it is actually less than 100 years old. The truth is that it goes back to 1897 and one William Irvine in Northern Ireland. He was the founder, and some of his early converts were Edward Cooney, Willie Gill, George Walker, Jack Carroll and James Jardine. I have thoroughly investigated the history. It is true and well documented in numerous articles in the newspaper *The Impartial Reporter* of Enniskillen, No. Ireland, copies enclosed.

Some in the fellowship say that Edward Cooney never existed. Contrary to this, however, Ken Paginton, a brother worker who attended McCordsville convention a few years ago, wrote a letter, copy enclosed, stating that Edward Cooney wrote the hymn Nos. 179, 182, 183, and 184. Also, Patricia Roberts wrote his biography, titled *The Life and Letters of Edward Cooney.*

So much about the fellowship has been kept secret and covered for over 90 years in this country, while it is common knowledge in the British Isles. You can only sweep things under the rug so long and then it begins to show. If you don't believe the fellowship is less than 100 years old, can you find even one of the following dated before 1897? A hymn written by a friend or worker; a photograph of a worker or friend; a workers list; a convention announcement or speakers list; the name of a friend or worker; any convention, funeral or meeting notes?

The earliest workers' list is dated 1905 and it records the date the workers went into the work. William Irvine heads the list and there were none who went before 1897. William Lewis stated to a reporter of *The Minneapolis Star Tribune* on Nov. 2, 1986, "Since early workers followed a Scottish preacher in Ireland before the turn of the 20th century, they have spent their lives traveling from home to home with little more than their clothes." Some workers say the fellowship came down from the apostles—John Badertscher told me the facts contained in *The Secret Sect* were true. William Lewis, an overseer, says he does not preach that one must be in this fellowship to be saved. In the past year, it has been my pleasure to meet many Christians, who are not of the fellowship.

Although the unity in the fellowship is often mentioned, there is little harmony in many areas. The east and west do not agree regarding divorce and remarriage, serving the emblems, ladies hair styles, Christmas, dress codes, and the list goes on and on. The workers don't even agree on doctrine. One lady asked a brother worker about the necessity of women having long hair and he said it was doctrine, not tradition. Another brother worker told her it was tradition, not doctrine. It seems the only things fully agreed upon are just some forms or methods: the two and two ministry, and the church meeting in the home.

It is not my purpose to discourage anyone from going to meetings, but I would encourage everyone to know what they believe and why. We are personally accountable to God for our actions and beliefs. Since this fellowship claims to follow the New Testament only, every belief should have its root in the Scripture. I encourage you to examine and test every belief you hold by the standard of Scripture. The workers cannot be our standard, as much as they would want to be. It is irrelevant what some man or woman thinks or feels; or the length of time a belief has been held; or who else holds that belief; or that a belief was passed down from another worker. The important thing is: What Scripture justifies the practice or belief? The only standard for God's will is the Word of God as recorded in the Scripture.

I am so very thankful I know, at long last, the true meaning of grace; "For by grace are ye saved through faith; and that not of yourselves: it is the gift of God" Ephesians 2:8. That salvation is a free gift we cannot do anything to earn or merit, Romans 5:15-18. "...the gift of God is eternal life through Jesus Christ our Lord" Romans 6:23. We cannot work our way to heaven. I know that I am not worthy of this free gift, but I am so very thankful for it. I want to do everything I possibly can to please Him for His "unspeakable gift." Jesus paid for the sins of all men when He shed His blood and died upon the cross. Jesus said, "I have finished the work which thou gavest me to do" John 17:4; "It is finished..." John 19:30. We can not do anything to add to the work Jesus finished. Jesus' resurrection was proof God accepted the price He paid for our Redemption. He opened heaven's doors. Without Jesus' finished work there would have been no route to heaven for mankind. That's why He said He was the way and that nobody could come to the Father, unless they went through Him. I now know the way is the Savior—Jesus Christ.

I am also so very thankful that I understand more clearly my God and Savior Jesus Christ whom I worship. I believe that Jesus is the Son of God and that Jesus is also God the Son. The Bible is so very clear on the deity of Christ. *The Prophets called Jesus God:* Isaiah 9:6, 40:3; Jeremiah 23:5-6; Malachi 3:1. *The Angels called Jesus, God* in Matthew 1:23. *The disciples called Jesus God:* John in John 1:1,14; 1 John 5:7; 1 John 5:20. Thomas in John 20:28. Stephen in Acts 7:59. Peter in 2 Peter 1:1. Paul in Philipians 2:5-6; 1 Timothy 1:17, 3:16; Titus 1:3-4, 2:10-13. *Some Jews called Jesus, God* in Luke 7:16. *The Father called His Son God* in Hebrews 1:8-10. *Jesus said He was God* in Revelation 21:6-7.

I did not write this letter to preach to anyone. I just wanted to let you know that I still love and respect all of you, as always. Please don't grieve for me...it is well with my soul. Please keep in touch, as all of you mean so very much to me.

Love, Peace, Mercy & Grace.

July 1, 1993

Address:
Don Ford
P.O. Box 255
New Castle, IN 47362

Chapter Sixteen

Lloyd Fortt
A Letter to Ernest Nelson, Paul Sharp, and the Friends

Thirty one years ago, in the final meeting of the second convention then held at Silverdale, I stood as the meeting was closed in prayer. The message had included Revelation 3:20, and my own prayer was to the effect that I opened my heart's door wide for Jesus to come in and sup with me. So began my journey of concern for the truth; a journey not yet at it's end.

Often as I prepared to read, and often in prayer alone, I asked, "Father open the eyes of my mind and spirit that I may understand." Nevertheless, some things puzzle me yet. With all sincerity and sobriety, I am concerned for the truth, because eternity is a very long time if one is wrong and misses the mark. Please bear with me as I share with you some of the things that trouble me. I look to discover sound and solid understanding, by whatever means possible. It is my hope that you may be able and willing to help me sort these things out correctly. I have not felt free to share these problems in meetings before, as I wish to direct them to the stronger saints alone, those most likely to be able to answer. This will contain a lot of quotes of scripture, so as to save you time in looking them up yourself, but if it appears that I have made any errors in the quotes, I may fail in the attempt to save you the time.

Ephesians 4:4-6 *There is one body, and one Spirit, even as ye are called in one hope of your* calling; *One Lord, one faith, one baptism, One God and Father of all, who is above all, and through all, and in you all.*

It is evident by this that there are not many choices of methods of salvation, but one alone. In my search of scripture, sometimes I wonder, as did Pilate, what is truth? In answer, Jesus said:

John 17:17 *Sanctify them through thy truth: thy word is truth.*

2 Timothy 2:15 *Study to shew thyself approved unto God, a workman that needeth not to be ashamed, rightly dividing the word of truth.*

Psalms 119:9 *Wherewithal shall a young man cleanse his way? by taking heed thereto according to thy word.*

The Bible has been my guide, as I have felt that my salvation is much too important a concern to entrust it to the opinions of others. But sometimes a brother can be of great help to clarify some things, only that advice, I think, is to be checked by scripture. I believe that God's word is the only safe refuge.

Acts 17:11 *These were more noble than those in Thessalonica, in that they received the word with all readiness of mind, and searched the scriptures daily, whether those things were so.*

2 Corinthians 13:5 *Examine yourselves, whether ye be in the faith; prove your own selves. Know ye not your own selves, how that Jesus Christ is in you, except ye be reprobates?*

By this I know that an individual self-examination is correctly in order, but how does one perform such an examination? What does it mean "Jesus Christ is in you?" How can one be sure that Jesus Christ is in him? Is there some unique feeling that shows the presence of Christ inside, because even though I had prayed that Jesus come in and sup with me, in all honesty I didn't feel so different afterwards. Does this mean that He did not come into my heart?? If so, how does this square with this scripture:

1 John 5:14-15 *And this is the confidence that we have in him, that, if we ask any thing according to his will, he heareth us: And if we know that he hear us, whatsoever we ask, we know that we have the petitions that we desired of him.*

Could it be that my prayer for Jesus to come into my heart was not according to God's will? If this is a possibility, what about this scripture:

2 Peter 3:9 *The Lord is not slack concerning his promise, as some men count slackness; but is long-suffering to us-ward, not willing that any should perish, but that all should come to repentance.*

Could one use God's law of righteousness as a measure to see if he is in the faith?

God's law of righteousness was given to the Jews through Moses, as recorded in the first five books of the Bible. One could measure his own standing before God by God's law; the result of such a self-examination would show the degree to which he is able to please God. I don't fare well at all. I find that I cannot pass the very first of God's commandments perfectly, and even if I could keep that one point, I surely have to admit to failure when I get to "Honour thy father and thy mother." While I looked at God's law, I did notice something, besides that I am a sinner. Though the law contains many points, scripture consistently refers to the law in the singular form, as a unit. The significance, I think, is that if I dishonour my father, for example, I am guilty of breaking the law; just as guilty as one who has committed murder. Conversely then, if I have committed murder, I am no more guilty than one who has dishonoured his father. What does scripture say in this regard?

James 2:10 *For whosoever shall keep the whole law, and yet offend in one point, he is guilty of all.*

Does this mean that there is no degrees of sin before God? My tendency has been to grade sin; to say that one sin is far worse than another. I think that I have been wrong in doing so. This is important for me to grasp, because if there are little insignificant sins, they could get ignored easily. Also, if there are no grades of sin, then a sin such as hating a brother one time for one second is as bad as what Hitler did to the Jews. My conclusion of self-examination by God's law of righteousness is that I am a sinner, and in no wise will I enter the kingdom of God by keeping His law.

One might try to argue that the law was given to the Jews, and I am not a Jew, but does this exempt me?

Romans 2:12 *For as many as have sinned without law shall also perish without law: and as many as have sinned in the law shall be judged by the law;*

Romans 3:20-26 *Therefore by the deeds of the law there shall no flesh be justified in his sight: for by the law is the knowledge of sin. But now the righteousness of God without the law is manifested, being witnessed by the law and the prophets; Even the righteousness of God which is by faith of Jesus Christ unto all and upon all them that believe: for there is no difference: For all have sinned, and come short of the glory of God; Being justified freely by his grace through the redemption that is in Christ Jesus:. Whom God hath set forth to be a propitiation through faith in his blood, to declare his righteousness for the remission of sins that are past, through the forbearance of God; To declare, I* say, at this time his righteousness: that he might be just, and the justifier of him which believeth in Jesus.

Romans 3:31 *Do we then make void the law through faith? God forbid: yea, we establish the law.*

Galatians 3:24-25 *Wherefore the law was our schoolmaster to bring us unto Christ, that we might be justified by faith. But after that faith is come, we are no longer under a schoolmaster.*

Ephesians 2:8-9 *For by grace are ye saved through faith; and that not of yourselves: it is the gift of God: Not of works, lest any man should boast.*

What is this faith through which we are saved by grace? In meetings I have often heard that faith is belief in the unseen. At the Prince George convention we heard about faith and how it comes to us. In my notes I have written, "Faith is believing what you do not see. When we first come to meetings, and before faith comes, we must almost like the messengers, or trust them, then faith will come." I not only like the messengers, but I love them, and yet the faith or trust I have in them doesn't seem to fit the bill.

I'm going to get a bit simplistic, or stupid here, and so I apologize up front, but in order to illustrate what my problem is: no one can see the wind; will belief then in the wind save? Again, and even worse, no one can see Satan, and of course belief in him will not save anyone. Obviously, the object of the belief is crucial; yet scripture does agree with the worker, that faith is believing what you do not see.

Hebrews 11:1 *Now faith is the substance of things hoped for, the evidence of things not seen.*

Hebrews 11:7 *By faith Noah, being warned of God of things not seen as yet, moved with fear, prepared an ark to the saving of his house; by the which he condemned the world, and became heir of the righteousness which is by faith.*

Hebrews 11:8 *By faith Abraham, when he was called to go out into a place which he should after receive for an inheritance, obeyed; and he went out, not knowing whither he went.*

Hebrews 11:17 *By faith Abraham, when he was tried, offered up Isaac: and he that had received the promises offered up his only begotten son,*

Hebrews 11:18-19 *Of whom it was said, That in Isaac shall thy seed be called: Accounting that God was able to raise him up, even from the dead; from whence also he received him in a figure.*

What is common to both Noah and Abraham? Noah was warned of God, he believed God and staked not only his own life on what God told him, but the lives of his house. Abraham was promised some things by God, he believed God to the point of unquestioningly offering up the one in whom the promises were to be fulfilled, believing God to be able to deliver on His promises anyway. They both believed God, and obeyed Him without question. The object of their faith was God. they believed what God told them even when it seemed illogical or impossible in the human sense.

If a definition is good, then it should make perfect sense when substituted for that word; Ephesians 2:8 (substituting) *For by grace are ye saved through believing what God has said even if it seems illogical or impossible; and that not of yourselves: it is the gift of God:*

So what then is grace?

Esther 2:17 *And the king loved Esther above all the women, and she obtained grace and favour in his sight more than all the virgins; so that he set the royal crown upon her head, and made her queen instead of Vashti.*

One element shown here about grace is that Esther received the royal crown even though she was not entitled to it, out of the king's favour. Grace here is equated with favour.

Galatians 5:4 *Christ is become of no effect unto you, whosoever of you are justified by the law; ye are fallen from grace.*

Neither Christ, nor grace is of the law, both are separate from the law to those who are under grace.

Romans 4:4 *Now to him that worketh is the reward not reckoned of grace, but of debt.*

Romans 11:6 *And if by grace, then is it no more of works: otherwise grace is no more grace. But if it be of works, then is it no more grace: otherwise work is no more work.*

Romans 3:24-26 *Being justified freely by his grace through the redemption that is in Christ Jesus: Whom God hath set forth to be a propitiation through faith in his blood, to declare his righteousness for the remission of sins that are past, through the forbearance of God; To declare, I say, at this time his righteousness: that he might be just, and the justifier of him which believeth in Jesus.*

Grace in these verses is contrasted with debt. In other words, if the reward is worked for, then it is received as payment or wages. So, grace, not being of debt for work that must be performed, must then be a free gift.

What is forbearance? An example of forbearance would be: if I were struck in the face for no reason, and though thus being entitled to strike back in retaliation, instead, I held back from retaliation of any form; a quality that Jesus showed always.

To summarize: grace then according to scripture, is a free gift of favour that holds back God's just retaliation for sin.

Ephesians 2:8 (substituting meanings) *For by a free gift of favour that holds back God's just retaliation for sin are ye saved through believing what God has said even if it seems illogical or impossible; and that not of yourselves: it is the gift of God:*

1 Corinthians 6:11 *And such were some of you: but ye are washed, but ye are sanctified, but ye are justified in the name of the Lord Jesus, and by the Spirit of our God.*

What does it mean, "ye are sanctified"?

To sanctify is to make holy; a process, as is denoted by the word "make."

What does it mean, "ye are justified"?

To justify is to acquit of guilt; a declaration of a position of righteousness.

According to scripture then, in the name of Jesus, the believer is washed, and begins the process of sanctification: he is justified, or declared righteous, having the righteousness of Jesus through faith in His blood. This is done by the Spirit of our God, the comforter who was sent by Jesus to dwell in the believer, and to guide him into all truth.

What does the Bible say that God told us to believe in order to be saved? In other words, what are we told is to be the object of our faith through which we have access to God's saving grace?

John 3:16 *For God so loved the world, that he gave his only begotten Son, that whosoever believeth in him should not perish, but have everlasting life.*

1 John 5:10 *He that believeth on the Son of God hath the witness in himself: he that believeth not God hath made him a liar; because he believeth not the record that God gave of his Son.*

Acts 4:10-12 *Be it known unto you all, and to all the people of Israel, that by the name of Jesus Christ of Nazareth, whom ye crucified, whom God raised from the dead, even by him doth this man stand here before you whole. This is the stone which was set at nought of you builders, which is become the head of the corner. Neither is there salvation in any other: for there is none other name under heaven given among men, whereby we must be saved.*

John 14:6 *Jesus saith unto him, I am the way, the truth, and the life: no man cometh unto the Father, but by me.*

The object of Noah's, and Abraham's faith, as shown before, was God: the object of our faith as shown in the above verses, is to be Jesus Christ. Does this then constitute a change in God's mind?

Malachi 3:6 *For I am the* LORD, *I change not; therefore ye sons of Jacob are not consumed.*

What then is the record that God gave of His Son; that which, if we believe not we make God a liar? It seems to me that the following verses are part of it.

Acts 20:28 *Take heed therefore unto yourselves, and to all the flock, over the which the Holy Ghost hath made you overseers, to feed the church of God, which he hath purchased **with his own blood.***

Titus 2:13 *Looking for that blessed hope, and the glorious appearing of the great God and our Saviour Jesus Christ;*

John 20:27-29 *Then saith he to Thomas, Reach hither thy finger, and behold my hands; and reach hither thy hand, and thrust it into my side: and be not faithless, but believing. And Thomas answered and said unto him, My Lord and my God. Jesus saith unto him, Thomas, because thou hast seen*

me, thou hast believed: blessed are they that have
not seen, and yet have believed.

Hebrews 1:8 *But unto the Son he saith, Thy
throne, O God, is for ever and ever: a sceptre of
righteousness is the sceptre of thy kingdom.*

John 1:1, 14 *In the beginning was the Word,
and the Word was with God, and the Word was
God. And the Word was made flesh, and dwelt
among us, (and we beheld his glory, the glory as of
the only begotten of the Father,) full of grace and
truth.*

John 1:3 *All things were made by him; and without him was not any thing made that was made.*

Hebrews 1:2 *Hath in these last days spoken
unto us by his Son, whom he hath appointed heir
of all things, by whom also he made the worlds;*

Genesis 1:1 *In the beginning **God** created the
heaven and the earth.*

Isaiah 9:6 *For unto us a child is born, unto us a
son is given: and the government shall be upon his
shoulder: and his name shall be called Wonderful,
Counsellor, The mighty God, The everlasting Father, The Prince of Peace.*

How can Jesus be God?

By human reasoning, it is impossible that Jesus
is God; it is illogical; just the kind of thing that
Noah and Abraham believed when *God* told them.

Who raised Jesus from the dead?

John 2:18-22 *Then answered the Jews and said
unto him, What sign shewest thou unto us, seeing
that thou doest these things? Jesus answered and
said unto them, Destroy this temple, and in three
days **I will raise** it up. Then said the Jews, Forty
and six years was this temple in building, and wilt
thou rear it up in three days? But he spake of the
temple of his body. When therefore he was risen
from the dead, his disciples remembered that he*

had said this unto them; and they believed the scripture, and the word which Jesus had said.

Acts 10:40 *Him* **God** *raised up the third day, and shewed him openly;*

Romans 8:11 *But if the Spirit of him that raised up Jesus from the dead dwell in you, he that raised up Christ from the dead shall also quicken your mortal bodies by his* **Spirit** *that dwelleth in you.*

According to scripture, Jesus raised Himself, God raised Him, and God's Spirit raised up Jesus. Was Jesus then raised from the dead three times?

What does God tell us about His Spirit?

Acts 5:3-4 *But Peter said, Ananias, why hath Satan filled thine heart to lie to the Holy Ghost, and to keep back part of the price of the land? While it remained, was it not thine own? and after it was sold, was it not in thine own power? why hast thou conceived this thing in thine heart? thou hast not lied unto men, but unto* **God**.

Romans 8:9-10 *But ye are not in the flesh, but in the Spirit, if so be that the* **Spirit of God** *dwell in you. Now if any man have not the* **Spirit of Christ**, *he is none of his. And if* **Christ** *be in you, the body is dead because of sin; but the Spirit is life because of righteousness.*

Proverbs 3:5 *Trust in the* LORD *with all thine heart; and lean not unto thine own understanding.*

James 1:5-6 *If any of you lack wisdom, let him ask of God, that giveth to all men liberally, and upbraideth not; and it shall be given him. But let him ask in faith, nothing wavering. For he that wavereth is like a wave of the sea driven with the wind and tossed.*

Matthew 7:22-23 *Many will say to me in that day, Lord, Lord, have we not prophesied in thy name? and in thy name have cast out devils? and in thy name done many wonderful works? And then will I profess unto them, I never knew you: depart from me, ye that work iniquity.*

Until I worked alongside of a man, whose name was Jesus, I never paid much attention to what scripture says about "another Jesus." You would be amazed how many people have the name Jesus; apparently a popular name in Central America, and South America, not to mention the Mediterranean area. This is however, not of a religious usage, of course.

Does one then just call the name "Jesus," and therefore have the correct "Jesus"? Does it not make good sense that one must know who the Biblical Jesus is?

To Jehovah's Witnesses, Jesus is the Archangel Michael, and was raised in spirit only.

To Mormons, Jesus is the spirit brother of the devil.

To Christian Scientists, Jesus didn't really die, but hid alive in the sepulchre.

The Bahgwan Rajneesh said, "When you call Jesus, really you have called me; and when you call me, really you have called Jesus." (utter BLASPHEMY)

2 Corinthians 11:3-4 *But I fear, lest by any means, as the serpent beguiled Eve through his subtilty, so your minds should be corrupted from the simplicity that is in Christ. For if he that cometh preacheth another Jesus, whom we have not preached, or if ye receive another spirit, which ye have not received, or another gospel, which ye have not accepted, ye might well bear with him.*

Galatians 1:8 *But though we, or an angel from heaven, preach any other gospel unto you than that which we have preached unto you, let him be accursed.*

God's Word say that the Father is God, Jesus is God, and the Holy Ghost is God. Also God says that there is one God. Again, God says that He raised Jesus, Jesus raised Himself, and God's Spirit raised Jesus. In Romans 8:9-10, the believer has God's Spirit in him, the Spirit of Christ in him, and Christ in him. Only in the context that the one living God is Father, Son, and Holy Ghost, can I make any logical sense from these verses of scripture. Now, if these were the only verses of scripture that present this view of God, I may be able to somehow come to a different conclusion of what God tells of Himself, but I find that scripture is absolutely full of verses and concepts of this view of God. To write more of them will soon make this a book rather than a letter, but if you will look into this for yourself, with prayer, you will see what I mean. Just because we as finite beings, find it difficult or impossible to understand all about God, who has the power to create all, which also we cannot understand, does not mean that His Word is any less true. We do not make it true by our belief, it is already true.

According to God's Word, having the correct Jesus is absolutely crucial, and essential to salvation. The teaching of Who the Way, the Truth, and the Life is makes the difference between Biblical truth, and damnable heresy. A gospel devoid of the Biblical Jesus, is also devoid of offering salvation, being Christ-less.

Prince George Convention 1989	**What does God say?**
Abraham made a commitment to God, he was faithful in building altars for sacrifice and had great security because he was faithful.	Romans 4:3 "For what saith the scripture? Abraham *believed God*, and it was *counted* unto him *for righteousness*."

Prince George 1989

We need security; if we make a commitment, we will have security.

Paul finished his course, he was committed to the race. He had only the course in view, it was his goal.

Faith is believing what you do not see. When we first come to meetings, and before faith comes, we must almost like the messengers, or trust them, then faith will come.

There are two things to believe in order to come to the position of faith, 1) What Jesus did for us, and 2) That this is the way of God.

Faith comes first, and then there is the battle over willingness.

Silverdale l968

If you want to know true Christianity, its those that follow Jesus. Jesus is the way, he left only one set of footsteps. (Paul Sharp) [Do the footsteps save, or the one who made them?]

Gospel of faith in the messengers and hard labour.

What does God say?

1John 5:12 He that *hath the Son hath life*; and he that hath not the Son of God hath not life.

1Corinthians 2:2 "For I determined not to know any thing among you, save *Jesus Christ*, and him crucified."

Romans 10:17 "So then faith cometh *by hearing*, and hearing *by the word of God*."

Romans 10:17 "So then faith cometh by hearing, and hearing by the word of God."

Jo 14:6 Jesus saith unto him, I am the *way*, the *truth*, and the *life*: no man cometh unto the Father, but by *me*.

Ephesians 2:8-9 "For by grace are ye saved *through faith*; and that not of yourselves: it is the *gift of God*: Not of works, lest any man should boast."

John 14:6 "Jesus saith unto him, I am the way, the truth, and the life: no man cometh unto the Father, but by me."

Gospel of Jesus Christ and freedom from sin

Galatians 1:8 "But though we, or an angel from heaven, preach any other gospel unto you than that which we have preached unto you, let him be accursed."

Paul, Ernest:

The responsibility that you carry is indeed an awesome one. The history of that which you call "The Truth," (though you claim no name) is out. God has seen to it that deceit is stopped. You have a choice, while you yet have breath, but soon you will confess to the eternal and living God. It is my prayer for you that God will have mercy on you both, and give you space to repent, and to know the real Jesus Christ. I would remind you of the thief on the cross at Jesus' side, who was promised paradise that very day, though he had no time for works of righteousness, nor baptism, he recognized Jesus, and repented of his ridicule, confessed Jesus as Lord, and called on Him for remembrance. It is not by the works of men, but by the work of the one and only God-man, Jesus Christ, on our behalf that we can be set free from sin. May the love of God so pierce your hearts that you receive the one in whom is life.

Lloyd Fortt

Chapter Seventeen

Dale Gardner

My parents professed when I was about 4 and I professed at age 12. For the next 30 years I blindly followed the teachings of the "workers" with confidence that I was in the only true way of God. Then came a series of events that woke me to the fact that many of their teachings and actions are not in line with the word of God. Finally, the discovery that many of the "workers" are child molesters and fornicators, some for as many as 40 years and protected by the senior "workers," was the catalyst that caused me to recognize that I was part of the "congregation of the dead." Prov. 21.16 We made a prolonged effort to convince the church that these matters needed to be examined and then taken care of as the scriptures direct. As a result of our efforts, our elder, Ralph Crist of Colorado Springs, told us that he could not go against Murray Keene and since Murray did not want me in the meeting I was not to come back to meeting.

It took me several years, after 30 years of indoctrination, to finally understand that the little group who call themselves the friends is not "The Truth" and "The Way," as they so confidently claim. I am very thankful that I now understand that the Truth of God and The Way of God are not defined by God as the "friends" or as the church of Christian Conventions as the "workers" named it for the government of the USA. It is now so clear to me that the church of God is made up of people scattered over the face of the earth who love the Lord their

God with all their heart, soul and mind and love their neighbor as themselves.

I'm very thankful now, that I was put out of the "church," as it was the experience I needed to wake me from the sleep that the workers are so gifted in producing among believers. I would like to say to any who have left or are thinking of leaving The Church of Christian Conventions, that it may be a slow process to wake from the sleep that the congregation of the dead produces. Although it may be a slow and painful process, it is so worth the pain. I now have a wonderful freedom to learn to worship the Father in spirit and in truth, free from the control of one of many cult religions whose poor members call The Truth.

I would certainly recommend that you separate from the deadness of this cult and search after God with all of your heart. He promised that if you do, you will find Him!

June 30, 1993

Address:
Dale Gardner
12680 Herring Rd.
Colorado Springs, Colorado 80908

Letters to Workers

1/24/92

Dear Selma,

In today's mail we received a copy of a letter you wrote to Tharold on March 4, 1991. Your clearly stated conviction that "Threshingfloor may be doing us a favor by bringing some of these things out into the open so we are forced to deal more thoroughly with them," brought great relief to our heart. I have prayed many times that some worker or workers, old or young, male or female, would simply be brave enough to earnestly contend for the faith once delivered and express their concern about sexual immorality in the church.

If, as a people, we do not handle these matters by God's directions we will surely pay a great price. Are you aware that unrepentant child molesters (workers) have been concealed by the overseers of the east for over 40 years? There are a number of workers under Taylor Wood who have been hidden and moved from place to place for many years.

We were put out of the church several years ago for exposing child molesting workers to the church. We then made an in-depth study of the situation and have a great deal of information about the matter, which we have shared with others. We talked to a number of victims, parents, etc. and we feel a great need to see these men stopped from the evil deeds that they continue over and over from state to state.

If you should wish to talk to us in person about this matter, we would be glad to fly out and visit you. Also we would be glad to speak to any of the friends and workers about what we have found. Do you have any suggestions on how we could help in this matter? We wish to thank you for your courage and concern. I believe that your actions brought thanksgiving to our Father's heart.

We also received a three page letter addressed to Sydney February 11, 1991. We could not read the name at the bottom. It was about how some young sister worker handled informing the church of immorality in their field. We again were thankful and wonder if it was your letter?

I hope that the circulation of these letters does not put too great a pressure on you, Selma. Please remember the similar position Jude and John were in before the church and I hope that brings some comfort if you are upset. We love you dearly for your effort and concern. Please write!

Love,
Dale and Janet Gardner

August 31, 1988

To Taylor Wood and the Church:

We have sought the counsel of many friends and workers, and over and over we are advised to write to you, Taylor. We know that you are aware of how disappointed we are with the outcome of our meeting with you at Elizabeth convention in Colorado this year. We were so glad when the workers called us and asked us to come and tell you how Ira Hobbs lasciviously (Mark 7:22, Galatians 5:19, Ephesians 4:19 I Peter 4:3, Jude 4) treated our young daughter several years ago. The three of us who talked to you together all felt great disappointment in your reaction to our despair. We still do not understand why you would not gather the other witnesses who had agreed to testify of similar problems concerning Ira and his concupiscence (Colossians 3:5, I Thessalonians 4:5). Some of the scriptural guidelines that we have found include the following: Matt. 7:15-23; Matt. 18:15-17; Acts 15:4,12,22; ICor. 5:2,5,6,13; II Cor. 11:12-14; Gal. 5:19-21; II Thes. 2:3,4; II Thes. 3:6,7; I Tim. 5.20-21; II Tim. 3:4,5; Titus 1:13-16; II Peter 2:1-3;

II John 9-11; Jude 3,4; Rev. 2:2,6,14,15,20; Rev. 3:1,8,15,16; Deut. 13:14; Judges 19:30; Judges 20:1,7,8; Jer. 23; Ezek. 34. We plead with you to make it known to Ira and the church that the accusers, the accused and the witnesses need to gather and proceed with handling this problem by the directions and instructions in the word of God.

We also know that Horace Burgess has been involved in concupiscence and lasciviousness and uncleanness (Romans 1:24; Ephesians 5:3; I Thes. 4:7) with young girls for several decades. We know those who are willing to testify before the church about him. Again, we ask that you make it known to the church that his problem needs to be openly examined by the victims, accusers and witnesses. Horace was in our home about 12 years ago, and we wish to tell what happened there.

I want to mention a situation that should help us to understand why these things need to be handled openly before the church as in Acts 15:4,12,22,23. It has been known by some of our ministry for a number of years that Roy Dietzel, who until recently was head worker of Nebraska, was involved in lascivious behavior. This knowledge was kept hidden in direct disobedience to the word of God, I Tim.5:20,21. Because a number of Nebraska elders were godly, wise, and brave enough to stand against those who had hidden this evil, the case was tried. When accused, he denied guilt, but when tried before the church, workers, elders, elders' wives, and the sister workers whom he had fondled, he confessed his lie and admitted guilt. He was then removed as overseer of Nebraska, but for some reason that no one seems to understand, he was sent to Colorado to be in the work. The truth of the situation became known to some and a wise young couple expressed that Roy and his companion, Gilbert Reese, could not spend the night in their home and it evidently became clear that something would have to be done. It was reported that Roy had been put out of the work. We now understand that he was sent to Missouri to continue in the work. Many friends and workers shake their heads in disbelief when they hear these things, and we wonder what we are doing to ourselves. If this case had been handled properly, years ago, several sister workers would not have had their precious lives blighted by this man of flesh and pleasure-Jude 11.

Another situation that is of grave concern to many in this area involves a Colorado worker, Kenny Wahlin. He has been accused, by Frank Caler of Colorado Springs, of lasciviousness towards his daughter. Because Frank's daughter and my daughter have both been advanced on by men who represent themselves as servants of God, we have become convinced that God's word teaches that we must earnestly contend for the faith once delivered (Jude 3), and there are certain men crept in unawares...Jude 4. Together, Frank and I went to Kenny and talked with him. Frank visited with Kenny first in private for several hours. Then in the presence of Frank, a Colorado elder Ed Atkinson, and myself, Kenny confessed that he repeatedly through the years had involvements with many girls, women and sister workers that were lascivious and wrong. He expressed to us that he would write a letter confessing his actions to Frank, myself, George Gittens, and Gilbert Reese. Our meeting was on a Sunday, and he said he would write the letters on the following Tuesday. We waited for a week, the letter did not come, so Frank called him on the phone. Kenny expressed that he had decided that he would not make known what he had lasciviously done in the past with females. We understand that he has been reprimanded by the workers and that he is to continue in the work. How can it be that he should be allowed to continue in the work, going into the homes of unsuspecting parents of girls and young women? It seems very clear to us that he needs to be rebuked before all that others may fear (I Tim.5:20,21), and then be removed from the ministry. If he lives pure as a friend and gains a good testimony wherever he decides to work and make a living, then, after a period of time, he might be fit for the ministry. We wonder if the verse in Proverbs 21:16 does not apply to our family today. The way we are handling these problems would make it appear that we are of the congregation of the dead.

Again, I plead with you Taylor, that you will make it known to the church that we must seek God's help and guidance to remove ourselves from this horrible condition that we are in, and openly investigate cases like these before the whole church. If we do not follow His direction and word, how can we ever become a pure people for Him? Why do we not seem to understand that mercy is the twin of truth, and if we do not place mercy at one end of the balance beam of God's judgement, and truth at the other end, then we will never arrive at true mercy or truth in our fellowship?

It would seem to us that the key to this problem is simply for our ministry to openly acknowledge that there is a major problem, and that the ministry would openly invite any testimony and witnesses that would help us to follow God's guidelines in these matters. We pray that those who read this letter will become very concerned, and earnestly search these matters out and encourage our ministry to be open about these problems, as God was when he revealed like matters to his people in His written word. We will be glad to explain in more detail to any who may wish to question us about what is happening here in Colorado. We would also very much appreciate help from others in regards to witnesses and testimony as to what these men have been involved in in other states. We are finding witnesses both in Colorado and other states, and wish to present the evidence openly to the church that we would follow God's established procedure in His Word.

We hope that all would earnestly pray for God's mercy and help for His people. It appears that our condition is very similar to the condition of God's people in the time of Nehemiah. Let us show God that we care and want His direction and help before he finds it necessary to separate us from Himself, (Jer.3.8; Hos.2.2; Rev.3.16).

Please write to us Taylor.

Signed by: Dale Gardner

Chapter Eighteen

Submitted by Grace Gardener
Letter Written by Fern Strouse, an Ex-worker

Dear Friends,

Colorado!! I understand the sexual situation there and have you all in my heart and prayers. Your concerns are my concerns, and I know what you are up against in not being heard by the authorities in the church. I read an account, on a similar situation, of a priest in the Catholic church. He had messed with a number of altar boys (he thought he was giving them love—a *distorted thinking!*) The Bishops wouldn't hear the victims so they went to the law. The collected victims were granted a total of one million dollars from the church for damages and to pay for *long-time* counseling. I doubt that you will move the workers to do anything. They are too far into denial, too lacking in knowledge of emotional damage to the victim, and too far into religious pride and insecurity. This is where the prayer of Jesus fits so well, "Father forgive them, they don't know what they are doing *in this type of problem.*" Workers have joined the world in playing the game of "blaming the victim" and minimizing the deeds of the abuser.

I understand sexual abuse so well—it's in my family. A nephew was "mildly" abused by his grandfather at age 6. Grandpa's reward to him for the sexual deed was ice cream and cake. This nephew went for alcohol treatment at age 13, weight kept going up, until at age 27 he is over

300 pounds and has been to alcohol treatment twice in the last 3 years. Thus, I join the professionals who say, "There is no mild abuse, only severe damage to the victim." This is soul murdering and needs to be stopped at any cost. If a child has to live with this "dirty secret" (and when it involves a minister it involves God, so is the most damaging form of abuse) it will kill him emotionally. It will show on him or her at school. They could be sent to the school counselor and it would have to be reported to the law by the counselor. The law may declare homes and parents unfit that allow such in the home, and put the children in foster homes. How can I impress the seriousness of sexual abuse of children in any form or degree? This dirty past enters into married life and hinders, divorces come. Victims develop serious emotional eating disorders, often turn to alcohol and drugs, and become sexual abusers themselves. I learned recently that a nine year old girl was molested in a cornfield on convention grounds over thirty years ago. It came out in her alcoholism counseling. The worker married later, molested his own children, and spent time in prison.

I doubt that the law can do much about the grown women who have been abused unless they can prove rape. Women need to learn to speak up and to use their fist on the end of the nose of the abuser. He really isn't God's true servant. I highly recommend that the victims attend a twelve step incest survivors group, and get to counseling for sexual abuse. (Lutheran Family Services is good.) The counselors can determine the amount of the emotional abuse, advise you on the law, and would likely even testify in court on behalf of the victim. Professing counselors would be out as they are bound by the authority of the church. Shop around

until you find a good one—many went into counseling because of their own abuse, so readily
understand. Would you want your children to testify in court? It would help the healing process if
you get it all in the open. This undercurrent hassle,
over it all, isn't good for children either. The law
may not send the abuser to prison, but there may
be counseling expenses covered, limits put on the
abuser—like not to stay in homes where there are
children, not be able to attend convention, etc. In
some states, the law says it has to be reported
soon. Only the victim can tell what really happened. Really, it is doing the abuser a favor to stop
him. This is an addiction that starts often with just
touching, and goes farther and farther. The abuser
has to do this to survive emotionally. It is very possible that he was sexually abused himself.
Professionals say that very few abusers get help—
they are only treated. They cry and repent and may
want to be different, but they have sexual addictions and can't change.

The victim needs to know it is a courageous act
to turn in their abuser, even if it is their favorite
worker. They may be saving others from the pain
they have borne. If these victims become abusers,
what will the church come to? Someone has to
break the addiction. I dealt with 70 victims during
my 30 years in the work, besides my family.

An ex-worker, still caring.

February 2, 1992

Chapter Nineteen

Kent E. Griggs

For thirty five years I believed I had led a "normal" but somewhat strict childhood. I knew I had been raised in a "church" that met in the home, had no name, and sent out "God's disciples" two by two just as Jesus had done two thousand years ago. These tenets I believed without question, and until I read **The Secret Sect**, believed "The Truth" was God's one true way. The shock of finding out that everything I "knew" was true was based on lies was like finding out that $2 + 2 = 5$, which meant the whole equation of life was different. The weight of the world left my shoulders when I found out I wasn't a sinful person and was not "condemned to an eternity in HELL" as I had been told repeatedly in my childhood years. I am not a religious person, but felt the need to learn more about how I was raised, what I believed, and why did I have such destructive and dysfunctional attitudes about life. Twenty years of drug use, alcoholism, and failed social and personal relationships had made me eager for the truth. I am not going into the history of the church, but only tell of my experience.

From my earliest memory visiting workers in the home and getting ready for convention were the highlights of my young life. The joys of "anticipated spiritual healing" were felt throughout the house. It was a time for new convention clothes, notebooks for convention notes, haircuts, and the warning about the belt, if we were not on our best behavior. My sister and I lived in fear of the thick

black cowboy belt with the silver buckle and tip
that would sting and welt the flesh. I was probably
only hit with the belt 3 or 4 times, but the threat
was always there, conveyed with a glance or glare.
Convention was exciting, seeing my friends, the
meals with the clanging of pots and pans and the
humble murmur of 600 saints and servants waiting
to sing "grace." I remember the thrill of getting a
"job", helping peel potatoes, serving food, or helping with the dishes. Jobs were assigned by a
worker, and it seemed the hotter or harder the job,
the more of the "right spirit" was shown to the
world. The meetings were a time for "spiritual healing" for adults, but were a time of stress and terror
for the children. Hard benches, humidity, and repetitive "fire and brimstone" preaching either lulled
children to sleep or kept them, rapt, on the edge of
the seat with fear of "eternal damnation" or the
more real fear of one's parents if they felt the child
was not paying attention.

After the night meeting there was cocoa and
doughnuts, and as I grew older this was a time to
"pair up" and sneak off for some heavy petting and
kissing. Romance in the "Truth" was often a long
distance affair with me writing letters to a girl all
year, but only seeing her at convention. Often
one's feelings had changed and sometimes the girl
had found someone new who lived closer. Then it
was time to try and find another girl and start the
whole letter writing romance again. I feel this lack
of commitment in my adolescent years has followed
me my entire life. I have lived "in sin" with several
girls, but these relationships, like my marriage,
were passionless and of short duration.

Other memories of convention include the intense feeling of comradery among the young men
in the "Truth." I believe most of us felt persecuted

in the everyday world, but when we got together it was a contest to see who was enduring the most pain, suffering, and self denial for "Christ's sake." I remember when I was about 10 years old having a contest with other boys, rubbing our knuckles in the grooves of a cinder block wall to prove how able and willing we were to endure pain. Whoever had the bloodiest knuckles at the end was the winner. That pain was very visible and real. The pain caused by being different in the world was not so visible. When one feels different they tend to direct their anger at themselves. The conflicts I had were about being too spiritual for the real world, and too worldly for the spiritual world. I felt like an outcast from both worlds. Because participation in sports, clubs, or dances was frowned on by the workers, (and my father used to be a worker), I feel many of the children were socially and politically stunted. I didn't know how to deal with girls or school work (these things were not important), and I had no clue about politics or current events. It was during these times of conflict I drank my first beer and smoked my first joint. I felt the need to belong somewhere and the "stoners" weren't going out for sports or clubs either. I was almost 14 years old. For the next 22 years I never looked back.

I professed at Utah convention when I was 12 years old. I remember going to my bed that night knowing I should pray, but I didn't know what to pray for. I started worrying that same night about giving my testimony the following week. The next 2 years were spent leading a double life. I tried hard to be submissive and "bending to God's will." I tried to be a "light unto others," to stay on the narrow path and to "deny myself so that His will could be done." IT WAS HELL!!! There was a constant knot in my stomach from worry of having to speak and pray in meetings. I would try to find something in the Bible that might somehow relate to something I had done, or might do, and hope there would be a moral to the story that had affected me, so I could learn to be more humble and submissive. I knew if I practiced more self-denial I could be more humble, submissive, and Christ-like, and DAMN this takes up a major part of your life when you are only 12 years old.

On the other hand it was 1970 and mini-skirts, free love, hippies and dope were everywhere. At a time when one's identity, whether "hawk or dove," was easily distinguishable, I had no identity. I couldn't hang out with the "jocks" because I couldn't go out for sports. I couldn't hang out with the "brains" because I couldn't join clubs and worldly education wasn't important. I couldn't hang out with the good kids because they were Catholics, Protestants and "sinners." The only place I really fit in was with the other social misfits and drug users. I would go to school half an hour early just so I could get "stoned." It was something I could excel at and when I was "high" worldly and spiritual problems didn't matter. For the next 20 years I got "high" every day and there was no "new high" I wouldn't try.

I never heard a worker ever say anything about alcohol or drug abuse, but I know I wasn't the only professing child with this problem. The names are not important, but I can only think of one person professing in my age group that didn't try drugs. I would steal pills from the medicine cabinets where we went to meeting. We would sneak off and get "high" after Wednesday night meeting. "Sings" and potluck dinners were a chance to see who had the best drugs. There was nothing we wouldn't try, from sniffing paint to eating pills (we didn't know what they were) just to get "high."

I never heard a worker say anything about homosexuality, incest, or pedophilia, but these too are real problems in the "Truth." I believe that the workers thought all sex was wrong so these dysfunctions were not any worse than normal sexual relations. All sex was to be denied except for procreation. Workers and "Elders" sometimes used their power to seduce other men, women, and children. I should know—My father is a documented pedophile. I don't remember my father ever abusing me sexually, but this may be a classic case of denial. My father was a child molester when he was a worker before I was born. The documented incidents of molestation involve a 12 year old boy who was repeatedly abused over a 2 year period. My father would sneak into the boy's room and molest him while the family was asleep in the other rooms. When the "head worker" was told, his response was "Well...the workers aren't married and sometimes these things happen." I didn't know this until I happened to contact T.F.M. in August 1993. I had been told by my mother in 1984, after their divorce, that my father was a homosexual who hadn't made love to her since 1968, and she showed me a letter he wrote to prove it. As I remember, the letter was mostly evasive and a denial of the issues except for the reference to something that had happened before they were married (I think now that this was the mentioned molestation). With regards to this he had written, "well...maybe in that way my head's not screwed on right." That is as close as I have had to an admission of guilt. I heard rumors of other incidents, but like usual the truth was suppressed by my father, the workers, and the victim. Looking back now, I can think of other times when maybe things were not quite proper. As an "elder" my father was often the chaperone for camping and ski trips. The parents thought their children were in such good hands. They didn't know how true that was. My father was always willing to lend a hand to young men in their time of need. (Now it looks more like *his* time of need.) Looking back, they all had the same type of dysfunctional personalities. They always looked poor and hungry with an eager to please and never question attitude toward my dad. This abuse will probably continue until he dies, gets killed by an irate parent, or goes to jail. At this time, he is still going to meeting, giving his testimony, and is in apparent good standing with workers and other members of the "Truth." It's like he has no regrets about all the lives he has destroyed. I don't think he knows a 29 cent postage stamp is all that stands between him and prison.

We had Sunday morning meeting in our home in Utah, and Wednesday night meeting in our home in Colorado. I've learned now that it was a "privilege" to have a meeting and be an "elder," but to me it just meant more chores. The house had to be vacuumed, furniture had to be moved to make room for the folding chairs, and I had to be showered and sitting quietly half an hour before meeting started. On Sundays, my father would cut the crust off of a piece of bread and put it on a plain white plate. He would take a small glass and fill it with Welches grape juice, and then both would be placed on the coffee table in the middle of the room. (Chairs were lined around the outside of the room rather than in rows.) When the sacrament was brought to the table, all horse-play stopped and we would sit quietly hoping to gain "the right Spirit." Being the son of an "elder" meant I had to work that much harder to gain parental and worker approval, and I was often told to be a "good example" for others. When there are 20 people singing in your living room, the whole neighborhood can hear, and as I got older this was an embarrassment when my friends would walk by. People already thought I was weird for having such short hair and an out-of-date wardrobe, so the singing was just another nail in my coffin. I never preached to my friends because I did not know what I believed, and even if I did I thought them all to be "sinners" with no hope of salvation.

The meetings in the home are basically the same world-wide. The worker or elder would choose a hymn to start the meeting and then ask if someone else had a hymn they would like to sing. Then he would say "let us pray" and all who were able would kneel in front of their chairs. As a child, looking around, making faces, or not showing the "right spirit" was good for a knuckle rap on the head. I think I still have lumps from this. One by one *all* professing would say a short prayer. There were no set prayers and I would just repeat things that I had heard since childhood. The elder was always the last to pray, praying a little longer and louder than everyone else. When he would finish all would say "Amen" and return to their seats. Another hymn would be chosen and then it was time for "testimonies." This was my own private hell from week to week. On Sundays after the elder would speak, we would usually sing two verses from a hymn before passing the "bread and wine." All persons baptised and in good standing were allowed to take part.

The elder was the last to partake, and then he carried the "bread and wine" from the room. When he returned we would sing the last two verses of the hymn and meeting was over. Everyone from the smallest child to the oldest widow would shake hands, thank each other, and leave. No one made too much small talk because they didn't want to lose the "spirit" of the meeting. Sometimes after Wednesday night meeting, (basically the same without the sacrament), the families with younger children would stay after for ice cream or a root beer float. It seems to me that if there were workers or elderly saints present that root beer or ice cream were never mentioned. As a child it was always best to be "seen but not heard" when visiting saints or workers were present. "Being seen and not heard" was one of the major rules of growing up. I believe this is one of the reasons I am so unassertive and accept many things as "that's just the way it is." Another main rule for the children was "to always clean your plate and be thankful for what you have." To this day it is hard for me to leave anything on my plate. I am overweight and still won't leave the table until my plate is clean.

Prayers before meals were either given by professing family members or sang together as a family. The larger the family, the louder the prayers. We were also expected to read a chapter from the Bible and say our prayers every night before going to bed. We were expected to rise early enough in the morning to read the scriptures and pray before going to school. Prayers were not usually of thankfulness, but rather asking to be more "submissive to God's will," "a better example unto others," and to be a "light unto others in this world of darkness." Prayers usually started with, "Our Heavenly Father," and ended with, "This we ask for Jesus sake." Prayers before meals usually include the phrase, "Bless this food to our body's use." I never heard "The Lord's Prayer" until I was a teenager, but these other phrases I still remember 25-30 years later.

I remember traveling long distances to go to meetings. Every 3 weeks in Utah, we would drive 100+ miles one way to go to meeting in Kemmer, Wyoming. A little old lady named Ivy Miller lived there and was the only "friend" for miles. People came from all over to meet in her home. (The workers must have had their eye on her estate.) Wednesday night meeting in Utah was 20 miles one way, and in Colorado we would think nothing of driving to Denver, Albuquerque, or Cheyenne for "Special Meetings." Special meetings were like a one day convention with workers, bag lunches, and the excitement of seeing friends, (Girls), that you only saw once or twice a year. We would also drive to Chugwater, Wyoming, Salt Lake City, Utah and the western slope of Colorado for convention. Many of our vacations were spent going to conventions or visiting "friends" in other states. When one is a "friend" they are welcome at meetings worldwide and our trips were often plotted around where we would go for Wednesday and Sunday meetings. It is scary to look back and know that there were children all over the world who were as regimented, humiliated, and terrified as I was. Wherever we went I could fit in with the "friends" children because we were all like little robots trying to win parental and worker approval. My parents were far from the worst and I knew of some kids that were beat almost weekly, whether they needed it or not. The children learned, not through support and encouragement, but through fear and forced submission. A proper outward appearance was needed so one could blend with the other terrified, brain-washed children of the "Truth."

Of all the abusive families, Dave and Donna R. were the worst. Dave was the only father that scared me more than my own. He would get a PSY-CHO glare in his eye and seemed to thrive on beating his many children into submission. He would make the entire family watch when he would kill the pet chicken for the dinner table. He would hold the chicken by the head and swing the body in an arc so when the body hit the ground "it would run like a chicken with it's head cut off." Where Donna ruled her house with an "iron fist," Dave ruled it "with a club." I don't think Dave and Donna were raised in the "Truth" and that is why they dealt such harsh punishment on their children. They knew the "sinfulness" of their young lives and beat the children into "holy submission" for the benefit of their own salvation. I can only hope that the children realize what a dysfunctional up-bringing they had and don't pass the abuse on to their own children.

Many parents that were raised in the "Truth," like my own, had no clue as to the "worldly" pressures put on their children. Parents had never smoked, drank, or done drugs, and like the workers could not intelligently interact with their children on these subjects. They pretended that these other problems did not exist. If you didn't talk about sex, you couldn't get pregnant. If you had short hair, you didn't do drugs. If you didn't talk about physical and sexual abuse, it never happens. Civil rights, war, poverty and politics, starvation and shattered lives did not exist for "we are not of this world." This blanket denial of problems has resulted in generations of children who are politically, socially, and sexually ignorant; who believe that if they turn their backs, cover up, or ignore a problem that it doesn't exist. This is the way I behaved most of my adult life. I had never voted, didn't watch the news, and never really had a strong opinion about anything. I was proud of being a slut who would screw anyone. I figured I was "going to hell," so my motto was "LIVE FAST—DIE FAST." I just *did not care.* I ran with bikers, hookers, and other social outcasts. I had *very* long hair, pierced ears, and tattoos. I had a BAD attitude about myself, others, and the world. I still have the hair, tattoos, and earrings, but after reading the information from T.F.M., I now realize most of my problems are rooted in my childhood in the "Truth." I think if I had been allowed to join sports, attend school functions, and was encouraged to do well in school, my life would have been different. I'm thankful I'm not in prison or dead from a drug overdose or motorcycle crash. I have a much better attitude now, and would be interested in corresponding with other ex-2x2's who went the same rebellious route as me, or parents who feel that is the way their children are heading.

Address:
Kent E. Griggs
12633 Fair Oaks Blvd. #136
Citrus Heights, California 95610

Chapter Twenty

Sandi Gunther
Fourteen Years a Two-by-Two

I was not raised as a Two-by-Two. I had never met one. So how did I become one? Here is my story.

I was an only child and my father died when I was an infant. I lived with my mother and step father. My step father died when I was 17, leaving me to care for my mother who, by then, was very handicapped with multiple sclerosis. Just before I turned 20, my husband and I were married. Because of Mom's MS, she asked us newly-weds to live with her. We all agreed it likely would not be a good idea, however, we thought we should give it a try anyway. My husband and I cared for my mom for one and a half years before telling her that we must establish a place of our own. We moved to an apartment and that was the beginning of Mom needing a full time housekeeper/lady sitter. Many lady sitters came and went over a period of about one year. Then Mom hired a single lady who was in her thirties. This lady was a Two-by-Two.

My step father had been a Catholic. He married my mother when I was seven. When I was nine, my Mom and I took a few lessons from the priest and we both became Roman Catholic. We attended Mass each week. In my early years the Mass was in Latin. I did not attend a Catholic school, and as a result, my knowledge of Catholicism was very limited. After my step father died, I continued to take my Mom to church. Once I was married, I no longer went to church. Mom rarely went, as she was not able to go by herself. Enter the Two-by-Two lady sitter. She agreed to work for Mom if she could have every Sunday morning and evening and every Wednesday evening off and four special days each July. As the lady sitter did not drive, some of her "friends" picked her up for the meetings. Soon the "friends" began taking Mom to the Sunday Gospel Meeting. After about two missions Mom professed. I was shocked! She told me "Now, I have peace." Apparently, I said "I bet!" I felt betrayed. She had led me into Catholicism and even though I didn't go to church any more, I felt, when she professed, that I had been dumped!

Six years went by. I still knew very little about this "church." My Mom never suggested that I attend. Another "church" lady, who was by then my children's baby sitter, would frequently invite me to the Gospel Meetings. I attended once. There were a lot of old grey-haired people there. I couldn't understand the preaching and I found it quite boring. A few months passed. One day two ladies rang my doorbell. Somehow I knew these were Workers. I invited them in and we visited. I remember asking if they were mother and daughter. The younger one laughed out loud and the older one (not old enough to be her mother) was certainly not laughing. They had laid their "business card" on the coffee table when they came in. We continued talking, mostly about nothing. Finally I said in a snarky voice, "Aren't you going to invite me to your meetings?" The older one pointed to her card on the table: "Well, there it is," she said. After they left I thought that since they had made the effort to come to my house, and my baby sitter continued to invite me to the Gospel Meetings, I would go again. Anyway, it would likely please my Mom. So I began to attend the Gospel Meetings, taking my two boys, then about four and six, with me. My husband was not interested (thank goodness). Besides my going to the Gospel Meetings, the Workers began visiting me about twice a week.

It took me several meetings to figure out what they were talking about. I remember them talking about sheep in one meeting, but they seemed to mean people. If they were talking about people, why did they say sheep? Eventually, I did catch on to their lingo. But before I did, I joined a local ladies' Bible group to see if I could learn something about the Bible. It seemed to me that everyone at the Gospel Meetings could completely understand what was being said. It must be because they are all familiar with the Bible, I thought. So if I could learn a few things from this neighbourhood ladies' Bible group, then I might be able to understand the Gospel Meetings. I mentioned to the Worker that I was in this study group, and she told me it wasn't necessary and I should just keep coming to the Gospel Meetings. I began to feel that God was dealing with me; but to "join up" was no easy decision.

An isolated incident happened. A neighbour lady had become a close friend of mine just about this time. One day, for no reason apparent to me, she called me and said I could no longer come for coffee and we could no longer be friends. I was devastated. What had I done? Where could I turn for comfort? It was Wednesday and although I had never been to anything other than a Gospel Meeting, I decided to go to the Wednesday night meeting. I phoned my baby sitter, as I knew they had a meeting in their home. Her daughter answered and I asked her if I could come. She said she would call me right back, and she did. (I think she contacted the Workers to see if it would be okay. So I attended my first Wednesday Bible study. Somehow I expected it to be a different type of meeting. I thought everyone would be sitting around a table and one person would be teaching from the Bible. I listened as each one gave a testimony. I couldn't believe the humility of the men. That is what really spoke to me. I began to cry and could not get control. I used tissue after tissue. In the middle of the last hymn I was so embarrassed that I got up and walked into the kitchen. Later in the kitchen the "Worker I knew best" put her arms around me. No doubt the whole group, in fact all the friends, had great hope for me after that Wednesday night!

There was another newcomer at the Gospel Meetings. I frequently tried to talk to her alone but a professing lady, who by that time was friends with both of us, was always present and I could never talk to this other newcomer. I even mentioned to "my" Worker that it seemed I could never talk privately with the other new lady. She said we were both like spiritual babes. She suggested that babies didn't play together until they were a few years of age. Finally, we were both at preps cleaning a brother Worker's cottage when I asked the other lady if she was going to profess. She thought she might and suggested to me that I could always profess and if I didn't like it, I could always quit. That sounded sensible to me. So I gave myself a few more weeks and I took that "stand to my feet." I remember it was quite a tearful experience and I did feel close to God.

Once I professed, I learned that I was expected to be in Sunday and Wednesday meetings, as well as the Gospel Meetings. I took my place in each, just like a good little Two-by-Two! By convention time, my hair was barely long enough to put up.

My husband couldn't believe I was wearing a bun on my head! I didn't explain to him that I had professed—he would never understand. He didn't keep me from the meetings and took the attitude of "to each his own."

I remember once after I professed I was with a lady (a worldly friend of mine!) who commented to me: "You know, Sandi, just because you joined that church, you don't have to let yourself go!" Another time, early on, I was shopping. My hair was up but was really still too short to have a proper Two-by-Two hair style. It looked awful and I felt awful. Two teenagers passed me and burst out laughing. I felt sure they were laughing at me. I mentioned this to "my" Worker and she just smiled and said I looked just fine.

On another occasion, perhaps a year after professing and when I had figured out how to do my hair, I stopped to see the folks where I used to work long before I professed. Quite out of the blue, this former co-office-worker said "Sandi, what do you think your best (physical) feature is?"

I said, "Well, I guess my hair is."

"Right," she said, "So why do you wear it that way?" I just smiled.

At my first Sunday morning meeting, I took note of how things were done. I was coached a bit first. "My" Worker told me to be ready to give a testimony based on what I had been reading in the Bible. She explained the emblems and said that until I was baptized I would not take part in them. Of course, she attended my first Sunday morning meeting just like she had that first Wednesday meeting. My Mom, too, was in this Sunday meeting. Although she was no doubt pleased that I had professed, I don't believe she said that to me. So, at that first Sunday meeting I was really watching. I looked to see if it was okay to cross my legs. I was not impressed that everyone drank from the same cup. I shook hands with each one after the meeting and joined in with a pleasant word or two with each. I was being moulded to the image of the perfect professing woman.

All the friends were very nice to me and my two boys. The boys had attended every Gospel Meeting and fellowship meeting with me. My husband didn't object to their going. We were included in potluck suppers, going away picnics, birthday parties and dinners and lunches from time to time. Once there was a surprise birthday party just for me! I got the impression that a lot of social activity was the norm. As my husband was not interested in socializing with the friends, I went it alone. How could I have a social gathering, in turn, for the friends that had been so kind to me? I decided that I would have a quilting bee. I invited all the ladies, a few at a time, to work on the quilt. The quilt was then given from all the ladies as a gift for a young friend who was soon to be married.

It took me a few years to realize that a lot of socialization didn't go on unless you were part of the "in" crowd or from a big professing family. The early attention that I received was because I was "new". About four years after professing, I was invited to a special "parents" meeting. Most of the people there were couples. A special sheet of information for parents was given to each couple. Those, like me, who weren't a couple, were to read the sheet of information at a couple's house on another occasion. Non-professing spouses were not to see this information. I, unfortunately, never did get to read it. I felt just awful at that meeting. At the coffee social after the meeting, couples visited with couples. They stopped to say "Hi Sandi," and moved right onto another "couple." I felt terribly alone. I left early and drove home in tears. Over the years, off and on, this continued to be my experience. Conventions were often very difficult especially in the evening when everyone visits in the yard, sipping on juice or soup.

About two months after I professed, I began to hear a message that no doubt was given before, but I had not "caught." That message came in several ways to my ears. Once, at a "friend's," I heard someone referring to outside teenagers as "the worldly kids." I remember I blurted out a half laugh as she said that. Then I felt embarrassed when I realized that that was part of the Two-by-Two "talk." Now that I was "in" (professing) I was beginning to hear a lot of that kind of message. By now I had been to my first convention and it was time for a new mission of Gospel Meetings. I began to hear clearly, for the first time, that this "way" was the only true way; that it was from the beginning and that all other churches and preachers were false. What? I could hardly believe my ears. These were beautiful people. The best I had known. In my eyes they were perfect. If they believed this was the only way, then they must be right. That left me with a problem. I didn't believe it. In the Gospel Meetings, it became more clear. Unless you hear the gospel story from these true servants, you cannot be saved. What? I had professed and I hadn't heard "that message" before. And further, once one had found the true way and had left it, one had no hope of salvation. To me that translated that if I left this group of people, I would go to hell! So, I continued on, hoping and praying that one day I would get this necessary revelation. I continued on, thinking that I was the only one who did not believe "it." My boys never did profess. I didn't talk to

them about the Bible, nor did I do any Bible studies with them. Looking back, I'm sure I felt I
couldn't push something on them that I didn't believe myself.

There were times when I fit in quite comfortably. There were times when I was quite uneasy.
Often, even though I normally function in extrovert
mode, I was unable to look another in the eye. I
felt my service was poor. It was hard to read and
pray. The Bible made little sense to me. I did learn
a lot about the Bible at first but that was not hard
to do. I had not even heard of the Gospels of Matthew, Mark, Luke and John before I met the
Two-by-Two's.

Before I continue on with my experience of how
I learned the real truth and am now in the fortunate
position of being an ex Two-by-Two, I will relate a
few true stories which I will never forget.

My mother had not been able to attend convention for several years. I asked the Workers if I could
tape record the speakers for my Mom since she was
not able to use her hands to read notes. The
Worker I asked, a fairly senior one, said he would
check and get back to me. The answer came back
that I could not record the speakers. I asked why
and he said "Because it might get into the wrong
hands." Looking back, I wonder why that didn't
sound strange to me. One would think that if God's
true word is being preached, there would be nothing to hide. Isn't God's word able to stand against
any test?

Having professed about 10 years, I decided to
"do something" with my hair. I had noticed a few
ladies had done a bit of scissor snipping on their
hair. I cut my bangs so they would give my hair a
fuller look. They were not curly and unless you
looked quite hard, you might not notice they were

cut. I blended them in and sprayed them down. I did look better and some said so. Soon after the "cutting" the Workers asked if they could come for lunch. I knew somehow that this lunch was about "bangs." Sure enough, one of the Workers stated that they were visiting a few of the married ladies who, apparently, had done as I had. He said, "We want to keep the standard high." Convention was in about two months and I told him I couldn't have them grown out by then and that I really preferred them the way they were but that I guessed I would begin growing them. The following year, he came up to me at the convention and in the sweetest, slowest voice he said: "We certainly appreciate your hair."

At that moment, I was reminded of a Worker who said: "Hey, no rules." That particular Worker, a few years earlier, was showing me a photo of his brother's wedding. His brother was wearing a full beard.

I asked him "Is your brother professing?"

"Yes," the Worker replied.

"But," I said, "He has a beard!"

The Worker took one step back, raised his hands shoulder high and stated: "Hey, no rules."

I thought to myself "Ya, right."

On another occasion, I had the Workers over for lunch. I was mentioning how "people of the world" are always getting us ladies mixed up because of our appearance. I proceeded to tell him a story of my experience in Hawaii. My professing mother had been in a wheelchair for a number of years and she wanted to take a trip to Hawaii. So she took me and a Two-by-Two nurse along to assist her. One day I left the condo and went down to the local pineapple stand. I stated that I wanted to buy a pineapple. Another man who was working out of the same stand asked me "Are you here in Hawaii with your husband?"

I replied "No, I'm actually here with my invalid mother and a nurse. Why do you ask?"

"Well," he said, "I'm looking for couples who would be interested in the condominium time sharing plan."

"Well," I said, "That lets me out, my husband is not here." I purchased the pineapple and I left.

(At this point I should tell you that I weighed about 50 pounds more than the nurse. Her hair was almost black and mine is reddish brown.)

A couple of days later, the nurse went to buy a pineapple. Stepping up to the pineapple stand, she asked to buy a pineapple.

The other man said to her "Are you here in Hawaii with your husband?"

The pineapple man said "No, no, you remember her. She's here with her invalid mother and a nurse."

The nurse said "Well, er—not exactly. I'm the nurse."

So, a few years later, I'm telling this story to the Workers and one of them said in a most gentle, soft manner, "Oh, yes, they would recognize the same spirit."

Much to my own surprise I blurted out "Spirit, nothin'—it was the bun!" There was no response from the Workers.

A few years later, I was re-telling this story to some elders in my city. They were siding in with the Workers that it was our spirit that those men in Hawaii saw. They were mocking me as I grew angrier, trying to get them to see that there can't be much spirit in saying "I'd like to buy a pineapple." I pressed them for several minutes to admit it was our appearance that they recognized. These elders continued mocking me with their verbal teasing and body language. Finally, in exasperation, I snapped my fingers and said "If this group of people can be this ignorant on something that is so logical, I could be out of there right now." At that point, their demeanour changed, but they would not verbally agree that it was our appearance that confused the two men.

Not so long after I professed, I heard one of the friends, who was raised in "The Truth" state that in the area where he came from, the worldly people called the friends the Two-by-Twos. I remember he had mentioned that his father had always said, "I'd rather be a Two-by-Two than a one by nothin'!" That actually spoke volumes to me. That was the first time that I heard those words Two-by-Two. But they stuck in my memory bank for future use. His father's comment was also one of the first indications I had that the "friends" thought they were a cut above the rest.

In 1991, a "friend" mentioned to me that an elder's wife had read the book called *The Secret Sect*. She also stated that the elder's wife would not show her the book because we were not supposed to read it. In July of 1992, after 13 years of trying to believe that "the way" was from the beginning and that other churches were false, I decided to see if I could find the notorious book. I went to the library. I asked the librarian. Nothing. Dead end. I pretty much decided that I couldn't get the book because the "friend" that told me about it wasn't positive of the title and she never mentioned an author. I was disappointed but I decided to stick around in the library anyway and pick up a few books. There on the shelf was a book called *Sect, Cult and Church in Alberta* by William Edward Mann. On one page, reference was made to Two-by-Two's. I couldn't believe my eyes. On several other pages, the book referred to Cooneyites. But who were they? I decided that if something was written about Two-by-Two's in this book, maybe the library would have other books on Two-by-Two's. The librarian directed me to The Encyclopedia of American Religions. I began my search. I thought Two-by-Two's were only called that in a little part of Canada, so it never occurred to me to look under that name in the encyclopedia. I began at the beginning of those two volumes, and after about three hours of looking—there it was: "the Two-by-Two's." It stated that the group had been started in the late 1800's in Ireland by a man named William Irvine. Boy, what a shock! At the bottom of the article, there were references to a scant few articles that had been written. I immediately asked the library to acquire these for me. The first one arrived about two months later. Each successive article led to another. One day the library phoned and said they couldn't locate a certain article, but they did have access, through the National Library in Ottawa, to a book called *The Secret Sect*. What good news! I read the book and began pondering all that I had learned. I knew of Threshing Floor Ministries, but I was not able to acquire their address until after I quit professing, some eight months after I had learned of William Irvine.

So how did I get "out"? *The Secret Sect* was so well documented, I did not doubt it. Of course, I never did believe "the way" was from the beginning. One thing still bothered me. The people seemed happy and nice, and the Workers always pointed out that no committees were needed because God was the leader. Days, possibly weeks went by as I thought about this. How did the system work so well? It came to me. The word I was

looking for was CONTROL. I knew that I was not presenting myself to be who I really was. I I knew that
to profess I had to exercise control of my every
move, every appearance, every word. And then I
thought of the few times that the Workers exercised
their control over me. I realized that it had all happened to me in a very subtle way. It was subtle
control. It was becoming harder and harder to profess. I needed out. I wanted out. But I was afraid.
Even though I never believed the fundamental beliefs that the Workers seemed so sure of, I still had
fear. "What if the Workers are right? Will I go to
hell?"

The week before Easter 1993 was very difficult. I
could think of nothing else but my agony of living
a lie. The lie was that by my life I was saying that I
believed what the Workers were preaching. I could
no longer live that lie. Easter Sunday was the last
meeting I attended. I decided not to go to the Gospel Meeting that night. That afternoon I visited my
mother, who by this time had been in a nursing
home for nearly 20 years. As I sat by her bedside
she said "What are you thinking about? Your face
looks terrible." I was so preoccupied with all of
this grief that my grief was clear to her on my face.
I had no idea when I was going to "get out." I
thought I would stay in, possibly a few weeks or
months. But when Mom said "What are you thinking about?" I just replied "Well, Mom, if you must
know, I'm thinking about leaving the church." She
looked surprised and started to weep. I asked her if
she believed that this "way" was from the beginning and that since neither of her husbands had a
chance to know the Workers, if she thought they
were going to hell? She did not answer either way,
but the look on her face was good enough for me.
We finished our visit and I immediately went and

told my best "friend." I told her I could no longer live what, for me, was a lie.

The next month was both beautiful and difficult. This, only an "ex" will understand. Unlike some, I did not leave because of the preaching of incorrect doctrine. I did not know that the Workers' interpretation of the Bible was twisted. Little by little, the right people came into my life. I read and read and read. I talked and talked and talked.

One day I was reading a book on cults. It stated that one way to identify a cult was if it's members don't believe in the Trinity. I had heard that word—Trinity—but I didn't know what it meant. The cult book referred to John 1:1 and 1:14. I looked it up in my King James Version Bible—the same Bible I had used for 14 years. The Holy Spirit immediately revealed to me that Jesus was God! Well, I began to read my Bible and for the first time in my life it made sense to me. I couldn't put it down!

Perhaps, reading and studying and praying for a whole summer doesn't appeal to you, but that's exactly what I did. I read from the KJV Bible, and *The Living Bible*. I read books on cults, material from Threshing Floor Ministries, and material from MacGregor Ministries (Box 294, Nelson, British Columbia V1L5P9). I read the books *The Church Without a Name, Has the Truth Set You Free?, The Grace Awakening, Coping with the Cults, Toxic Faith. The Subtle Power of Spiritual Abuse, Shame and Grace, Why Can't I Be Me?*, and a few more. I listened to Christian music, John McArthur tapes, and tapes about cults. I wasn't able to get enough! I've attended several different churches and have met some wonderful, kind, understanding people. I've talked to and met with several like me who have got out. In all of this, the thought was real to me that I was one who never believed the basics that the Workers preached. After I found out about the cover-ups, it still took me over eight months to leave! My mother is my only relative who is a Two-by-Two. I often wonder, "How could anyone get out who has been raised in it, believes it, who is surrounded by those in it?" I will pray daily for the many who are still deceived.

The best part of all of this is finding out who Jesus is; He is God almighty Himself. This means that God not only gave his son to be my substitution on the cross, but He gave Himself. I tried to tell one "friend" still in "the way" that Jesus was God Himself. She, like I, had never heard of that. She said, "So what if He is God? What difference does that make?" I said "It makes all the difference in the world." Only the Holy Spirit can make this clear to each individual. That in itself makes this revelation very, very special.

God revealed something to me about three months after I "got out." It was something that I should have been thanking Him for and that I had prayed for, for over two years. On this particular day, I was preparing to get dressed. My thoughts were on nothing spiritual at all. A strong message came to me all at once. It wasn't exactly words and yet the message was very clear. God reminded me that I had prayed many times to be "shaken up"; that I would get close to Him, that my "walk" would be right in His sight. It was like He was saying to me, "Woman, don't you recognize all that has happened to you these past few months? Don't you understand I have given you what you asked for?" In gratitude I fell to my knees and thanked him. I was praying, crying, thanking Him and laughing with joy all at the same time. It was an incredible experience. To Him I am grateful.

Now at last I am free of legalism, free of lies, free of scriptural abuse and I am free to praise the Almighty for all He has done for me. For the first time in over 14 years, I can honestly say that I am thankful for what I have been brought out of and what I have been brought into.

Now I know that it is JESUS who is THE WAY.

Address:
Sandi Gunther
1527 Lee Grayson Crescent
Regina, Saskatchewan
S4X 3Z9

Two weeks after I quit professing I received a letter from the Worker I professed through. The letter read:

Dear _____,

I'll have to say I was SAD to hear you had declared yourself to no longer be a part of the fellowship. If there is any thing I can do to help re your feelings or questions...please feel free to share. May I ask you one question for your own consideration...Have you been reading the "Thoughts of men"...regarding God and or His Way...if so we will think like men think. Or have you been reading the "Thoughts of GOD" (BIBLE) re what GOD thinks about man & His purpose for him. If so we will think like God thinks!

    Love,

    _____

Upon receiving "my" Worker's letter I responded:
(My letter shows that I did not yet know that the
Two-by-Two doctrine was twisted.)

Dear _____,

I will always have a special place for you in my heart. I respect you and appreciate your diligence in what you believe in. Thank you for your note.

About three years ago, as you will recall, we met for lunch in a restaurant to discuss the problems I was having in professing. I had previously expressed to you in a lengthy letter my concerns and unbelief. You explained a lot of things to me that day we met for lunch, and at the time your comments seemed to help, but in actual fact my unbelief returned.

I have never accepted in my heart that this is the only true way—that all other ways and ministers are false. I don't believe I understood that message before I professed. Then, after I professed, I began to really hear that message. By then I felt it was too late. I simply tried to believe because I was afraid if I left I would go to hell.

I am not one who can tell a lie. For me to live something that I did not believe was the ultimate lie. Can you imagine my agony? Here I was, one of the most honest people you will ever know, living a lie. Don't get me wrong, _____. The Way is beautiful and probably the best. It is certainly not a lie for those who believe. It just seemed to me, as I listened more and more, that "The True Way" was THE main message preached and if that's what I need to believe, and I don't believe it, then I lie by living a life that says: "I Believe."

You might not believe this next sentence, but it's true: My prayer life is honest and sweet now. Needless to say, I never fooled God before.

Throughout my days, now, I hear His still small voice and I respond immediately. He knows me and my honest heart. To Him I am grateful.

Your friend,

_____

Nine days after writing the above letter, I received the following reply:

Dear _____,

Thanks for your lines! You have ACKNOWLEDGED your condition (unbelief)...WONDERFUL!...The FIRST STEP towards restoration! You feel you have & want to have an honest heart before God...WONDERFUL! (GOOD SOIL) IF YOU KEEP YOUR HEART soft AND LISTEN FOR HIS VOICE (only) and are responsive to it (Heb. 4:7) and read HIS word (only)...and come faithfully to the throne of grace...ONLY the right things will come to be in the end!

It would be nice to chat "face to face" again some day IF YOU WOULD LIKE TO...if so drop me a line as it would be possible to work something out from (preps).

Love you!

___

I did not respond to the invitation to meet "face to face" nor did I write the worker again.

About one week later, however, I bumped into another worker who knew that I was "out." The worker was very anxious to talk with me. We chatted for 45 minutes. I told the worker that I stayed in out of fear—fear that if the workers were right, and I left, I would go to hell! To this the worker responded: "You should feel fear, if I were in your shoes I would be afraid!"

A few weeks after that "confrontation" I was reading a book that was speaking of the Trinity. Finally, I found out who Jesus is and learned about Salvation! This news was "WONDERFUL."

At the time of writing this I've been "out" for five months. Things are just now starting to be normal. GOD TRULY IS GOOD!

Chapter Twenty-One

Following are responses to a questionnaire received several years ago and reprinted by permission of the author, who asked that he not be identified by name.

Origins

When I was a young boy I was told by my mother and grandparents on several different occasions that the Truth was started by Jesus when he was here on Earth. His life was an example for us to follow and the manner in which He sent out the twelve apostles was the identifying link between His following and the Truth today. Little importance was placed on the fact that a direct unbroken line of descent may or may not have existed, however, the impression I was left with at that time was that the Truth *had* been in existence since Christ.

During my second year of college, I engaged in a religious debate with my roommate one evening. In the course of explaining the beliefs of my religion and it's continual existence from the time Jesus was crucified, he brought something to my attention that I was unaware of called: "The Dark Ages." When I questioned my parents as to how our religion could have existed continually all through the years, they explained as best they could with the knowledge they had at the time. Their impression was that the Truth apparently had died out and came back, at least one time perhaps more, but the most recent reemergence of the way was in Ireland or Scotland during the nineteenth century. The manner in which it reappeared was described as being revealed by God to a few men who were humble, worthy, and willing to restore the original way of God to the Earth. No details of the revelation were known, nor were the names of the original ones who were involved in this event. Although I believed this and all other information I was told, I felt disappointed that no one had bothered to relate, what I thought would be a beautiful and inspiring story to others down through the years so we could find joy in this knowledge today. When I expressed my feelings in this regard to my parents and others, the response was something to the effect that the original workers were so humble that they did not want to be revered for being the first ones and thus remained unknown.

If the workers had presented William Irvine as being the one who God chose to reveal his way to, and from there he converted Walker, Gill, Jardine, and others, I would have had no problem in believing this at all.

Where doubts would have been raised would be in the explanation of Irvine's subsequent expulsion, which would appear to be a "no-win" situation. If one were to claim that God did in fact reveal his way to Irvine, and everyone believed this and followed his teachings, then at what point does another person, whom God has not established direct contact with, make the determination that Irvine is no longer in tune with God, but has instead started teaching his own views and ideas. It would seem to me that if one were to truly believe in Irvine's first revelation, that you would have no choice but to believe in all succeeding revelations also.

On the other hand, if one were to claim that Irvine and the other original workers established the Truth through their interpretation of reading the scriptures, then by admission the whole concept would be nothing more than another religious group's opinion, and without divine inspiration, would certainly be subject to human error.

William Irvine's name was unknown to me until seeing it written on a poster that was being carried by an elderly man who was picketing outside Casa Grande convention a few years ago.

The only thing known to me with regard to Edward Cooney, was that he was an old-time worker who went "astray" and that he apparently was well known enough that the name "Cooneyites" was attached to the group.

I remember George Walker always being referred to as the head worker of the United states. I may have even met him when I was a boy, although I'm not sure. I am certain, however, that he was a very good friend of my grandparents and stayed with them in their home on many occasions.

The other names I recognized (Jack Carroll, John Hardie, Wilson Reid, Willie Jamieson and Willie Gill) as being those of old-time workers, but nothing more.

No, I did not know of anyone in the CCs who went back to Ireland for a visit or to obtain information.

Name

"The Truth" is the name by which we referred to the church.

My grandmother told me the story about George Walker registering the Truth as "Christian Conventions" during World War II. The knowledge of this did not alarm me because I was told that the name existed for registration purposes only and had no importance at all other than to allow for the recognition of Conscientious Objectors. Except for this, I never heard the name Christian Conventions applied to the church.

Other names: Most commonly "Two by Twos." My mother told me that when she was little that they were referred to as "Blackstockings," but I have never heard this reference made. There were always numerous localized names attached to groups derived from the owner's name of the home in which the meetings were held, i.e. Clement's religion, Jenson religion.

Other Churches

My feelings toward other churches: They were all "lost sheep" and it didn't matter whether outsiders went to church or not. I was taught that there were two classifications of people: those who knew Christ and belonged to our church, and those who didn't know Christ and didn't belong to our church. It was immaterial whether outsiders had any religious affiliations or beliefs, if they were not members of our group they were simply "lost souls."

Now I am of the opinion that God will judge us by our lives, not by our affiliation with a certain religious group. I don't believe that just because you are a member of the Truth that you are going to Heaven any more than I believe that just because you are not a member of the Truth that you are going to Hell.

What I was told about other churches: that they were all false doctrines taught by false prophets. I cannot now worship comfortably in a church building or under a paid minister. Regarding the paid clergy today, I have no feelings really one way or the other. I have not found a new church home.

Leaving the Christian Conventions Sect

I professed just after turning thirteen in the summer of 1970.

In my immediate family my mother and my older sister were both professing at the time. All of my life I had been told that the Truth was the only true way that existed, so there was never really a question of whether or not I would profess, but merely when.

My father was the son of a Lutheran minister and my mother's parents are both in the Truth and have been members since the 1930's. Although my mother professed as a little girl, my father didn't join until 1974. My two younger sisters still belong and my older sister and myself do not.

A few years ago I began to have questions regarding the Truth's origin, or at least the early years. In fact, I had made it a point to ask as many old-timers as I came in contact with in the way, to recall anything they could along those lines. Needless to say, I came up with very little information dating back to 1920 and nothing at all prior to that.

Since our church kept no records, my only hope was to talk to someone who could relay something that they were told even perhaps, as a child. Slowly I began to realize that the chances of my coming up with any information were remote.

Then one fall at convention, I saw a poster carried by a man who was picketing just outside the grounds. On it was written something to the effect that William Irvine started the Truth in 1899 and claimed years later that it was a "great experiment." When I saw the reaction this brought from the workers, I concluded that although unknown to me, the information on the poster might be considered "sensitive." Another contributing factor to my leaving the movement would have to have been a discussion with a worker who was staying in my home one evening. The topic was the day of the week that Jesus was crucified and the amount of time He spent in the tomb. I had always been told He was crucified on a Thursday, but this worker was of the opinion that it occurred on a Wednesday. When I inquired as to the opinion of the other workers, he said there were those who agreed with him and those who agreed with my view and it appeared to be evenly divided.

It became apparent to me that there was definitely a lack of unity with the movement on interpretation of scriptures as well as the establishing of policies and the enforcement thereof. My conclusion was further reinforced by learning of the disparity that existed with regard to how matters of divorce and remarriage were being handled, both locally and across the country.

There was a situation in our area where a woman married a divorced man and was told that not only would she lose her privilege of taking part in the meetings, but she could no longer attend at all! Also, within the past few months several elders of the meetings were told to shave off their mustaches because they were supposed to be examples. Of what, I'm not sure.

In light of the events that had taken place, I began to have doubts as to whether or not this movement was really under the direction of the Lord. Remembering the name I had seen on the poster, I began to research Irish and Scottish history trying to find the link between the movement and William Irvine. As the information began to unfold, I was amazed at the findings and the entire picture suddenly became crystal clear.

Given time to digest this wealth of information, I determined that my personal position did not coincide with the radical and self-righteous views of those within the movement.

I feel pity towards those who are being deceived and appalled at those doing the deceiving.

I have never heard what they thought about me when I left. I don't know what reason they gave for my leaving. I still see some of my friends and our relationship seems to be unchanged.

Yes, I know of others who have left, but its' hard to say how many. While in the movement you would hear of those leaving from time to time, but some would return after a few years. There are ones who become inactive through a lack of willingness to submit and others who give it up for good and break all ties.

Family members still in the C.C. sect: Mother, grandmother, grandfather, two sisters, two great aunts, three second cousins, four third cousins.

The only one with whom it seems to have made a difference (in our relationship), would be my mother. At present, it would appear she has little use for me.

Yes, I was encouraged to read the Bible for myself. Yes, my scripture reading raised questions in my mind about what the C.C. workers preached or told us to believe.

My beliefs were fairly close to the universal beliefs on most of the terms (listed) with the exception of The Trinity, Justification and Atonement. These were very seldom covered in the workers sermons, so my knowledge of them was very limited.

Yes, I prayed for strength, guidance, forgiveness and mercy.

I hoped that I was saved, but I wasn't sure. Basically, you had to give up all the things of the world, as well as the desires for them, and live your life in the pattern of Jesus. If you did this then you would have a chance of salvation, but not even all in the truth were going to be saved.

Teaching regarding the Blood of Christ: That it was shed for us that we might have an opportunity to obtain salvation, if we lived right.

Meaning of Baptism: Basically it meant that no longer would I be asked: "When are you going to be baptized?"

One Sunday, after meeting, the elder announced that there would be a baptism the following Sunday afternoon. Before I left their house, the elder's wife asked me if I would like to be baptized and I said, "Sure". It was held at the home of an insurance executive who had a swimming pool in his back yard. There was a service before the baptism but I have little recollection of what was said. After the service Johnny Porterfield baptized about eight of us.

Meetings and Conventions

Feelings toward meetings: The meetings were the only proper way to have fellowship.

I attended Sunday morning meeting and Sunday afternoon Gospel meetings when they were held. Growing up I also attended Wednesday night Bible Study.

How did meetings make me feel? Good.

Most of the unusual events that took place in meetings were in the form of disturbances caused by people who were allowed to take part in prayer and testimony that were incoherent due to either senility or mental conditions.

Conventions were an event that brought increased strength and faith.

The incident of the poster that I have described earlier comes to mind as the most unusual event that I have witnessed at conventions. I should note that this was not a one-time occurrence but has taken place at all conventions and Special Meetings in this area since.

Conventions attended: Antioch, Nebraska; York, Nebraska; Callaway, Nebraska; Black Hills, South Dakota; Chugwater, Wyoming; Bird City, Kansas; Elizabeth, Colorado; Casa Grande, Arizona.

General Perspective

There were schisms that existed at times between members in the Truth, but nothing extraordinary that probably would not be present in other religious organizations today. I would consider most of the issues to be petty and of personal nature rather than religious. I cannot recall any problems among workers that I was personally involved with of which I could relate first-hand information. There were often rumors circulated around regarding friction between workers or disagreements relating to the handling of certain affairs, but these issues were rarely the topic of open-air discussions between members. If one were to question a relative or another member in the Truth as to why a worker "stepped down" or was transferred, the typical response was something like: "It was for the best," or "It's not to be discussed."

I was impressed by the way the members cared for each other and were very supportive in time of need. This was readily apparent in times of sickness and death among the members.

I did not care for the radical views and the judgmental attitude displayed by some of the members.

I felt that the workers had made a great sacrifice in serving the Lord and were very sincere in their efforts.

Did you note differences in house church groups when traveling? Some church groups would kneel to pray and others wouldn't. Also, some groups would stand to speak and others would not.

The Workers

Generally, the Workers would stay with us on two or three occasions a year and each visit would consist of one or two nights.

I really cannot complain of being mistreated by the workers at all, nor did I ever have a conflict arise between myself and a worker. There was one occasion when I was in college where an older sister worker came up to me after a gospel meeting in front of everyone and asked me what my problem was. To which I responded that I wasn't aware that I had a problem. Of course she was referring to the fact that my hair was long and I was growing a beard, although she didn't say as much. She told me that I should stay away from the other young people in the Truth until I straightened up lest I would be a bad influence on them. Although I felt the issue was mishandled badly, I did not hold this against the Truth, but instead attributed it to a basic lack of class on her part and the inability to handle situations with the least bit of wisdom.

Did you consider for the work? No, although when I was growing up and discussions would arise as to what my sisters and I would choose for a profession in life, my mother always said that if it were up to her that her first choice would be that we all would go into the "work."

Differing status of women and men workers: I observed nothing other than the obvious status of Head Workers and elders leading the meetings.

I knew several workers who have stepped down for various reasons and their treatment afterwards

directly relates to the reason behind their departure. Those who have left to care for parents or
have had health problems of their own are generally still in good standing. Usually members and
workers alike mourn the loss of a worker who steps
down to get married, but they seem to remain in
good standing also. That leaves us with the ones
who leave for reasons that are never told, or at
least never talked about, of which a portion of
these will leave the movement altogether and will
be remembered as one who "lost his vision".

*Were you aware of the struggle among the work-
ers to gain favor with the head workers?* No.

Money given to workers: I never kept track of
the money I gave nor did I deduct it for tax purposes. I can say that it wasn't very much but I felt
like it was for a good cause.

Did you know where the money went? No.

Was an accounting ever given? No.

Were you ever asked for money? No. In fact one
contribution was turned down by a worker because
I had a television in my home.

Other Issues

I was basically content until a few years ago
when I became uncertain on several issues.

Changes I have seen: I have seen the pressure
taken off listening to radio and hair styles and dress
liberalized somewhat.

Did you ever vote in an election while a C.C.?
Yes, I elected not to go back!

Did you serve in the military while a C.C.? No.

Did you socialize with other C.C.s? Yes, but I
also socialized with many people who were not in
the church and had many close friends who were
non-members.

How were your children affected by being in the C.C.s? Not adversely I'm sure, they are still very young.

Would you say more children leave the C.C.s or stay in it once they have grown up? Judging from the status of my contemporaries I would have to say it's running about half and half. As far as what is happening to children today, I really don't have an idea as to what the ratio is.

How did the women you knew feel about not wearing jewelry and makeup? I don't know.

Dress code: Whenever issues of dress came up you could count on the term "modesty" to be mentioned in there somewhere. Primarily it affected the women in the church as they were not to wear pants or shorts in public and their dresses were to be below the knee. I do remember someone mentioning that men were not to wear short-sleeved shirts to meeting because it was disrespectful.

Women's feelings about long hair: Some agreed with the idea and some didn't.

Were you able to establish any close friendship within and/or without the C.C.s? Yes, both.

Reaction when questioned about your church: As a child I was embarrassed, but as I grew up it didn't bother me as I became aware of churches that were even more weird than we were.

Did you feel persecuted? Did you consider this a mark of the true way? No. No.

Did you note any effect on your personality, physical and mental health? I would say it had little effect on my personality and no affect at all on my health.

What aspects of the C.C.s made you believe they were the only true church? The fact that there were no records. The method of sending forth preachers. The absence of taking collections. Church in the home.

Did you at anytime feel brainwashed? Somewhat. When you were told not to question things in reference to doctrine or decisions of workers and not to research church origin.

What would you tell anyone today who was thinking about joining the C.C.s? "Think again. Read the book that Doug Parker wrote."

What would you tell anyone who is currently in the C.C.s to help them see the truth? I would probably also suggest that they read the book.

What do you think would happen to the C.C.s if the truth was made known about them to the general public? I think it would lessen the chances of winning new converts from outside the movement.

How do you think they would react to such an expose? I think that a great deal of them would become inactive in the movement, but the radicals would remain un-phased.

Do you feel that such a public expose of the true facts would be beneficial? I feel it would be beneficial to some and perhaps harmful to others. I think there are some within the movement that are not capable of withstanding such a discovery. I don't know, if I would encourage such a revelation.

Were you ever aware of any child, or marital abuse? No.

Were you ever aware of any sexual abuse by the workers, or any sexual relationship among the workers—homosexual, or otherwise? Yes, I have heard stories of homosexual relationships among male workers. There was one instance where two workers used my grandparents home while they were gone for several days to seclude themselves. Also, my father had an experience that left little doubt in his mind that the worker that had approached him was gay.

Did you ever hear any workers preach on, or condemn, homosexuality? I have never heard the subject addressed from the platform. I did hear a worker condemn this type of activity in a discussion once but was never taught that it was wrong as a part of religious doctrine. Perhaps it was taken for granted as a moral issue, like murder or stealing.

Chapter Twenty-Two

Dr. Greg Harvey

It is the sincere desire of this writer's heart that the following might encourage each and every reader. Praise be to God for "light after darkness" and "peace that passeth all understanding."

The house has been quiet, except for guests stopping in the past few days as my lovely wife and two beautiful daughters attend their second annual 2x2 convention of the summer. My heart is pained to see them "pressing into the way" in response to my decision to withdraw twenty two months ago. The pain and separation this has brought into our family and marriage is incredible and I pray, as did the Apostle Paul, that "doors may be opened" and that I may "make it manifest as I ought to speak" concerning Christ; His abundant love, His "unspeakable gift" and saving grace. Indeed, I have, for the first time in my Christian experience, learned to trust my Lord fully and to know the reality, and necessity, of living just one day at a time.

I "professed" thirty years with little evidence of the Holy Spirit's power working within my life to control sin or overcome the emotional scars related to childhood family dysfunction; this in addition to being tossed about by frustrations, inconsistencies and contradictions. What a contrast and joyous blessing now to finally experience what God had intended all along; freedom from all psychological burdens from the past, near complete (and effortless!) power over patterns of sin, in addition to a joyous peace that accompanies an ASSURANCE OF

SALVATION. (This rather than merely "hoping" to be saved.) Indeed, we ARE "saved by grace through faith, and not of ourselves, it is a GIFT OF GOD!"

My life was changed most by simply being brought to the understanding that I AM SAVED. The freedom from wondering and worrying brings the fullness of peace Paul speaks of and a love for that incredible provision. This love, in turn, prompts one to desire to walk in accordance with our profession—it's no longer a "have to" (codes, traditions, legalism, etc.) but a "want to" as we recognize all God has done and planned for us.

Another major turning point for me was to be brought to a fuller understanding of the HOLINESS of God. As one realizes that NO SIN can stand in His presence, it follows that sin in my life causes separation from the very God of Heaven. My limited understanding of this truth in the past allowed me to continue in and repeat patterns of sin while mistakenly believing I would still be "OK" because, after all, I was part of the "perfect way of God."

A clear definite perspective of who Jesus Christ is has been a wonderful blessing as well as a seed for victory in my life. To understand, for the first time, that the very GOD OF HEAVEN came to earth and bore the shame of the cross in addition to enduring separation from the Father, (the ONLY period of separation in all eternity, past, present, and future), and that very separation was required to atone for MY SIN! What an AWESOME thought!

Another seed for victory was planted as I attended a Bill Gothard seminar last summer. We were reminded of the COST of grace and that once God's Spirit comes to dwell within our lives we become DEAD TO SIN—it no longer has the rule over us. We were encouraged to memorize Romans 6— and what a helpful uplifting chapter that is! One wonders why Romans 6 has not been studied in Wednesday night studies even once during the past twenty years!?

Though there has been much pain and separation, God has provided abundantly. A very special family of Christians encourage, support, and uphold me continually at our small rural community church. I have the privilege of helping teach the adult Sunday school class which takes me "beyond myself" as it is necessary to spend many hours each week in preparation.

I will close with a few "coping strategies" which have been helpful for me. Finding a compatible body of believers with whom to have weekly fellowship and becoming involved in the ministry of the church has been invaluable. The need is SO GREAT—God needs us to employ those gifts and talents He has blessed us with to help others—and what a blessing when we do. I find it helpful to pray audibly OFTEN—while driving, working alone, exercising, etc. MY ONLY radio is Christian broadcasting and only music hymns of praise, worship, etc. This keeps me encouraged in a spiritually bankrupt environment. I enjoy a TV/VCR for videos which are of spiritual value. Regular aerobic exercise and lots of "B" vitamins as well as a healthy diet helps keep the stress under control as we leave the world of meetings!

Please feel very free to phone, should you have ANY need or reason to do so. We do need one another in this difficult "spiritual crossroads" experience.

May God's presence be VERY REAL to each of you.

Business Phone: 509-486-2991 (Washington).
If not available, I will return your call.

Letter Dated March 8, 1992

Dear Workers,

Thank you for your recent note. Please understand, my not being in meeting has nothing to do with *offense* but *altogether* to do with *inconsistencies* and *contradictions*—some of which have plagued me for many years. I harbor no hard feelings toward anyone in "the way."

By way of history, I was born into a marriage that lasted scarcely a year after my birth. My mother was forced to work full-time and I was raised, for the most part, by "sitters." My step dad came into the picture when I was three and though a good provider, there was no love relationship between us. I cannot remember my step dad *ever* giving me a hug or speaking anything endearing to me. Unfortunately my mother was not demonstrative in her love either. My *only* real "love" person, as a child, was my grandmother. However she lived many miles away so I only saw her one or two times each year.

At the age of eight I can remember spending time in the woodlot behind our home wondering what life was all about—wanting to know if there was a God. I asked Mom if I could begin attending church and she began taking me to a neighborhood Church. I went along at first then later my younger sister started. Not finding much warmth I tried a second and then a third church and was about to be baptized therein when my mother asked us kids to go to meetings with her. She had known of "the way" as a child and felt our interests would be best served there. I was 13-1/2 then in 1961.

I was overwhelmed by the friendliness of the people—they seemed to take a real interest in me. I was extremely vulnerable since I hadn't known much of love in my boyhood home. Six months later, near my 14th birthday I "stood up" at Milltown convention. The only thing I knew about "the way" that night was that it had "started with the apostles and continued" and I felt *really loved* by a number of the "friends." I stood up as a result of a feeling based on emotion plus having the assurance that "the way" was nearly 2000 years old. I knew *nothing* of doctrine, only that I had accepted Jesus as my Savior.

Not long after, some of the sister workers gave me a Bible handbook and concordance. I enjoyed using these until Dan Hilton told us, from the platform, to burn our Bible related books since the Bible itself was all we really needed. (inconsistency #1) I didn't burn my gift books, but felt somewhat guilty whenever I would use them.

During the succeeding 5 years I observed a number of fairly minor inconsistencies but nothing that really "rocked the boat." I often wondered why some of the "friends" celebrated Christmas while others were outspoken against it, for example. If "the way" was perfect, why weren't the friends all doing the same things? What *was* the position of "the way" on certain observances such as Christmas?

In the fall of 1966 I started college in eastern Iowa. It didn't take long to notice that "the way" in Iowa had some different practices from "the way" in Washington. Some women still wore black stockings and long dark skirts. There were *no* radios or other music components in homes or cars and boys and girls didn't go swimming together. Why were these ultra conservative practices adhered to in the *Midwest* but not in the *Northwest*? I said little but my peace was definitely disturbed. These were not major doctrinal issues, of course, but to a teenager with barely five years "professing" behind him they were quite troubling.

Trying not to let the little differences bother me, I continued on. A few years ago rumors began circulating that "the way" perhaps wasn't as old as I'd originally been lead to believe. Some said the rumors were without merit and—since I didn't want to believe them anyway—I basically ignored them. Eventually, the evidence was overwhelming that "the way" had been started by a William Irvine in Scotland in 1897. This has now been confirmed by several individuals, articles, letters, etc. This confirmation basically "undid" me. Apparently *many, including workers,* have known this for years and yet the myth was, for whatever reason(s) perpetuated. Everett S. told me in June 1991 that he had been told this by Jack Carroll in 1957—*four years before I professed!* (He also said it took him 10 years to get over the shock.) I guess what bothers me about this most is that I feel I have been the victim of a cruel hoax—as I stated earlier, one of the two reasons I started in "the way" was due to it's succession back to the apostles. It had to be "right," was my reasoning if it went back to Jesus himself. *But it didn't* and now my rock of spiritual reality was crushed—if that wasn't so, *what else* might come to light that would shake my faith?

For years I have struggled with the concept that "the way" was the *only way.* For most of my years in "the way" I naively believed that the really sincere Christian folks I'd meet and come to know (outside of "the way") would eventually "profess" as I knew it to be and *really be saved.* A little over one year ago one of the "golden" people died—but he *hadn't "professed" yet!* Was he in hell even though he'd been a Bible reading, praying man who confessed Christ faithfully in the community? I could not accept that he was. This issue of "the way" being the only way was discussed with four workers with 25-40 years experience each. Three of the four have affirmed what I'd been lead to believe in past years—that *the seed must be planted by a worker for salvation to result.* One of the four said "not so" and Everett S. went so far as to say my friend *could not* be a saved man. As a result of this *major* inconsistency between what workers think as well as what I read in my Bible, my confidence in "the way" "bottomed out." I have discussed the "only way" issue with many of the "friends" and it has been of *great interest* to note that *each* has felt there are those good people not in "the way" who *are saved.* This is a *major inconsistency* in itself—the belief system of the "friends" not lining up with that of the workers. I read that *Jesus* is the *only* mediator between God and man. (I Tim. 2:5)

There are a number of other significant inconsistencies as well. Tharold feels that if a person really "has it," nothing can cause him/her to lose it. (Doctrine of eternal security) According to Dan Hilton, however, we can lose it *at any time.* Some workers believe that Jesus had a divine nature and some say a human nature. The Scripture must be strictly adhered to in the matter of divorce and re-marriage said one sister worker, but another said each case must be considered according to circumstances. Howard Mooney has often told us that there is "perfect harmony" among the workers and yet two of the workers I spoke with were extremely critical of certain other workers. Can you not understand how all of this might be somewhat *unsettling?* I have *despaired* for *months* wondering *who* or *what* to believe.

A Scripture often quoted with regard to no collections has been Matthew 10:8—"freely ye have received, freely give." Having studied this passage using the Greek, I find this verse has *nothing whatever* to do with money but refers instead to freely pouring out—without reservation.

These inconsistencies and contradictions can be "swept under the rug" but that doesn't make them go away. A sister worker told us last June that four families, including twelve children, had discontinued meetings in her field alone that year due to these and other questions. I appreciated her honesty in stating that there would be more "go out" unless these legitimate questions are confronted and dealt with.

There seems to be an abundance of "codes" (traditions, dogmas etc.) which people in the "the way" faithfully adhere to without giving much thought as to whether or not there is a scriptural basis. The main concern seems to be that "good feelings" prevail and that no-one "rock the boat." In reality, feelings are very fickle and not to be trusted. They are governed by intuition and emotion and we must rule over them with sound Godly reasoning and scriptural knowledge, lest we become "slaves" to our feelings.

The depth of pain and disappointment all of the above has brought into my life's experience is indescribable—and, of course *I am to blame!* I am to blame that I was misled regarding the origins of the faith. I am to blame for *observing* inconsistencies and contradictions and wanting to separate myself from the frustration and stress that were a result. I am to blame for seeing things in the scripture that didn't line up with what I was hearing or seeing lived out in friends and workers. I am also to blame for attending a small, country, community, non denominational, Bible teaching Church—it doesn't claim perfection but does offer a measure of encouragement and fellowship which I sorely need during this major unsettling experience. (This is a major source of embarrassment to my family.)

The ache deep in my chest overwhelms me at times. I can no longer be the Spiritual head of my home which I am supposed to be—there is lack of respect for and a pernicious stigma attached to those who leave "the way." Our close marriage relationship is all but gone. My *only hope* is that in time there will be an acceptance of me again as I seek to live a Christian life apart from meetings. Matt. 10:34-36 has been *very real* in recent weeks—for the first time my being a Christian is *really costing me something.*

Please know that all of this has nothing to do with unwillingness to serve God or submit to His will for my life. BY FAR the course of *least resistance* would be to go back to meetings—but I cannot now go back—and the measure of peace (passing all understanding) that I feel (though very *alone* in my choice) is very real for the *first time* in my Christian experience as is the power to rid myself of some of the "weights" that have held me back for 30 years.

I love you and wish the best for you.

Chapter Twenty-Three

Olga D. Hawkins
Letter to Mr. Fred C. Hanewell and Wife,
Dated September 17, 1959

My dear friends —

Today I shall try to answer some of the questions asked in your letter received last week. It would be a long story to tell you some of the things that led to my own questionings of things that were being done on the inside. Perhaps I should say it was an "inquiring mind and a refusal to be satisfied with evasive answers to sincere, honest inquiries."

I am enclosing a paper that may supply the answers to [much] that you wished to know. This paper came out 7 years after the one [which] is in your possession, the one that I circulated several years ago, [as I] felt that the things that were being done were so wrong.

I have been out of fellowship with the C.C. organization 15 years, and it seems it takes years and experiences to cause a real concern and questioning, but in spite of the time element, a few here and [there] in all parts of the world wish to know the facts.

Some one said that there are 3 sides to every story—my [side], your side, and the facts. All I am interested in is conveying the latter. The young chap who compiled the enclosed, as well as many in his country knew some sad experiences, but perhaps all has taken place to open their eyes to the truth of things as they are, for which all should be grateful.

Having been in fellowship with them since 1911 I knew much of what had been going on inside, and since it has been of earthly origin and very deceptive at that, its no small wonder that it has taken the turn it has.

Its just too bad that so-called "workers" still continue to cover up and deceive, and while there may be some of the younger ones who are ignorant of things, this cannot be said of the older ones. Some of the older ones in your own country have seen and know of these papers and will some day have to answer for themselves.

Mr. Parker was in our home 5 yrs. ago before that paper ever went to press and had he been older and in fellowship with them longer, it could have contained a great deal more. I have correspondence from the Gov. and other sources regarding statements they have made which have been enlightening to me, and while for a time it did cause heartache and bitter disillusionment, I have learned through the past to quietly and calmly reason things out and have tried in a small way to make known these same facts to others so that they would not support or uphold the wrong.

It was my privilege a few weeks ago to visit with some in Alaska and in the western states who have given thought to these things and I know there are many in other places who are doing likewise.

You mentioned that you may in the not too distant future come to these shores, and if so, I would be glad to meet you and speak face to face. My best wishes and greetings to you both and I shall be glad to hear again from you.

Sincerely yours,
Olga D. Hawkins

Chapter Twenty-Four

Joetta Swartz Heiser

I hardly know where or how to begin "My Story!" I surely wasn't looking for "a way out" like many of those still associated with 2x2's have said; nor was it that I just wanted to take my own way. It's very frustrating when I don't have an opportunity to even tell others the way I feel because most communication has been cut off. My decision to leave has been misunderstood, misquoted and speculated about a lot; so I feel in this way I can perhaps set the record straight.

I was raised in the fellowship called "The Truth." My parents remember when they first started going to meeting; however, it was their parents who took them. It's always assumed when you grow up in this fellowship that you will eventually profess too. For a child growing up in "the Truth" there is somewhat of a fear about the whole thing because you're aware that it is a way of sacrifice. You have to be different from your friends at school, not attend school functions, dress differently, wear your hair differently; in short stand out to prove that you're a "separated people" and to be an example to the world. Not a real attractive proposition for someone who's growing up and facing many pressures just discovering who they are. The burdens placed on the shoulders of the young people are not balanced by the positive attention they may get at meeting from the friends and workers. I feel this whole thing about submitting means to the other friends and workers ideas of what's right; but not necessarily God's or backed up by scripture. It means because some people may not like certain things; you can't like them either. I had wondered for years why bowling was such a sin. I've never really gotten a definition why it's wrong; but know it was something I couldn't do or if I did, had to be done rather secretly! Then I would hear over and over again how the Truth had no rules! Why I didn't think that through logically years ago still amazes me.

When I was fifteen years old I went to my home convention in the Midwest. During the summer prior to the convention I'd been what the workers call "troubled." I'd kept that entirely to myself because it was such an uncomfortable thing and not something I felt I could share with anyone. I'd thought so much about eternity and being with God forever. I remember relating that to the song "Always!" Some of that song says, "I'll be loving you always, etc. Not for just a day, not for just a week, not for just a year, but always." I started thinking about eternity not just lasting a year, not a hundred years, but just going on, on and on. I could not (and still cannot) comprehend that. The thing that really concerned me was that if I didn't profess and went to Hell there would be burning not just a year, not just a hundred years but on, on and on. That terrified me so much! I had gone to school for eight years in a small school. In fact there were only thirteen kids in my eighth grade class. My freshman year, I went to a consolidated school where there were about 125 students in my class alone. That was a big step attending such a big school my freshman year. Now here I was so concerned about my soul for the future but what about my second year among my peers. I knew my appearance would have to take on a DRASTIC change;

and I felt so inadequate for the task ahead. Yet there was no peace whatsoever for me if I didn't profess. I guess it was the biggest choice of my life thus far, and I felt all alone in making it. On Saturday of the convention, the tension built higher throughout the day. By the evening meeting I was a nervous wreck. I felt I was being forced into a situation that was impossible. I remember crying through the entire meeting. I was so scared; yet what could I do? It seemed to me that there were so many negative, uncomfortable things; yet the reward was eternal life. How could I speak and pray in meeting? How could I bear the reproach of my newfound friends at school? I found myself in the quandary that most kids raised in the fellowship must find themselves. I guess my fear of fire, overcame MY fears because I managed to stand up when the last song was sung. I know it was a shock to most people because I had fairly short hair and looked quite different from most professing girls/women. I felt though, if this is what I have to do to be saved; then this it is. I had the most horrible headache and it persisted through the sleepless night. I remember taking more aspirins than was recommended, just so I could tolerate the next day, I felt some relief because of my decision yet *so* burdened by what was ahead.

It was as difficult at school as I'd expected. I tried to wear my hair up (after it got long enough). I remember there was one girl in particular who rode my bus who always made snide remarks about my hair when I wore it up. This was also the age of mini-skirts. I remember the frustration of shopping for a skirt or dress that was long enough to be acceptable. I'd come home and rip out the hem and face it so it would be longer. One year at convention, a sister worker took a few of us girls aside and told us how our testimonies were marred because of our short dresses. I went to convention that year to be encouraged to endure being different from those I went to school with; and I was even "shot down" there! It started feeling pretty hopeless. This worker told us that even a dead fish could go with the current; but it took a live one to swim against it. I repeated that to myself so many times; trying to take comfort from it, but really finding none. Another year one of the girls wasn't allowed to be baptized because her dresses weren't deemed to be long enough. Yet I and some other girls with dresses shorter than hers had been baptized a year or two before this. I could NOT understand the justice of that. It was like they were discouraging us from spiritual growth. Most of the professing girls who met the workers' criteria for being acceptable were such outcasts—even amongst the friends. I remember a professing aunt of mine talking about a girl who looked like a sister worker but was a teenager at the time. This aunt said she was ashamed of the way this girl looked when she'd run into her on her lunch hour at work. She sure didn't want others to know they attended the same church or in fact even knew each other. If you're a misfit even amongst the friends, what do you think you are when you're out in the world with ALL kinds of people?

The Sunday morning meeting I went to had some wonderful, wonderful people. I have fond memories of so many of those people and I feel certain they have a wonderful reward. They were mostly quite elderly people and they were genuinely happy to have a young person in the meeting there. I never felt condemned by them; they were just so glad I was there and that was a real encouragement to me. I remember though when I was about six years old, wondering why so many of them cried in Sunday morning meeting. You could just about predict how each testimony would start out. "I've failed so much this week." The prayers were the same way, full of remorse for their failures of the past and a desire to do better. But the next week; the very same sentiments were expressed. As a small child I used to wonder what they had done that was *so* bad that they had to cry every week. I spent most of the meeting trying to figure out what it was; after all, most of these people were old and I just couldn't imagine them having the energy to commit too great a sin. I felt *so* sorry for them.

I went through high school professing and they were more difficult years because I was the only one professing at my school. My future husband came with my professing cousin to my high school graduation. We started dating steadily and were married less than a year later. I was grateful to have a professing husband and a professing home. I can't think of anything real eventful to say about those years. There were lots of adjustments during that time as there are for all newlyweds. We attended meetings regularly but it seemed like there were some things missing. It was during this time that the pressure on us seemed too great and for a period of a year or so, that we quit going to meeting. I think both of us knew that the day would come when we HAD to come back. Our only choice was when—but again eternity was the big fear. When we were married nine years, our first daughter was born. I started feeling quite guilty during this time. I'd had infertility problems and we'd given up thoughts of having children. During this time however, I'd prayed many prayers. It was always that if "You'll give me a child lord, I'll raise it in the Truth." Therefore, I felt an obligation to remember that vow. I professed very early in my pregnancy and again "grew my hair out." We had two more daughters after that, so these were extremely BUSY years. There isn't much time for anything but cleaning and cooking and more cleaning and cooking when you have little ones around.

A few years ago, some people moved into the house across the road from us. This couple and their young daughter were from California but had been driving cross-country hauling freight for several years. Since it was time for their daughter to start school, they decided to buy a home and the wife stay home. Her husband was gone a lot and her life had changed so drastically. She was a very private lady, very quiet but sometimes she'd call me and say she needed a little "girl talk." We became friends though we weren't in and out of each others homes a lot. During this time she asked me about schools, about the Dr. we went to, which grocery store I favored, etc. One day she told me they were looking for a church. I was speechless, what could I say? I didn't know how to begin to tell her what we believed or to welcome her to attend meeting with us. You see, she was white, but her husband was black. I did not think she would be welcomed by some of the friends because of her biracial marriage. Also they smoked and I had no idea how to broach that subject with her. In short I felt, they would not be considered "suitable candidates for the Gospel." (Yet I'd read many times that God is no respecter of persons.) I dismissed all that, but for awhile was quite upset about this discrepancy. They hadn't lived here too long, when she got sick and just couldn't seem to get better. One day her car broke down about four miles from home and she called me full of apologies and asked if I could pick them up. The girls and I were so shocked at her appearance. She'd lost some weight before, but had since lost more. Her color was bad and she sounded terrible. I called her often and a few days later she called to say that the doctor was putting her in the hospital. Her husband came home to take care of things. They diagnosed her with bronchitis but before she left they did a routine chest x-ray and discovered she had an inoperable tumor on her lung. The tests came back that it was malignant and it was growing very rapidly. She began radiation treatments, then chemotherapy. The treatments slowed the growth and from what she told me I thought things were going fairly well. Over a year after finding the tumor, her health began to fail rapidly. Her husband didn't realize how bad she was and she was very unselfish and didn't want to worry him. One day she called and asked me to pick her little girl up from the bus that night and bring her to our house. She said I just can't take care of her any longer. We talked every day by phone but I hadn't been to her house for awhile, she usually came here. I went over then and was appalled by the way she looked and by the condition of the house. There were dirty dishes around and it was obvious that they'd eaten a lot of cold cereal prior to this. Despite our daily phone calls and my asking how she was and if she needed anything—this was how things REALLY were. She was quite sick at her stomach and couldn't keep food down by now. I cleaned the house the best I could in the short time I had and tried to interest her in some food. I did pick her up a few things at the grocery store and then called her doctor from my house. He told me the cancer was growing again and it was a matter of weeks! I was afraid for her to stay alone and tried to get her to let me stay with her but she assured me over and over that she'd be fine. Her husband was on his way and arrived home a day or so later. I called him and said I don't think you realize how ill she is. Don't leave her again, please. He called her doctor and they went to his office. He told them that the time was short and they needed to get her affairs in order. This was on a Friday morning and Monday afternoon, he called to say he thought she was dead. We went over and he and the little girl were standing in the kitchen with their arms around each other crying. We went to the bedroom and she was lying there with a horrid expression on her face. Her eyes were set and staring with the look of pain on her face. I think we knew before I took her arm to feel for a pulse, that she was in fact dead. She looked so bad. She was completely bald by now and so thin she was like a skeleton. Her eyes were the thing that really got to me. I felt like she was looking through me and accusing me. There wasn't time for me to think of myself though. They hadn't discussed any future plans at all, so it was a time of asking and suggesting. I called the mortician, the family she had, went through her purse, helped to pick out her clothes to be buried in, etc. I didn't sleep for two nights because all I could see was her pained facial expression. I felt better once we saw her at the funeral home; she looked more peaceful. During all this time, though, I could not dismiss from my mind the fact that I'd let her down spiritually. I'd not had any comfort whatsoever to offer her during her sickness. I had no comfort to give her husband, child and family. I remember having some thoughts about God I wasn't very proud of during this time. I just couldn't understand why she wasn't given a chance and was I the one who should have given her the chance to at least attend meeting?? The workers came for a visit not long after that and they had no answers and no comfort for me. Then we had visiting workers for special meetings so I asked one of them I had a great deal of confidence in; again nothing!! I really felt empty spiritually during this time. How could I go to meeting and try to praise a God that didn't seem kind and merciful after all? It was so hard to hear about a loving God during this time—love for whom?

Another year passed and some of the friends around here had a potluck at a state park nearby. We attended and there were volleyball nets set up and people playing games and having fun. It was a nice relaxing summer day for people to enjoy. However, some of the girls there, forgot themselves and dressed suitably for the occasion. THEY WORE CULOTTES. It was pretty obvious from the atmosphere that there were some unhappy campers there concerning the dress!! You could see whispering behind hands, buzzes here and there!! Disapproval prevailed. I wore my old faithful denim skirt, so I wasn't targeted and neither were our girls. There were two sister workers there too but they weren't the only ones suffering self-righteous indignation! We stayed awhile but were invited to a potluck where my husband worked, so we left soon after dinner. We didn't have time to change clothes so went in the same ones we'd worn earlier. The difference in the atmosphere of the other place was *so* different. Nothing illegal or immoral was going on there; but we just had a good time. There wasn't any self-righteous judging and was it EVER pleasant. I was *so* amazed at the difference! We had a visit from the two sister workers that week and they talked about how disappointed they were in the girls' culottes. I was told how nice I looked in my denim skirt. (If they were trying to make me feel good—it back-fired!! It made me sick to my stomach!) I said I felt that the judgmental attitude that others displayed was more out of place than the culottes!! Well every home had to be visited and every girl talked to about what they were wearing. Such a production made, when the issue was modesty. The girls were much more modest in my opinion with their culottes than rowing a boat with a skirt on—to say nothing of safety if they fell out of the boat!! What really got us was that Deuteronomy 22:5 was quoted. I'd been told by a brother worker over 15 years ago that the passage about man not wearing that which pertaineth to a woman and a woman not wearing that which pertaineth to a man, was dealing with cross-dressing and homosexuality—not women wearing slacks!! Yet this just kept coming up again and again. When we asked why it wasn't necessary to build a battlement around the top of your house like it says in another verse in this same chapter; we were told that what was an abomination to God should not be touched!! This troubled us all summer and yet we kept plugging along.

As we left for convention that year; I knew I needed help like never before. I just didn't know what was happening in my life but some of the things I thought were really settled, were suddenly causing a lot of unsettling thoughts. I prayed very earnestly for there to be something at convention to help my troubled soul. However, though I enjoyed the social part of convention; it seemed somehow like the salt had lost its savour. It was bland and blah and lifeless.

I began examining things like I never had before. I'd always felt and been told that to ask questions was like doubting God—a very dangerous place to be. Yet something drastic was happening in my life and I HAD to get to the bottom of this. I'd often been comforted in the past when I'd seen discrepancies in the government. My generation saw reports on organized crime operating openly. Bribes being taken by police chiefs and those in higher authority. We saw Nixon involved so deeply in the Watergate break-in that he resigned from office to avoid being kicked out. I recall after President Kennedy was shot, hearing that Lyndon Johnson may have been involved so he could become president! I was quite young at the time; but remember being *so* shocked. I put men who became president right up there with Abraham Lincoln and George Washington. Men who were honest. That they were selfish and dishonest was more than I could imagine. The Vietnam War brought more accusations; more discrepancies among Government officials. To think that our country has left prisoners of war in some of the countries where they fought is so repulsive to me. There have been the Iran Contra Affairs, the Supreme Court nominations and many more I'm sure that I'm leaving out. In short, men of clay were having to defend inappropriate actions. Their offices no longer protected their wrong-doing. I also discovered that honesty and politics should not be used in the same sentence! They were poles apart. During all these episodes, I would console myself with "But isn't it wonderful, I'm in the perfect way. Things are crumbling in Government, but I have TRUTH." That was a very great consolation to me. Honesty also became more important than ever before.

Someone mentioned to me, again, the book *The Secret Sect*. Like most professing people, I'd felt I wanted no part of such a book. Now I felt I should at least read it. However, I was NOT ready to believe it. I read it with a very jaundiced eye. Finally, I could see it WAS well-documented. Many of the things the book said, I knew to be true from past experiences. The fact that I'd always been told that the Truth was from the beginning of time and that now I could see there HAD been a founder was just one more letdown in life. The thing I thought infallible was built around many tales. I felt devastated and heart-broken and I literally did not know which way to turn. Someone pointed out that MEN had let us down; not God. I began turning to the scriptures and really examining them to see what they REALLY had to say, I was again surprised to see how many things had been taken out of context, twisted and inappropriately applied. More and more of the foundation was crumbling but I surely felt more shipwrecked than ever. During this time I prayed more sincerely than I ever had in my life. I asked God to help me through this because I did not know which way to go. I also asked Him to help me not be deceived because I felt very vulnerable. I wanted during this time nothing more than to prove that the accusations in this book were WRONG! But it was not to be. The workers visited someone else we knew who had many of the same questions we did during this time. I prayed again that the workers would show us where we were wrong and I honestly thought they would. But it was not to be. Again there was no comfort there; obvious cover-up was going on. Questions were not answered, and issues were skirted. I was reminded of politics again and it wasn't a pleasant comparison! The lady at this home was verbally attacked by the Overseer of the state in anger and accusations. This "Man of God" didn't have the verse that says "a soft answer turneth away wrath," in hand when he talked to this couple. We were devastated again to think that those we thought had answers—didn't!

A bit later a delegation of four workers came to our home to discuss things. We weren't verbally attacked this time, BUT there were no answers given to some of our questions, evasions to some of the others, and in general just disappointment!! We were still attending meetings at this time; but it was almost more than I could do. When I'd hear some phrases I'd heard all my life repeated, it was all I could do to stay in my chair. I usually spoke the most during this time about LOVE. I'd noticed how important that was in Jesus' time and in his thoughts. How he tried to convey that to the apostles and how he didn't shut out anyone. I finally got to the point where I could no longer go. I'd stay home on Sunday morning and READ, READ and RE-READ my Bible, searching for answers. I began seeing the similarities between the Pharisees and many of the people from meeting. I'd always heard it was the inside that was important but I knew from experience that the outside got a lot more attention. I'd felt too that many times I attended meeting trying to concentrate so completely on keeping a right attitude and trying to be right within; but something on the outside was condemned which nearly quenched my spirit. Where was the love? Where was the confidence in God that He could control situations and people? Where was the part about letting HIM complete the work in our lives? That was given over to the workers to do. I'm NOT trying to condemn the workers here, don't get me wrong. I know many that I feel to be very sincere, very diplomatic—but I've known others to be just the opposite. I cannot escape the verse which says there is no mediator between us and God save the man Christ Jesus. I've heard that quoted many times; yet I knew the workers DO act as mediators. At the same time this is said they will talk about Catholics and how they have to go through the priest or the pope and how wrong that is—yet we have to have workers' approval to get baptized? Also during the time when we weren't professing we bought a television. We never hid it but kept it in our bedroom. We were told that the workers would really love to put a meeting in our home but as long as we had the television they just couldn't do it. I felt so guilty about that television and yet I didn't watch it and actually my husband seldom did either. It became for a period of time, a real thorn between us. I felt we should get rid of it but he refused to. Yet when I thought logically about it, IT really wasn't a big issue—but others were trying to make it one. We were controlling the time we spent watching it but they were telling us we didn't have enough judgment to control it. No, I didn't spend much time watching it; but was I any better reading a book for several hours at a time or talking on the phone than I was watching a TV program?? We asked the workers when they visited what really was the difference in reading a book or watching the same movie on TV? We got shrugged shoulders for a reply.

Well I have a tendency to get sidetracked very easily. I did find a church just a few miles from our house. We all attend it together as a family and are very happy there. The children are learning things about the Bible for the first time in a church-like setting. Our oldest daughter said she learned more from the week at vacation Bible School than she'd ever learned at meeting. She's rather jealous that her younger sisters are memorizing the books of the Bible, something she doesn't know. We appreciate that our children are being taught and they are considered important right now, not just for the future of the kingdom. They are learning at their own age level just like at school. We love the feeling of learning ourselves too. We've had to tear ourselves away from reading our Bibles sometimes because there are chores to do. NEVER have we felt this enthusiasm for spiritual things. We're like sponges absorbing liquid and our appetites are being satisfied so completely. I come away from church knowing I'm far from perfect, but that I can rest now in Jesus. I have confidence in what He has done for me, not in what I am going to do for Him in the week ahead. Grace is such a new concept for us and not one we learned at meetings. We never realized we are saved by grace through faith and not works. In fact we were shocked to hear a worker tell another that yes, we are saved by grace. But when we mentioned our surprise at that to someone who professes; we were asked where we'd been all these years? Where indeed? At meeting!! Not only had we not heard that, another couple our age hadn't, my parents in their mid-seventies hadn't and several others whose privacy I respect hadn't either. A worker recently told us that we needed to "sit through a mission." When we reminded him that we'd sat through mission after mission ALL OUR LIVES, he still felt we needed another. I might add, this worker DID verbally attack me and I have six hours of his last conversation with us on tape, if anyone is interested. This worker made some rude comments about our church and pastor to us, so we asked him to make those comments to our pastor's face instead of behind his back. He did agree to meet with him and that was done here in our home. During that discussion the worker told our pastor that the women at meeting dressed conservatively but that it was a choice, not enforced. Now I ask you to search your memory and think about it a bit. Was it choice or force when the sister workers mentioned above visited the individual homes and discussed the wearing of culottes? Was force being applied there or not? Will those girls openly wear culottes again around friends or workers? I'm sure you all have experiences of similar treatments. Also, the girl who wasn't allowed to be baptized because her dresses were too short, was that force or choice? With our choice of having a television, we lost the opportunity to have a meeting in our home. It's an either/or situation, no doubt about it. These are BIG discrepancies we're talking here. Also if discrepancies here; how about in the way scripture is interpreted?'

I've also been considering some of the negative thinking that many people who go to meeting teach their kids. We may not agree with something that we must do at meeting—for an example, let's say you don't make your professing teenage daughter wear her hair up except to meeting or if there are friends or workers around. Remember: God sees all—He knows. You think it's a ridiculous rule and unscriptural, but not something you have a choice about. Think about the message you are "teaching" here. You as a parent are caving in to peer pressure—you don't have the backbone to stand up to others about a situation you don't agree with. Yet the next thing you try to teach your child is "you don't have to be like everyone else. Just because your friends at school are drinking, smoking or having premarital sex—you can be different." Is it any wonder so many of the young people go completely wild in their teenage years or that once they're out from under parental control they exercise *no* control. They've been taught by parents' example to cave in to peer pressure and to not exercise their own true emotions. An outside change does not evoke an inward heart change. Until friends and workers begin to understand that, I expect there will be continued heartache for parents and children alike in these important growing-up years; and sometimes I think it follows them all their lives. I was recently reading a book in which the author mentioned that when he was a child and others asked him if he was a Christian he would say yes. I don't drink, don't smoke, don't curse, etc. Well, he said one day he looked at his dog Ralph and realized that Ralph didn't drink, didn't smoke and he'd never heard him use foul language—yet Ralph wasn't a Christian. The author was saying it's not an outward thing but it's an inward change that has to come about. It's a relationship with Christ which makes us a Christian—that and nothing else.

In conclusion, the turn of events this past year have been surprising indeed. I feel that the prayers I prayed both privately and at meeting have been answered. I'd so often prayed to have a closer walk with God and I feel that has taken place. I never in a million years thought it would take me out of the way I knew of as Truth, in order to achieve this closer relationship. I feel my focus has changed so much this past while. While I felt so unworthy, so inadequate before; now I can worship knowing He is worthy; what He did was adequate. I don't have to concentrate on my lack but I can love and appreciate the fullness of His sacrifice. I can rest in that and let Him bear the burdens that I was trying to carry.

I don't want this to sound bitter or angry because I'm not. I feel sorry for those frustrated years I spent trying to reach God on my own. However, if I'd never had those years I wouldn't feel the spiritual freedom I now have and appreciate so much. My goal is to help others that are burdened and overcome with a system. Many are trapped and like I, cannot imagine a way of escape. With me it finally got to the place where I had to ask myself, "are you willing to risk the disapproval of friends, workers and family to try to find your own personal relationship with God." Again I find myself thinking of judgment day. It won't be the workers or friends judging me there (however, I sure have experienced that judging here in this life). It'll be God's approval I'll desire. I've heard so many times recently that if we want to have a personal relationship with God—"get rid of the middleman!" When I think back to times I've been discouraged by workers or friends judgmental attitudes, I realize it was almost impossible for me to read and pray during that time. I felt too unworthy to reach God because I'd been told I'd done wrong. It's very comforting now to be able to go to God like I would a friend and lay my burdens on Him and know He cares. I read over and over in the Bible that God is a caring, loving compassionate and merciful God, yet I never felt that way about God while I was in the 2x2's. I felt over-burdened so much of the time that there was very little joy to experience. I'm just trying to put first things first in my life and in doing that I had to go it totally alone for awhile—just me and God. I found I had to stand alone because my husband, my children, friends, workers, family no one but God really understood where I was. It took that time alone with just God and myself and coming to terms with Him FIRST. When I really got that relationship in the proper order, then I could concentrate on the other relationships. There are still many in my family who do not understand and do not choose to understand. That has hurt and hurt very deeply that they cannot take into account my past and remember that I have always been honest and sincere. They have allowed their thoughts to become clouded by the *smear campaigns* others have unjustly launched. Instead of coming to me and asking me what has happened, they take other people's word. We find ourselves questioning if we'd be welcome at hospitals or funerals of people from meeting. We still care and love these people but are unsure how we'd be received. Yet in being treated unkindly and unfairly, we've felt pity and sympathy for them. Praying for others who treat you badly, does help overcome bitter feelings. In closing, my prayer for ALL people is that we'll have God's guidance and do His will. In finding Him, you too, may have to leave the spot you've known for years, the friends you've always had, past relationships may be dissolved. In general things and life may be turned upside down. Are you willing for that? It's not easy and you will be shocked at some of the things which happen. However, with God's help, we can do anything. Who is your confidence in? Is it in yourself, is it in what you've always known and the way your family has always worshipped? Is it in the workers, or is it in sincere people you have always known? Or is it in God totally? We must all ask ourselves these questions and sometimes we're really surprised at the answers we get. May God be our guide and our help and may we learn to trust Him totally.

June 30, 1993

Address:
Joetta Swartz Heiser
6301 E. U.S. 33
Churubusco, IN 46723

Chapter Twenty-Five

Connie Kamp Jacobsen
My Testimony

*Note: Because this is a one-sided "conversation,"
I realize there's a danger of giving a wrong impression.
I do not write to make "foolish argument," to justify
the choices I have made, to "convince" anyone that
I am "right," to imply that I have all the answers,
with the intent to "preach" at anyone nor out of
any "bitterness." I do not consider that I had "a bad
time of it" while I was professing. —CJ*

Early History:

Both sets of my grandparents met up with The Truth in their early married years. My father was born and raised in The Truth. My mother was one year old when her parents heard "the gospel" and her mom professed. She was two when her dad professed and they started having Sunday and Wednesday meetings in their home. My mom professed when she was 12 and my dad when he was about 14. It was customary, then, for young people to travel to an upcoming convention and stay with local friends in order to help out at the preps. My folks first met when my mom went down to Manhattan to help there.

We moved around quite frequently when I was a child and, except when we lived out on the farm, we generally had at least a union meeting in our home. For many of those years my dad was the elder—either of the meeting in our home or in a

widows home nearby. The workers stayed with us
often. My three older siblings and I were all raised
(as my parents had been before us) to believe The
Truth was the only true way of God and that the
workers were a continuation of the ministry which
Jesus had established when He was on the earth.
We grew up with a great respect for the workers
and friends in The Truth. We were taught the value
of fellowship and only missed a meeting when we
were sick. Most years we attended at least two
complete conventions and got to as many of the
Montana special meetings as weather and Dad's
"eldership" responsibilities permitted.

We grew up in a home where the Lord came
first. Our parents taught us the importance of a
right heart condition before God. Their lives were a
testimony before us that God was worthy of our
very best. As young teenagers, or younger, we all
professed and continued on faithful to our profession through the years. As young adults we each
chose, as our life partner, another person who had
been born and raised in The Truth and with time
began to raise our own children with that same
heritage.

I don't know if it's possible for a teenager with a
heart for pleasing God to be raised in The Truth
and not be very conscious that God could call them
into the work. Certainly, through my teen years and
into my twenties, this possibility was very much on
my mind. I prayed about it often. I never thought or
dreamed of what lay ahead for me in life without
being conscious that God might have different
plans for me than my own dream of a hardy professing husband, an open home and several
children.

Since the workers often speak of receiving the
call to the work at some convention, I also prayed

specifically before and through every convention I
went to in those years that I would be listening for
God's call and if the work was His choice for me, I
would hear and would be willing to respond to that
call. It was unsettling living through those "early
adult" years wanting to make plans for the future
yet knowing *my* plans might not be God's plans for
my life. Sometimes I'd get impatient and instead of
remembering that God has His own perfect timeta-
ble, I'd even pray, "Father, If you want me to give
my life in the harvest field, please let me know
NOW so I can settle it... so my life doesn't have to
continue on hold."

But God didn't call me (or Brian) into the
work—and after Brian and I had been dating for a
time (at the age of 23) we began to talk of marriage. As we made those plans for our life, for the
first time I felt settled and at peace with God about
His plan for my future—that our plans were not being made in spite of and in direct opposition to a
"higher call," but that in marriage we were re-
sponding to God's call for our lives. The hymns we
chose to be sung at our wedding were "Together
with Jesus" and "Lord, Help Us Be Lights" (both
were from sheet music and were not in the hymn
book). We chose those hymns with great care. It
was our prayer and purpose right from the start that
our home and our lives would be dedicated to and
used by God to further His kingdom.

Five and one half years later (about 9-1/2 years
ago), when we were expecting our second child,
Brian quit taking part in the meetings. He continued to come to most meetings with me, but he
basically set his Bible on the shelf and left it there.
I was heart-broken and (though I really didn't recognize it for what it was for quite some time) I was
VERY ANGRY. We had made our plans to marry and

raise a family knowing that The Truth was important to both of us and that we wanted to raise our children to know and love God, too. How could he just turn his back on this most important part of our lives?! For almost a year, every time I attempted to draw near to God, I became so upset because of Brian's choice (a choice that I didn't understand and that he chose not to talk to me about) that I found it almost impossible to either pray or read the Bible—a situation that, of course, concerned me a great deal.

Finally, though I wasn't even consciously aware then that the verse was in the Bible, the Holy Spirit was able to teach me the lesson that "man's anger does not bring about the righteous life that God desires." —James 1:20. I acknowledged the anger I was battling. I began to see how destructive that anger was and how I was allowing the choice of another person to hinder my own relationship with God. I was not responsible for Brian's choices nor for his life and I had no control over his choices, but I finally realized that I did have the choice as to whether I would allow it to affect me and my own relationship with God. With that realization, I at last felt like a very heavy burden had been lifted from my shoulders. It didn't change the circumstances—I still had a husband who didn't have a love for The Truth; who was not involved in teaching the children about God; who didn't care to read and pray with me, etc,—but I had at last come to understand that his decision was between him and God. My only responsibility was to maintain my own relationship with God, to teach the children and to pray and Pray and PRAY!!

So, I began to pray that God would give Brian a soft, seeking heart and that He would draw Brian to Himself and reveal His truth to him. I prayed that I, too, would know God's truth and that He would give me wisdom in my dealings with Brian and that NOTHING in my life, service, attitude or spirit would be hindering God's ability to work in Brian.

Questioning

As time went on, different issues came up—issues that sometimes seemed to pit my love for the fellowship against my commitment to my marriage. Brian became less willing to attend meetings with me. Eventually he was only coming with us to the Sunday morning meetings (most of the time) and joining us for a few weekend meetings at the conventions we attended. Brian knew I loved God and he knew how important that relationship was to me. He also knew how I valued the fellowship of the friends. But I loved Brian, too, and I was committed to my marriage. I had made vows before God "for better or worse." As these issues came up, so did many questions: What was God asking of me in this? What "example" would really touch Brian the most? I tried to seek God's guidance and respond as He would lead me—but often I was torn because I knew how it would *look* to the friends and workers if, for instance, I chose, on occasion and according to what I believe was God's dealing, to put my marriage and my husband's desire to spend time with his family before getting to a meeting. (For several years when our children were young, Brian's job kept him away from home 65 to 80 hours (or more) a week. He often went several days without even getting to see the kids while they were awake and our opportunity for "family time" was extremely limited.)

I spent much time trying to search out and study what the Bible said was my responsibility in the position I found myself. I found in God's Word that women should be in subjection to their "unbeliev-

ing" husbands and that their adornment should be
that of a meek and quiet spirit. (I Peter 3). God
knew my heart. He saw my faithfulness in prayer
and studying His Word. He knew my love of meeting together with other believers, but He had also
laid out some specific commands for wives and
husbands. His Word had to be my guide—commands such as: "What therefore God hath joined
together, let no man put asunder" —Matthew 19:6
(Which spoke to me to mean, especially not the believing wife by her choices and actions, or lack of
commitment and submission.); "Not forsaking the
assembling of ourselves together" —Hebrews
10:25; "wives be in subjection to their own husbands (in everything.)" —I Peter 3:1 (and Ephesians
5:24) and other instructions as well. With the pressure in The Truth to conform to an acceptable
lifestyle, I often felt that many of the friends and
the workers failed to understand how all these various aspects had to mesh together in order for my
life choices to be pleasing to GOD.

Just as the accepted standard "lifestyle" didn't
necessarily match up with what God's Word and
the Spirit asked of me in my personal life experience, I also found this to be true in the matter of
the outward conformity of appearance. Throughout
the years of my "profession," I never had the conviction—that many in The Truth have—that any
outward conformity of appearance is Biblical other
than the instruction to be moderate and modest. In
fact it was the manner in which all this "need" for
outward conformity was upheld by many in The
Truth that caused me to first begin questioning the
teachings in The Truth; I KNEW my heart condition
before God. I KNEW the reality and the depth of my
personal relationship with Him. Yet, I heard time
and time again how necessary this unity of appear-

ance and lifestyle was. Once at convention a worker (one with considerable authority in the area) even went so far as to say that anyone who wasn't conforming to some specific things was nothing more than a fake. Several of the things he mentioned applied to me—either in actuality or in the fact that, though I was choosing to conform to what was accepted and expected in order not to offend anyone, I had no conviction from God that those things were necessary to salvation. As I have said, I knew my relationship with God was no pretense. I knew I was not a fake in God's eyes.

We were taught in The Way that women were not to wear makeup and jewelry and were not to cut their hair. This was generally accepted by the friends and workers as the Biblical view. Since it seemed to be such an important issue to many, it concerned me that I didn't see these portions of scripture in the same way. But even with continued study and prayer my convictions remained the same. It was said that God's reason for these restrictions was that those things were vainglorious and would put a woman's focus on herself rather than on God. Actually, in time, I came to realize that dressing and looking "plain" had nothing to do with whether or not a woman was "vain." In fact, that enforced emphasis on outward appearance actually could make a person more self-focused. Some women in The Way had marvelous, *manageable* hair. They could fix their long hair in 50 different ways that all looked pleasing. Some women also had been given a natural glow of "built-in makeup" by God. Others had limp, unmanageable hair and washed out complexions.

While the "beautiful" woman (or ANY woman who is content with the accepted standards of appearance) can become self-righteous in "willingness to submit to God's plan," the "naturally plain" can become buried in self-consciousness and low self-esteem. Either situation hinders a woman's ability to do the work God calls her to. I fit into that category of the limp, washed—out and buried in self-consciousness and I chose more and more with time to "buck the system." I found with a little makeup and my hair trimmed up and permed (though I still knew that I was not and never would be a "raving beauty"—nor was that my goal) some of my self-confidence was restored. Contrary to what we'd been taught, this did not create a problem of "vanity"—it simply freed me up to turn my focus away from myself and onto God and His will for my life.

I had come to realize that my love for God was revealed in my obedience to HIM: to His commands in His Word and the Holy Spirit's guidance in my life; rather than my hair style, the shoes I wore, how inflexible I was in the matter of NEVER missing a meeting or any other such issue. So, why did I keep going to the meetings? Because I believed with all my heart that The Truth was God's True Way; because I loved God and desired with all my heart to serve Him and bring joy to His heart; because I wanted my children to come to know and grow to love God as I did and because, in spite of these discrepancies of understanding, I loved the fellowship, I loved the meetings, and I loved the friends and the workers.

Still, I didn't understand this discrepancy of thought and it bothered me greatly. In fact, discussion of these points always disturbed my peace and caused me to go back to God's Word and back to my prayer closet again. I would receive fresh answers from God that confirmed my understanding and brought me peace again. Then, repeatedly, I would find myself losing that peace and getting stirred up in my heart as I sat in a meeting or engaged in conversation and heard the thought expressed again that anyone who wasn't living according to the accepted outward standard was unwilling—lacking self-denial and understanding. I began to feel that these man-made restrictions were hindering God's ability to build in my life. I remember once thinking that I knew how Abraham had felt when he said, "Oh let not the Lord be angry, and I will speak yet but this once"...as I returned again and again to pray to God about these same issues and to seek answers in His Word again. (God is so good!—He was faithful every time to show me answers in His Word to confirm my understanding about these things.)

Every child of God has certain standards in his life. Some are specifically commanded in Scripture, some are as a result of personal direction from the Holy Spirit for the individual and some may just be a matter of personal choice. As long as that personal choice doesn't violate or compromise God's Word, each believer should be free to make those choices. "Accept one another, then, just as Christ accepted you, in order to bring praise to God," — Romans 15:7. In The Way I didn't see that kind of Scripture-directed acceptance of one another's God-given, God-directed and God-accepted differences. Rather, I saw a pervasive attitude that all believers would ("by virtue of the Spirit working in them") be living according to a pre-determined set of standards—in spite of the fact that Scripture makes it clear God accepts our unique personalities and differences (and even endows us with different spiritual gifts).

In addition, this emphasis on standards that could be measured by other men also concerned me because it was even obvious within The Way that man's judgment was often faulty. I refer to the instances of respected elders who have been found to be seriously lacking integrity in their business dealings, embezzling funds from their employers, cheating on their taxes or abusing their children; as well as respected workers in high places of authority involved in sexual immorality. (It further bothered me that many in The Way seemed to find it easy to continue to uphold compliance to the "standards" as proof of a person's love for God in spite of the evidence to the contrary in such happenings.)

Breaking Away

About four and one half years ago as I realized the desperate situation I was in—caught in between my own God-given conviction and the conviction of others—I finally came to the place where I began to pray earnestly to God, in almost every silent prayer, that He would show me HIS truth; separate from my own ideas, separate from other men's ideas, separate from empty traditions and separate from Satan's promptings—and that He would give me the courage to stand up for His truth. While I prayed this prayer (almost daily for about two years) I still felt assured that this was God's Only Way. I didn't know how God would answer my prayer, but I didn't for a moment imagine it would take me out of The Way. I continued to encourage others to keep on going in The Way. As God made it increasingly clear to me that He had other plans and another place for me, I was gripped by fear. This Way was all I knew about serving God. I began to pray, "Lord, if what I have been striving to fulfill all my 23 professing years is not your will for my life, then—what AM I supposed to do?!!"

With time I came to understand that the very issues that I didn't see as Scriptural were, in fact, the
very basis of The Way for many. I came to see how
destructive the harsh, and often inaccurate, judgment of other people had been. My heart broke
when a worker sat at my kitchen table one morning
and told of refusing to allow several teenagers to be
baptized—young people, with a love for God and a
desire to obey His commands, pleading their cause
only to be found "unworthy" by another person's
standards. Where was the scripture for this? Where
was the emphasis on a person's personal, heart relationship with God? Where was the Holy Spirit's
work and power in this? We have seen this kind of
treatment bring immeasurable pain to many and
even shake some people's faith to the point of turning them completely away from any endeavor to
come to know God. Many have gone away with an
aching heart, misunderstood and confused; but
have simply been written off by others in The Way
as bitter, contentious, or unwilling. This all troubled me very much. I knew it was not the way
Christ would have handled things if He had been in
our midst. If it wasn't Christ's way and we were
"following" Him, how was it being justified?

I often tried to talk with different ones (both
friends and workers) about my concerns. Some
didn't share my concerns. Others indicated that
they did share those concerns, but the very system
itself demanded conformity and few were prepared
to speak out about these injustices. In The Way,
people were not encouraged to talk about things
that could be viewed as "controversial" or "contentious argument." Often the answer to such
questioning was, "You must just believe in faith."
But, Jesus never asked anyone to walk in blind
faith. Paul told the Romans (10:17), "Consequently,

faith comes by hearing the message and the message is heard through the word of Christ." The Bible is also very clear on the need of seeking understanding and knowledge: "Do your best to present yourself to God as one approved, a workman who does not need to be ashamed and who correctly handles the word of truth."—2 Timothy 2:15. "You must teach what is in accord with sound doctrine."—Titus 2:1. "It is not good to have zeal without knowledge..."—Proverbs 19:2. And in Paul's second letter to Timothy (3:15), "...from infancy you have known the holy Scriptures. which are able to make you wise for salvation through faith in Christ Jesus." We may not be able to see it or touch it; we may not be able to comprehend it; there may be no human logic to explain it—but we can and must base our faith on what God's Word tells us—about Himself, about His plan of salvation, about His promises. His Word is truth!

My assessment of The Way is not intended to be a judgment of anyone's heart condition before the Lord. I know that I had a real, personal relationship with the Lord when I was "professing." I am certain this is true of many still in The Way, too. By contrast, though, some we've met in recent years, who had been professing for many years—and had been highly respected by both the workers and the friends, now say their "service to God" was nothing more than an empty form all those years! Even though at the time they truly believed they were faithfully serving God, now having come to understand the gospel story in a new light and having come to know God personally, they understand that all they had before was a form. That is the very thing the Bible warns about and that we fear when a system places a lot of emphasis on salvation by works rather than salvation by God's grace.

In January of 1991, after much agonizing, soul-searching and prayer, I finally made the decision that I would not be returning to the meetings. I had come to feel that just by virtue of attending the meetings and taking part there, I was upholding ALL of what the system stood for. I knew I could no longer do that—not before my own children, not before my "unprofessing" husband, not before others at the meetings, not before "outsiders" and (most especially) not before God.

What Next?

At that time, I still had a distrust of "organized religion" and the paid clergy, and I didn't know where God would lead me. However, knowing, as I've already mentioned, God's commandment for His people to not forsake "the assembling of ourselves together," and also knowing the benefit to me personally that this "gathering" had been and could continue to be. The most difficult part of making that decision not to return to the meetings was the thought of walking away from the possibility of any further godly fellowship and the study of Scripture with others in God's family.

During the month or two before I made my final decision not to return to the meetings, I had read a book about becoming an authentic Christian, one on religious "addiction," and I had ordered *The Secret Sect* and *The Church Without a Name*. When they arrived, I read them and then ordered and read through all the turn-of-the-century newspaper articles which have been compiled about the beginning of The Way in Ireland. I realized The Way was not as unique as it is claimed to be. In spite of the disdain those in The Way often show toward any other religion that has been "started by man." The Way has that same history. Not only was it started less than 100 years ago, but even from that beginning this "unchanging way" has seen many changes.

Within a couple weeks of making my decision, I knew that I was not content or prepared to go without godly fellowship unless I had first made an intense (and unsuccessful) search to find it. We had heard about a non-denominational church in our area and had met some of the people who attended there whose values we admired. We decided to attend one of their services. Making the decision to go to the church and then actually walking into our first service were among the most difficult decisions and endeavors of my life. The things we'd been taught all of our lives about the danger and falseness and emptiness of "organized religion," didn't just go away when we left The Way or when we chose to enter a church building. (Some people have even experienced physical illness of one sort or another as they enter a church for the first time.) I went there trusting that God would not forsake me in my sincere desire to live for Him, nor take away my ability to discern His truth, just because I was walking into a church building.

There were many things about the place of worship and the form of worship that were VERY different from what we were used to in The Way: the passing of a collection plate; the paid clergy; the joyful, exuberant praise and worship time; baptisms in a baptismal; and many other such issues. What amazed and delighted us, though, was the manner in which the pastor upheld the truth of God's Word; the apparent unity of the congregation in their love for God, their zeal to serve and worship Him, their honor of the Word of God; and their recognition of the need to allow His Word and Spirit to shape and control our lives. (We now know those things are not true at every church. For many it has taken a lot of searching to find a church where the pastor and the people truly uphold the Word of God.)

Over time, we have also gotten involved with smaller mid-week Bible study groups and have gotten better acquainted with many other Christians. As our understanding of God's Word has increased and as our fear of "organized religion" has been dealt with, we have come to experience a measure of joy and peace that we NEVER knew before. We have come to realize the benefit of fellowship with so many other wonderful, godly people we missed out on while we ignorantly practiced separation from the Christian "world." (The "world" that Christ warned his disciples about was the self-serving, self-sufficient element that failed to acknowledge Him as their King and Savior. He did not warn them against other believers who were worshiping the same God, though in a manner which was different and unfamiliar to them. In Luke 9 the disciples spoke to Jesus of a man driving out demons in Christ's name. "We forbad him, because he followeth not with us." Jesus told them, "Forbid him not: for he that is not against us is for us.")

"Rebuttal" to The Way

Many people like to blame what they call the "hateful books," which have been written about The Way, for our choice. However, as I mentioned, neither Brian nor I read any of the books—nor even knew much about them—until after I made the decision to leave the fellowship. Many people have told us that if we had only put more into our service to God, we would never have "lost our love to do His will." Does my testimony tell the story of someone who was insincere in seeking to give my very best to Him? Many people think our decision to leave The Way was about unwillingness and a hard spirit. Does my testimony tell the story of someone who has failed to seek God's guidance in life and who has bitterly rejected the Word of God because it didn't fit in with my own plans? I never doubted God or His Word. (And, today, I understand that it was for similar reasons to the things that caused me to question that caused Brian to "give up." He saw too much of what we had been raised to believe was "the truth" that didn't seem to agree with what he read in his Bible. His conclusion at the time was that none of it made sense. His joy in the Lord now is a fresh marvel and delight to me every day! God is so good!)

Many have told us that they know The Way is God's only way because of the peace and joy that they have in The Way. To them I would ask: *"Who or what does God's Word teach us is the giver of our peace and our joy? Should we place our trust in God or in a way? Does your peace and joy truly come from your system or way of worship, or does it come from your relationship with God Himself?"* (In Luke 10 when the 70 came back, their joy was in having power over the demons. Jesus had to tell them their emphasis was misplaced—that they were rejoicing in the wrong thing. Just as this was possible for believers in Jesus' day to have a misplaced focus to their rejoicing, so it is still possible for us today.)

Brian and I also know a great peace and joy and a deep love for the brethren in Christ, but there are literally millions of cult members—from Mormonism, Jehovah's Witnesses, Christian Scientists, Unity, The Way International, etc., etc.—who would attest to the same thing and who use that as proof of the "rightness" of their way of worship. It's true that a right relationship with God brings great peace and joy, but evidently the father of lies—Satan, himself—can even make the people he deceives think they know this very same peace and joy. In Jesus' intercessory prayer to His Father recorded in John 17, he prayed, "Sanctify them [make them holy] by the truth; your word is truth" (v17). None of us should be content to trust our "feelings" alone. The important thing (the only sure test) is how our beliefs and our lives stack up to God's unchanging, inerrant and infallible Word. (And how essential for us to remember that every verse in the Bible does indeed fit together perfectly with every other word of Scripture. If a person's interpretation of a verse does not tie in with the overall context of the entire Bible, the verse is being taken "out of context" and something is wrong with that interpretation.)

Jesus commanded us to follow Him. It has become very real to me that there is a great difference between seeking CHRIST and seeking a WAY (or method) through which to reach God. Jesus did not say, "I am showing you the way" or "I am pointing out the way" or "I am guiding you along the right path," but.,. "I AM the way.") God doesn't always accomplish things in the same way. (Consider His various ways of conquering the enemy in the Old Testament and the different ways which Jesus and the New Testament Church used to reach, heal and convert unsaved people.) Yet, God's character and His truth remain forever unchanged. Those character traits are the things we strive for in order to be "followers of God."—Ephesians 5:1 "...Be perfect, therefore, as your heavenly Father is perfect."—Matthew 5:48; "he that is chief among you, let him be as he that doth serve...I am among you as he that serveth."—Luke 22:26-27; "Forgiving one another, even as God for Christ's sake hath forgiven you."—Ephesians 4:32; "as he which hath called you is holy, so be ye holy."—I Peter 1:15; "But the fruit of the Spirit is love, joy, peace, patience, kindness, goodness, faithfulness, gentleness and self-control. Against such things there is no law." —Galatians 5:22-23.

We have come to understand that there is no single "religious method" to receive salvation. Paul encouraged the Corinthians to examine themselves to see whether they were in the faith—it wasn't a matter of looking at the "system" they were in or at any outward standards they were upholding, but rather of looking at their heart condition before God. Jesus told the Pharisees, "the kingdom of God cometh not with observation: Neither shall they say, Lo here! or, Lo there! for, behold, the kingdom of God is within you."—Luke 17:20-21. Christianity is NOT any sect or denomination or system of worship or service. It's a heart relationship (one person at a time) with the God of all the universe! Christianity crosses denominational, cultural, economic and any other lines which seek to classify men.

Jesus taught in Luke 17, two will be in one bed...Two women will be grinding grain, together; one will be taken and the other left. So it is with denominations, churches and sects in the world. I believe He could say today, two in The Way will be testifying in a meeting, one will be taken and the other left. Two will be "praising God" at Overlake Christian Church (the church we attend); one will be taken and the other left. Two will be witnessing to others about "serving God," one will be taken and the other left. Two will be living in a foreign country, seeking to "bring Christ" to a previously unreached people group, one will be taken and the other left. Why is that? Because salvation is not dependent on what "system" of worship or service we are affiliated with or what "outward forms" we conform to or who we "associate" with. Rather, it's a question of whether we've come to a saving knowledge of Christ and His truth. It's a matter of our heart relationship with God.

Jesus Is The Way

In pouring out His blood on Calvary's cross, Christ provided the way—the only way—for us to be born again and become a child of God. "Salvation is found in no one else, for there is no other name under heaven given to men by which we must be saved."—Acts 4:12. "Yet to all who received him, to those who believed in his name, he gave the right to become children of God."—John 1:12. Jesus paid the redemption price that we might have eternal life. "He suffered death, so that by the grace of God he might taste death for everyone." —Hebrews 2:9. "God made him who had no sin to be sin for us, so that in him we might become the righteousness of God."—2 Corinthians 5:21. Oh, that we would praise Him for that! Indeed, He is the way! Christ, the only sinless one took our sin upon himself and endured the punishment we deserved (death and separation from God). In so doing, He made it possible for us to receive His righteousness and thus be reconciled to God. "We have been made holy through the sacrifice of the body of Jesus Christ once for all."—Hebrews 10:9-10.

Salvation is a gift freely given by God, "For by grace [the unmerited favor of God] are ye saved through faith; and that not of yourselves: it is the gift of God: Not of works, lest any man should boast."—Ephesians 2:8-9. All that is required of us to receive that gift is that we repent (acknowledge our sinful state and our need of a Savior), believe in Christ and accept Him as our personal Lord and Savior—in faith, because "without faith it is impossible to please God, because anyone who comes to him must believe that he exists and that he rewards those who earnestly seek him."—Hebrews 11:6.

Any further requirements—food restrictions, circumcision, religious rites, methods of ministry, methods of assembly, appearance, etc,—turns the gospel of God's grace into a gospel of works or human effort. "And if by grace, then it is no longer by works; if it were, grace would no longer be grace." —Romans 11:6. Paul said: "Are you so foolish? After beginning with the Spirit, are you now trying to attain your goal by human effort?" —Galatians 3:3. In John 6:28-29 the crowds asked Jesus, "What must we do to do the works God requires?" Jesus answered, "the work of God is this: to believe in the one he has sent." And in Acts 20:24 Paul said, "I consider my life worth nothing to me if only I may finish the race and complete the task the Lord Jesus has given me—the task of testifying to the gospel of God's grace."

The Bible is also clear that man does not have the power to earn his own salvation, but must rely on God's grace. "How then can we be saved? All of us have become like one who is unclean, and all our righteous acts are like filthy rags; we all shrivel up like a leaf and like the wind our sins sweep us away,"—Isaiah 64:5-6. "God is light...if we walk in the light as he is in the light, we have fellowship with one another, and the blood of Jesus, his Son, purifies us from all sin. If we claim to be without sin, we deceive ourselves and the truth is not in us." —I John 1:5-8. "We all, like sheep, have gone astray, each of us has turned to his own way; and the LORD has laid on him the iniquity of us all."—Isaiah 53:6.

Godly Living

Though it is through this grace of God that we receive eternal life, believing this does not free us to live in sin. (By definition, if Christ is "Lord" of our life, He will be in control.) Jude warned the believers about ungodly men "turning the grace of our God into lasciviousness, and denying the only Lord God, and our Lord Jesus Christ," (v 4). And Paul said in Romans 6:15, "Shall we sin, because we are not under the law, but under grace? God forbid." In Galatians 5:13 he said, "For, brethren, ye have been called unto liberty; only use not liberty for an occasion to the flesh, but by love serve one another." and in verse 16, "Walk in the Spirit, and ye shall not fulfill the lust of the flesh."

It is God's desire and purpose that, from the point when we accept Christ as our Lord and Savior, we would continually be growing and becoming more like Him. "Do not lie to each other, since you have taken off your old self with its practices and have put on the new self, which is being renewed in knowledge in the image of its Creator."—Colossians 3:9-10. "We ought always to thank God for you...because your faith is growing more and more, and the love every one of you has for each other is increasing."—2 Thessalonians 1:3. "Consider it pure joy, my brothers, whenever you face trials of many kinds, because you know that the testing of your faith develops perseverance. Perseverance must finish its work so that you may be mature and complete, not lacking anything,"— James 1:2-4. "But grow in the grace and knowledge of our Lord and Saviour Jesus Christ. To him be glory both now and forever! Amen." —2 Peter 3:18. The glory does belong to the Lord. Our spiritual growth is also not a result of our own merit but comes by God's grace, for "God makes things grow."—I Corinthians 3:6 and "God caused the body to grow." —Colossians 2:19.

Though there will still be times when we stumble and fall, we don't need to be defeated by that because, in this also, God's grace is sufficient. Our recognition of our inability to live righteously in our own power is reason to rejoice! As Paul concluded in 2 Corinthians 12:9, "Therefore I will boast all the more gladly about my weaknesses, so that Christ's power may rest on me." In acknowledging our weakness and our dependence on Him, we open the way for His perfect power to work in and through us. Not as an excuse to sin, but giving hope in spite of our human weaknesses. Jesus told Peter, "Watch and pray so that you will not fall into temptation. The spirit is willing, but the body is weak."—Matthew 26:41. (He understands the weakness of our human state.) Jesus also told Peter, "Satan has asked to sift you as wheat. But I have prayed for you, Simon, that your faith may not fail, And when you have turned back, strengthen your brothers."—Luke 22:31-32. (He offers forgiveness and hope beyond the failure.) "For I know the plans I have for you," declares the LORD, "plans to prosper you and not to harm you, plans to give you hope and a future."—Jeremiah 29:11. "...God has said, 'Never will I leave you, never will I forsake you.'"—Hebrews 13:5. "If we confess our sins, he is faithful and just and will forgive us our sins and purge us from all unrighteousness." I John 1:9. Just as a disobedient child damages his current fellowship with his earthly father, but is still his father's beloved child, how much more this is so with our heavenly Father when we fail. As our Father, God will discipline us; He will rebuke us and correct us when we fall into sin, but He will never abandon us. We have His promise, and He cannot lie.

Jesus said, "Come unto me, all ye that labour and are heavy laden, and I will give you rest. Take my yoke upon you...For my yoke is easy, and my burden is light."—Matthew 12:28-30. Trying to earn our own salvation by our own performance, knowing that we will continue to fall short, is not a light burden. Trying to live a Christlike life by our own effort, knowing that we will never be able to do it perfectly, is not an easy yoke. I praise God that, by His grace, He has not left us in that defeated position. "Therefore [Jesus] is able to save completely those who come to God through him, because he always lives to intercede for them."—Hebrews 7:25. "Let us therefore come boldly unto the throne of grace, that we may obtain mercy, and find grace to help in time of need."—Hebrews 4:16. "I give them eternal life, and they shall never perish; no one can snatch them out of my hand."—I John 10:28. "These things have I written unto you that believe on the name of the Son of God; that ye may know that ye have eternal life"—I John 5:13 "To him who is able to keep you from falling and to present you before his glorious presence without fault and with great joy" —Jude 24. Oh, that we would learn to rest in His loving arms of grace!

Foundational Bible Truths?

We were always taught that there was a unity and a world-wide fellowship in The Way that compared to nothing else on earth. What we have come to understand is that while there is some measure of uniformity and conformity to some outward standards of living (thus giving the appearance of unity), there is no universal unity of thought about essential doctrinal issues amongst the friends and workers in The Way—with the exception of what they consider to be the two essential issues: meeting in the home and the two-by-two, unsalaried ministry. It is not that we think these two things are wrong in and of themselves for anyone who feels called to them, but we do believe it is a distortion of Scripture to claim that this method is the only possible way for anyone to serve God and receive salvation.

In fact, we have been amazed to see that the Bible just doesn't teach those "foundational truths" we were raised to believe in The Way. As we broke away from the training we had always believed and began to study the Bible for ourselves more thoroughly, it became more and more clear to us that we had been guilty of re-interpreting the Bible to say what we wanted it to say, rather than reading it to find out what God was actually saying through those pages! The following several paragraphs will address some of that convoluted thinking:

What about the supposed instructions for the workers to leave all? The only time Jesus ever told anyone to sell all their possessions before they could come and follow him was that rich young ruler (recorded in Matthew 19:16-26; Mark 10:17-27 and Luke 18:18-27). This man was operating under the false delusion that he was keeping all the commandments perfectly; though the Bible tells us, "If we claim to be without sin, we deceive ourselves and the truth is not in us...If we claim we have not sinned, we make him out to be a liar and his word has no place in our lives,"—I John 1:8-10. As we see all the way through the four gospels, Jesus saw right into the hearts of people - he knew this man's possessions were more important to him than his relationship with God. In this attitude, he was breaking the first commandment: "thou shall have no other gods before me."—Exodus 20:3. When that rich young man went away sad, still clinging to his earthly riches as the most important thing in his life, everyone around him saw what Jesus had already known.

In Matthew 19:27 (just after this incident with the rich young ruler) Peter said to Jesus, "We have left everything to follow you!" What did Peter mean by this statement? In Jesus' response to Peter he said, "every one that hath forsaken houses, or brethren, or sisters, or father, or mother, or wife, or children, or lands for my name's sake, shall receive an hundredfold, and shall inherit everlasting life."

Let's look at this closer: Did Peter literally leave his wife to go and follow Jesus? Was Jesus instructing the apostles that day that they needed to literally leave all in order to go and make disciples? Hebrews 13:8 tells us, "Jesus Christ is the same yesterday and today and forever." At the sermon on the mount, Jesus said, "whosoever shall put away his wife, saving for the cause of fornication, causeth her to commit adultery."—Matthew 5:32. Also, that same 19th chapter in Matthew that we have already been looking at, starts out with Jesus having a discussion with some Pharisees about divorce. Jesus made the statement that day, "Therefore what God has joined together, let man not separate."—Matthew 19:6. Would the same Jesus who made those statements then turn around (21 verses later—or even an eternity later, for that matter) and tell the apostles to leave their wives and their children? Would he ever tell anyone to sever their commitment to their spouse and their children? Did Peter (also called Cephas according to John 1:42) literally leave his wife? Not according to I Corinthians 9:5 where Paul said, "Don't we have the right to take a believing wife along with us, as do the other apostles and the Lord's brothers and Cephas?" (That's a pretty interesting statement for Paul to make, in light of the teaching in The

Way that the workers are to be homeless and unmarried, and that this is so because it most closely
follows the example of the New Testament church!)

Yes, it's true that, though there are no longer
any married workers in The Way, at one time there
were a few. (Why has such a change occurred in a
"changeless" way?) Several of the friends and workers have assured us when this question comes up
that workers could still marry, but it is just so difficult and impractical. Wait a minute! Isn't that the
same argument I've heard friends and workers ridi-
culing when it's made by anyone outside of The
Way? (Not to mention that we know of several accounts of people who were in the work, got
married and wanted to continue in the work, but
have not been allowed to.) Would Jesus have set in
place any plan that would later prove to be too impractical and difficult? If it was a task too difficult
to perform as a married man, would Jesus have ever
called any married men to fill that place?

Why does sexual immorality continue to surface
among the workers? It's true that in I Corinthians 7
Paul told the Corinthians, "An unmarried man is
concerned about the Lord's affairs—how he can
please the Lord. But a married man is concerned
about the affairs of this world—how he can please
his wife—and his interests are divided...a married
woman is concerned about the affairs of this
world—how she can please her husband." But Paul
also said, "Now to the unmarried and the widows I
say: It is good for them to stay unmarried, as I am.
But if they cannot control themselves, they should
marry, for it is better to marry than to burn with
passion." and, "It is good for a man not to marry.
But since there is so much immorality, each man
should have his own wife, and each woman her
own husband." We have already seen that Jesus did

not forbid married apostles—does that restriction for workers in The Way today create an environment that leads people into sexual immorality? Paul warned Timothy about those that would abandon the faith in later times. One of the ways Paul identified those people was to say, "they forbid people to marry."—I Timothy 4:3. Is an enforced unmarried ministry really following the New Testament church most closely, or does the teaching in the Bible show that decision should be left up to each individual to make between themselves and God?

What about literally leaving homes and giving up all possessions? In Luke 5:28 it tells us that "Levi (also called Matthew) got up, left everything and followed [Jesus]." What did that mean? Just after this, we are told that "Levi held a great banquet for Jesus at his house." If Levi had literally left all, he would not have been able to throw such a party and he'd have had no home to invite anyone to. Perhaps in The Way today, a person's family and/or friends may have some sort of "sending off" hymn sing or potluck for someone going into the work, but no worker himself would be able to do what the Bible tells us Levi did that day—he would not have the funds or the provisions, let alone the house! Did Matthew literally leave all behind to follow Jesus the way workers are required to do today?

If the Apostles had no home and no means of providing for themselves (let alone anyone else) why did Jesus entrust the care of his mother to one of the apostles when he was crucified? Jesus understood perfectly the position and the role of those 11 apostles that day. If Jesus had instructed his apostles to leave their own mothers because it was too difficult to devote their lives to the ministry while being tied to such family responsibilities, why would he have turned around and "saddled" one of them with his own mother? There were many other disciples of Jesus who could have taken on this responsibility—not to mention Jesus' own brothers. Why would Jesus have placed his mother under the care of someone who had no means of provision? And if, when Peter spoke in Matthew 19, he meant that John—as well as the other apostles— had literally left all, how could John have then taken Jesus' mother into his own home? (As it says in John 19:27.)

In Luke 14:26 Jesus said, "If anyone comes to me and does not hate his father and mother, his wife and children, his brothers and sisters—yes, even his own life—he cannot be my disciple." But this same Jesus said in Matthew 5:43-45, "You have heard that it was said, 'Love your neighbor and hate your enemy.' But I tell you: Love your enemies and pray for those who persecute you, that you may be sons of your Father in heaven." and, "Honor your father and mother." —Matthew 15:4. Was Jesus literally telling his disciples that they must "hate" their families? Of course not, or Jesus would not be the Unchanging One the Bible tells us He is. The actual thought Jesus was expressing here was that we must put him first in our lives and love him more than even our closest, dearest loved ones and family members if we are to be his disciples.

Again in Luke 14:33 Jesus said, "In the same way, any of you who does not give up everything he has cannot be my disciple." These verses are often used in The Way as additional proof that the workers need to literally give up all to go into the work. Interestingly, these same verses are also used in The Way in dealing with the need for the friends to surrender all to Jesus in the figurative sense of

putting Jesus first before all else in their lives.
These verses can be used this way for the friends
since all agree that "disciple" refers to any follower
of Jesus, not just the apostles. Were the words of
Jesus ever meant to apply in a literal sense to one
group of believers and only in a figurative sense to
all other believers?

What about this whole concept of two "classes"
of believers? Does the Bible really teach that kind
of division? Jesus' final words to his apostles before
he ascended to heaven were, "Therefore go and
make disciples of all nations, baptizing them in the
name of the Father and of the Son and of the Holy
Spirit, and teaching them to obey EVERYTHING I
have commanded YOU."—Matthew 28:19-20. With
that commandment of Jesus in mind, what part of
Jesus' teaching can be considered as only applying
to the apostles?

In Mark 16:19-20 it says, "After the Lord Jesus
had spoken to them, he was taken up into heaven
and he sat at the right hand of God. Then the disciples went out and preached everywhere, and the
Lord worked with them and confirmed his word by
the signs that accompanied it." There is no indica-
tion of two "classes" of believers here, either.

Paul encouraged Philemon (v 6) and the rest of
the church at Colosse, "I pray that you may be active in sharing your faith." Philemon was the slave
owner of Onesimus—he was not a "worker;" he
had not sold all, yet Paul was exhorting him to go
and spread the gospel.

In Acts 11 it tells us how the church at Antioch
got started. It was during the time that "a great persecution broke out against the church at Jerusalem,
and all except the apostles were scattered throughout Judea and Samaria,"—Acts 8:1 "Now those who
had been scattered by the persecution in connec-

tion with Stephen (Acts 8) traveled as far as Phenice..."—Acts 11:19. It was those scattered disciples who carried the gospel message through the land to the Jews and established this church in Antioch while the apostles were still in Jerusalem.

Philip was called an evangelist (Acts 21:8). He was a married man, he traveled around preaching and teaching, leading people to a saving knowledge of Christ and baptizing them. (Some have told us that he was endowed with special responsibility as one of the seven "deacons" appointed in Acts 6, but how many times do we have to insert some special information not found in the Word of God, or adjust something in the Bible to make it fit our beliefs before we begin to question if possibly it is the beliefs themselves that need some adjusting?)

The Bible tells us that all believers receive certain gifts from the Holy Spirit (Romans 12, I Corinthians 12, Ephesians 4, etc). However, our special area (or areas) of giftedness does not preclude our obedience to God in all areas—that is, being gifted as a teacher does not exclude us from God's command to "serve one another," having the serving gift does not exclude us from "encouraging (or exhorting) one another," and so forth. Some people are specially gifted as evangelists (preachers of the gospel), but there is nothing in the Bible to indicate that people with the gift are given a set of life style requirements which differ from the requirement of all believers to "live soberly, righteously and godly." Can the division of the people in The Way today into "workers" and "friends" really find a comparable match in the New Testament between "apostles" and "saints"? "For there is one God and one mediator between God and men, the man Christ Jesus."—I Timothy 2:5. "But you are a chosen people, a royal priesthood, a holy nation, a people belonging to God, that you may declare the praises of him who called you out of darkness into his wonderful light."—I Peter 2:9. Does the teaching in the Bible really uphold this separation of God's people into different classes?

What about the need to meet in a home ONLY? In Luke 14:52-53 it says of the disciples (earlier mentioned as "the Eleven and those with them"). "Then they worshiped [Jesus] and returned to Jerusalem with great joy, And they stayed continually at the temple, praising God." In Acts 2:44-45, "Selling their possessions and goods, they gave to anyone as he had need. Every day they continued to meet together in the temple courts." In Acts 5:12-13 it says, "And all the believers used to meet together in Solomon's Colonnade. No one else dared join them, even though they were highly regarded by the people."

In James 2:2 it says, "For if there come unto your assembly a man with a gold ring, in goodly apparel." The Jewish New Testament uses the word "synagogue" in the verse. The Greek word which was translated here as "assembly" is *"sunagoge."* It means an assemblage of people; specifically, a Jewish "synagogue." I made a study of the Greek word and found it was used 58 times in the New Testament: 56 times it was translated into the word "synagogue" and referred to a Jewish synagogue; 1 time it was translated as "congregation" (in Acts 13:43, speaking of the gathering at a Jewish synagogue) and then James chose to use the same word when writing of a gathering of believers. Paul told Timothy, "All Scripture is God-breathed and is useful for teaching, rebuking, correcting and training in righteousness, so that the man of God may be thoroughly equipped for every good work."— 2 Timothy 3:16-17. Does James' God-inspired choice of wording here indicate that James, or God, was overly concerned with the location where Christians would gather to worship their Lord and King? Jesus said, "For where two or three come together in my name, there am I with them."—Matthew 18:20. Was the New Testament church as concerned with the place of worship as the people in The Way are today? Does the Bible provide appropriate proof (and instruction) that the only accepted place of worship is in a home?

As always, I don't discuss these issues to make personal attacks on the people in The Way, but only to help bring to light the truth about these matters from a Biblical perspective. Satan is a master deceiver. From man's first encounter with him in the Garden of Eden, he has been twisting God's Word to trip people up. He appears as an angel of light—making it possible to deceive those very ones seeking to know God's truth (if they are willing and content to accept anything less than what the Word of God proclaims as their basis of "Truth"). To me, that is the most tragic thing in all of this—the wounded that fall by the wayside discouraged and confused and defeated, people who were desirous to establish a relationship with God and live for Him and please Him but who get tripped up by the deceiver and turn away to nothingness, or even turn from one deceit to another.

Seek the Lord

God says, "Call to me and I will answer you and tell you great and unsearchable things you do not know."—Jeremiah 33:3; "Ask and it will be given to you, seek and you will find, knock and the door will be opened to you,"—Matthew 7:7. And we have God's assurance: "'You will seek me and find me when you seek me with all your heart. I will be found by you,' declares the LORD"—Jeremiah

29:13-14. Life's answers aren't found only by special interpretation of a certain person or group of people. They do not lie within ourselves, either— that is just another deception of the enemy first used in the Garden of Eden: "'You will not surely die,' the serpent said to the woman. 'For God knows that when you eat of it your eyes will be opened, and YOU will be like God, knowing good and evil.'" —Genesis 3:4-5. (This idea of all answers being found within us is very popular in America today, It has also been taught for centuries in the religion of Eastern Mysticism.)

We must turn to God! All of life's answers are wonderfully provided in the pages of God's Word! God does not lie and His character is unchanging. He speaks to us through His Word. Through the pages of Scripture, we can come to understand who He is and what He promises to those who are His children and we can claim those promises in our own lives when specific need arises.

The Word of God is not confusing, hidden or convoluted when it is interpreted as it was written. We are wise to take advantage of the knowledge others have gleaned from years of studying God's Word. But we must always beware of any person or group who claims to know and be "the only way." (There are many who make this claim; but it is only God—not any man or group of men—who holds the key to the only way, through the shed blood of Jesus Christ our Saviour on the cross of Calvary!) Pray to God as the Psalmist prayed, "Open my eyes that I may see wonderful things in your law."—Psalm 119:18; learn from Christians of long ago and from Christians of today, read Christian literature, listen to Christian radio, talk to Christians in your workplace, in your neighborhood and in your school and, finally, (like the Bereans) search the Scriptures daily to see if the things you have heard are true. Rest assured that "God is faithful to his promises and loving toward all he has made."—Psalm 145:13. "Whoever comes to me I will never drive away,"—John 6:37. He will answer when we call to Him! He will never disappoint us!

The enemy is very real. If he tried to tempt Jesus into sin, he is certainly going to attack us, too! We need to be aware of his tactics and be prepared soldiers. We need to run to God, claim our redemption through the shed blood of Jesus Christ and make Him the Lord of our lives. God's Word says, "You, dear children, are from God and have overcome them, because the one who is in you is greater than the one who is in the world." —I John 4:4. Satan has no power over God's Holy Spirit within us... nothing "will be able to separate us from the love of God that is in Christ Jesus our Lord." —Romans 8:39. We can put our trust in our God, nothing is too difficult for Him! How can we possibly praise Him enough!?!

Assessing "False Religion"

In The Way, we also had a very low opinion, even a distrust, of all "organized religion." Much has been said over the years and continues to be said, from the platform and among the friends and workers, to encourage and feed that distrust. People who have come out of "organized religion" into The Way have often done so because they personally have seen or experienced something they didn't feel fit in with Christianity. (I in no way mean to imply that all is well in the "religious world." Just as I believe it is wrong to generalize that all organized religion is corrupt, so I recognize it would be wrong to generalize that it is all "pure.")

Though it's not true in all cases, with our better understanding of the religions of the world, it has been interesting to hear how many of the testimonies, of people who have come out of organized religion into The Way, even include involvement with one or more "cults" (like Mormonism, Christian Scientists or Jehovah's Witnesses). The negative experiences in organized religion for some others in The Way has come from the Catholic Church. While I haven't done any sort of an extensive study of the Catholic Church, I believe they endorse a correct view of Jesus, but they do not understand the gospel message of the Bible. They have added "idol worship" in the form of worshipping Mary, the mother of Jesus, and all their "Saints;" and they have added a long list of unbiblical "requirements" like penitence and confession before a priest, though the Bible clearly teaches, "there is one God and one mediator between God and men, the man Christ Jesus."—I Timothy 2:5.

It's from these people who have suffered through negative experiences in other churches and have shared those experiences with the friends and workers that we in The Way (who never had any personal involvement in another church) shaped our understanding of "organized religion." But, for each person who comes out of such "organized religion" because of a negative experience, how many others are still in a church because their experience has been positive; because they know the truth of God is being upheld there, they love the fellowship with other believers, they see the good works of Christian living being done from their church through believers in Christ and they know the fellowship and teaching is helping them to grow in the Lord? Many in The Way are convinced, because of their own experience in it, that the "problems" seen in The Way by those who have left are not true or, at the least, were an unfortunate exception rather than the norm in The Way. Isn't it possible (and, in fact from our own experience we know it to be so) that the same could be said by those in other churches?

We were often taught in The Way that salaried pastors were just "in the business for the money." Obviously, as we see too often in the news, there are *false prophets* seeking to make merchandise of God's Word—and doing a, regrettably, successful job of it. But I do not believe that is the "norm." There are, of course, ex-workers that none of the friends or workers would want to see upheld as the "norm" in The Way, either. Human nature is human nature and Satan is alive and well. Jesus warned about false prophets and those who would call on His name and even do great things in His name, yet who would never really know him. This sort of activity should not come as a surprise to anyone, that's the very reason we must be careful not to put our trust in any man or in any system, but must trust in GOD, and God alone.

In fact, more often than not, a pastor's salary is purely a matter of faith that God will provide, because the first factor in determining the pastor's salary is how much money is given and, then, what other needs the money might be required for. We were also taught that people are put under compulsion to give to churches. The statistic that, across the board, only 20% of the people provide 80% of the funds given (and 50% of the people give nothing at all) proves this is just not true. Pastors do talk about money and they do ask for money for the needs they see, but such requests are generally understood by Christians to include the biblical direction that, "Each man should give what he has

decided in his heart to give, not reluctantly or under compulsion, for God loves a cheerful giver."
—2 Corinthians 9:7. (There are many other issues regarding the beliefs held in The Way about organized religion that we have since learned aren't necessarily true, but I won't take the time and space here to mention any more.)

Unity Within the Brotherhood of Believers?

I believe a lot of misunderstanding comes from the belief that there is to be perfect unity within the body of believers—but what about this matter of unity? We don't have to look very far to see that all Christians did not see eye-to-eye on everything even in Scriptural times! Was the lack of divisions and disagreements something that Jesus promised to those that would follow Him? Consider the record God left us of the New Testament Church (the body of believers who enjoyed and sought out and benefitted from the fellowship with one another because they each one had, individually and in their own heart, made Christ their "Head"—exactly what Christ's "Church" continues to be today). Even at that time, it was no perfect picture of unity: the 12 jockeyed for a place of honor, Judas (who was never really "following" Christ, although he certainly appeared to be) sold Jesus for 30 pieces of silver, Peter denied Him, John Mark turned back and Paul and Barnabas had a falling out; Paul reprimanded Peter because he was trying to force the Gentiles to follow Jewish customs (and that wasn't the only time that issue came up!); Ananias and Sapphira lied to God in an endeavor to appear more "righteous" before other men; Peter was criticized by others when he brought the message of salvation to Cornelius' home; the Corinthians were quarreling amongst themselves and withheld their affections from Paul—and this list could go on and on!! No, being believers in Christ does not guarantee freedom from strife within the body of Christ. Paul told the Galatians (5:15), "If you keep on biting and devouring each other, watch out or you will be destroyed by each other." Nor, does it guarantee sinlessness. Paul said, "For what I want to do I do not do, but what I hate I do."—Romans 7:15.

Anyone looking for a group they will be in perfect agreement with will be disappointed. All of us would desire that kind of agreement even with our own spouses, but it often eludes us—even if we both love God and also love one another with all the love we are capable of. We don't have that kind of perfect and total agreement with our own parents, not with our children, and not with our best friends, either. So how can we expect more from a "random" group of God's family at large than we have in our own circle of immediate family and close friends? If we set unrealistic expectations (of divine behavior) from a group of God's not-perfect-just-forgiven children, we are setting ourselves up for disappointment, and also setting up for failure the opportunity to fellowship with others of God's family, before we even walk in the door and get acquainted.

There is a reason why God put verses like the following in the Bible: "How can you say to your brother, 'Let me take the speck out of your eye,' when all the time there is a plank in your own eye? You hypocrite, first take the plank out of your own eye, and then you will see clearly to remove the speck from your brothers eye."—Matthew 7:4-5. "Therefore, as God's chosen people, holy and dearly loved, clothe yourselves with compassion, kindness, humility, gentleness and patience. Bear with each other and forgive whatever grievances you may have against one another. Forgive as the

Lord forgave you. And over all these virtues put on love, which binds them all together in perfect unity."—Colossians 3:12-14. Unfortunately, all of us need these reminders much too frequently!

What is Truth?:

But what about those disagreements or divisions? In regard to some of those differences of opinion, we have been directed in God's Word to be careful not to judge, as in the following passage. "Accept him whose faith is weak, without passing judgment on disputable matters. One man's faith allows him to eat everything, but another man, whose faith is weak, eats only vegetables. The man who eats everything must not look down on him who does not, and the man who does not eat everything must not condemn the man who does, for God has accepted him. Who are you to judge someone else's servant? To his own master he stands or falls. And he will stand, for the Lord is able to make him stand. [What an amazing promise, by the way!!!] One man considers one day more sacred than another; another man considers every day alike. Each one should be fully convinced in his own mind. He who regards one day as special, does so to the Lord, for he gives thanks to God; and he who abstains, does so to the Lord and gives thanks to God."—Romans 14:1-6.

But there were other divisions that were not handled in such a manner. Why? Because, "some people are throwing you into confusion and are trying to pervert the gospel of Christ." "I am astonished that you are so quickly deserting the one who called you by the grace of Christ and are turning to a different gospel—which is really no gospel at all." "They were not acting in line with the truth of the gospel." (from Galatians 1 and 2). When division comes, the consideration of any child of God should be: Is this just a matter of a person's individual choice before God? Am I being judgmental when this particular matter is just between this other person and God? Am I exhibiting the *"agape"* love described in I Corinthians 13 to my brothers and sisters in Christ? Or are we talking about a perversion of the gospel? Is this an issue that I can't embrace nor choose to be silent about; but one which I must speak out against?

This idea of standing up for God's truth against any perversion of the gospel is not a matter of age and/or years in God's family, either. Paul directed Timothy, "If you point these things out to the brothers, you will be a good minister of Christ Jesus...Don't let anyone look down on you because you are young..."—I Timothy 4. And, what is this gospel that Christ's disciples are each responsible to keep pure? If each is responsible to know and uphold this truth, then each one must study what God's Word teaches for themselves. What did Jesus teach would bring salvation and eternal life? What did the Apostles teach? What WAS the gospel message of the New Testament Church? It is not enough for anyone to just be trusting the teachings and the interpretations of Scripture from others, but he must be making a study through God's Word as the Bereans who "were of more noble character than the Thessalonians, for they received the message with great eagerness and examined the scriptures every day to see if what Paul said was true."—Acts 17:11. These were new converts eagerly receiving the word, yet searching the scriptures to prove for themselves that what they had been taught by that great teacher, Paul, was true. Paul did not reprimand them or accuse them of being contentious; rather he commended them for their diligence and their understanding that it was God's Word which is truth.

I have appreciated thinking of it in this way: Jesus said the most important commandment is to, "Love the Lord your God with all your heart and with all your soul and with all your mind and with all your strength." If we love Him in this way, and the more we come to know Him through prayer and studying His Word, the less tolerant we will be of any perversion of His gospel. He said the second greatest commandment is to, "Love your neighbor as yourself." Again, if we love God as Jesus commanded, we will also "love one another, for love comes from God."—I John 4:7; and if we love others in this way, we will be much more tolerant of one another's differences. We will not be allowing our individual direction from the Holy Spirit, or our differences of opinion on matters that are not specifically addressed in the Bible and are not essential to salvation, to be hindering our ability to "live a life worthy of the calling [we] have received, [to] Be completely humble and gentle; [to] be patient, bearing with one another in love. [making] every effort to keep the unity of the Spirit through the bond of peace,"—Ephesians 4:1-3.

Paul put it this way, "therefore, I urge you, brothers, in view of God's mercy, to offer your bodies as living sacrifices, holy and pleasing to God—this is your spiritual act of worship. Do not conform any longer to the pattern of this world, but be transformed by the renewing of your mind. Then you will be able to test and approve what God's will is—his good, pleasing and perfect will. For by the grace given me I say to every one of you: Do not think of yourself more highly than you ought, but rather think of yourself with sober judgment, in accordance with the measure of faith God has given you. Just as each of us has one body with many members, and these members do not all have the same function, so in Christ we who are many form one body, and each member belongs to all the others. We have different gifts, according to the grace given us."—Rom 12:1-6.

It is true that some religious sects today have a totally faulty basis of doctrinal belief (a perversion of the gospel). Some have literally rewritten their own "translation" of the Bible so it will say what they want it to say; some only use the Bible as a token and have chosen to use their own literature in place of the Bible to back up their doctrine and others have just reinterpreted the Bible according to their own beliefs instead of basing their beliefs on what the Bible really teaches. Anyone trusting in these false writings and false systems without that personal heart relationship with God would obviously be living with a false hope.

As long as the devil is free to prowl around "like a roaring lion looking for someone to devour," there will be confusion in the "religious" community. Jesus and the apostles repeatedly warned about false prophets and teachers and there are records of false prophets throughout the Bible. "Satan himself masquerades as an angel of light. It is not surprising, then, if his servants masquerade as servants of righteousness."—2 Corinthians 11:14-15. Paul also warned the Colossians (2:8), "See to it that no one takes you captive through hollow and deceptive philosophy, which depends on human tradition and the basic principles of this world, rather than on Christ." What better way for Satan to keep men from following Christ than to confound the thinking of the very ones who are seeking to "find" God, so that they believe a counterfeit instead of the truth; and thus, never come to a saving knowledge of Christ?!

However, many of the denominational divisions that exist today have come about because of people's differences of opinion on these "non-essential" issues. Human nature tends to enjoy fellowshipping with others who think just the same as we do, and the tendency also is not to stop and consider if the difference in belief or understanding is really essential to salvation or if it is an individual matter between a person and the Holy Spirit. Many Christians today are encouraging the dissolution of the denominations. This is not out of a desire to compromise God's plan of salvation (may it NEVER be so!) but, out of a recognition that if God accepts some of our differences, can we do less? Even when churches are still connected to one denomination or another, it is true that there is much more acceptance of non-essential differences with other churches and much less division between denominations, than there have been in times past,

Jesus said, "you are the light of the world...let your light shine before men, that they may see your good deeds and praise your Father in heaven."— Matthew 5:14-16; and in His intercessory prayer, He prayed for all believers, "May they be brought to complete unity to let the world know that you sent me and have loved them even as you have loved me."—John 17:23. A united body of Christ means a glorified King! (And, tragically, when we as believers engage in needless sparring and hissing at one another, we become Satan's greatest "advertisement" against Christianity to the unbelieving world around us.) "For our struggle is not against flesh and blood, but against the rulers, against the authorities, against the powers of this dark world

and against the spiritual forces of evil in the heavenly realms,"—Ephesians 6:12. Oh, that we would
all remember who the enemy is! That we would be
putting on that incredible armor God has provided...including the shield of faith (in God and His
promises—with which we can extinguish all the
flaming arrows the enemy hurls at us), the helmet
of salvation (our assurance against the lies and
doubts Satan tried to plant regarding our position in
Christ) and the sword of the Spirit (which is the
word of God) and that we would be prayerfully
seeking to keep the unity of the Spirit through the
bond of peace. Then...to God be the glory!!!

Our present joy!

We have now found a world-wide fellowship
which truly compares to nothing else on this earth!
We've often had visiting pastors—from other
churches throughout the U.S. and even from other
countries—speak at our church. We've also been
listening to Christian radio and reading a lot of
Christian literature. It has been a joy to us to see
the unity of thought and understanding that does
exist from Christian to Christian—from church to
church, pastor to pastor, and generation to generation—when they are standing on that same Rock
foundation of Christ, the Word. The words of Deuteromony 6:4-9 have taken on an entirely new and
living meaning in my life during these last months:
"Hear, 0 Israel: The LORD our God is one LORD:
And thou shalt love the LORD thy God with all
thine heart, and will all thy soul, and with all thy
might. And these words, which I command thee
this day, shall be in thine heart: And thou shalt
teach them diligently unto thy children, and shalt
talk of them when thou sittest in thine house, and
when thou walkest by the way, and when thou liest
down, and when thou risest up. And thou shalt

bind them for a sign upon thine hand, and they shall be as frontlets between thine eyes. And thou shalt write them upon the posts of thy house, and on thy gates."

Some might even say that we have become "obsessed" with living for God. (What a blessed obsession!!!) Our desire is to know God's Word more fully, so that we may "be throughly equipped for every good work."—2 Timothy 3:17 and to truly be Spirit-filled, that we "might walk worthy of the Lord unto all pleasing, being fruitful in every good work and increasing in the knowledge of God..." —Colossians 1:10. We rejoice in learning more and more of the truth of God's Word and our most valuable friendships are those where we have the freedom to share and discuss these things of God.

Just as Jesus taught, "Not every one that saith unto me, Lord, Lord, shall enter into the kingdom of heaven; but he that doeth the will of my Father which is in heaven."—Matthew 7:21; so we understand that not everyone who calls themselves a Christian has truly accepted Christ as Lord and Savior, but we rejoice in this world-wide fellowship—it's called Christianity! It's a group of people of all ages, from all cultures and from all walks of life who uphold God's Word as truth—our most valuable "possession"—and who lift up the Lamb, our precious Savior Jesus Christ, as our glorious Lord of lords and King of kings! "Wherefore God also hath highly exalted him, and given him a name which is above every name: That at the name of Jesus every knee should bow, of things in heaven, and things in earth, and things under the earth; And that every tongue should confess that Jesus Christ is Lord, to the glory of God the Father." Philippians 2:9-11. PRAISE HIM!!

Address:
Connie Jacobsen
13813-125th Ave NE
Kirkland, WA 98034

Connie's Recommended Reading List
(listed approximately in the order in which I read them)

This is in no way meant to be a complete list or the only books worth reading on these subjects, (Others may have a totally different list—equally good or much better—which they would recommend.) Though I may not agree with all the content in some of these books, I still believe they have each had some merit in helping me make my transition to experiencing "life more abundant"!!

Honest to God? Becoming an Authentic Christian by Bill Hybels
Twisting the Truth by Bruce Tucker
The Secret Sect by Doug and Helen Parker
The Church Without a Name by David Stone
Has the Truth Set You Free? by Gene and Grace Luxon
Toxic Faith by Stephen Arterburn & Jack Felton
Beyond the Battle for the Bible by J. I. Packer
How to be a Christian Without Being Religious by Fritz Ridenour
Essential Christianity by Dr. Walter Martin
More Than a Carpenter by Josh McDowell
Your God is Too Small by J. B. Phillips
The Knowledge of the Holy by A. W. Tozer
And I highly recommend all of Kay
Arthur's studies, including:
Lord, Heal My Hurts
Lord, How Can I Ever Be Righteous?
Lord, Teach Me to Pray
Lord, I Need Grace to Make It
Lord, I Want to Know You

One final book I will mention, which I read about seven months before I left "the fellowship" (while I was still encouraging other people to "keep on keeping on" in The Way):

Bradshaw on: THE FAMILY by John Bradshaw

(This is a "secular" book—not religious literature—about "functional" and "dysfunctional" families, I read this with amazement and distress, as I continually found myself recognizing traits within the "dysfunctional" family profile as matching the family connections within my "spiritual family" of "The Truth"—not exactly a picture of "God's family" as He intended it to be.)

If you have any questions or comments please get in touch with us. We welcome the opportunity to visit about the things of God and we often find that in the endeavor to respond to another person's comments or questions to us, we are led through some studies that prove to be very interesting and profitable to us! Finally, Ephesians 6:18 says, "And pray in the Spirit on all occasions with all kinds of prayers and requests. With this in mind, be alert and always keep on praying for all the saints." We praise God that we can be continually praying for all the saints...not because of our own abilities or our own righteousness, but because the One to whom we pray is GOD! He is All-knowing, Every-where-present and All-powerful! So, please know, as I have written this I have prayed for God's guidance and I have prayed and continue to pray for those of you who will read it. May God richly bless you!

Chapter Twenty-Six

Dennis Jacobsen

Asked to write a letter to be compiled with the experiences of others, I gave the request a great deal of consideration. My conclusion is this: if reading my account might somehow help another over the same depression as I faced, caused by a "religious experience," it is worth any criticism I might face from anyone for giving it!

Once I was, perhaps like you are yet, a fully dedicated and fully persuaded believer of a fellowship group which I knew only as "the Truth" since birth. As such, I thought the system, method, fellowship was of Divine, rather than human, origin, and therefore "perfect." You have the testimonies of many claiming it is and works "perfect;" none dare say it is not your right to know how, when, and where others believe it has failed completely. In this collection of compositions, you will read of a number of such times and occurrences. Like others, my account is true and factual.

Wanting to be "right with GOD" (and man, I might add!) I "professed" as a lad of 11, was baptized at 15, was raised in what I understood to be a typical devout "believer" lifestyle. Beginning college with a burning desire to study Aero-Space Engineering and Dynamics, "workers" made me feel with subtle words, ways and means that I would not obtain approval with either GOD or them in fulfilling such ambitions. I was aware that most "older" workers opposed advanced education at the time, and I quickly became both fearful and resentful as a result. As a result of the conflict, I did poorly in my first experience with higher education at college.

Combined pressures resulted in rapidly increasing stresses. They grew from continued unexplainable restrictions, rules, and/or opinions, frequently inconsistent, and apparent ignorance or blindness to certain facts by the very ones I loved and trusted the most, (the "workers" and my parents.) They were those from whom I wanted complete approval. I was then and remained for many years completely "co-dependent." I wanted approval from GOD (imbedded into me as given via both workers and parents.) I wanted to pursue the engineering and math skills I felt were given to me by GOD but which I felt were ridiculed and contradicted as being given from GOD by a number of workers. Wanting to apply myself, do well, and please my parents, I felt a strong conflict with workers, some of whom told me I was wasting my time.

One way which I could safely "grow up" and still experience some freedoms, as well as obtain day to day subsistence, was via the army draft experience. Knowing it lay ahead of me anyway, I "volunteered for the draft" as a means of escape, which none could fault nor intervene.

Many experiences came my way during those next two years, good ones, bad ones, necessary ones, and ridiculous ones! I obtained and lost my first boy-girl relationship during those years. More questions arose than I could find answers for in my mind and soul. While in the army, I grew to want my religious group's approval (which I had been fully indoctrinated to believe as synonymous with GOD's approval) more than anything else.

It is widely known amongst the group that such total and complete approval is restricted to dedicated "workers." It is considered "THE Work," not just, "one" of many. I offered for that work. Sometime later in the middle of my 23rd year of life, I was accepted, and went into that work, expecting true willingness for service (sacrifice?) would bring an end (if not answers) to all my internal questions, while helping others find "truth."

During my years in that work, I both wanted (and sought) to "fit in" in every way possible. Each year I became more and more aware of inconsistencies, and previously unknown facts and found even more questions arose in my mind than answers to previous questions, all which required extensive rationalization, i.e., condemnation of Church buildings in the light of conventions, ridiculing/accusing others, where we ourselves might be guilty of the same, misuse of scripture, feigning unity, etc., etc.!

Finding myself with even more questions and doubts than ever, I felt perhaps it was because I remained unwilling to leave even homeland, friends and kindred for the LORD's sake and thus was not completely "submissive" to the will of GOD.

One statement used frequently was that someone was "too smart for their own good!" because they raised questions that caused discomfort or uneasiness in "older" companions which they could not or would not answer. Therefore, I chose to channel my own intellect into language study, and sought answers to my questions by prayer, meditation and the learning of the scriptures. In complete submission, I offered to work in other lands, amongst other customs and people.

It became my part, when not working on some project for conventions, to speak publicly of religious things to people in 11 states, and 4 countries outside of the United States. Gradually I became very aware GOD has people outside the group I had long assumed to contain the only ones saved. That awareness had begun in the army and grew the most by contact with religious people during my last years in that work.

Eventually I knew that I could not uphold myself as an example as I felt certain "older" workers did of themselves and expected me to do of myself. I felt I was awaited to follow after their examples, which I began to see was not safe to do. After physical injury while in the work abroad, and many disappointments; burdened by quantities of yet additional questions—always more questions than answers—I left the work after 6 years with far more sorrow in my heart and soul than I had upon entering it, for none of the nagging questions about the validity of "the work" (for me) had been answered positively.

In leaving the work, I had overseeing workers, in both my homeland and newly appointed country, beg me to reconsider and either stay or later ask me to return to the work. I knew I was unable physically, emotionally, and every other way to do so. I chose a year later to marry and settle down. Even then, prior to my marriage I had an overseer write, pleading with me not to marry but to go ahead and complete an education, whereupon I would see that returning to the work was the only answer for my life!

It was impossible to follow such contradictory advice to that which I had received from others 10 years earlier. I married, and I immediately became aware of discrediting reports spread about me by certain workers, two of whom had previously first begged me to continue in it, and then only a short while before my marriage asked me to reconsider and return to that work.

I continued to have and ask questions, often which had no answers nor responses. (Since excommunication, questions go more unanswered!) Once I was told by an overseer to just accept that "workers" were given unexplainable understanding denied "saints" because they had better vision than "saints."

While in the work, I had experienced that such was just not true, but I tried to accept and believe it anyway, thinking that it must have been because I was somehow wrong in my soul. From meetings, to home-life, to conventions, I let my light shine to the best of my ability, very conscious of it being limited by my own humanity. I continued to believe GOD to be one, yet consisting of three, The Father, The Son, and The Holy Spirit as I understood Mabel Gibson to have taught when I was a child, both of the latter submitting to the Father. I continued to believe the Son, though one, consisted of two, 100% human, 100% Divine (GOD). I thought I believed as most other workers in these matters, and I have been very surprised since that others have been excommunicated for holding such a belief as this.

Thus even as a child I knew GOD to be one, but plural. Fire, Wind, Water, all examples of GOD. One but plural. A physical example to me of my Spiritual GOD is an egg: yoke, white, and shell, each different, each with a place to fill, but all egg. My GOD is Father, Son and Holy Spirit, All GOD, but each with an orderly place to fill in accordance with and subject to the FATHER's will.

I knew my gift of eternal life to be by GOD's grace, through the substitute sacrifice of Jesus Christ. I knew Jesus' righteous life was imputed to me when I accepted His sacrifice made for me. I knew my own works are what earn me eternal "reward" which is different from GOD's gift to me of eternal life, that is totally unearned, and undeserved by me.

To help people understand my faith and understanding regarding the gift of eternal life, I use an example. Picture a great magnet with a powerful draw passing over a pile of rusty metal shavings with minds and feet of their own! All are free to make a decision to run away to escape. Some think, "If I am drawn to this greater power, I will lose my individuality, and be unable to do my own thing," and run away. Others think "But I like being as I am, and don't want to leave this environment," and run away. Yet others, feeling the draw of this powerful magnet think, "I am so rusty, I must get polished up somehow first, then I can be acceptable," and run away. All shavings left, misshapen, rusty, are taken exactly as they are, drawn to the magnet, to be under the control of the magnet thereafter.

The Father (the Will of GOD) draws all. The devil tries to interfere using first our flesh, or the world, and then the concept that we need to do something in the matter! If we aren't deceived by anything else, he makes us think we have at least a need to "submit," and thus have a part in our own salvation. It is just not so. GOD saves all by His grace, His substitute sacrifice of part of Himself as also our kinsman redeemer, and imputed righteousness for all, who, though tempted to run away, reconsidered and did not make such unwise decisions.

We (my wife and I together!) attended every meeting possible, made every sacrifice possible to be in meetings and support the fellowship. We sought to support that work in every way possible, thinking perhaps our own children would one day make such a choice for their lives, with better results than I.

We invited as many as possible to meetings, seeing some converted to the group, supposing them to have final assurance of salvation. One day in early 1987, thinking myself in the very center of the fellowship, I was falsely accused. I merely denied the false accusation by saying it was not so. I ought to have known better, but I naively thought all efforts made to live in a way as to gain eternal reward, could not be hid, that truth would be revealed, and that anything more than "Yea" or "Nay" to the accusations was unnecessary.

Instead false accusations grew, were distorted, and soon spread like wildfire. I offered to do (and did so as soon as possible!) whatever false accusers asked of me to make things right for them in their own eyes, both directly to them, and in front of certain workers as witnesses, and was told that with such intent I would be called "a brother." However, I was immediately excommunicated, being called a drunkard, extortioner, liar, idolater, and every other label except fornicator (of which they said they were glad to be able to say they did not believe me guilty!) I was told that GOD and His people saw me as such things now, and that until I repented publicly of those things, I was too wicked to be allowed to attend any of the meetings or be amongst GOD's people!

According to Jesus own teachings I knew myself to be nearer guilty of adultery, or fornication than any of those other things. I was hurt and shocked! I could not believe that such false judgment and accusations would be allowed to stand. I encouraged my wife and children to submit to all things and attend meetings. Gradually the insinuations and soon outright statements made to drive wedges between my own wife and children and myself became so obvious to even them that they could no longer claim such a group as their own. I have been repeatedly accused of poisoning them.

In the years since, lies about me and what happened have been made and spread by people (both within that work and without) and appear generally accepted as true by many. Gradually time has exposed some of them, one by one, as corrupt, and sadly, more will follow.

At first, in despair, I fasted for a week! I prayed and wept frequently for months. New questions arose! How could such things happen, and what would happen to even my own children? I tried writing letters, communicating, to make things right. Gradually and from a great depression, I became aware, "sometimes it is impossible to fix what you haven't broken!"

Meanwhile, during this time, someone mailed me a copy of *The Secret Sect*, which at first I did not even desire to read. As time passed, I read every word, very thoroughly and carefully! I was shocked, but because of first hand knowledge, previous questions, and experiences, I immediately knew "the vast majority if not all of what was written there is true!"

Still I rationalized to excuse "The Truth!" More lies were spread worldwide about me and mine. I sought and found more information and undeniable documents. From the accumulated copies of articles from the *Impartial Observer*, newspaper accounts from the first of the century to government documents, to other books (*The life and Ministry of Edward Cooney, Has the Truth Set You Free? The Church Without a Name.*). Others who knew of my experience and who had similar experiences began to contact me. I was shocked at first, then I began to understand, and before I was 50 years old, all the years of unanswered questions were answered!

If you, dear reader, have unanswered questions that you might wish to ask me, if I know their answers, or even where to find them, I will respond with no beating about the bush! I love all those who "we" (for now my wife and children are also free!) left behind (in what I now believe to be largely a cult of exclusive, pseudo-christianity) more than ever. We now know how bound many really are by legalism, private (human) interpretations of scripture, and traditions of men and feel only love and pity for everyone connected with it!

We have finally been set free from bondage and all the hurt and heartache. For some, ignorance will remain bliss—continuing to consider certain traditions of men as true standards of GOD's righteousness, convinced their's is the only true way—while never having assurance of salvation or their own Christianity in their hearts and minds. Such people are only to be thought of with compassion. Even with their many questions, they want to find a contentment and a degree of peace in remaining ignorant.

However, from my own experience of once being in an almost identical condition, I firmly say it was not the "peace and contentment" from GOD and the "eager anticipation" which now is within me! For any as yet unaware of it, "eager anticipation" is the 1610 English meaning of the word "hope," not today's current concept of "wishful desire!"

In closing, if any reader recognizes one's own religious condition as:

- filled with questions and lacking knowledge or answers;
- bothered by inconsistencies, gossip and/or deceptions;
- aware that their "hope" is only a "wishful desire" and is not an "eager anticipation!";
- living with a "peace" born of submitting to a religious system and its ministry;
- thinking "safety" and "contentment" is in "fitting in" and not rocking the boat nor asking questions;
- feeling they must "obey" teachings not clearly understood to be saved;

from experience I can say, "you have not yet found the 'Truth that sets you free!'" I feel compelled to also express to you, "don't settle for anything less no matter who tells you otherwise!" Only those nearby Jeremiah heard what he said from the pit where supposedly "true believers" had cast him!

In His Love,

Dennis Jacobsen
804 Si Town Road
Castle Rock, Washington 98611

June 8th, 1993.

Chapter Twenty-Seven

Rhetta Kent
Personal Testimony

I was born and raised in the church calling itself the Truth. I was never read to from the Bible nor taught, or talked to about God or the Scripture. I was expected to learn everything from Gospel Meeting, examples, and the Spirit.

I don't remember when I professed, but I do recall I felt I had to do it by the time I was twelve because my mother expected it. I felt no moving from the Spirit to do it, I just wanted to please my mother.

I would read and pray but never felt in contact with God. This always bothered me. I never felt moved to be baptized because there were things I just couldn't agree with. I can vividly remember laying awake at night filled with fear as each day shortened my life and took me closer to death.

Fear of an uncertain salvation and fear of Jesus was always with me. One time I had to enter a tavern to use their phone and I wondered what would happen if Jesus came back while I was in there. I was afraid I would be sent to Hell.

I was always bewildered by all the hiding of things from workers and other friends. I also wondered why nobody ever helped anybody. The ONLY help I ever saw offered was a ride to meetings. I never witnessed any monetary help, food, clothes or physical help even though I felt that those should be part of a Christian's life. The friends and workers depend on the SPIRIT to provide these needs. I have heard workers bragging from time to time that professing people aren't poor or hurt in storms or troubles, although, I know that isn't true. Professing people try to give the impression that they are normally well set financially. They say this is proof that God cares for his people.

While I was in college I began dating a divorced man. One day I came home from school to find Everett Swanson and his companion waiting for me. They gave me a lecture about my sins and told me I could no longer take part in prayer, testimony or hymn choosing until I proved my repentance. I had to break up with my boyfriend there in front of them. My proving of repentance went on for a few months until Everett Swanson and Tharold Sylvester decided I could take part again. By this time I really knew I didn't agree with the church. I did not feel they had the right to condemn a divorced person who did not know God. I was still troubled as to why prayer and Bible reading were so empty.

I felt like "to make it in the WAY" was just a matter of minding all the rules and it was never really learning the Bible or knowing God.

After I graduated from college I made the decision to leave the church. I did this slowly by just missing meetings here and there. I wasn't sure what was right or how to find God, but I was sure the WAY wasn't right.

Then I met my husband-to-be and my parents came unglued because he was divorced. He talked to my parents about us marrying and my mother told him they would have no part of it. My mother contacted the workers and was told not to acknowledge or attend our wedding because if she did that would be agreeing with it. So, we just went to Idaho and got married.

My mother didn't have a lot to do with me and wouldn't speak to my husband at all. It was over a year before she finally started to acknowledge him. Then when our first child was born, she slowly started accepting my husband.

As more children came, a total of three, I felt more and more moved to have contact with a body of believers for the sake of my children. My husband wanted no part of it, but said he wouldn't stand in the way of the kids and I going. I didn't even know where to start looking for a church.

When our children were 6 months, 2 years and 4 years old, I went to work for a medical center. Through that job I became best friends with a fellow employee who is a Christian. I shared all I was struggling with her and my total non-belief in churches because of being raised in the WAY. She patiently listened, shared her church growth and experiences and when the time was right she invited me to her church. The kids and I went one Sunday and were touched by God. We never stopped going. After we had gone twice, my husband asked to go also. I became a REAL BORN AGAIN CHRISTIAN after attending about two months. My husband gave his life to Jesus after attending about 10 months.

My mother continues to make comments every time we visit about how perfect and wonderful and right the WAY is and how far off base I am. They believe God punishes anyone who leaves the way by financial ruin, broken marriages, problems with children, job loss or illness. I have MS and have been told by my mother it is my punishment for leaving the WAY. Yet, my mother was involved in a car accident and was sued horribly and never saw that as punishment. She also hid the accident from everyone possible.

In 1976 the workers pulled the bread and wine from the Sunday Morning Meeting in Omak, Washington because the friends didn't have the "right Spirit." Nobody really knew what they did wrong. A few months later they put it back, but still nobody knew what they had fixed.

In Tonasket, there was an older couple who had married. The workers made them split up because one had an ex-spouse who was still alive. So, they moved apart and the man died a very broken and lonely man.

Address:
Rhetta Kent
1809 Plath
Yakima, WA 98902

Chapter Twenty-Eight

Carla Knott
Letter to the Friends

Dearest Friends,

I have never liked the idea of a typewritten letter sent out to several people at one time, because I felt the personal tone was not there. However, I chose to do so as there are several of my friends, who have known and loved me, that I wished to have a copy of this letter.

First of all, I want to say how deeply grateful I am that you all have proved your love to me over the past few years. They have not been easy years for me and you know what I have struggled with for so long. I value you so much and only hope our friendship will continue. Your prayers and thoughtfulness toward me have truly been a blessing to me. Thank you.

I just want to let you know I no longer choose to be a part of "the truth." I know this will stir up a lot of feelings in you, but please let me say it is not because I have been offended out of this church, that I have come to this decision. This did not happen overnight. I know God's purpose over these last trying years has brought me to this point, and I truly rejoice in the freedom I feel and have come to know since I have learned the true meaning of what grace and mercy really are. From all that has happened in my life these past three years, I have come to see that God is far greater than I ever imagined. I realized I was trying to limit Him in how, where, when and who He moved through and to. I have come to realize clearly I cannot do this, nor should I ever believe I could ever do so. His ways are mysterious and He works in ways we wouldn't always agree with. God's grace is not based on man's ideas of fairness. The Holy Spirit has placed people in my life that have truly shown me His Spirit lives richly and fully in them, using their talents to help me and others.

It has been a truly difficult, but exciting time for me in the discoveries of the riches of His grace and mercy. I know many of you probably will not agree with me, and I understand that. I only hope you will study for yourselves and discover what it means to us to be loved in such an unconditional way. He loved and died for us in our unlovable and undesirable state. What joy that gives our hearts when we realize we can openly glorify and praise His name for all He has done for us.

I have been attending a Bible church for the past several months and have truly been amazed at the wealth of the lessons of grace and mercy preached and practiced in this church. No church is perfect, but there is a lot to be said for those who can pray together openly for each other, sing with true songs of *praise* to His Holy name, and truly love one another through their experiences. Giving thanks is a separate function, and praise and thanks together truly show Him how we long to glorify Him in our daily lives for all he has brought us through. There is much about what I have found in this church I would like to share with you, only if you wish me to do so. I only know in my heart this is where I need to be. I became a member 1 week ago.

I do not expect a reply to this letter, unless you choose to reply. I would be happy to answer any questions you may have. However, I have faced many angry confrontations and ask you, as a friend, please don't expect me to enter into that anger with you. I know you believe in Jesus, in His life, burial and resurrection, and in my mind that makes us brothers and sisters together with others that believe, and that have Him a part of their lives. I will be happy to give you scriptures to back up my decisions. I only hope you will continue to love me as I love and respect each of you. Thank you for what you have meant in my life thus far.

With Love in Him,
   Carla Knott

July 29, 1991

Chapter Twenty-Nine

Dale Knott

Letter dated March 30, 1992

Greetings Friends,

On a flight from Phoenix, Arizona to Los Angeles I served a cup of coffee to a nice young lady. That meeting would change my life. She was the first person that I had met that I am aware of who was in the truth. We became good friends and it was through that friendship I started to attend gospel meetings, Wednesday night Bible studies and Sunday morning meetings. I met many wonderful, dedicated people through that experience. I studied with workers and after a period of time, I professed. That was February of 1979. It is hard to believe it has been thirteen years. I will always be grateful for the experiences of those years and still admire and appreciate the ones who were involved.

The purpose of this letter is threefold. I have agonized over whether to pen these thoughts. A couple of the friends questioned the reason for an "exit" letter in the first place. I appreciated that concern as it really caused me to search my heart to examine my motives. Purpose number one would not in and of itself justify a letter. That would be to simply state that I attended my last meeting June 30, 1991 and have decided not to return. I was told by an overseer that some who believed Jesus was fully God had been asked to leave the fellowship. They were excommunicated. I knew that if I did not leave on my own that I would probably be asked to leave, as I believe with all my heart that Jesus was God come in the flesh. I will mention more on that later. The delay in this letter is due to the fact I really wanted to give the decision lots of time. Please know that I don't write you that I am leaving because I think it constitutes an earth shattering announcement. It is just that after thirteen years to merely not show up without any word from me would not say much for the depth of my feelings for the many friends I made and those terrific people I have met with. One I know of called everyone in his field when he decided to leave meetings. I would prefer that approach myself, if not for the fact that I know many would be uncomfortable. I will opt for a letter and at the same time apologize for it being so impersonal.

Through this experience I have been made aware of a number of folks who have left the fellowship. Their reasons are varied. some who had been told this way went back to the apostles found it has a very well documented history and identifiable founder, through the book, *The Secret Sect*, by Doug and Helen Parker. These facts were also verified through newspaper articles and first hand accounts of folks at that time and now. Some were in situations where love and compassion were not shown as is so clearly commanded in the Bible, and in fact the lack of love was justified, and resulted in the hurting of friends and loved ones. Some have left because of immoral behavior of church leaders that went unchecked and biblically un-corrected. There are other reasons, but there is a common thread that runs through each experience. That is that no *one* experience led to the people involved choosing to leave. That initial experience naturally led to further study, and further questioning, which uncovered other serious considerations.

The second thread of commonality, was that after the person left meetings, people would speculate as to why that person left without ever consulting that individual, therefore misrepresenting the true fact. That leads me to my second purpose which is more of a request.

As our friends, or even merely someone who hears of Carla and I, my heartfelt hope is that you always allow us to speak for ourselves. I have heard a lot of speculation since Carla's decision to leave last Fall. None of it has been accurate. There is no need to speculate, our home will always be open to anyone who would be interested in visiting with us. We welcome you to come, write, or call anytime. You may also feel free to give anyone a copy of this letter and in that way allow me to speak for myself.

For those who know us, and have wondered about us, and would be concerned, maybe I should just say this. At the Mt. Peak convention it was said that Carla was "doing good physically, but not so good spiritually." It is unfortunate that what I mentioned earlier concerning speculation without consulting the one involved has occurred in this case. Someone had spoken without having the facts. The person who said that has not visited with Carla about where she is spiritually at any time. It is even more unfortunate that this was a member of our own family. So maybe it is needful that I say Carla is doing really well on both fronts. Many of you knew Carla was battling a serious disease. I am thrilled to say, and grateful to God, that with much courage on her part and help of capable loving people she has found healing; long awaited, but welcome all the same.

It has also been said that I have "been intentionally working weekends to avoid going to church with Carla." That also could not be further from the truth. I know how many of you feel about churches that are outside the home being false. To you this will bring little comfort. We have found a beautiful family of believers right up the road from us at Midlothian Bible Church. We have found much love, wonderful Bible teaching and opportunities to reach out to others. We could not be more grateful for our new church home.

Before I close with purpose number three, please allow me to express my deepest thanks to those of you who know us and some who may not, as our lives were touched by many. In particular, I would like to express my love and gratitude to those in the last meeting place we attended; Mansfield. On that last Sunday morning in June, I paid special attention to each testimony. I shook hands and bid a good morning with more focus on each one, as I knew I might not return. For all those we have met with in the Dallas area, I want to say your lives have changed mine. Thank you.

Now, finally, for purpose number three. This will be the most difficult to communicate and not offend. Let that be a testimony to how strongly I feel about what will be my last testimony to you, so to speak.

The journey that led to my decision and this letter began with something that took place almost two years ago. That experience caused me to seek counsel from overseers, workers, elders and friends. I gave this thing lots of time. The explanations that came from those discussions really concerned me. Those talks led to other issues as well as doctrines of the fellowship coming to light; primarily and most significantly, the things said to me about the person of Christ. I would be dreadfully wrong in not making that a part of this letter to you. I hope

as well that if you can see where I have missed
something in the scripture, you will feel compelled
to let me know. We know that is at least part of the
purpose of scripture. II Tim. 3:16.

I would like for you to consider that the one
most important question we can ask ourselves regarding salvation is this: Who was/is our Savior
Jesus Christ? Without an answer to that question,
nothing else falls into place as He is the Chief Cor-
nerstone. On the other hand, with that question
answered, all the cogs fit and the machine runs
smoothly and eternally. It defines who we believe
in, knowing that if we worship anything but the
true Christ we worship an idol. It was that question
concerning Christ that I never asked the workers
about thirteen years ago. I take full responsibility
for that. I felt the Bible was so clear about the person of Christ, it just never occurred to me to ask.

I have sought the counsel of many since I first
heard that the leaders of the fellowship do not believe Christ was fully God and equal in *all* ways to
God the Father and God the Holy Spirit. Out of the
visits I remember two in particular. I was told by a
brother worker that, "I believe and as far as I know
those in the truth believe that Christ was a created
being." Secondly, I was told by one with great responsibility that, "Christ sweat drops of blood in
the garden because he feared losing his salvation."
I had never heard these things before. Having
trusted the workers for so long, I asked for teaching
and began to dig into the scriptures on my own.
That was *my* biblical responsibility. I was told some
had been asked to leave the truth because they believed or taught that Christ was fully God. I will
continue to welcome teaching from those concerned, but that seems pretty straight. I am always
open to biblical proof of that teaching, and I have

made that clear to those involved. The Bible, however, must be the standard. Again, our home is always open to anyone who might help me see where I have missed something.

In short, I believe Christ was/is fully God and I have always believed that. He is one of the three persons that make up the Godhead. I simply believe John the first chapter when it says the Word was God and the Word became flesh and dwelt among us. It was Emmanuel, God with us, God Himself who came to live on earth so He could relate to us and become the perfect sacrifice for us on the cross, an understanding intercessor for us in heaven saving us from our sins. I do not believe some created being could ever accomplish that. I do not believe that trusting in that same created being could ever save me.

This subject could fill books, so I will not attempt to do it justice here. My earnest prayer is that if any of you who believe what I was told and can show it to be true biblically, that you will share that with me. If you should find it in your heart to ask the workers about Christ, I can only hope that you will give me equal time to make the case for His being God and not created. I am genuine in that request. You will not be encouraged to contact us. You may even be told that in the last days there will be those that cause many to fall away and that is how Carla and I should be thought of. It is likely that you will be told that we have not been willing for the Holy Spirit to reveal His truth to us. I do not believe the Spirit will reveal anything that cannot be read in the scriptures. I believe the scriptures are complete. Some who have left have even been said to be of the devil. That way of thinking saddens me. From my perspective, I can only encourage you to examine your beliefs

in the Christ *you* believe in and trust to save you. I
hope you will give it the consideration it deserves,
knowing no one can do it for you. Please know that
one reason Christ died for us, was to tear the cur-
tain in the temple in two so we could do what the
old law could never allow us to do; that is to draw
near to God. Before, sin separated us, but now
through the perfect sacrifice for sin we can cry
abba Father. We need no intercessor but Christ our
Lord. He is found in the Word and imbedded in our
hearts through belief in that Word.

Just please know again we are here if you wish.
Truth can withstand any amount of honest examina-
tion. We are encouraged to do just that; examine.
Paul admonished the church in Thessalonica to
"Prove all things; hold fast that which is good." I
Thess. 5:21. I am grateful for that admonition.

Much love,

A second letter dated October 19, 1992

Dear Friends,

It has been since my letter of March 30th that I
wrote you last. The purpose of that letter was to
share with you the fact that I had decided to leave
meeting and say a few things in that regard. At that
time, I really didn't consider another letter. As time
went on, I couldn't see not writing you again. I
want to thank you in advance for your time.

I know that many of you will question my motive. I know that many of you already have. I don't
blame you. Why would any sane person take the
time to write and send out over 250 letters to people that for the most part don't care to receive
them? If you have made up your mind about what
motivates me, I hold little hope of you opening
yourself to what I would like to share. But in hopes

that some will read on and trust me, I promise to open my heart to you as honestly as I know how. My motive? Honestly, I care.

I would like to thank those of you who responded to my letter. Your concern and the frank way you shared with me was appreciated. I received replies from five states and two foreign countries. Thanks!

I want to talk to you about a group of people who are greatly misunderstood. There are a growing number of people leaving the fellowship now that certain truths are emerging. I only request an opportunity to share some thoughts with you about us. When others speak for us, it only prevents us from speaking for ourselves. First let me give you a couple of examples of the kinds of things that are being said. These kinds of statements have become far too common. Sadder still, they are, as a whole, untrue. These excerpts are taken out of context. I would be glad to share the complete letters with you if you like. The first is from convention notes. Because they are notes, the wording is a little choppy.

"I John 2:19 'They went out from us because they weren't of it.' How can we leave? If of us they'd [have] continued. [They do] Not feel as God's children, so [they] goes out. Love's not in those who go out. Not of right spirit when they leave. One time [they] loved it, but [they] goes out. Lost something previous, before they went out." From a saint's notes from a Texas convention 1992.

"When a person quits meetings they don't read their Bible as much and they don't pray as much etc. We drift from God." Everett Swanson in a 1991 letter.

I hope we agree that for anyone to speak this way is sad. I only hope William will discourage this kind of thing from occurring at the upcoming Mt. Peak convention. I would be glad to speak to the convention about ex-fellowship members. Worse than that, these kinds of statements are so untrue. How would Everett Swanson know how much someone spends with their Bible or how much they pray? I know how untrue these statements are. I have come to know many who have left. Let me tell you a little about them, if I may.

Over the past year, Carla and I have been really blessed. Many who have left the fellowship have stayed in our home. Still others write and call. We have met with some as we travel. Do some leave for wrong reasons? Sure they do, but I haven't met them. I have met lovely, caring people who hold their Lord first in their lives. Who share with us the joy and fulfillment of their relationship with the Creator. Who love the inspired Word of God and believe it is infallible. I can only say there is no resemblance between these people and the things being said about them. I would love for you to get to know them.

If you have had friends, family, or people in your meeting to leave, I would encourage you to visit with them. Share with them with an open heart, the Bible being your standard. I guarantee a blessing.

Would you allow me a personal note in concerning being misunderstood? It is still being said by some who you trust far more than you trust me that I left because of "family" problems. You can imagine how difficult that misrepresentation is to overcome. I want to make it clear again. No doubt that things concerning the handling of Mt. Peak convention concerned me and caused me to begin to think about some issues, but the final decision was based on what came to light later. They were doctrinal considerations, the foremost being the fellowship's beliefs about the person of Christ. Another said I left and wrote my letter because I was angry. I really am not angry. My overriding feeling is gratitude. I have never met the person who said that. I would like to. I think a visit would be helpful.

I only hope that you will make informed decisions about those who choose to leave the fellowship. I only appeal to what is fair. I know things that are not true are being said about me and others. Our home is open to anyone. You will be welcomed with open arms and a hot cup of coffee if you are so inclined. Come and see us!!

Can we spend just a minute together on this subject of standard? Do you believe the Bible is the infallible, inspired Word of God? Do you believe the absolute standard by which everything should be measured is the written word of God? If your answer is no, then I encourage you to pitch this letter and letters you receive from me in the future as we have no common ground on which we can communicate. If your answer is yes, you do hold the scripture to be sufficient, read on if you will.

Would you agree with me that every time we have a thought or experience concerning the things of God that we should measure that thought or experience against the Word of God? Would you agree that when we read material that is written about the scripture or when we hear a worker speak that we should always test that message by examining the scripture to see that it is so? The Bereans did in Acts 17 after Paul spoke to them. And Paul was an apostle! If you do not agree, would you share with me or just consider within yourself why you do not? I just want to ask you, is what a worker says your standard? I would like to give you just a few examples of some of the things I have heard workers say that concern me. Again, I have nothing but love for the workers as people, but this stuff is far too serious, in my view, to ignore. See what you think and check it with the scripture.

- In a Sunday morning meeting a saint spoke on how the Bible should be our standard and nothing else. When William Lewis gave his testimony, it was on how his "experiences verified what he believed." Friends, our experiences cannot be the standard. We end up with as many religions as we have experiences. We must judge our experiences by the standard of the Bible. We cannot judge the Bible by the standard of our experiences.

- At Texarkana in the summer of 91, Dale Spencer spoke on the servant in Gen. 24 who went out to find a wife for Isaac. He said the servant was a foreshadow of the workers. Again, I personally like Dale Spencer, but he does not have the authority to make the Bible say things it does not say. When we take that kind of liberty, we can make the Word of God fit our personal agenda rather than us fitting into the Word of God. I realize most will say that for me not to see workers in the servant is a lack of revelation and willingness to trust the workers. You are right, I only trust the scripture and you have to go beyond the scripture to believe what Dale said.

- In a gospel meeting June Douglas spoke on the good Samaritan. Again, June knows I love her, and she has been in our home several times. Again, June made the Samaritan man out to be a worker bringing the gospel. Again, that is going beyond what is intended. The meaning of the story is that we would love our neighbor and not be religious on the outside as those who passed by, but live our beliefs in good deeds for others. We can often bring out thoughts that are not authorized by the text that are beautiful and helpful, but they should always be identified as such.

I hope that at convention, meeting, special meeting, or gospel meeting that you will always measure everything with the scripture like those Bereans did when Paul spoke. There is a saying and it is true, concerning biblical study.

If the literal sense makes good sense, seek no
other sense lest you come up with nonsense.

I know the workers discourage reading books written to help us in our understanding of the Bible. They even, regrettably, discourage the use of anything but the KJV. Why? William Irvine did the fellowship a huge disservice when he started this way. He left the Faith Mission Church where he got his education and promptly said all churches were wrong. As well, everything written to help us study the Bible was wrong. Let me just say, William Irvine was wrong and the fellowship's doctrine is paying the price. At the same time, William Irvine instituted the "Living Witness Doctrine." That doctrine said that a person could only be saved through a worker. That gave workers far too much authority and made them the standard. The implication is that the workers have something that the saints do not. There is no biblical justification for that. The Bible makes us responsible for our own salvation dependent on no one but Christ. These two doctrines are dangerous and have been a detriment to the fellowship over the years.

I hope you will not hesitate to read other Bible translations and books written about the Bible. The newer translations are much easier to read and present a more accurate representation of the original text. The KJV is so beautiful and I love it, but for study others are better. One argument is that man has changed the other translations to mean what they want them to say. Did you know the KJV has been revised many times to keep up with what we have learned to help us in translation? Did you know that you would not even have been able to read the original KJV because it was so deeply entrenched in the Old English style of the time? Workers say we should not read books about the Bible because they (workers) are against biblical education and those educated scholars are false and not led by the spirit. (Interpretation is, workers are the only ones who are led by the spirit. Living Witness Doctrine again.) Using that argument, they cannot endorse the King James Version. It was written by the best educated scholars of the early 17th century for the King, James. Can you imagine the workers accepting a biblical translation ordered by President Bush to be accomplished by our country's best biblical scholars? I doubt it very much, but that is exactly what happened in 1611.

In closing, James Walden spoke of the fact that the fellowship was seamless. It is not. There is deep division over things like divorce and remarriage. There are many changes ahead as the worker's teaching on divorce and remarriage has changed. I encourage the workers to include the saints in the process. Especially the elders. Elders should hold a much more biblical place in teaching and leadership than they do in the fellowship. There is even division over who Christ is. Some workers say He is God, some say He was created.

Think of it, workers disagree on who the person is that constitutes the very foundation of the way. Elders, I encourage you to get involved. Ask questions of workers.

Please understand that those of us who have left did not do so for trite, insignificant reasons. We feel passionate, as a result, about sharing with you. Give us an ear and an open heart. compare what we have to say with the scripture.

There is a substantial amount of information now available to those who have the heart to search for the truth. The teaching of the workers has been documented as well as the irrefutable truth that this way was started by a man named William Irvine in 1897. It did not exist prior to that time. No, not even in the New Testament. This is not for profit. I would like to offer to pay for any materials you might order. It will be the most rewarding thing you can imagine. Just request an order list from:THRESHING FLOOR MINISTRIES, P.O. BOX 9899, SPOKANE, WA 99209

I will be back for another visit soon. In the mean time, I encourage you to call me if you like. I love you very much.

Address:
Dale Knott
1530 Indian Creek Dr.
Midlothian, TX 76065

Chapter Thirty

Life History of Cherie Kropp

My parents, Dot and Ray Berry, were both teen-agers when their families first came into contact with the workers. I was born in 1948 in Martinez, California and was raised in a professing home. I inherited my beliefs from my loving, God fearing, faithful parents. While my grandparents had asked the questions, and searched until they found an-swers that satisfied them——I had the answers without ever asking the questions. In other words, I knew what was "right," but not why. For a time, I accepted these hand-me-down beliefs as Absolute Truth without question. I was taught and believed that the 2x2 fellowship was God's only true way, and that it came down in an unbroken line from the apostles.

When I was ten and my brother, Galen, was six, we moved from California to Jackson, Mississippi, my mother's home state. Within the year, our new home became the first convention to be held in the state of Mississippi. With this privilege came cer-tain status. Galen and I found we were expected to be "good examples" (role models) to other children of professing families. While this role suited my brother to a "T," it far from suited me! Most any professing child knew he was supposed to be an ex-ample to the "world"; we were also supposed to be examples to all the professing children. We set the standard, or so we were told! Often, the bottom line was, before you act, ask yourself: "What will people think—if I do this?" What a killjoy! I resented being forced to act out this role I did not choose and for which I was entirely unfit. With a child's tunnel vision, I only saw what other kids could do that I couldn't. I didn't realize how much our parents permitted that other parents didn't permit.

My very closest friend was my first cousin, Judy. There were just three weeks difference in our ages, but we lived 180 miles apart. Judy and I discussed professing and decided we would hold off; that neither of us would profess until late in our teenage years, after "we had some fun." However, when Judy was 12, she reneged and professed. My mother told me I shouldn't profess "just because Judy did." I didn't plan to, but to my surprise, two weeks later at convention I felt really moved and wanted to stand up. I cried all through the song when they tested the meeting, but remained in my seat. However, the next year when I was 13, I couldn't hold out any longer, and I professed. Galen was 9 when he professed. It was years before I could pray, as many often did, "Thank you Lord, for showing me your true way..." I'd have preferred He held off until I "had a little fun." I sometimes wondered what my life would have been like if I had not been born to professing parents. Would I have chosen to be a part of this fellowship if it just "came across my pathway" one day later in my life?

My brother and I had looked forward to this move, but had no clue of the tremendous adjustment it would be for us. We moved from a city environment where we had lived ALL our lives, to the country. There were NO playmates near our new home. Not one! We were bored out of our minds! Neither of us was athletically inclined or lovers of the outdoors. We both took refuge in books and in playing the piano. For years, we were the only children in our meeting. In fact, the closest children of professing parents lived 60 miles away! When we moved to the country from the house we were renting, all the Mississippi and Alabama workers came and stayed at our place, as well as many friends. They swarmed everywhere, busy building the new convention grounds. Galen and I were right there in the middle of things, helping too.

One time I was helping Miss Mable, a sister worker, get a tent ready for the visiting brother workers to sleep in. After we set up the same THREE beds in THREE different spots, and made them up THREE different times, Miss Mable decided she better make sure they were a comfortable praying height. So she dropped to her knees and put her elbows on the bed in a prayer-like stance. Immediately, she declared, "Nope, this won't do. All these beds will have to be lowered." Nothing would do, but unmake the THREE beds AGAIN and lower them. Trying to dissuade her, I said, "Oh, I don't think they're too tall!" She replied sharply, "Well, you're just a little girl. You don't know anything about conventions!" Maybe not, but I was sure learning! Her comment cut me to the quick and moved me to tears. I ran off immediately to cry on my Mom's shoulder. Mable told Mom later that she had "used grace" in dealing with me. She never apologized. The elder of our meeting was also helping her move and remove the three beds. I felt his sympathy, and he accurately predicted to my mother, "Be a long time before that little girl gets over that!" About 25 years—that's all! In retrospect, I see that she really did me a BIG favor. I grew up with an accurate picture of workers, and I never became a worker worshipper.

From that point on I recoiled and kept my distance from ALL workers. They drifted in and out of our home, but I never let any of them get close to me. I didn't write to any of them, found them extremely boring, and was uneasy in their presence. I trusted very few of them. It was a no-win situation. They had the power to criticize and find fault with me AND they would always be "right," because workers are always "right."

Before I reached my teenage years, I had concluded from personal observation that workers were only human; they were not on a higher plane than the friends, and a far cry from being perfect or infallible. I had seen some express feelings, or act in ways that were not, to my way of thinking, particularly Godly. Workers and Saints alike were at times irritable, tactless, rude, thoughtless, bossy, jealous; got angry, offended or miffed; made mistakes, blunders, goofs and screwed up; were critical, scornful, judgmental, hurting other's feelings without apologizing; were afraid of other workers; and resented anyone challenging their word or authority. Sometimes they gave good advice, and sometimes not so good. In short, I learned they were no different from other human beings, something many friends do not realize today.

Mississippi has around 100 friends total and usually six workers, so the workers stayed with us a LOT. When the workers were there, my brother and I had to sit at the table after we were through with our meal for what seemed like an eternity. We rarely made a peep. It wasn't that our parents told us not to talk—we just didn't care to. It would prolong the boring time at the table! Most workers were not good conversationalists. Often there were long uncomfortable pauses, and laughter at unfunny things that I stubbornly refused to even crack a smile at. We endured these endless, dull meals wondering how much longer before we could escape to our rooms and pick up our books, through which we lived vicariously.

Sometimes after the meal was over and cleaned up, everyone went to the living room and chairs were arranged in a circle around the room. Instead of multiple conversations going on simultaneously, one person would speak while everyone looked at him. Then someone else would say something, and everyone would focus on that person. Frequently, there were uncomfortable pauses, and nervous laughter at nothing. Being shy, I never ventured a word, lest all those eyes turn on me! To this day, I get terribly uncomfortable and ill at ease when I'm sitting in a group in a circle, and there are not multiple conversations going on.

For a time, can-cans were a fad so they were considered the height of worldliness. Can-cans were stiff half-slips usually made of a net-like fabric that made a skirt stand out. The sister worker in charge of the dining tent always held a meeting for the waitresses at each convention. Without fail, Miss Minnie would comment in an acid tone, "Of course, it would not be appropriate for anyone waiting on tables to wear *can-cans* or *spike* heels." Long after can-cans and spikes went out of vogue, Miss Minnie continued to make this comment.

Although married couples sat together during meetings at both Alabama and Mississippi conventions, the men and women were segregated in the dining tent! All the women sat on one side, while the men sat on the other. To enter the dining tent, the women had their door; and the men had their door. The men and women didn't even stand and mill around together while waiting to enter. One table was especially designated for mothers (but not fathers) with babies and small children. Many a mother had a terrific struggle at mealtimes, especially if she had more than one small child to feed by herself. I could never understand why this separation existed. It just didn't make sense! There was a strange undercurrent in those two states, and perhaps others, concerning male-female relations. Workers would say from the platform that convention and meetings were not the place to meet and socialize—yet they didn't allow some to participate, who married outside the fellowship! If convention wasn't the place to meet—where in the world *was* the place, I wondered? Some workers discouraged boys and girls from mixing and talking.

Once, my husband Dave and I invited two Dallas teenagers, a brother and sister to go with us to MS convention. Mr. Charles, a brother worker, was there who had made it his personal responsibility to do all he could to prevent marriages "for the kingdom's sake." He spied Andy talking to his sister. He went over to them and said something to the effect: "You know, this really isn't the place to be talking to girls." Andy looked puzzled for a moment, before he asked, "Not even to my SISTER?" We had a good laugh over that! Mr. Charles also put in an unwelcome appearance at my side one night while I was talking to a teenage boy after the last meeting. He let us know it was past the time (9:00 p.m.) when we should be in bed. Lights weren't even out yet! I was scared to death he would tell my folks. My heart sank the next day when I saw who was to baptize me—Mr. Charles!

Most of the Bigshot Workers who are invited to a convention arrive by the weekend before the convention is to start. Galen and my bedrooms were always earmarked for visiting workers, so we had to move out to the dorms more than a week before convention started. The highlight of the whole year for most of us was getting together at convention with other young professing kids. We usually dreaded returning "to the world" (school) and leaving this warm, safe environment, the only place where we fit in and were one of the group.

For the first few years, the women all slept in the house at Mississippi convention. The first year, I staked out my bed in a cubby hole in the attic under the eaves. I was saving the two other beds for some of my friends. Miss Mable (Killjoy) came along and discovered my plans and objected strenuously. She told my Mom that my friends and I were all in a clique, and she didn't approve of cliques. Mom told her, "Mable, EVERYONE is in a clique!" She compromised. My friends and I got two beds, and Mable put two girls of her choosing in the other bed.

After they built the women's dormitory, I had a particular bed I always slept in each year with my cousin, Judy. The beds were built in squares, in groups of four double mattresses. Four double beds on the top bunk and four on the bottom. Everyone slept with their heads together—perfect for talking! One year the sister worker in charge of sleeping arrangements, Miss Evelyn, asked me for whom I had saved the three beds around me. Just an ordinary, reasonable question. Little did I realize what my answer would bring about. I rolled off the names of six of my friends, and she wrote them all down. Next thing I knew, an old lady had climbed up the ladder, plunked down her suitcase, and started to make up one of the beds I had saved! When you have a year's worth of girl-talk to catch up on, the last thing you want is an old lady hearing everything you say. This would NOT do! Immediately, I marched off to inform Miss Evelyn about her mix-up. To my surprise, I found she had *assigned* the lady to that bed—even though there were plenty of other beds available! I asked, "Why did you do that? I told you I was saving them for my friends!" She replied softly, "Because it's best this way." Not a little bit distressed, I ran off to tell my mother about the way my plans were being disrupted! Mom found out Miss Minnie, the can-can sister worker, was behind it all, and Miss Evelyn was just her pawn. Seems Miss Minnie thought I was "taking on a little too much authority" for a teenager! Those were her exact words. She actually felt threatened by a 16 year old! I KNEW Miss Evelyn was too sweet to do something like that. She was one of the few sister workers I ever found genuinely nice at heart

Things went from bad to worse! Miss Minnie decided she would teach me a lesson and show me who was in charge. My friends arrived for whom I had saved the beds. They were assigned to sleep at a friend's house!!! Not only were they sent completely off the convention grounds, but they were sent *12 miles away—out of the county!* UNBELIEVABLE! I was dumbfounded, and I objected strenuously! We had ALWAYS slept together, etc. The girls tried to shush me up and told Evelyn they just wanted to do whatever was best—to sleep wherever they were needed, to fit in, etc. Baloney, I thought!! It never occurred to me to say, "Well, I've decided I want MY room back. You'll just have to find another bed for that visiting worker you put in there!" Miss Minnie taught me a lesson all right, but it wasn't the lesson she had in mind. I learned from her that the workers could be downright petty and MEAN. This means they were not always "right." I trusted the workers less and less. It was becoming crystal clear they were not a cut above as some thought.

I allowed a professing girlfriend to have a great deal of influence over me, something I have regretted exceedingly. I suppose I had a crush on her. I yearned for her approval, and I thought the way to get it was to copy her actions, likes and dislikes. She was the most negative person I have ever known. She seemed to only have two reactions; either she loved or hated everything—mostly she hated. She was extremely critical of the workers and scorned them out loud. A real actress, she would put on the most gracious, respectful, interested face and smile when she ran into a worker at convention, and seem so genuine in her conversation; but the minute their backs were turned, she would scowl and mutter all sorts of hateful things about them. So, we had in common that neither of us had much respect for the workers, and we both saw all sorts of flaws and inconsistencies with the fellowship. We were both rebels and didn't fit the mold they were trying to force us into. My experiences had confirmed to me the workers were not exceptional, so I followed her lead and took up the habit of scorning them also.

I was under her influence until I was in my 30's. Once she told me not to talk so loud, and to this day people often have trouble hearing me. One day I woke up and realized how much I had allowed this person I didn't really care for all that much to rule my life. After that, I made a conscious effort not to let the fear of "what she would think" guide me. I lived in fear of being on the receiving end of her scorn, even when my better reasoning told me I was doing the right thing! I know firsthand that scorn is a TERRIBLE habit that is extremely hard to let go. There is no doubt in my mind that it is a weapon of Satan—since it is the opposite of love, mercy and compassion. I was determined to instill a guilty conscience in my children concerning the practice of scorn. I often prayed that God would protect and keep my children from ever coming under that sort of bondage to anyone and to keep them from "sitting in the seat of the scornful." So I taught them from a young age to recognize scorn and that scorning others was terribly wrong. They still tattle: "Momma, he/she's scorning me."

It is considered an honor to be chosen to wait on the workers' table. Even though I was the daughter of the convention ground owners, and gave up my room for two weeks, I was never offered the position. I guess Miss Minnie never thought I was fit for that honor. However, I didn't feel slighted in the least—I was actually rather relieved because I never wanted to. NOT at ALL! Looking back, I see they usually put the girls they were grooming for the work on that table, like my cousin Judy.

Entering adolescence, I went through the usual period of pursuing, investigating, measuring, and evaluating the beliefs and values handed down by my parents. I had no problem accepting and following the teachings of my parents that were supported in the Bible. But I argued and argued about any teachings that had no Scripture to justify them. I was usually quelled with something to the effect, "When you are on your own, you can do what you want do, but as long as you're living under this roof....etc."

My FIRST serious disagreement involved the interpretation of the Old Testament verse that forbids women to wear the apparel of men. It all began about the first week of school when I was in the seventh grade and 12 years old. As I breezed through the kitchen on my way to catch the school bus one morning, I remembered to inform my mother, "I'm supposed to have a pair of gym shorts

before next week." BIG MISTAKE! This innocent statement was to have far reaching effects. A brother
worker sitting at the breakfast table with my parents
commented something to the effect that if HE had a
daughter, SHE would certainly never put on a pair
of shorts. I HAD to take gym class—it was *required.*
The thought of being the only girl taking gym in a
dress or skirt put me in supreme agony and anguish. I desperately wanted to be like the others
and not to stand out! I couldn't bear to think about
it. Salvation comes in unusual packages. Volunteers
were requested to work in the school cafeteria and
they would be relieved of taking gym class. So for
the next six years, until I graduated, I served in the
cafeteria line without pay, receiving in return only
a free and plentiful lunch. However, I was given a
grade for gym, a class I never took. Those high
standards were never let down by me—I never
wore a pair of those "worldly" shorts in a class of
all girls—but what was the outcome? Dishonesty. I
was a party to deceit. I took a grade I didn't earn
because I was MADE to do something I didn't agree
with, didn't understand, wasn't willing for, and
thought utterly ridiculous. I wanted to run track,
but I wasn't willing to do so in a dress. I was prevented from doing the one thing at which I
excelled modestly, and for years I was bitter that I
was forced to give it up.

Did they really think God "who looks on the
heart" would be pleased with something wrenched
from a child who wasn't willing to give it? What
value is any service, when it isn't given from the
heart in love and willingly? Little did I know I had
just begun a collision course where I would often
battle traditions and inconsistencies for which there
was no Scripture. I passed up going on our Senior
Trip to the Gulf Coast, because I knew I would be

the only girl who wasn't wearing shorts. Ironically, I was allowed to wear a swimsuit.

I could quote the verse, "Jesus is the same yesterday, today, and forever" from the time I was a small child. I naively thought this meant the fellowship was the same in every location in every way. I have lived in four different states (California, Mississippi, Texas, Oklahoma) so I know this is far from being the case. Further, I knew that practices were not only different from state to state, but also from worker to worker! I was especially resentful when I could not do something I would have been allowed to do in California or Texas, like wear my hair down. I bitterly resented being robbed of this right.

When we left California, Mom and I left behind our slacks (which we only wore fishing or to the farm), our Christmas tree decorations, our radio, and probably more that I didn't realize. As children, we thought we left them behind because we didn't have room in the trailer. Little did we suspect the real reason was because in Mississippi, they were not approved. Later, I found out my parents had been uneasy about taking their movie camera, projector, screen and films of the family trips, scenery, baby's first steps, etc. However, they did. When Mom told one sister worker about them, she suggested they talk to a brother worker about it. However, they never did, because they fully expected him to say they should get rid of them, and Mom refused to do that.

I wouldn't describe my childhood as unhappy, but I wasn't happy either. Certainly I felt loved and wanted by my parents. Both our parents inspired my brother and me with self-confidence and self-esteem, one of the greatest gifts a parent can give a child, I am convinced. I suppose I was depressed, extremely bored and just plain lonely. As a teen-ager, I felt repressed, suppressed, depressed, oppressed and I expressed it. I blamed it all on Mis-sissippi, my parents, and the workers, and lived for and dreamed about the day I would leave that state behind. Whenever I didn't get to do what I wanted, I would comfort myself thinking about my plans to leave home and Mississippi just as soon as I possi-bly could. I didn't want anyone around telling me when and what I could and could not do. This was one reason I chose not to go to college.

It seemed I was nearly always mad at my folks about something. It has long been my fear that my own children would treat me the way I did my par-ents. Although I know I richly deserve it, I don't know if I could stand it. I never found a friend at school that I felt very close to. When we moved from California, I had been a ring leader since first grade and was the president of my fifth grade class. I had thought being the "new kid" at a new school would be fun. NOT! The girls in the new school had been friends since they were babies in the Baptist church nursery. They had formed a tightly knit group that was well bonded (cemented?) which rarely opened its arms to anyone outside their faith. Nor was living way out in the country favorable to making close friendships. Of course, I wasn't al-lowed to date any nonprofessing guys; and professing guys were very few and far between in Dixieland. In 1963 when I was 15, I went to work part-time in a dime store where the radio played all day long. Since we moved from California, I had not heard the radio play, so I had been totally igno-rant of the current popular songs the other kids at school discussed and sang. Being familiar with the songs made me feel not quite as "out of it."

Since my parents didn't object, long before I left home I had been openly wearing cosmetics—sparingly, as did the other professing girls my age also. Looking back, I am surprised the workers didn't say something. They sure didn't allow makeup in many other areas of the USA. I remember one time I deliberately baited Miss Mable, the bed-moving sister worker. I was 15 and had been baptized two weeks prior. I heard her coming my way, so I got out a compact and began to carefully powder my nose looking in the mirror and ignoring her. She said, "Well, I thought you were saved from all that!" I looked at her coolly and said, "This is my MOTHER's compact." That shut her up. It was the truth!

When I was nearly 17, we made our first trip back to California, where there were loads of young professing kids. Several of the friends where we spent the night had sons a couple years older than me, who enjoyed my Southern accent. Of course, there wasn't much my sharp eyes missed. I duly noted each and every difference in the do's and don'ts; coulds and could nots; have and have nots. Like how many girls wore their hair down, and how short it was. While some did have very long hair without bangs, one girl's hair barely covered her ears in a pageboy. She claimed the beauty shop cut it off before she knew what happened. That excuse wouldn't wash in Mississippi—where it was a sin to GO to a beauty shop! I took notice of all the radios, stereos, and even a TV in one home, which were openly displayed. Before we came back home, I trimmed my hair the shortest it had ever been, and was crushed when I wasn't allowed to wear it down anywhere in public. MAJOR discontent entered my life after that trip! And I became more determined than ever to leave Mississippi, preferably for California, just as soon as I possibly could.

On the way home we were involved in a head-on collision. The impact caused my face to strike the hard, metal dash and my lower teeth went entirely through my bottom lip twice. Two of my upper teeth were chipped off and all my front lower teeth were knocked out. I also had a one-inch gash in my chin. Stitches, oral surgery, caps, root canals and braces and plastic surgery followed. And to add insult to injury, I had just had my braces removed before we left! Barely a month later, in this condition, I met my husband-to-be, Dave Kropp. I had just turned 17, he was 21, and it was the summer of 1965 at Texarkana, Texas convention. His parents moved to Oklahoma where they had family when he was four years old. They began to attend gospel meetings, and professed soon after. At the time I met him, he was working in Dallas for Texas Instruments and lived in an apartment with three professing roommates who were all worried about being drafted. Sure enough, when he returned from convention, his draft notice was in his mailbox. SHOOT! He was to report to the army in six weeks. He came to see me twice before he left for Vietnam for a year. I was hoping he could come to our convention, and was warned that if he did we couldn't sit together, even though he wouldn't know another soul there. We planned to be married sometime after he returned.

Judy called me one day and said "Cherie, have you seen the newspaper?" I said "no." She said a picture of Dave and an article was on the front page of the Memphis newspaper. A reporter had interviewed Dave in Vietnam and many newspapers across the country carried the report and Dave's picture. Friends all over recognized the article was about a professing Commanding Officer. He received hundreds of letters. My fiancee was a hero!

For years afterward, little old ladies would come up to him at convention and smilingly say, "I've got your picture in my Bible."

The year Dave was in Vietnam was the longest year of my life. While he was gone, in 1966, I graduated from high school. My parents were willing for me to attend a local junior college nearby or business college, but I only wanted to leave MS and be my own boss. I went to work in an office, where fortunately, another girl worked who also had a fiancee in Vietnam. We became very good friends and did things together which helped while away the time. Soon after I went to work I went shopping for a radio. I bought the smallest one I could and kept it in my car. When my brother discovered it and ratted on me, I assured my parents I had never taken it in the house on those holy grounds.

During my last year at home, my relationship with my parents smoothed out. I don't know if they gave me more freedom, or if I grew up some, mellowed or what. But it was a time of peaceful waiting. We actually grew fairly close. Not that I wavered in my intention to leave Mississippi or anything like that! In nine months, Judy and I had saved enough money to venture out on our own. Our goal was to move to a city where there were lots of young friends, as well as fewer 2x2 restrictions. Dave had a job waiting for him in Dallas, and he urged us to move there. Since my Dad was from Texas, and we had several relatives living there, we often attended Texas conventions. I knew Texas was far more liberal, so Dallas sounded OK to us. My parents approved our choice since Daddy had two professing sisters living there. Judy's parents were opposed, and tried every way possible to talk her out of moving. Judy had not yet discovered that parents could be wrong. She continued to feel terribly guilty even after we moved, but hid it from me. On the other hand, I had no doubts, whatsoever! After all, where did the Bible say, "Thou shalt not move to Texas"? If it was so terrible, why did several ex-workers, my uncle included, make it their home? Apparently my folks thought it was OK, or they would never have encouraged us to move there!

After Dave returned from Vietnam and was assigned to San Antonio for his remaining six months duty, Judy and I moved to Dallas, 400-600 miles from our homes. Dave drove 280 miles to Dallas every weekend. Judy and I leased what we considered to be a lovely apartment. I was shocked when Judy's sister worker aunt considered it extremely "worldly," all because it had a swimming pool. This was a new one on me. Judy and I were both professing, but we also had big plans to do "whatever our hearts desired." However, we actually did very little different! Dave escorted us to the drag races a couple times. I tried one cigarette which came in a "Welcome" sack and nearly choked to death. (I'm allergic to smoke) We both began to wear mascara and bought some very modest two-piece swim suits. We brought our radios "out of the closet." We had attained our lifelong dream. AT LAST—we were on our own! We were heady with our new freedom, high on being career girls in a big city, being our own boss, going to bed when we pleased, doing things our way, etc. We thought we had no one but ourselves to answer to, but found this wasn't exactly the case when we skipped a Wednesday night meeting. The Relatives all called pronto.

However, all was not well on the horizon. Before we had hardly settled in good, Judy's sister

worker aunt (now deceased) and companion descended upon us. She was hardly in the door,
before she went into her preamble. It was something like: "Judy, when I get to Heaven and you're
not there, I would always feel very badly unless I
spoke to you about this." She then proceeded to
throw a hissy fit right in our living room! We
should be ashamed that we even THOUGHT about
moving away from Mississippi! Surely, we weren't
so ignorant that we didn't KNOW it was a SIN for us
(and Judy in particular) to leave a place where
there were so few friends, and move to this "worldly" state where they didn't need any more friends!
Oh, she really read us her "right act." Judy and I
were so dumbfounded at this unexpected tirade that
we both went absolutely mute, while she raved on
and on and on.

Furthermore, Aunt Sister Worker had talked with
several very wise friends who said they would
rather have their daughter live ANYWHERE but in
Dallas, Texas; that it was a horrible, wicked,
worldly, evil, &*%$# city! And, what on earth pos-
sessed us to choose it over lovely Mississippi,
where we were so needed? She intimated she *knew*
for certain we had been doing things we shouldn't.
But we both *knew* there was no way she could
have known about the few questionable things we
had actually done or tried in private.

Aunt S.W. suggested (demanded) we have a Bible study, and she chose a particular Scripture
passage for reasons known only to her. The four of
us each read a few verses. I didn't see any connection in the study and her former ravings
whatsoever. During a lull in the conversation, I figured I might as well make the best of a bad
situation and ventured to ask a question I had long
wondered about: "Where does the Bible say it is

wrong to wear make-up?" Apparently my spiritual understanding was retarded. She seemed exasperated and pointed to one of the verses we had just "studied," and said, "Haven't you been listening? Isn't that what that verse XX says, which you just read?" What was plain as day to her was clear as mud to me. Bewildered, I hardly opened my mouth again that evening. I have wished since that I could remember which Scripture she referred to... Aunt S.W. hinted that she was, of course, guided by divine intuition. And she was gracious enough to let us in on some of that knowledge. Oh yes, she knew all about how extremely unhappy and miserable Judy had been since the day she came to Texas! Didn't Judy realize that this feeling would only escalate? That she could only look forward to being more miserable in the future? Things only get worse when you're out of God's will, you know. Why Judy's only hope was to pack up and go back home to Mississippi right this minute. And she would be glad to help her—let's go call Judy's parents right now and ask them when they could drive over and move Judy back!

Although we had been blissfully happy with our lives before Aunt S. W. arrived in righteous indignation; and even though Judy and I knew each other so well we could often read each other's minds, Aunt Sister Worker was so convincing that I even began to wonder about Judy's state of mind, as Aunt S.W. elaborated on the lengths and depths of Judy's unseen misery, unhappiness, shame and guilt, etc. Maybe Aunt S. W. was right? Maybe I had read Judy wrong—maybe she WAS miserable. Surely NOT! We knew each other so well—how could I have missed it? For once, I couldn't read Judy's expression and her face gave me no clue as to her feelings! Our apartment was so small that the two of us could not get out of Aunt S.W.'s presence without it being very obvious we wanted to talk about her. So finally, while we prepared supper in the kitchen, I opened a cabinet door so Aunt S.W. couldn't see us, and whispered, "Do you really feel like she said?" "NO WAY!" Judy stormed. I was extremely relieved, to say the least.

That night Judy and I sacked out on pallets on the living room floor and gave the workers our bedroom. Aunt Sister Worker sent her companion in to ask Judy wouldn't she like to sleep in the bedroom with her Aunt so they could have some time alone? Judy politely refused. Judy said to me disgustedly, "No way am I going into that lion's den!" The companion returned a short time later and begged Judy to trade places with her. Judy's lovely gracious, southern manners came to her rescue. She replied so sweetly in her southern drawl, "Why, Alice, there's no way in the world I would be able to sleep, knowing a sister worker was sleeping on my floor, while I slept in a bed!" I nearly applauded. Right on Judy! Not one to give up easily, Aunt S.W. sent the companion in a third time! Again, Judy adamantly refused, and Aunt S.W. finally gave up. Suffice it to say that any remaining illusions I harbored about workers being infallible or being privy to special revelations died with that visit!

After she left us, Aunt S.W. called Judy's parents and told them Judy had gone stark, raving, wild, and that they better get themselves out to Texas FAST. Furthermore, Judy was sporting a most "outlandish hairdo" and was wearing ridiculously short dresses! Ironically, Judy had selected her dress for the Aunt's visit with the greatest of care. It was one she had worn in Mississippi, and was the longest one she owned! A week later, both our parents and Aunt S.W. converged upon us at Texarkana, Texas convention. The folks were prepared for the worst possible scenario. However, they scratched their heads in perplexity as they found the same, sweet Judy sporting the same hairdo she had worn in Mississippi before she left, wearing some of the same clothing. She didn't appear changed in the least.

I never really understood the bee that Aunt S.W. had in her bonnet that weekend until this year! Aunt S.W. had long entertained visions of Judy becoming a sister worker, and had been "grooming" Judy for the work for years. Therefore, she viewed me as no small threat to her plans, a very bad influence, and a very real ENEMY.

Texas didn't disappoint us!! There was liberty in TEXAS and life was much more to our liking. TEXAS was my hero, my deliverer, my liberator, a breath of fresh air. I finally felt as though I could BREATHE! For me, Texas still stands for freedom! Joe Crane was the head worker in Dallas when we moved there and for several years after. Joe was a very good speaker, a real comedian and was actually FUN to be with. A worker who cut up and whose jokes were actually funny! This was certainly a new twist for a worker! Imagine a worker you enjoyed being around and listening to! Judy was amazed beyond words! In Texas, it was not a sin to own or listen to a radio! Some girls wore their hair down. One could go bowling, skating or swimming without censure. Workers never said a word about women wearing red shoes—any color shoes for that matter, hairpieces, spike heels, styles that were in fashion, etc. Joe Crane even teased the boys and girls about their sweethearts. Back home, the workers wouldn't have thought of mentioning any boy-girl relationships. Why they didn't even mention an impending marriage until it was a fact.

We noticed these lovely wood cabinets in the majority of the Texas friends' living rooms, often taking up one entire wall! *Stereos* were everywhere! It was not uncommon for the emblems to sit upon the stereo during meeting in the elders' homes. I heard about a man who moved to Dallas from another state who was outraged at this practice. He thought it bordered blasphemy. Stereos were common place because the Overseer of Texas, Gus Jensen, adored music. Eventually Gus left the work and married. Hubert Childers took his place and went about gradually shaping the Texas friends to fit his mold and standards. Right up there near the top on his list was "eliminate all stereos." Some moved them OUT, and others moved them further IN—to their bedrooms.

Within the year, Dave and I entered into Holy Matrimony, and Judy entered into a new lease with a new roommate. I became worried about her when she started missing meetings. I believed some people in her apartment unit were having a bad influence on her. When she found herself in a financial strain, I encouraged her to move home. I hoped her folks could get her back on the right track. She decided to move back to Mississippi and asked her folks to come and move her things back. Guess who was visiting them at the time? Aunt Sister Worker. They insisted on bringing Aunt S.W. with them, because "she knew the roads." I told Judy I would have refused if SHE had to come. But Judy was depressed, and it didn't seem to matter to her. I missed her sorely. However, moving back didn't do the trick. Within a year after moving to Mississippi, she quit professing, and married a divorced man who had custody of his three children. She helped raise the kids (now grown) and they all regard her as their mother. They have been married over 20 years now. Judy never reprofessed.

Hubert rearranged the meetings so that we were a part of a meeting composed entirely of young couples where the oldest one was 35! We were all pleased and proud of our meeting. Dave and I were offered one of the rotating Wednesday night meetings, with the stipulation that I let down some of my hemlines. There were many other young couples in the area with whom we went out to eat, had get-togethers, New Years Eve parties, etc. We exchanged dinners with over thirty different families. We were quite content with our lot in life. We were "Texans by choice," if not by birth, and proud to be identified as one.

Our families did not celebrate Christmas in the same way. I had never so much as heard of ANY professing people who didn't exchange gifts at Christmas time. I loved that time of the year, and looked forward to it. I simply couldn't imagine life without Christmas gifts. On the other hand, Dave had been raised in Oklahoma where Christmas was no different from any other day—no gifts, cards, decorations, dinner, special eats, etc. In fact, celebrating was considered sinful! We didn't discover this until the first Christmas we were married which was a disaster. I happily bought presents and gaily wrapped them and left them laying on the fireplace hearth in the living room. Whenever someone was coming over, Dave would hide all of the presents. We resolved to ask the workers about this before the next Christmas rolled around.

When Hubert Childers and Lecil Sullivan came for a meal, we each told them exactly how our family had viewed and celebrated Christmas. Our problem was obvious. We told the workers we had decided we would do whatever they suggested. My parents had decided they would also. Neither Dave nor my parents thought we would ever celebrate another Christmas with gifts. I still appreciate what Hubert said. "There is never ever anything wrong in giving gifts—at any time." He asked Lecil if he agreed. Lecil did. He also told us that when we had children, we would need to be "wise with the little ones" with regard to Christmas. That settled it for us. Dave's parents told Joe Hobbs, an Oklahoma brother worker, what Hubert said. Joe replied, "Oh, I'm positive Hubert would never have said that. They must have misunderstood him." The misunderstanding was all in Joe's mind. A clear example of the unity that doesn't exist.

Dave's sister married an "outsider." She continued to take part in meetings in Dallas. However, Joe Hobbs sent word through her parents that she wasn't to take part in meetings when she was visiting in Oklahoma. Neither was she to wear "those high heels." And they were only medium high! I wonder if Joe had something against Texas or a particular Texas worker. Apparently, unity wasn't high on his priorities.

I worked for ten years after we married. While I was the Contract Manager for the M-K-T Railroad, I learned to scrutinize the fine print in contracts. When I scrutinized the Scripture, I expected everything to be clearly spelled out in its fine print. NOT! I had seen too many errors in the workers' judgment too many times to believe everything they said was right. Neither did I believe their interpretations were without error, *especially* when they could not support them with Scripture. I had faith in the Bible, but what I did NOT have, nor does the Bible recommend, is faith in the word of men!

I worked under a wonderful, brilliant lady at Katy Railroad who became my mentor. She was the first employee I'd ever worked around who truly worked "for the company," putting the company first. Many times she accomplished minor miracles or the seemingly impossible. I watched her closely for clues to her method. Her secret was quite simple—she asked. She "knocked" on doors that appeared to be closed up tight with no admittance, and they often opened right up to her. All because she asked and didn't assume. She didn't take "no" for an answer, didn't go by what others said, and insisted on seeing for herself. Her motto was: "Never assume nothing!" She also got a great deal accomplished because she didn't insist on taking the credit herself. She knew more was accomplished by leading, planting ideas, and praising—than by driving, pushing or force. Raye had many enemies because she was always being noted for some new accomplishment or brilliant idea. One of her most remarkable feats was how she dealt with her enemies. She is the only person I ever saw who truly practiced "Love Your Enemies." Over a period of time, I witnessed her love one enemy lady to the point they became close friends! She eventually had her eating out of her hand! When we sing the hymn "Strong in the strength of gentleness," I always think of Raye. *She made others strong; her strength was in her gentleness.* She taught me by example that gentleness is stronger than force. She became the first female Vice-President of the M-K-T Railroad. Every time she was promoted, she pulled me up with her into the position she vacated. Besides my parents, there has never been a person who has taught me any more valuable lessons about life than she did. Many, many times I have been thankful for the seven years we shared.

Dave worked at Texas Instruments and went to college. He graduated in 1976 with a Business degree, majoring in Accounting. Our son, Kelly, was born in 1977, two weeks before our tenth wedding anniversary. We loved Dallas and didn't plan to ever leave it. We had even bought our cemetery plots in Restland, where "One Call Does All." HOWEVER, in 1979, Dave took a new job with Continental Can, and we moved 140 miles east of Dallas, to Longview, Texas. Population 72,000, quite a change from Big D. Krista was born a month later.

We lived in Longview for nine years, and didn't plan to ever move from there. The fellowship in Longview was sort of dead—very different from Dallas. Over the years, we became close friends with two couples, but on the whole, we didn't find the friends very friendly and they rarely invited anyone over. Our elder never once invited us for a meal, except to a pot luck they held for the whole church. Consequently, most of our friends were "outsiders." We opened a custom picture frame shop and later added country craft supplies, which I managed for 5-1/2 years.

One lady who worked for us was a member of the Church of Christ. I had a great deal of respect for Mrs. Dodson, and the feeling was mutual. I was impressed by her sincerity, values, lifestyle, and conduct. We sometimes discussed things we had noticed in our Bible studies. After going to gospel meeting with me to hear some sister workers, she confessed that she just could not understand how we could believe in women preachers because of the verses: *"I suffer not a women to teach, nor to usurp authority over the man, but to be in silence"* 1 Tim. 2:12, and *"Let your women keep silence in the churches: for it is not permitted unto them to* speak," 1 Cor. 14:34. This was the first time it really hit me that the practices of having women preachers was at odds with these Scriptures. I gave her some notes I found regarding women preachers, confident they would convince anyone.

Her husband, Mr. Dodson, was a college speech professor, and had studied to be a preacher. He wrote me a letter concerning the notes I sent. He shot down the notes with very reasonable, valid points. He showed how one would have to "leap" to conclude these Biblical women were ministers from several of the passages given in my notes. For instance, Anna the prophetess, who was living long before Jesus ever sent out the disciples, etc. I was quite surprised. I began to seriously question whether or not women preachers were "right."

Given the notes and Mr. Dodson's reply, one brother worker recommended not replying. He indicated it was like "casting your pearls before swine." Given the same, a sister worker who had been a recent college graduate and who had traveled all over the world, replied, more or less, that women preaching was "right" (1) because it feels right and (2) because it has endured. If it wasn't right, it wouldn't endure. Another brother worker showed through various other passages that Paul didn't REALLY mean that women shall not teach. Part of his reasoning was based on differences he attached to the terms keeping "silent" and keeping "silence." He went to great lengths to prove this passage didn't mean what it said. So why do they take the passages about long hair and jewelry at face value? Why don't they look into them long and hard, and prove they didn't mean what they say? The inconsistencies were beginning to drive me crazy!

Except for Hal Lindsey's best seller *The Late Great Planet Earth*, I had never read any religious books. I was enthralled with it and didn't realize I shouldn't be reading it. I loaned it to some of the other friends and gave it to a sister worker for her opinion. I was anxious to learn the workers' position on the rapture; pre or post. I expected her to take the book with her when she left and get back to me after she read it. About 5 minutes after she took the book to the bedroom, she came and gave it back. With a bored manner, she dismissed it saying that it was just like all the rest of books written by worldly men on that subject. She hadn't even read it! I thought her reply was very strange, to say the least.

As long as I can remember, I used to "space out" in meetings into a fantasy world where I daydreamed, to escape the boredom. After I professed, I struggled to break this habit. For 20 years or more, I went to convention after convention and could not remember a single thing I heard. I'd wake up about the last meeting and scold myself, "Well, Cherie, you blew this one, just like all the others, didn't you?" Eventually, I began to make a concentrated effort not to tune out the speakers, and to listen carefully and take notes. I found the same old things were being said most of the time. I rarely heard anything I didn't already know. Time after time, I left feeling puzzled with precious few notes. I can only remember three outstanding sermons during those barren 20 years that have stayed with me. Later, I was shocked when I came across all of them almost verbatim in books by outside Christian authors! Some suggested something wasn't right within me, but I didn't believe that. Not after praying so very diligently and earnestly for food for a whole month before I went. And I really did listen intently to every speaker. God promised that *"if we ask any thing according to his will, he heareth us"* (1 John 5:14). Was I the only one who felt like they were in a famine? I remember identifying my soul with the word "barrenness."

I went to one convention with high hopes but left feeling particularly empty. I reported to my mother that all we heard about was The Convention itself. How they had looked forward to it; how it was such a privilege to be there; how it could mean so much to us; that it could be our last; that it could be ever so meaningful if we let it; that it could bring about great changes. They talked about what they hoped to get there; what we could or should do with what we heard there; what God thought about The Convention; speculations on what would happen after we left there; pity for outsiders who knew nothing about Conventions. The Convention was like a book with only a prologue and epilogue, and no material in between. The Convention was idolized, glorified, honored and worshipped, but where was the spiritual food I was so hungry for? Conventions were devised and created by men. They were never commanded in the Scripture. It seemed to me man was worshipping his creation, The Convention, more than his Creator.

It wasn't only at conventions, however, that I found no food. After I opened our shop, it was a tremendous effort to get the family ready to go to Gospel Meetings or Wednesday Night Meetings. It became harder and harder to push ourselves to make an effort to go to these places "for nothing." We were expected to attend two Special Meetings 100 miles away, and in 9 years, we made maybe 5 out of the 18 expected. Eventually, we attended only the Sunday meeting, and the one Wed. Night meeting held in our home once a month. We rarely went to any gospel meetings, unless they were SUPER convenient. I didn't know it, but I was starving spiritually.

Mrs. Dodson loaned me some religious tapes that I really enjoyed and found informative. For my birthday, she gave me the book *Righteousness Inside Out*. I couldn't refuse it! It opened up Jesus' Sermon on the Mount to me in a way that I'd never experienced before. I wondered how could this man write such a wonderful, enlightening book, and not be saved? I realized there was no way I would ever have heard everything contained in that book from the workers. No worker ever speaks over an hour, and the workers never continue a sermon, so no subject was ever covered in depth. I began to realize teaching was not the strong point of this fellowship, nor its priority, nor would it ever be! Yet the Scripture said, *"And he gave some, apostles; and some, prophets; and some, evangelists; and some, **pastors and teachers"**;* Eph. 4:11, 1 Cor 12:28. The workers are evangelists preaching to those who are "lost." Where were the teachers? Who is teaching those who believe? No one! In this fellowship, the position of the evangelist is combined with that of pastors and teachers. Where is the Biblical authority for that??? No wonder there isn't any food.

My son was close friends with a neighbor boy his age. His mother, Doris, and I became close friends. I had not thought it possible for an outsider to truly understand my lifestyle, but she had been raised in the Assembly of God Church, which had many of the same rules as I observed, so she understood quite well. She raved over a book she had just read and practically *insisted* that I read it. It was *Ordering Your Private World* by Gordon Mac-

Donald. Since I had pressed various books on her, it seemed only fair that I read one she recommended. Again, I marveled that an "unsaved" man could write such a spiritually enlightening book! I knew his message was "right on" because I had picked up on some of the same things myself. These books I was practically forced to read opened the way to where I began to read other Christian books also. Here I found a spiritual feast outside, where no one was supposed to know anything!

I was totally shocked one day when Doris told me she was just "hungry" to learn more about the Bible. Here my friend was spiritually starving, and I hadn't even realized it! She had attended a couple of meetings with me and declined more, saying she wanted more than the milk they preached! Milk, huh? Supposedly, I had God's answer at my fingertips, and she wasn't interested in it! From another woman who worked for us, Gail, Doris learned about an in-depth Bible study. I had a hard time thinking of Doris, Gail and Mrs. Dodson as "unsaved" just because they didn't attend the same church I did, so I just didn't think about it. Their sincerity and actions told my heart otherwise. Then, Doris dropped her bombshell on me. She announced she wanted *us* to attend. To say I was extremely reluctant about complying with this idea of hers, was to put it mildly, but I finally agreed. I believed if we studied together, perhaps I could help them see the way I believed was "God's only right way."

The study is called Bible Study Fellowship (BSF for short). It isn't a church, but a completely independent Bible study. It's interdenominational, that is, it is not affiliated with any particular denomination. Your church affiliation is irrelevant, as it is in a college class. We three enrolled, but just Gail and I were placed and Doris was put on the waiting list and never did get placed that year. Disgruntled and extremely uncomfortable, I attended the first few weekly sessions, hoping fervently that they would find room for Doris soon. I told myself I could drop out any time I wanted to. After all, this was HER idea, not mine! Under "Amount of Previous Bible Study, I brazenly checked the category "extensive." I was certain the study would be a cinch for me as I would probably be the only one who had ever studied the Bible much anyway! NOT!

Was I in for a surprise! On the first day, 300 ladies showed up—without any advertising. They all heard about it by word of mouth, like we had! I wondered how they could draw 300 ladies who wanted to learn more about the Bible, and yet often the workers couldn't get even one outsider to come? The study that year was the "Life and Letters of Paul" (Acts and Paul's epistles). Talk about thorough! I didn't feel a part of the group, but more like a spectator with different goals, taking what I wanted out of the sessions. Two entirely different camps: Those who THOUGHT they were saved—and me, fortunate enough to be in "God's right way." You can imagine my surprise when many of the ladies had BETTER answers than mine to the questions!!
     Well, I'd certainly never studied the Scriptures like this before! They called it "expository" which meant studying verse by verse, chapter by chapter, and we also learned about the relevant culture and history. I really looked forward to going to BSF each week, a feeling I never had about going to meetings. I remember hearing a professing man say, and I believe he was totally sincere, "There is no

other place on earth I would rather be than in this meeting today." I thought, "Boy, I sure couldn't say that. I'd rather be most ANYWHERE than here." But I COULD say that about going to BSF! For the first time, I found myself actually *wanting* to study the Scriptures. In meetings, we only got bits and pieces, and no overall view of the Scripture. Through BSF, many puzzle pieces began to fall in place, and my understanding grew and I reveled in the experience. Finally, I found spiritual food—and look where it came from!! I later told Harry Brownlee I attended BSF and that I had learned more in those studies than in all the meetings I had sat through in my whole lifetime put together. Now, I am a real champion for BSF, and I encourage EVERYONE to attend. For one nearest you, call or write Bible Study Fellowship, 19001 Blanco Road, San Antonio, Texas, 78258 (512) 492-4676.

When we studied Paul's letter to the Galatians in BSF, I recognized the friends and workers! They had fallen headlong into the same error as the Galatians had; that of believing certain "works" were required to merit salvation, or that salvation is conditional upon works, that we have a chance at eternal life because of Christ' sacrifice, and if we work hard we may be rewarded with salvation. In other words, Christ didn't finish the work of salvation, and we must do so. *If we must work for our salvation, why did Jesus need to die?* Paul adamantly stated it is *"not of works."* We can't work for it—it is God's free gift (the meaning of grace) to us through faith. I also learned about the nature and work of the Holy Spirit, who had been a vague enigma to me. He guides all believers into *all truth*. Since we have the source of wisdom and guidance *in* us, we don't need anyone else to tell us what we should and should not do!

I read *The Hiding Place*, the biography of Corrie Ten Boom. Corrie and her sister were some of the most tenderhearted, Godly women I had ever EVER heard of. Their actions revealed beyond all doubt to me that the Spirit was surely dwelling in them. I read the story of the founder of BSF, Audrey Weatherell Johnson and about the Christian Martyrs. After I was in BSF for two years, it began to dawn on me that those ladies had the Holy Spirit dwelling in them, and anyway, who was I to say whether or not they did or didn't?? I came to the conclusion that there were definitely others who were saved besides those who were in the same fellowship I was, and I began to look upon these women as my "sisters in Christ." I also looked back at all the really good people I had known in my lifetime (that I had thought were not saved) and saw them in a new light. Why, some I had mourned for were probably in heaven! Many folks I know now are also going! What JOY! Heaven was going to contain far more people than I had formerly thought, and that was GOOD NEWS to me! I never had been too sure I would like being cooped up with just the friends anyway. I began to resent the friends and workers making fun of other Christians. I still felt this fellowship was "right" for ME because it was the closest way, but that it very well might not be the "right way" for my children.

I began to feel an urgent need to teach my children all about the Scriptures. I wanted them to be well grounded and to know the basis for the 2x2 teachings. As I faced this task, I felt very helpless. Where to start? The Bible was a maze. How could I be sure I taught them everything, with the right emphasis? If only there were some sort of outline, guidebook or map for professing parents! I decided I would write a Daily Bible Study Program geared solely for children of the friends and use my own children for guinea pigs. Friends who had children similar ages were enthusiastic, and wanted to try it out. They encouraged me so I began. I told one worker about my project, and he said he thought it was a splendid idea!

My goal was to write one lesson a day. I started with the subject "church." And I realized with surprise, that the point of the verses in Acts 17:24 and Acts 7:48, *"Howbeit the most High dwelleth not in temples made with hands"* was not that church buildings were sinful or false. But rather the point was where God does live; i.e. in the hearts of His children: *"That Christ may dwell in your hearts by faith"* Eph. 3:17. It was saying "You're looking in the wrong place—he's not over there—he's inside you!" I saw that the 2x2's had distorted the real intent of this passage. Their emphasis missed the point entirely. They had "magnified a pine needle to 70 foot tall!" It wasn't saying God abhorred church buildings! Studying churches lead me to temples, tabernacles, synagogues, the old law, and eventually back to the nature of God, where I should have started in the first place. I found myself spending half of each day and often longer working out these lesson plans. I was thoroughly enjoying it and learning hoards myself. I had never enjoyed studying my Bible before. I had often wished I did, but I didn't. While I was enthralled, my kids were less than enthusiastic about being my guinea pigs!

I had never believed God intended for women to keep their hair uncut and pinned up! I never could understand why women weren't supposed to wear CERTAIN cosmetics, no pants, and CERTAIN types of jewelry. After I left home I began wearing even more makeup and also slacks or shorts when I thought the occasion warranted it. I was sure the Scripture passages they gave for long hair, slacks and jewelry didn't mean what they claimed they did, but I didn't know what they DID mean! The whole business about jewelry was so inconsistent! How was I supposed to explain why I didn't wear necklaces or earrings when I wore hair jewelry, huge elaborate pins, a gold wedding ring with diamonds, and a gold watch? And I sure wasn't going to give up any of them, just to be consistent with their incomprehensible interpretation!

Up until I was 21 years old, I had never heard of any friends or workers who believed women's hair should never be cut. All the other professing girls I knew trimmed their hair, and most kept it about 6-8 inches past their shoulders. So I naively thought girls did this everywhere. Dave objected when he found me trimming my hair after we were married and told me he had heard Joe Crane say, "Shame on a woman who would put the scissors to her hair!" I told him to work out his salvation, and I would work out mine.

Since the sixth grade, I had worn my long hair put up. At first it was only in a pony tail. During my teenage years, I longed to wear my long hair hanging loose, (not pinned up on my head). After I left home, I knew I would feel ashamed if some of the friends saw me with it down. So fear of what others would think kept me from doing anything much to my hair. I also had several bad experiences with hairdressers, and beauty shops intimidated me. I'd never had any qualms about cutting my hair, probably because my mother had kept my hair trimmed and thinned all my life since it was so thick and hard to manage. In my 30's I developed what the dermatologist call a "liver spot" on my forehead, and I began to wear a few wispy bangs to cover it up. Later, Doris tried to persuade me to give her hairdresser a try. She didn't have to try too hard! Freda layered, permed, and fixed my hair to where for the first time in my life, my long hair really looked good worn down. I began to wear it down to work and gradually extended that to almost everywhere I went, except to meeting. I noticed some of the friends attitude cooled towards me after I cut bangs.

I began to wonder how sincere Christians of other faiths interpreted 1 Corinthians 11:1-16, the hair chapter. I asked Mrs. Dodson and Gail what they thought those verses meant. They both said they believed those Scriptures were meant for the people of that day—not for us in our day. Well now, I had never thought of it in that light! That sure explained how they could do otherwise in good conscience. Our BSF study of Corinthians had a reference to a book by G. Campbell Morgan. For the first time, I went into a religious bookstore in search of a book that wasn't a Bible. I hadn't any idea there were so many helpful books available. I found the book, and it confirmed the answer the ladies had given me. It was really quite simple! The 2x2's believe the instructions found in this Corinthian passage were intended for ALL women believers for ALL times. Others believe these instructions were intended only for the first century believers to whom the instructions were originally written (the Corinthians). Whereas 2x2's believe this Scripture pertains to the present; other Christians believe it pertains to the past. The 2x2s had not considered the cultural context, historical background, or the occasion and purpose for which the Scripture is written. They hadn't even considered WHO Paul wrote the letter to the Corinthians TO!

That was like reading mail addressed to someone else, without taking that into consideration!

I realized something was terribly wrong with the system. The best explanation I could come up with was that it had "fallen into the ditch" or derailed. At this point, I still believed it was what the workers said it was: God's only way which came down from the apostles. Therefore, I believed I HAD to be in it if I wanted eternal life, and, of course, I wanted eternal life. When it is this fellowship or hell—there is no real alternative. However, I was certain the workers had misinterpreted some things. I also thought there must be a good reason *somewhere* for the requirements I didn't understand or find Scripture to back up; but the reason must have been lost somewhere down the line, while the tradition was passed down.

Meanwhile, Dave's employer was involved in a hostile take-over and they moved the entire accounting office to Omaha, Nebraska. This was comparable to the North Pole to us! He began to look for another job. We had said many times we would NEVER move to our home states. Well, he was offered two positions: one with a competitor in his home state, and another in Dallas, Texas. I was thrilled. If we had to move, Dallas was my choice. Then the Oklahoma company offered to buy our house, at a time when the real estate market was very slow! It was like the Red Sea opened up for us, and there was dry land clear to Oklahoma City (OKC). Dave accepted the job in Oklahoma, which was the position he actually preferred. It was 1988, the year I turned 40 and the kids were 9 and 11. Dave went off to OKC to begin his new job—one year to the day that we had moved into the dream house we had built and planned to stay in forever. The kids and I stayed while I liquidated our custom picture frame and craft shop. We moved four months later.

Since Dave grew up in Southeast Oklahoma and his parents still lived there, I knew firsthand that Oklahoma was extremely legalistic. History seemed to be repeating itself. We were moving our kids to a repressive state when they were about the same age I had been when we moved to Mississippi! Before we moved, the kids and I took a trip to OKC. While there, I really outdid myself getting to a gospel meeting. Dave had to work. I hardly EVER drive after dark, but I did. I drove on strange freeways, in a strange city, at night, completely across town with my two children, and I was coming down with the flu. That's how anxious I was to meet and greet the friends in our new home city. After meeting, two workers we knew spoke to us. That was it! That was our welcome! We hung around for awhile, but not another person ventured to speak to us. I found out later several knew who we were. I was very disappointed, to say the least! The prospects ahead were looking dimmer and dimmer...

However, my spirits began to rise when I found out there were no less than SIX malls and also SIX meetings in the OKC area—as many as there were in Dallas! Since I would not be owning and managing a time consuming business in OKC as I had for the last five years in Longview, I would have time to develop new friendships with the friends! Why, it COULD even work out to be similar to our happy days in Dallas! This just might not be so bad after all. I really shouldn't prejudge OKC. Maybe things have changed. A former Texas worker was the overseer. Maybe they had loosened up some. I bought a country sign to hang in my OKC kitchen that sym-

bolized my hopes. It said: "Sit Long—Talk Much."
My hopes would soon be dashed.

Back at home, Doris began to seriously quiz me
why women weren't supposed to cut their hair,
wear jewelry, make-up, etc. She found out I didn't
believe it was necessary. So why was I doing it? I
felt foolish, and in January of 1988, I vowed to myself I would get to the bottom of all this. I WOULD
find out exactly why women had to have long hair,
and wear no jewelry, slacks or makeup. I WOULD
discover what exactly God required of a woman, in
order to be saved. She asked me, "Did you ever
wonder if 'it was meant to be' that I came into your
life?" I had.

I had often heard it said: "The truth is so simple
a child can understand it." Yet, here I was 40 years
old, no longer a child, and I still could not comprehend it. Furthermore, NO ONE COULD (or would)
EXPLAIN it to me, in a simple way that created conviction in my heart—much less, convince a child! I
resolved: I was GOING to understand this faith I was
a part of, if it was the last thing I did. Armed with
Jesus promises in Matthew 7:7, *"Ask and it shall be
given you; seek and ye shall find; knock and it
shall be opened to you,"* I prayed for guidance, and
firmly believed God wanted me to understand His
will and way, and that He would enable me to do
so.

Dale Spencer and Herbert Nelson, brother workers, came to our area. Both were excellent speakers
and I often listened practically spellbound. I did
some serious studying and came up with all sorts of
inconsistencies between the system's requirements
regarding women and Jesus' principles. I typed my
thoughts and gave them to Dale for his evaluation,
and later the workers came over to discuss my
notes. Dale agreed with me that long hair wasn't

necessary for salvation. He also volunteered a most interesting statement: "Even though some will say otherwise, long hair for women is NOT "doctrine"! As to why women are to wear their hair up, Dale said, "Some believe women are to wear their long hair pinned up, because the Bible says long hair is to be a covering for the head—NOT the back." I burst out laughing. It was incredible and so stupid that it was funny! He had quoted the Scripture earlier to me about *"wresting with the Scriptures,"* so I exclaimed, "That is a good example of *'wresting with the Scriptures!'"*

I pointed out the 2x2 fellowship had fallen into the ditch; that women are forced to look odd to the point of appearing "dorky"; that the rules prevent some women from obtaining jobs for which they are well qualified; single women who really need good jobs to support others. That requiring this extreme of women is a far cry from *temperance*; that these enforced traditions are making women appear as Pharisees who did *"all their works they do for to be seen of men: they make broad their phylacteries, and enlarge the borders of their garments*, Matt. 23:5. I knew many women who refused to come into this fellowship solely because of these customs. It really concerned me because these customs were keeping some from eternal life—people I LOVED, like my cousin Judy. I knew many others also who had told me this was their reason. I pointed out how these customs were counter-productive to what the workers' hoped to accomplish in their missions. To him, those women who looked "dorky" were those "who hold high God's standards"; and those I said went "to extremes" were those who "bent over backwards to be right." Then he named off some of the few nice looking women in the group we both knew.

I had invited the workers over, prepared to brighten their day with new and additional light with far-reaching ramifications for professing women. I thought I would be providing welcome data they had never before stumbled upon, and with which they would be delighted. *Ha!* They were even resentful! I had believed that the workers valued truth above all else. After careful examination, I believed they would drop any belief which proved to be "untrue" and embrace the new truth. I received replies to my questions like: "This is the way it is" or "This is what we believe this means," with no explanation as to why my points were incorrect. I soon saw it was useless to argue or ask any further questions or to press my points—these traditions were written in stone. I sat there mute with disappointment while the workers droned on and on. Naively expecting my newfound information to be accepted with open arms, my illusions were fast falling down like Humpty Dumpty, and "couldn't be put together again." It was an understatement to say I had seriously misjudged their values and priorities. I was devastated when I learned how far off I was.

I have since come to realize that the workers believe they have a monopoly on Truth—that is, there is no truth other than theirs and they alone have been given True Revelation. Believing they are in a "way" founded by Jesus Himself, they are supremely confident of their mental capacities and judgment. Extremely zealous guards of the system's status quo, they simply block out and ignore counter considerations. Therefore, from their point of view, the only possible right response is to agree with them! Even though they have no Scripture to verify this, many workers believe they stand in God's stead or are his representatives. So they view anyone disagreeing with them as disagreeing with God. Undoubtedly, to disagree with God would be foolish, but to question man? Ps 118:8-9: *"It is better to trust in the Lord than to put confidence in man. It is better to trust in the Lord than to put confidence in princes.*

In the end, Dale summed up my problem. This matter was my personal "thorn in the flesh" which I needed to accept and submit to. I must have looked strange, because when they rose to leave, one of them eyed me carefully, and asked hesitantly, "Are you all right?" I felt completely drained and just wanted to be by myself. I said, "Yes." He asked if I was sure. I was! They let themselves out the door, and I went into depression and probably shock accompanied by a migraine headache! I had gone from being super high to super low in thirty minutes. I was utterly crushed. I went to bed to keep from thinking and to get away from my thoughts and despair.

I had foolishly hoped for so much! It never entered my mind I might meet with this type of response. My hopes weren't just doused—I felt as though freezing cold *ice water* had been thrown all over me. I walked around in a dazed depression for about a week. Dave was away working in OKC. I didn't go to any meetings for the next eight weeks. This was the FIRST "Leave of Absence" I had ever taken from meetings. No one called to check on me. They probably thought we had moved away. I realigned my assumptions with the "real truth" I discovered that day. I tried to reconcile these inconsistencies in my mind. Finally an explanation cropped up in the form of a sneaking suspicion: Perhaps the reason things are the way they are is just because the workers WANT them to be this way, regardless of what the Scripture says. And they have no good reason. I wrote an analogy titled "Would You?" on this subject, showing the double standards.

Dave soon became tired of being an Oklahoma bachelor and accused me of "resisting" this move and dragging my feet. Certainly I was NOT anxious to leave Texas. But finally, when all our possessions were loaded onto a North American moving van, all four of us went to gospel meeting that night. Mainly we went to see everyone for the last time. Dale then realized I had been living in town for the last 8 weeks and hadn't been to a single meeting—positive evidence of a deeper "problem!" No doubt, he was relieved that "problem" was taking herself off to Oklahoma where he wouldn't have to deal with her!

In the very first Sunday meeting we attended, a man said in his testimony that while we weren't subject to terrible persecution like they had in Bible days, still persecution did occur in the lives of God's people at times. For instance, it was hard on the children at Christmas time when everyone else was celebrating and receiving presents, but they didn't, etc. Immediately, I was assaulted by a child on either side elbowing me sharply in the ribs, and whispering in alarm and distress, "Does this mean we can't have CHRISTMAS any more????"

We were well respected in California, Mississippi and Texas. After all, Dave was THE Vietnam hero, and I was the daughter of convention ground owners. Dave's parents, as well as his sister and husband with three professing children, were also living in this same state and had a good reputation. Even so, we found ourselves ignored by many of the friends. Many Okies at gospel meetings didn't speak to us or try to make our acquaintance. Eventually, I decided I would meet THEM. At each gospel meeting I would go up and introduce myself to a few of the friends. Some said, "Oh yes, we know who you are." Although Harry Brownlee disagreed with me, I believe the reason we were not accepted was because my daughter and I didn't meet and follow the Okie standards for women's outer appearance. It griped me because we were compelled to place hypocritical license plates on our cars which read: "Oklahoma is OK!" It was NOT!

Some of our friends from out-of-state visited us. The mother and daughter dress very plain, and wear their hair slicked back in buns on the back of their heads. On the way to gospel meeting, I thought about warning the family not to expect anyone to come up and introduce themselves after meeting, but I kept my mouth shut. Was I ever in for a surprise! I couldn't have been more wrong! The entire meeting practically fell all over themselves shaking their hands and introducing themselves to OUR guests. What was the difference? Their outward appearance!

I had been aware that SOME of the Eastern friends didn't believe the Western friends were saved, and in particular the California friends, but it was news to me that the salvation of the TEXAS friends was suspect. While discussing the upcoming Oklahoma conventions, an Okie told me dryly, "Perry is the true Okie convention; Bradley is infiltrated by TEXANS!" I brightened at that! That convention was the first time I felt "at home" since moving to Oklahoma!

Intentionally, we had never told our children about most of the do's and don'ts; could and could nots; have and have nots; and all the other idiosyncracies we didn't agree with in the fellowship. I didn't want them to feel guilty doing or not doing these things. I believed the way to see that these things were eradicated was to eliminate the guilt. I hoped they would forge ahead and help to break down these ridiculous traditions. We also never taught them that the fellowship was "the only way," because I was afraid they might repeat that to their friends who would tell their parents that we thought they were not saved! I had done that as a child. What we DID tell them was that there were many "ways" or churches, and one must find what was right for them, and we thought this was the right one for us. When they accepted Jesus, we wanted them to feel a dimension was added to their lives by their own free will. I didn't want them to feel as I had growing up: that the truth bore an invisible sign stating "living prohibited"; that everything pleasurable was a sin and forbidden; to feel a great impoverishment, instead of a blossoming and a fulfillment, accompanied by joy. When a child is forced to give up what they never had, they often feel cheated, stripped, violated. I know—I've been there. I was cheated of my childhood. We allowed them to do most anything any good parents would have permitted. They didn't feel different from other children.

Krista has naturally curly, extremely thick hair which tangles easily. She is also extremely tender-headed, unfortunately. Combing her hair every day was no fun for either of us. One day when she was just 3 or 4, she threw her brush down on the floor and shouted, "I HATE my hair!" My mother and I both burst out laughing—our sentiments exactly about our own hair!

We usually spent the weekend with Doris when we visited Longview. I was combing out Krista's long hair, and Doris came bounding up the stairs hearing Krista's screams, sure she had been badly hurt. Only to learn, "Oh, this is normal procedure when I comb Krista's hair." Doris was horrified, and called it child abuse. I laughed then, but I didn't forget what she said. What was abuse to Doris was the norm for many little girls raised with professing parents. But, it WAS abuse! Why was it considered necessary? Because I had hardened myself to her screams, cries, and tears, and grown immune to her pain, she was sure to picture God as being very mean, and wind up with a distorted, bitter view of Him. "If God's loves me, why does He hurt me so?" "**Above all else,** guard your heart, for it is the wellspring of life" (NIV) Prov. 4:23. How was I doing at "guarding her heart"? Pretty lousy. By blindly following this cruel custom beyond reason not based in Scripture, was I "offending a little one"? "But whoso shall offend one of these little ones which believe in me, it were better for him that a millstone were hanged about his neck, and that he were drowned in the depth of the sea." Matt. 18:6. One day my husband had all he could take. He grabbed the brush, hugged Krista to him to comfort her, and yelled, "STOP IT!! THIS IS CHILD ABUSE! It has GOT to CEASE—FOREVER. NO more, EVER." Compassion and reason were victorious over men's traditions that went against God's commandment of LOVE. The next day, Freda cut Krista's thick hair off above her shoulders, layered and thinned. If we err—it will be on the side of compassion.

All my life I had questioned and fretted over things in the fellowship that didn't line up. If this was The Perfect Way, as claimed, why did these discrepancies exist? There is no place for discrepancies in perfection! I knew all the do's and don'ts were what kept many people from becoming a part of God's only true way—people I LOVED. I was extremely concerned because I believed some would be lost eternally and all because of some man-made traditions that weren't even Scriptural! I didn't buy "some things you have to accept in faith." I accepted without question what the Scripture said, but I could NOT accept everything the workers said—especially when they could not support it with Scripture.

Off and on for years, I questioned and searched for the original intent of 1 Cor. 11:1-16, which is the passage used to require women to wear their hair long. I never received any answers that satisfied me when I asked workers questions about this and other prohibitions placed on women. I received many *replies* to my questions that were not *answers* that rang with truth. Since this fellowship claims to follow the New Testament teachings ever so closely, there SHOULD be a Scripture to back up every belief or practice. However, replies to certain questions never gave a Scripture as their reason. Some replies evaded my questions, while others attempted to divert my attention from the subject. Some replies were obviously faulty reasoning, merely experiences or analogies; others were verbal attacks on me personally. Some attempted to make me feel ashamed as if I wasn't worthy to have my question answered, or that I had committed a faux pas by asking. It was implied that my spiritual life was lacking or defective; that I wasn't what I ought to be, therefore, I had no right to ask the question.

To the question, "Why are women not supposed to wear slacks?" the following are examples of some replies that are not answers:

- "If you had the right spirit, you wouldn't even ask that question."
- "The reason you can't see it is because you're unwilling"
- "Some things we just have to accept in faith."

- "When you question, it shows you have a wrong spirit."
- "It's not good to argue/wrest with the Scriptures..."
- "Don't you think the workers know more about this than you do?"

Not one of the replies gave a *Scriptural* reason. When you are looking for truthful Biblical answers, fallacious reasoning just doesn't "get it." I felt I wasn't being leveled with and I was determined to figure out what was wrong with this type answer. So I studied the replies that didn't satisfy or ring with truth until I noticed there were *certain* questions that brought on this type reply, while other questions were answered with explanations of Biblical verses and precedent. Once I told John, a worker, "That answer is just a cop-out." He said, "No, it isn't!" and I said, "Yes, it is." I was at a loss as to how to reply and show what was wrong with his answer. All it would have taken to totally satisfy me was a Bible reference, provided it was interpreted in context. I was frustrated. How was I to get my legitimate, honest, sincere questions answered?

I looked up the subject "arguments" at the library and was referred to "logic." The logic book was an intimidating maze with all sorts of symbols and circles overlapping each other. I couldn't make heads or tails of it—it was way over my head. Soon I found myself enrolled in college taking "Introduction to Logic." Most logic textbooks (also debate, argumentation, rhetoric and speech textbooks) contain a section identifying faulty arguments. This section may be headed: fallacious reasoning, informal fallacies, deceptions in reasoning, obstacles to clear thinking, pseudo arguments, whatever. The word "fallacy" originally meant "deceive," but has come to mean errors in reasoning. More than 100 fallacies have been identified. Some have been recognized for so long, they are called by Latin names! Guess what??! Each of the unsatisfactory replies I had received were perfect examples of notorious fallacies described in my textbook. The workers constantly make use of these well known tricks of persuasion, crooked thinking and stratagems to divert, distort, confuse and persuade people to accept their viewpoint and customs. No wonder many answers didn't ring true or click! They were counterfeit arguments which are so well known they have long been identified by their own individual name!!!

I had found one of my answers, but I still didn't know WHY the workers did this! Why didn't they just give a straight Biblical answer? All I wanted was the plain truth. Why did these ministers of "the truth," resort to fallacious reasoning with certain questions and not with others? Why not just give the Biblical basis, and be done with it? That's all it would take to satisfy me and get me off their back! FINALLY, I knew "why?" *Because there is no Biblical basis.* And if there is no Biblical instruction, that means these beliefs or requirements are merely the preference or tradition of men! I wondered: How many of the beliefs I'd accepted in this fellowship truly had Biblical basis? I began to focus on and study into the beliefs that were peculiar to this fellowship, in writing my children's program.

Even though it was far from what we expected life to be like in Oklahoma, things went smoothly for awhile. Then an unforeseen, persistent hitch surfaced. Bear in mind that we were extremely liberal when compared to most professing parents. Even so, we had refused to let Krista pierce her ears which she had wanted to do since she was in pre-school. Krista began to *earnestly* question us, reason with us, and beg us to let her pierce her ears when she was in the fifth grade. She was the ONLY girl in her class who didn't have pierced ears. I can't begin to tell you how important this was to her. It was all she talked, lived and dreamed about. I showed her the two New Testament Scriptures on jewelry (1 Timothy 2:9: *"In like manner also, that women adorn themselves in modest apparel, with shamefacedness and sobriety; not with broided hair, or gold, or pearls, or costly array;"* and 1 Peter 3:3: *"Whose adorning let it not be that outward adorning of plaiting the hair, and of wearing of gold, or of putting on of apparel."*) Was I really so naive to think she would accept that?

"No problem Mom, I won't wear gold or pearl earrings. Actually, I like the painted, cutesy ones better. How come you and Daddy wear *gold* wedding bands and *gold* watches? Why is it OK to wear pins, but not necklaces, rings and bracelets when the only thing different is the way you fasten them on? How come it's OK to wear hair jewelry? And so on. I had taught her to think critically, to question, to reason...and look what happened! She was using it on ME! Talk about something backfiring...! They say, history repeats itself in the next generation. But I wasn't prepared for my children to press me for *good* reasons for customs I didn't understand or agree with!

I tried some of the worker's stock standard answers that hadn't satisfied me, but got nowhere. "Mom, that's silly! I mean, do you have a GOOD reason why?" I had drilled my children, "Don't believe it unless you see it in the Bible." And here I was. I couldn't see "it," and I was supposed to teach "it" to them—and convincingly too!! HOW?! How could I teach my children certain things were *imperative* to their salvation, when I didn't believe they were the least bit necessary? I felt dishonest. The words stuck in my throat. I couldn't do it. It was intellectual dishonesty. Meanwhile, Krista continued to beg and reason. "Daddy, you have your TV and you're not supposed to. So why can't I get my ears pierced?" To which her Dad replied, "Because you can't take off your ears and put them in the closet."

I could still remember exactly how I felt as a child when I was not allowed to do some things I felt were reasonable and which meant a lot to me. I was years in overcoming the resultant resentment, hardness and bitterness! However, due to my experience, I made a resolution that I would make sure MY children avoided the pitfall of being poisoned with bitterness, as is recommended by Proverbs 4:23: "**Above all else,** *guard your heart, for it is the wellspring of life.*" (NIV) I had no idea this hard-learned priority would conflict seriously with the workers' opinion. I agonized, "If we refuse, how will it affect her?" I identified my experience of not being allowed to wear my hair down or to take gym, with her intense unfulfilled desire to pierce her ears. I felt certain she would bitterly resent not being able to do this, just as I did. I certainly didn't want to be responsible for causing her spirit to become bitter. So I was willing to let her, and stand back and watch what happened! Wasn't that why I kept from them the knowledge of these unwritten rules? So they wouldn't feel guilty violating these customs? Wasn't this what I had secretly wanted my children to do? To challenge the old traditions? Break new ground? Harry Brownlee said if she was his daughter he would tell her she could do what she wanted AFTER she left home—but until then, etc. This is faulty reasoning called the Fallacy of

Time. Piercing her ears at 18 could NEVER make up for the pain of being the "odd man out" NOW.

Why must the children suffer for the parent's faith? Why are they forced to give up what they never had, and aren't willing to give? How could the God who looks on the heart be pleased with something a child was forced to give up? Why must this fellowship present God and Jesus to the children as someone mean who takes away everything enjoyable? A God who robs them of their childhood pleasures? How can we disregard God's commandment to *"guard your heart above all else"* in favor of following hard, uncompassionate traditions of men that have no Biblical basis? It's not only the Pharisees who: *"...reject the commandment of God, that ye may keep your own tradition"* Mark 7:9. Well, Dave finally agreed to let Krista pierce her ears. She was on Cloud Nine and thought he walked on water. I told Harry of our decision and said, "I consider guarding her spirit against bitterness far more important than two tiny holes in her ears." I spoke from experience.

Oklahoma City has a terrific Christian radio station. A couple of my friends were fans of Dr. Dobson, so I began to listen to him. After Dr. Dobson went off the air, Malcolm Smith came on, a preacher with an English accent. I sometimes heard part of his program before I switched stations. Then, I began to listen to all of Malcolm's program every day. Then I began to arrange what I had to do, so that I wouldn't miss Malcolm's program. I was hooked! I learned some things from him every day. He was funny, informative and so knowledgeable. He has an extensive tape library. I ordered some tapes and enjoyed listening to them whenever I pleased about whatever subject I chose. So different from hearing only in meetings about whatever subject someone else wants to say to you!

Malcolm Smith's series on the Pharisees really opened my eyes to see that the fellowship was full of modern-day Pharisees! HORRORS! He also addressed the Galatians trying to merit salvation by their works while giving up their liberty. What were the requirements for women, if they weren't works???? If these things aren't required, I wondered, what DOES God require? What does He want of us? The age-old question: "What must I do to be saved?" What is essential? And what is commendable?

I decided to make a list of every single one of Jesus' commands in the gospels. To my surprise, I found Jesus made very few direct commands. Instead, Jesus usually said *"**IF** ye will be my disciple, then do thus and so..."* Like a shepherd, He gently leads and never drives or forces. He prefers people choose to do things for him out of love, instead of from duty, force or fear. It was a real eye-opener to me to discover that THE primary principle both the Old and New Testaments were based upon was the command to love God, and your brother as yourself. That meant this command was the most important concept in the whole Bible regarding our conduct. This was a new slant to me. From sitting in meetings all my life, I had assumed that self-denial, suffering and submission were the most important issues.

Avidly, I studied the Scripture, jumping from one subject to another, searching for understanding to something I couldn't identify. I knew I would recognize the answer when I saw it, but I couldn't frame what I was looking for in words. I was driven, seeking something vague, the answer to an unknown question. Eventually I realized my question was: *"What is the doctrine of this fellowship?"*

A stranger questioned my mother about her beliefs, and asked her if she believed in the Godhead. She didn't know what the "Godhead" was, and neither did I. He substituted the term "trinity."

"Oh, yes," she said, "We believe in the trinity." Later she wondered to me, "Or do we? I don't think I know what we believe about the trinity!" (Or anything else for that matter it seemed.) We looked up the definition of the trinity and the Godhead in the book, *All the Doctrines of the Bible.* We were astounded to learn that some believe God is composed of three entities: God the Father (which we had always believed); but also in God the Son and God the Spirit. Did that mean they thought JESUS was GOD??? It was inconceivable! Incredible!! Some find it hard to believe that this concept was utterly foreign to us. We had never, ever heard of it previously and had no idea *anyone* believed this anywhere. We were also totally ignorant of how many Christians believe this!

Some North Dakota friends told me their local newspaper carried an advertisement about a book about the fellowship! I was dying to read the book. However, I didn't know the name of it, and I didn't know how to get a copy of it. Many others have had this same experience. Some said it was a dangerous book; others burned copies given to them; still others said reading it only increased their faith. I had no idea what it was about. In 1990, we received a flyer advertising *The Impartial Reporter* articles which was mailed to many Oklahoma friends by Threshing Floor Ministries of P.O. Box 9899, Spokane, WA 99209. Through them, I FINALLY located the book: *The Secret Sect.* NEVER, EVER IN A MILLION YEARS would I have guessed what it actually contained. I had never in my life doubted that "the truth" was God's only true way, and the literal continuation of the apostles' ministry. Now I found out the truth: that William Irvine started this fellowship at the turn of THIS century. While it claimed to be 1900 years old, in truth, it was less than 100 YEARS OLD!!

We had been deliberately tricked! Betrayed! The agony of deceit is crushing and extremely painful. I felt as if a rug had been pulled out from under me. I felt robbed, ripped off, swindled, gypped, and cheated. We were intentionally deceived by those we trusted above all others—and furthermore, the practice continues today! The sole reason many of the friends chose this faith over other churches was because they believed it was the original apostolic church—Jesus' only true way which had continued in a direct line from the apostles through workers up to this very day! We were told and believed it was the only genuine church in existence. And that was a lie.

One thing is certain—NOW I can truly empathize with a child discovering there is no Santa Claus. The workers caution parents NOT to teach their children the false tales about Santa Claus. Then they go and teach the friends false stories about how this fellowship began. The child is hurt and devastated, likewise the friends. Discovering the fellowship is not of apostolic succession, and not even 100 years old, damages their trust in their parent or the worker. Why did they lie? The answer? Regret? Apology? NOT! Insult is added to injury! More times than not, the true story of the origins is denied. Some give insipid, ridiculous reasons so transparent a baby could see through them in an attempt to placate, mollify and soothe the outraged friends. It's a wonder some haven't been tarred and feathered or lynched for the countless lives they've wrecked and ruined! A Canadian lady raised in this fellowship suffered unbelievable misery because of this belief system. She wrote her life story and said that it was a good thing William Irvine was dead, because if he hadn't been, she personally would have gone to Jerusalem and killed him. Many can identify with her feelings.

I could no longer trust anyone, but God and the Scriptures to lead me—no matter how Godly a person might seem. No man is infallible. No man is a mediator between God and me. What if there were other things that were misrepresented or omitted? I began to check out EVERY THING I'd been taught in this fellowship—to see for myself if and where it was supported by the Bible. I discovered unexpected joy in proving these things; in exploring all my inherited, hand-me-down, unexamined beliefs and making them my own full personal beliefs; in knowing the Scriptural basis for all my beliefs. I proved: *"If ye KNOW these things, happy are ye if ye do them."* John 4:42; 1 John 2:26-27; 1 Timothy 4:7, Matthew 22:29.

Many other questions began crowding into my mind. What difference does it make that the fellowship was founded by a man, and not God? It's still "the closest way" isn't it? A neighbor and I were discussing the reasons we had chosen our respective churches. I was astonished when she stole my line! She said they chose to become a part of the Church of Christ because IT was "the closest way to the church of the New Testament days"! I pointed out they had a church building, while the New Testament Church met in homes. She didn't see WHERE the church gathered had anything to do with following closely! It seems "closest way" means different things to different folks.

On the other hand, reading *The Secret Sect* did clear up many mysteries for me. FINALLY, things clicked. The discrepancies and things that didn't line up, add up, match up or fit, existed because a MAN started this way, not GOD. Things were the way they were because a man started this fellowship. That's why there was no Scripture to support so many practices. They were just his interpretations, preferences and opinions! I always believed God could create a "perfect way," and that He had the power to keep it perfect. Yet the 2x2 belief system was riddled with imperfections and claimed to be God's only perfect way! When I learned it began with a man—well, it all made perfectly good sense. That's why everything didn't line up—because it is the imperfect creation of a man!

Though the facts in *The Secret Sect*, sounded very well documented, I am the type who has to see things with my own eyes, preferably in writing. I had in mind making a trip to Ireland some day to verify the facts. Then some of the friends shocked me with the information that Garrett Hughes had mentioned the beginnings at some of the North Dakota conventions from the platform! Garrett was one of the top Eastern USA Overseers! If anyone knew, he did, and he was telling it! No need to go to Ireland now! I also heard about an overseas worker, Joshua Gamble, who astonished everyone when he discussed the beginnings in a California convention. Some other ex-workers acknowledged that they became aware of the beginnings while they were in the work. After all this and more confirmation from additional sources, my faith in this fellowship had well-nigh slipped.

Fortunately, I discovered there was a whole network of friendly folks out there just full of encouragement. And finally, I discovered someone

who thought like I did: David Stone, author of the
book *The Church Without a Name*. Reading this
book was like reading my own thoughts in print!
What a relief! My "radical" viewpoints were held
by someone else! I give most of the credit to that
author for showing and convincing me that the
2x2's were not "the closest way." For pointing out
the 2x2 ministers PLUS church in home, PLUS following their man-made rules does not equal the
closest way. The workers have placed themselves
between God and man as mediators, when the Bible says there is no mediator between God and
man except Christ. Hats off to David Stone for driving these points home in a superior manner. I
believe I would have eventually figured these
things out for myself, but that book saved me
many, many years of frustration, and perhaps a
nervous breakdown!

We learned Harry Brownlee was to be over
Oklahoma. He stated in the first gospel meeting
that he was anxious to get to know each family,
and would be going down the friends list alphabeti-
cally, and spending 2-3 nights or more with each. I
planned to ask him several questions. We were no
longer keeping our discontent to ourselves, and
both our parents were getting concerned about our
spiritual state. Unknown to us, both our parents
contacted Harry and asked him to talk to us. Peri-
odically, I checked to see what letter of the
alphabet Harry was visiting. I found he wasn't stick-
ing to alphabetical order. Some friends he went to
quite frequently, while others he had never visited.
Finally though, they called and asked to come for
our promised visit. Would it be okay if they arrived
for lunch? Certainly. I studied and crammed so
much Dave said I was "prophesying." The workers
asked about Dave and seemed surprised to learn he

was at work. Harry said he knew we had some questions, and he knew we had read *The Secret Sect*. However, I didn't ask any questions during lunch because I wanted Dave to be present. After all, we had all evening (I thought). Well, about 3:00 Harry looks at his watch and jumps up exclaiming that they better run or they will be late, etc.

I was shocked: "Where are you going? Aren't you going to spend the night?" Harry apologized profusely for the misunderstanding, but no, they had other plans and they must leave immediately. I was dumbfounded. Didn't the true Shepherd leave the 99 to bring one back? More cracks became obvious in this "perfect" system. Harry went away to special meetings, to convention rounds, and overseas somewhere before returning to Oklahoma. Finally, I decided to write him and ask my questions, so he could come and be prepared to answer them. That letter has made the rounds, and is known as my "Dear Harry letter." I requested a detailed Bible Study, verse by verse, of 1 Corinthians 11:1-16. Finally, Harry and his companion arrived for an overnight visit. Harry never mentioned the study I requested, so I brought up the requirements for women. Further details of this visit are written in "Harry's Reply," which follows.

I asked Harry how he could reconcile preaching that "the truth" is the only right way to Heaven when it was founded by William Irvine around the turn of the century? He went into the story about how his family heard the gospel and wound up with something to the effect: "As to whether or not there were others before William Irvine, I don't know, because I have never looked into it. I am satisfied that this way is the true way of Jesus, and I don't see any sense in wasting time checking into it further." In the next breath, he assured us he was not claiming it was of apostolic succession. Talk about inconsistency!

I said, "Harry, you said in gospel meeting that there are only differences in tradition—not in doctrine. Tell me, is long hair for women doctrine?" He immediately said, "Yes." I replied, "Your former companion, Dale Spencer, stated to me that long hair for women was definitely NOT doctrine." Obviously Harry's claim was false—the workers didn't even agree on what doctrine consisted of! He ignored the inconsistency, and began to relate some amusing incidents about Dale.

I mentioned how the spirit isn't allowed to guide the friends in the 2x2 way. "Quench not the Spirit." I told him, "Believing as I do that others outside are saved, if I went to meeting dressed like I believe a professing woman should be able to do, you would ask me not to take part." He asked me how I thought I should be able to dress. I said, "No different from any other respectable woman in the world around us. I think a professing woman should be able to have short hair, wear jewelry and make-up." Harry said, "Cherie, you're wrong. I'd be *very disappointed* if you came to meeting like that, but if you had bread, I would NOT take away your part. If there is a gulf made between us, it will not be because I have pushed you away, Cherie, but because you have chosen to do so." I was quite surprised at his reply.

I invited two couples from our Sunday meeting over for dinner who had been friendly to us. I explained in detail why I wasn't coming to meeting anymore. Soon after, some professing Texas friends came to visit us and we went to Harry's gospel meeting that afternoon. I hadn't been to a meeting in three months. I was a captive audience and

Harry took advantage of it. He preached straight at me, addressing things he could only have learned from the two couples I invited for dinner for I hadn't even mentioned them to him. After meeting, our Texas friend jokingly said "Don't you need some water to cool those 'coals of fire' he heaped on your head?" I wasn't the only one who had noticed. Afterwards, Harry *thanked me* for coming to the meeting. I resolved that I would NEVER be a captive audience again.

I wrote both our folks letters explaining my decision. It was the first time either of our parents had ever heard any details about the 2x2 founder, William Irvine. My last Sunday meeting was Memorial Day weekend, 1990. Dave left a few months later. Dave's parents were upset; mine became progressively more understanding.

In 1990, both Galen and our family went to Mississippi for the Christmas Holidays. The folks had decided the convention grounds was just too much for them to take care of. Daddy was retired, and he didn't even have time to go fishing for taking care of the place. They were thinking of putting the place up for sale and moving completely off of it, if we all agreed. We did. They contacted William Lewis. My folks endured endless frustration, bewilderment and confusion due to workers being involved with the sale. Three workers were giving directions, approval, disapproval, orders and they didn't get together on their stories or instructions. It was unbelievable and somewhat traumatic. My folks said if they had it to do all over again, they wouldn't involve the workers at all. They would put their place on the open market. However, a year later, the sale was finally completed to some local friends.

To the surprise of many, my folks moved clear out of state to a suburb of Oklahoma City twenty miles from us. Within the year, my brother, also moved to OKC and bought a home. Not one of us ever dreamed that all the immediate Berry family would be living within thirty minutes of each other! Fancy that—in Oklahoma, of all places! Neither my mother or Galen returned to meetings after they moved to OKC.

Six months after I left, I sent a 6-page letter to my closest friends and relatives letting them know why I was not attending meetings. I received some nice and some nasty replies. Some who were already aware of the history and William Irvine wrote me about their learning experiences. To some, the idea that this fellowship had a founder was simply inconceivable. Others provided their viewpoints, arguments and expressions of regret, kindness, understanding, compassion, scorn, reproof, pity, judgment and warning. To show I was not nearly as gullible as some seemed to think and to show how very thoroughly I had investigated this matter before making my decision, I gathered up and sent them evidence proving William Irvine originated this fellowship around the turn of this century. This evolved into what is known as my 52-page letter (plus 22 attachments), which I sent out a year later.

What do I believe now? I can honestly say my faith in God is stronger than ever. However, I have utterly lost all faith in the workers and in the 2x2 belief system. I still profess to be a child of God. I believe the Bible is God's Word, and it is my guide for conduct and living. I believe Jesus Christ is the Way to heaven, through his sinless life and His sacrifice on the cross. I believe that God is interested in a relationship—not a religion. That salvation is by grace through faith and trust in Jesus Christ.

That belief involves our minds, emotions, and a commitment to a personal relationship with Him. That His church is a common fellowship composed of everyone who does that.

Irvine's experiment to "*restore*" God's true way to earth wasn't an original, unique or novel approach. It was the same ideal embraced by most of the leaders of the early 19th century: to restore the church to its original state; to restore the essential marks of the primitive New Testament church; to return to the faith and practices of the Apostolic Age; and to return to the simple teaching of the Bible alone for the Christians' guide and rule. They abandoned all man-made creeds, traditions, confessions, teachings and doctrines, and they took no name for their assembly. They called themselves "Christians" only; however, unlike Irvine's movement, they did not believe they were the only Christians.

Choosing a new church home was a family decision. We now regularly attend a Christian Church, a conservative group with many of the same principles as the 2x2 fellowship. The preacher openly refers to their founders, Alexander and Thomas Campbell. The preacher's style of preaching is usually expository. The kids are very content in the youth program, and have made many Christian friends. They both enjoy going on the trips and to church camp with the youth group. In the same service both children, at the ages of 13 and 15, made their choice to accept Jesus as their Lord and Savior and were baptized within 30 minutes, by immersion. There was no waiting; no conditions; no proving themselves; no promises required that they would or would not do thus and so! Both realize by their choice they entered a permanent *relationship* (not a religion) which will remain constant, regard-

less of what church or group of people, if any, they
choose to assemble with.

My motives are often questioned, so briefly I'll
state them. To do all I can to help others have a
closer walk with God. To do unto others what I
wish had been done for me. To do everything I possibly can to make the origin and history of this
fellowship common knowledge to every person connected with this fellowship, for they have a perfect
right to know all about it. I must speak the truth,
when keeping silent protects a lie and aids deceit.
If I don't, then I have joined the conspiracy.

May the Word of God be your guiding rule, and
the glory of God your goal. In essentials, may there
be unity; in non-essentials liberty; in all things,
charity.

June 1993

Address:
Cherie (Berry) Kropp
11117 Woodbridge Rd.
Oklahoma City, OK 73162

Letter to Harry Brownlee dated June 8, 1990

Dear Harry:
Your two visits have left us somewhat mystified,
and I thought perhaps it would be better to give
you an idea of the things we are concerned about.
You see, what you have said on your visits has not
addressed the things that concern us at all. You
seem to have a misconception of what our "problems" are.

Yes, we have both read *The Secret Sect* and *The
Church Without a Name* by David Stone. The scan-

dals do not bother us. I never expected perfection of the workers or friends, so their failures do not upset me unnecessarily. As I stated to you earlier, having grown up on a convention grounds, I never thought of workers as anything but human beings. The other side of that is, however, that I do not believe that every word that proceeds from a worker's mouth is a divine revelation of God. I have seen too much that came from them in way of advice, instruction or correction that was simply their own human opinion, or feelings.

What *does* bother us concerning the books is the fact that a man started this way, and decided at one point to say it was God's only true way to salvation, and began to perpetuate that belief. We know Jesus is the Way. We know in Jer 31:33-34, the new covenant promised that the law would be written in the hearts, and not be a "way" as the old law was. Everyone who wanted to know about it, and asked, would receive it in their hearts through belief. Then enter William Irvine who narrowed Jesus' Way down so that one had to be *in the way to the way*, before they could hope for salvation, even though it plainly says there is no mediator between God and man after Jesus' resurrection. The deception that was allowed to be made, inferred or preached also makes for resentment. We understand Garrett Hughes is confirming from the platform that the way was founded by a man at the turn of the century, at several conventions. But we've not heard of any others coming out with it openly.

We have heard various theories attempting to prove the Truth is Jesus' only true way, but have not found any that satisfies. They seem to be inventions or assumptions to explain an earlier failed assumption (that the truth is the only true way of God). Instead of concluding that this belief may be incorrect, one revises his assumptions so that he can still maintain that they are true—and that the original set of assumptions were at fault (that truth started with apostles and has continued throughout history, being the Truth as we know it today). Revising original assumptions is OK, and sometimes necessary—up to a point. A revision is certainly called for when one discovers that a basic foundation has a great fault in it; and that's just what we are trying to do. However, if you have to use theories with no scriptural basis to revise your original beliefs, in order to discredit evidence that would prove the assumption false (that this is God's only true way), it is only reasonable to suspect that one is simply refusing to acknowledge the contrary evidence, in order to believe what he wants to believe. Here is a natural example that I think parallels these theories:

A lie-detector expert announced the theory that plants react to the thoughts of human beings in their vicinity. She claimed that these reactions can be registered on a device similar to a lie-detector and attached to the plants. She also claimed that she had conducted many tests that confirmed this theory. However, when the tests were repeated for a well-known plant physiologist, no such responses were observed. The lie-detector expert explained that nothing registered because the plants had "fainted," fearing that the plant physiologist might harm them. She pointed out that the plant physiologist was known to dissect and incinerate plants when doing experimental work.

It is a rescue attempt for the lie detector expert to be able to keep her original theory—even though it was proven false. You can see how the threatened lie-detector expert is valiantly holding onto her theory—even though it has been proven false.

Are we not doing the same thing—in continuing to maintain that this is God's only true way—when a man, not God, declared it to be so?

The best theory seems to us to be that God raised up a Prophet in William Irvine. But, consider the end of that man. His prophecies did not come to pass. He did not pass the test of a true prophet stated in Deut 18:22. How can one reconcile that? Did any of the other prophets go crazy in the end?

They are just that—theories. To our way of thinking, it is a way (started by a man) among other ways (also started by men) on earth. Jesus plainly states the way one will know his people is by Love. He does not mention how one will know his "Way," but his people (disciples).

You continue to preach about Jesus' true way, as if there is only one way, while saying in the next breath that people ask you if you think this is the only way, and you tell them that you cannot say "yes" to that, because Jesus is the Way. What you want is for the listener to come to the belief that it *IS* the true and *ONLY* way, without your saying so. No wonder the man (you mentioned once) said he couldn't figure out what the message was when he sat in gospel meetings...that other churches laid it on the line. You must have accepted some theory you believe correct in order to continue preaching this.

From the things you have said the two times you have been at our home, it would seem you are attempting to persuade us that because the ministry "works," that it is the true way, (money is provided; that you were gone to the Layman's when the man threatened to kill you that night, etc.) Harry, all we want are scriptures for proof. Experiences do not prove anything to us. I have drilled into my children, "Don't believe anything people tell you about God, Bible, etc., unless you can find it in the Bible. If you are to believe it, it can be found in the Bible." We, of course, follow the same rule. This is why I am writing you mainly—so when you come to spend a few days, that you will have scriptures you can show us to prove your points, not experiences, or opinions. Because something "works" is not necessarily proof—so do the other denominations, or they would not still exist today; so do satanic cults "work." The Bible is our point of reference, and we would like to discuss it on these terms next time.

You will probably ask, "Well, do you know of something better?" No, we do not presently. But all we do know about other denominations has been gleaned solely from the workers' and other friends' very slanted opinions. I find I can no longer depend on others' opinions concerning salvation, but must see for myself. So the workers go out 2x2 like Jesus sent his disciples—he never told them to continue doing that for all times; so we meet in the home like they did in Paul's day—that was not a commandment either. It works, and works well, I'll grant. But I cannot see that it was made a necessity for salvation, or that it makes others who meet in buildings ineligible for salvation. There were no commandments on these issues.

We have no intention of putting you on the spot with our questions—a simple "I do not know" is a respectable answer to us, or a promise to look into a question further. We appreciate it that you do not consider "questioning" wrong; and that you will not stoop to an appeal to shame like, "if you had the right spirit, you would not even ask questions like that," as some have. We *must* come to terms with our questions concerning our faith, and we will with or without your help. We are sure you have insight that we have not considered, and that would be helpful.

If we have seemed reticent about asking questions, it is because you simply do not give us the opportunity, and we do not like to butt in. Simply say, "Now, how can I help you?" or "What is it that is bothering you?" Find out from us *directly* what those "problems" are—don't assume you know everything, and come in with the talk that leaves us bewildered, and wondering what on earth someone else said were our "problems"!

Scorning other denominations, their beliefs (washing each others' feet, for example), and the people who frequent them and who are doing the best they know how to do, does not prove anything to us—in fact, scorn turns us off. Constantly I caution my children against scorning. I feel it is a form of judgment and pride. It's putting another down so that one can elevate oneself. Is not the labeling of another church "false" a form of self-righteous judgment, especially under the circumstances of how the truth originated?

It also bothers us because we know we are not to judge others (and truly no man can—only his own master can), but that when one is part of a way that believes it is the only true way, *automatically*, one is judging those who are not part of that way. This is contrary to Jesus' teachings, it seems to us.

You mentioned you had not come to use authority and tell us what to do or not do; and that you felt one was to follow one's own convictions. However, I do not think you realize just how far apart our thoughts are on women's appearance. If I were to follow my convictions and continue to take part in meeting, it would cause problems, and I am not a trouble-maker. My convictions, in a nutshell, are that neither Jesus nor Paul ever intended for the women in the Truth to be any different *whatsoever* in appearance from any other *respectable* woman in the world (just like the men in the Truth do not look any different from other respectable men). Being the kind of person I am, naturally, I have scripture, not opinion or experiences, to back up my convictions. So, even though you gave me permission to follow my convictions on my appearance, I would rather discuss them with you first, because we seem to be poles apart.

You seem to be so aware, as some are not, of the need for the workers to dress nicely, use good grammar, etc., or, to appear respectable by men's standards, so as not to turn off listeners (cut off their ears?). But you appear ONE-sided in your viewpoint. It only includes the men. Your statement that the women are just lazy is why they do not look better, just made me want to cry. You just do not understand at all. You resent the wind in Okla. because it "messes up your hair"—you are saying it is trouble for you to comb your little bit of short hair—and calling women lazy in the same breath who have to somehow deal every day with hair they've let grow as long as it will grow, because they have been told that is what God wants. I'm sorry if that sounds rude. I do wish men could have to put up with long hair for awhile, so they could understand. I've noticed that, when wives become unable, because of health reasons, to care for their hair, that their husbands usually encourage and have them cut it off, rather than fool with it themselves. When the shoe is on the other foot, they can't stand the trouble it requires.

Previously, you stated in meeting that there exists "no inconsistency in doctrine and a whale of a lot of inconsistency in opinions." Yet, since Dale

Spencer disagrees with you that long hair is NOT doctrine, we DO have an inconsistency in the Truth in what is even considered to be doctrine! I realize Jesus never INTENDED there to be any doctrinal inconsistencies. Since there exists a "whale of a lot of inconsistency" in belief concerning hair (whether to trim or let grow to full natural length, whether or not to color, roll, perm, cut partially, wear up or down, etc.), it would seem this would have to be regarded as a matter of opinion—if your statement is true. This would seem to be borne out further in I Corinthians 11:1 and 16, where Paul discusses various "traditions" (Greek for ordinances) and "customs." However, I realize I rather put you on the spot, and did not give you time to reflect when I asked you whether you considered long hair doctrine or opinion.

If we take I Corinthians 11:1-16 literally to mean "long hair" for women, and not as addressing the problem of the wives' lack of subjection to their husbands (a problem of their spirit), do we not miss the whole point and intent of the passage? There is no other scripture that confirms this is a teaching that is to be taught literally and universally. There is no teaching of Jesus that recommends it be taken literally. There IS back-up teaching of Jesus concerning the attitude of husbands and wives. Paul even states it is not the custom of the other churches—yet the workers give this passage the interpretation of it being binding on all women today in the way. If it was so wouldn't Jesus have taught this necessity?

Have you ever noticed that the one English word "covering" found in I Corinthians 11:1-16 is used to translate THREE different Greek words, *each of which have an entirely different meaning each time they are used in this passage*—yet all three meanings were translated as the same word in the King James Version? And that "shorn" is the past participle of "shear" in Greek—and does not mean "to cut," but to shear to the scalp. The Greek language only has one word for wives and women—not two separate words, as the English language does (likewise for men/husbands). The translators of the KJV decided by context where to use the word "women" and "wives." This entire passage could possibly be referring to only husbands and wives. It certainly limits the necessity of head coverings to a certain time—while praying or prophesying, and was not an ultimatum for all time.

The words "Doth not even" in verse 14 is a translation of ONE Greek word *"oude,"* which means "neither, nor, not even," which means that verse could just have accurately been translated, "NEITHER does nature teach you..." or "Even nature DOES NOT teach you...," which is the exact opposite of what we take it to mean. The actual translation of "FOR her hair is given her FOR a covering" in verse 15 is "BECAUSE her hair is given her INSTEAD of a covering," in which case, hair and covering are definitely two DIFFERENT items, and not one and the same as we presently interpret.

This passage surely contains more than meets the eye, and is one of the most hard to understand in the New Testament. There is no way to know for sure what the reference to angels meant in verse 10. Yet, with all its complexities, the workers stick to an adamant translation of this passage that women are to have long hair, and some even that it should not EVER be cut. Truth can bear scrutiny— yet the more we scrutinize this text, the more confused we get. The portion of this letter related to I Corinthians 11:1-16 only covers a fraction of

this subject. I have much more research I could review with you.

The record for the longest hair is held by a man
in the *Guinness Book of World Records,* proving
man's hair will grow quite naturally as long or
longer than a woman's. "Nature" doesn't prove
what is shameful—shame is relevant to one's culture and tradition.

Has God ever been interested in literal things
only? Was he only interested in the Law being performed to the letter? Of course not. He has always
been interested in the heart condition of people.
Yet women everywhere wear this "symbol" (long
hair) and even though following worker's instructions, most have not the faintest idea what it all
stands for, and have no heartfelt feeling when they
fix it or care for it. What are we supposed to remember each time we care for it—that we are
subject to our husbands? Of what value is a symbol
if it has no meaning for the wearer? We have an
idea what we are to be thinking about when the
emblems (symbols) are passed around, and what
baptism is symbolic of. But no one, least of all the
women who wear it, know the significance of the
symbol they wear. Of what value is a symbol that
no one recognizes? Has not the wedding ring in our
culture taken the place of the long hair of the
Corinthian culture? (IF it was meant to be recognized as a token of subjection to one's husband?)

We cannot overlook the importance of rightly in-
terpreting figures of speech, and mannerisms of
expressions either. If someone were to read some of
our printed material two thousand years from now,
they might be throwing salt into their mouth every
so often, as we sometimes use the phrase "Take
that with a grain of salt." Without taking these figures of speech into consideration, the difference

between the almost right meaning, and the right meaning could be as far apart as the lightning bug and lightning!

Paul said in I Peter 3:3: "Whose adorning let it not be that outward adorning of plaiting of the hair, and of wearing of gold or of putting on of apparel, But let it be the hidden man of the heart..."

I believe this is an example of a case where the workers have maximized what Paul intended to minimize, through a lack of understanding of a common Hebrew idiom. An "idiom" is a manner of speaking distinctive of a certain people or language. In this case, the idiom was a manner of speaking which would minimize a first clause in order to emphasize a second clause.

We must take into account the idioms of Oriental speech. . . the "not" means, as often elsewhere in Scripture, "not only. . . but also" or, "not so much. . . as." An example of this is found in Luke 14:12 and I Timothy 2:9.

Today, in order to express the thought contained in this type of idiom, we would place the word "only" in the first clause, and "also" or "rather" in the second clause, as: "Let not a woman's adorning be (only) that of outward things—such as fixing her hair, wearing of gold or pearls, or apparel—but (also/rather) let it be the inward adorning of a meek and quiet spirit." In the use of this idiom, the emphasis is on the second clause, BUT IT DOES NOT FORBID THE FIRST CLAUSE. It is in addition to it. The emphasis is on the inward adorning, but the outward adorning is not eliminated.

The same type idiom was used by John when he said: "Let us not love in word, neither in tongue; but in deed" I John 3:18. The context speaks about a brother in need. If we have this world's goods and do not help him, we do not really have love.

We can tell him we love him—we can love in word—but this is not enough. Thus the instructions: "Let us not love in word (only), but (also/rather) in deed" If we take I Peter 3:3 and I Tim 2:9 to mean we are NOT to wear jewelry, do we not also have to not wear apparel, and to take John's meaning to be that we are not to tell our brother we love him? Another example is John 4:21-23. Jesus said that the hour was coming, and then was, that true worshippers would not worship at Jerusalem or in Samaria—that God must be worshipped in spirit and in truth. But after this men DID worship God at Jerusalem (Luke 24:52, 53; Acts 2; etc.) Recognizing the idiom, we realize that people would not worship at Jerusalem (only), but (rather) in spirit and in truth—regardless of location. We have to take this literally to mean no true believer can ever possibly worship in the physical city of Jerusalem, to be consistent with our interpretation of I Tim 2:9 and I Peter 3:3.

In Luke 14:12-14, we read: "When thou makest a dinner..call not thy friends, nor thy brethren...but call the poor, the maimed, the lame, the blind..." The idiom makes the first part into a strong negative in order to emphasize the second part. The meaning is "Call not (only) your friends, but (also) the poor, blind, etc." If this was simply a command not to call friends to supper, why did Jesus accept invitations to eat with his friends? And why do we today invite our friends and relatives to eat with us?

If these two verses (I Tim 2:9 and I Peter 3:3) are NOT expressing an idiom, but are actually forbidding the use of jewelry—then they are contrary to all the rest of the Bible on this subject. "For after this manner in the old time the holy women...adorned themselves..." I Peter 3:5-6. There is no denying that women in the old days wore jewelry. See Gen 24:22, 47, 53; Ex 35:22; Numbers 31:50; Is 3:21; Ex 32:2-3; Is 3:16-23; Song of Solomon 1:10; Prov 25:12; Jer 2:32; Is 61:10;. There are many other references to men wearing jewelry.

In Ezekiel 16:11, 12, the Lord took a cast away newborn baby and cared for her. As a woman he clothed her with ornaments...bracelets...chain...jewelry...earrings. If these things were sinful, would the Lord have given them, even in this parallel of the origin and history of Jerusalem? If these things were sinful, how could they possibly make the point that was intended in this passage—that of jewelry symbolizing his blessings upon Jerusalem? If jewelry was a sinful thing, why would a pure and undefiled bride be described as adorning herself with jewels? A bad thing does not symbolize a good thing. The holy city is described as having gates of pearl in Rev. 21:21. If pearls were unholy, what place could they have in describing the holy city?

If we interpret I Timothy 2:9 to mean that any wearing of pearls is wrong, we have a problem with the usual interpretation found in Matthew 7:6 where we are told not to cast your pearls before swine. Pearls here would represent things which are good, in contrast to swine—representing those who are unholy, unclean, evil. If wearing pearls was a sin in the sight of God, there would be no contrast or point in this saying of Jesus.

So far as scripture tells us, Jesus said nothing against wearing jewelry, gold or pearls. If we take this passage literally and as applying from then until now—what principles of Christ are we using to enforce it? Why do we not examine and accept the exceptions to this statement, as we do for "women shall not teach"? To be consistent, do we not also have to literally always require men to lift up holy hands when praying, as it instructs in the previous verse in I Timothy 2:8? If we're going to take these things literally, to be consistent, do we not have to take everything literally? Just like Paul told the Galatians—if you are going to follow the Law—you must follow the WHOLE Law."

What was the REAL intent of the passages? Could he not have said it this way: Gold and pearls and fine hairdos are not valuable spiritually as adornment; make sure you are adorned spiritually. Or like I Timothy 4:7-8 Adorn yourself with godliness, for gold, pearls and fine hairdos profiteth little.

You mentioned the black stocking issue...sad we didn't learn from that unfortunate experience. We have two more "black stocking issues" in our midst: that of insisting women not wear cosmetics or slacks. At one time these things may have been worn by undesirable types of ladies—but that is no longer the case. I won't elaborate on these things now, except to say there isn't a scrap of New Testament scripture to enforce these "absolute" unwritten rules.

You stated you thought it funny that the authors of the books could think that they could thwart God's true way, or something close to that statement. Harry, they want to HELP the truth! Their entire purpose for writing the books was to make others see that the truth is in need of the same thing the Pharisees needed when John the Baptist came: "Make his paths straight!" Their sole desire is for the truth to align itself with Jesus' teachings, so the people will depend on Jesus' blood and resurrection for salvation, and not their own works.

Harry, I know for a fact that there are more books about the truth being printed and written right now, which will be released in the not too distant future. They all have the same intent: to expose what is in the truth that is not in line with Jesus' teachings. Criticism can be taken two different ways—one as help, and the other offense. Can not the workers take the truth in these books and use it for constructive changes in the truth that are much needed? "Make his way straight"?

We realize you preach the gospel somewhat differently from many—that you acknowledge it is only the blood of Christ that saves one—not works; but, unless there has been a recent change, many others do not teach that, and are opposed to that teaching. There were murmurs against your preaching in that vein at Texarkana when you were last there for conv. Perhaps this is your way of doing what *you* can to align the truth with Jesus' teachings. But other things need to be addressed. It would be so much better if they were addressed BEFORE the friends get a hold of them. You know, most of us have no idea what our doctrine is. Isn't that shocking? But nevertheless, true. If we were asked, as I have been, we would be totally at a loss. I know, because I was, and I have asked others, and found this to be the absolute truth. This would be an excellent theme for a series of gospel meetings. But we have a problem in that what is doctrine differs from state to state, worker to worker, etc.

The things that bothered me a lot were the discrepancies I found in "the perfect way," "the way is the same," "the unity" and the "love among us." If the way was perfect, it would not have all these things that didn't line up; it was supposed to be the same from Jesus' day, and yet it is different from state to state, worker to worker, friend to friend; there isn't unity of doctrine, but differences, and not always unity among friends either; and the love that was to characterize his disciples was sometimes nonexistent among the friends. It all made sense, though, when I found this was a way started by a man—not God. You see, we expect so much more if this was truly God's way—I truly believe he could create a Perfect way, and thought that this was his way—but could not understand for the life of me how all these things could be imperfect about it, and it still be his perfect true only way! *The Secret Sect* answered that question that has bothered me since I was 13 years old.

I know many of these thoughts are quite foreign to you, and that you will probably think we are WAY off track. Don't blame the books—the books were not really the start of our problem. The problem stemmed from the differences we could see in what the truth was purported to be versus what it actually was. Sounds like the Pharisees, doesn't it? Perhaps we are the modern-day Pharisees. Perhaps we need a letter like Paul wrote the Galatians— maybe we've fallen into the same trap, of adding works to grace.

I am simply no longer willing to have men's will and traditions forced upon me, without explanation. I, along with many others, would just like to be able to live my life as my convictions guide me. Why does it have to be lived within the framework of rules, although not actually specified, which are as hardfast as though engraved in stone tablets?

The Sabbath existed for men, not men for the Sabbath, Jesus said. Should not also the way exist for men, not men for the way? Is the Way going to be saved, or the people in it? Is the way supporting believers, or believers supporting the way? The Way is not going to heaven—only the relationship between a believer and Christ will count in the end. The spirit is all that will return.

Communism, we learned as a child, was when the people existed for the government; democracy, when the government exists for the people. This truth is run like a dictatorship...the people have no say; they must obey, or be put out. Yet the New Covenant said the spirit would be in every man's heart and would guide him. In a dictatorship like is found in the truth there is no trusting the spirit—no room for the spirit to guide. We are all like dough, cut by the same cookie cutter, forced to come out identical. If one doesn't comply, one lost his place in "the only true way to heaven." But now, after people are aware of the real beginning of the way, people do not have to put up with that kind of rulership, inconsistencies, invalid reasonings, and with no explanations. They can decide whether or not this way is as good—or worse than another way. Why can't we trust the spirit to guide. Do we not want to be sure that we err on the side of compassion on uncertain things?

Did you ever stop to think that everyone with questions may be troubled with them, because the things they question go against the rule of the spirit in their lives? Are you not finding more and more people asking questions concerning the appearance issues for women? No one understands them, and the workers are unable to explain them. Parents don't expect a baby to obey things it cannot understand and do not punish it for same; why are women forced to obey/do things they do not understand? Will not the Heavenly Father also have mercy, as a parent, if understanding is not present?

We believe it would be in the best interest of all if you come by yourself, without a companion, when you visit us on your return.

Cherie Kropp

Harry's Reply:

RECORDING VISITS/CONVENTIONS: As we sat down that August evening, Harry said he would like to clear up something first before we started talking. He had heard that I had taped his last visit (a lunch), and he wanted to know if that was true.

Cherie: "I certainly did NOT."

Harry: "I didn't think you would do a thing like that, Cherie, but I had to make sure. I would have been very disappointed if you had."

Because he made a big issue out of it, we knew it really had him concerned. Later my husband, Dave, quizzed him about his concern from the angle that "If what you said was true, why would it matter if Cherie HAD taped the conversation?"

Harry: "Well, you see the spirit does not come through tapes (or notes either)."

He detests both of them, which seems peculiar to us, unless you have something to hide. It seems from his point of view that the spirit is only really transmitted on a one to one basis (rather like a germ is transmitted to people?). It doesnt through tapes. He also said that things said can be taken out of context if one doesn't know what was said before and after the recording/notes are made. We both disagreed, but not verbally.

Thinking of my grandparents in particular, I mentioned how nice it would be for the old folks in rest homes to hear the convention through tapes. No, he didn't think it was a good idea to tape the conventions, because things may be said that were not "right." (We should have brought up the fact that if the same folks had been healthier, and able to be at the convention personally, they would have heard the same thing that was not "right."...and what about all those who WERE there who heard the something not "right"?) It seems to me that the possibility of hearing something not "right" over a tape is far more damaging to the soul than it is to starve spiritually in a rest home. Why don't they just correct the problem—get the thing said "right" in the first place?

Previously, Harry had stated to us that he knows we have read the *Secret Sect*. My question was, "How can you reconcile preaching that the 'truth' is the only RIGHT way to Heaven, when it was founded by William Irvine around the turn of the century?" He said the first preacher his parents heard preach the gospel was Irvine Weir. They had also heard William Irvine. As to whether there were others before William Irvine, he didn't know for sure, because he had never looked into it. He, himself, was satisfied that this way was THE true way of Jesus. So he didn't see any sense in wasting any time checking into it.

However, in the next breath he assured us that he was not claiming apostolic succession. But he IS sure it is the truth. When pressed, he would NOT admit or deny Irvine as founder. He was slick. I could not pin him down that Irvine started this way. He took the attitude that it just didn't concern him enough to be bothered about looking into it. He did NOT say others had NOT told him about the first days or anything. Just that he had not personally checked into them. I wish I had pursued this angle. Each time he spoke of the "way" or the "truth" or "Jesus way" I made him define which way he was referring to: Jesus' Way or this fellowship of which you are a minister? I didn't let him pull any double talk stuff on me. I separated the two by calling them Irvine's way and Jesus' Way.

Since this time, he has come for another short visit, at my request. Then, he said that he believed God could raise up a prophet like he did in the old testament days and mentioned Irvine as a prophet with a revelation. And he asked if I didn't think God could raise up, etc. I replied, "Yes, I think he COULD, but I don't think William Irvine was such a prophet, because he didn't pass the prophet test—his prophecies never came true."

Overseers:

I asked him, "Who is your overseer?"

Harry: "Well, I look to Taylor Wood."

Cherie: "Who are the other USA overseers?"

          After he hedged a bit, I hand-pulled them out of him. "Isn't William Lewis one?"

Harry: "Yes."

Cherie: "And Garrett Hughes?"

Harry: "Yes, but poor old Garrett's health is gone."

Cherie: "Who will take his place?"

Harry: "Well, I believe that will be Leslie White.

Cherie: "And Therold Sylvester is one?

Harry: "Yes.

Cherie: "And Murray Keene?

Harry: "Yes."

Cherie: "Is that all?

Harry: "Yes, as far as I know.

Cherie: "So there are five total.

Misc. Questions Asked:

Cherie: "What commends us to God?"

Harry: "Belief and growth."

Cherie: "What is fruit?"

Harry: "Growth."

Cherie: "How does one grow?

Harry: "With works."

Cherie: "What are works?"

Harry: "Submission"

Cherie: "How does one get saved?"

Harry: "By repenting and accepting salvation by grace through faith."

Cherie: "We agree wholeheartedly on this, but Harry, you preach a different gospel than most workers do."

Harry laughed. "But it's true—I'm not one whit more saved today, than I was the first day I stood to my feet and professed. I remember when it came so very clear to me—Willie Jamieson showed it to me."

Cherie: "What does it mean SPECIFICALLY when it speaks of giving to others in the Bible?"

Harry: "It means to give to others spiritually. There are enough government agencies and others to help everyone naturally."

Note: I was trying to see where "love" figured in his scheme of things. I finally had to ask him, "What about love? Isn't that the MOST important thing of all?" He never mentioned it, until that time. I asked many more questions, but cannot remember them. I never did point out my views on these matters, just asked for his.

Cherie: "You stated in gospel meeting that there are only differences in traditions—not in doctrine. Is salvation by grace DOCTRINE?"

Harry: "Yes."

Cherie: "I know for a fact the workers at Texarkana convention two years ago where you preached that did not agree with you. There was some grumbling about it, and remarks like 'That's his opinion.' That shows there ARE differences in what is considered to be doctrine in the truth."

I can't remember what he said exactly. Usually he tried to get out with something to the effect that he couldn't help that, or do anything about it. Perhaps he is doing all he can to preach correctly, and realizes he CANNOT do anything else. He is practically 80 years, and had no pension plan or any provisions for his old age except in this way. He HAS to fit in with what those over him want him to do or preach. He's locked in.

Cherie: "You do SOME things differently. You are trying to preach correctly—salvation as a gift through faith. But you won't even put a hand to the plow to help in other areas of discrepancies. You just say 'I can't do anything about that.' I don't believe there is nothing you can do about these things. I think your hands may be tied—but I do believe there ARE things you can do."

Harry: "Like what?"

Cherie: "You could tell others how wrong it is to be judgmental. Impress them with the difference in tradition and doctrine. Most have no idea there is any differences. Everything is doctrine to them. They have doctrine all mixed up with 'commandments of men.' Encourage everyone to respect each others decisions on how they live outwardly, and what they choose to do and not do. Show them that there is no ONE way to do things that is always right for everyone, and that it is WRONG to judge."

Harry: Shakes his head, like no he couldn't do that, or that I was way off track.

Cherie: "Harry, you don't know how laid back these folks are in Oklahoma. My daughter and I had been here over a year before we found out it was a sin to ROLL your HAIR! Here we had our permanents, and hot rollers and curling irons, and probably mentioned them freely, offending people right and left, but not knowing it. Then I find out it is a SIN to even ROLL your hair

with a curler!! I can't tell you when I've
been more shocked!"

Harry: "Name me one person who believes that."

Cherie: "[name withheld]. Someone saw her in rollers, and she was so ashamed, even though
she knows in her mind that there cannot be
anything wrong with them. Having naturally curly hair, she has to do SOMETHING
to be able to get her hair to look halfway
decent. Yet she feels guilty for doing this
absolutely innocent, harmless thing, because that's what she has been taught. Oh,
and let me tell you what else. It's ok to roll
your hair in rags - make rag curls, or use
hose to rag curl hair, because rags or hose
were not specifically made to roll your hair
on, like a curler."

(Harry and the younger bro., were laughing hard at this.)

Cherie: "Rich, you don't know what you've missed,
not growing up in this! You just don't
know how tangled up this mess is! It's like
living in the dark ages here in Oklahoma,
compared to Texas.

"And the elders wives were told not to
wear colored hose.

"Another example: [name withheld] doesn't
believe in trimming her hair. Her hair is so
long it actually drags the floor when down.
My daughter has seen it down. The weight
of it causes her head to hurt, she gets headaches from the pins digging in her head
which are necessary to put it up, and the
first thing she does when she comes in after work is to take it down. She does this
because she WANTS TO? No, because she

thinks she is supposed to in order to be saved. Think of the horrible time she has in washing it - the amount of time it would take it to dry! That is ridiculous! This is what she understands the workers want and she thinks it is required for her salvation."

NOTE: Since this time, Harry has given the first girl I used for an example three compliments about liking her hair!! I clued her in on what he was trying to say. Harry's attitude on this type thing, is people look that way because they want to. I insisted to him that it is NOT. They think the workers want them to look the way they do, and the workers have to let them know they don't have to look that way either. He shook his head—indicating that wasn't his job or he couldn't do that. I told him they would NOT change unless they were told differently - and he still holds to the belief they look like they want to—telling them wouldn't change them. Not ALL of them, I said, but it would definitely set a lot of folks free.

I was ready to get everything out in the open and see what he would do with us. I told him we were tired of living two lives in order to avoid the rejection of the people in the truth. We wanted to live by our convictions, and not cover up what we saw no harm in. We want to truly let the spirit guide. Then I told him we saw nothing wrong in TV, or movies. With my husbands employer being Anheuser Busch, that drinking a beer was like drinking a Coke to us. That my daughter (11 yrs old) was at a dance that very moment, and that I would much rather her be at a supervised dance when she is older than in a car necking simply because there was no recreation deemed suitable by the workers for dating kids to enjoy. That I had been going to a Bible Study group with some ladies for four years, and would work my life around those studies until I completed them—they meant that much to me (I have one more year). That I had learned more in them than in all the meetings I had ever sat through ALL put together. That I saw nothing wrong in short hair, make-up, jewelry or women wearing pants. That I didn't believe this was the only way to salvation. I told him you can't be honest with your beliefs in this way. You have to conform, or your part is taken away. This way simply hampers my spirit.

Cherie: "Harry, if I went to meeting like I believe professing women should be able to do, and believing others outside of this way are saved—in other churches, you would ask me NOT to take part."

Harry: "How do you think you should be able to look?"

Cherie: "No different than any other respectable woman in the world around us. I think a professing woman should be able to have short hair, wear jewelry, make-up."

Harry: "Cherie, If you came to meeting like that and had bread, I would NOT take your part away."

Now THAT was the most surprising thing about the whole evening! I wonder how many other workers would have said that—very few I imagine. Or did he think (hope?) I surely would not take him up on it. But you cannot live by your beliefs, or what you understand in this way. You have to conform to the workers' interpretations, regardless of how you understand them. Should you ask the workers any questions relating to women, I hope you will ask them if you think people should live by their beliefs and convictions. Harry firmly believes that is what people should live by. Would they allow you or a woman to take part in meeting if they did wear short hair, make-up and jewelry? If they say NO, well, why would Harry Brownlee tell Cherie Kropp she could? Must not be doctrine if it is not the same everywhere??

Cherie: "It would cause you all SORTS of problems if I took you up on your offer, and I'm NOT the troublemaker type. I abhor strife! The friends would get all upset, and go to you, as well as your overseer. It would make far reaching waves and for lots of confusion. I can't see how it would help ME spiritually—or that it would further my relationship to God. And it would cause you lots of grief. Thanks, but I'm going to pass."

Harry hates rules and emphatically wished all of them could be abolished. He said they make Pharisees out of people. I heartily agreed, and said "Let's do it, let's do it." He laughed. The problem is that a lot of what he considers doctrine is what I consider rules and traditions. However, I think we may hate them with equal intensity! We were definitely together on this issue!

Cherie: "Harry, you said in gospel meeting that there are only differences in tradition—not in doctrine. Tell me, do you consider long hair for women to be doctrine?"

Harry, without the slightest hesitation: "Yes."

Cherie: "Your former companion, Dale Spencer, stated to me that long hair for women was definitely NOT doctrine."

Obviously Harry's claim was false—the workers didn't even agree on what doctrine consisted of! He ignored the inconsistency, evaded the issue, and attempted to distract me by relating some amusing incidents about Dale.

Cherie: "Do you think Paul's writings are applications of Jesus teachings, and therefore, may not always be applicable to everyone in all generations? Or is every instruction of Paul's just as applicable today as it was 1900 years ago?"

Harry: "Pauls words were inspired by the Holy Spirit, and as such are every bit as inspired as Jesus words; we are to give Paul's words the same importance as Jesus. All scripture applies to us."

Cherie: "If you think all scripture applies to us in this our own time, why didn't you give me a holy kiss when you walked in?"

Harry: "Well, we do kiss you in our hearts when we walk in. We are very grateful for each and every home that is open to us."

Cherie: "Why aren't you taking Paul's coat to Troas?" (II Tim. 4:13)

Harry: "Well, we do take the coats of others to various places when they ask us to."

Cherie: "Do you take wine when you have a stomach ache?"

Harry: "I would certainly have no objection to anyone doing that."

Cherie: "My point is you do NOT literally do everything that can be done which is instructed in the Bible. Why are some things performed LITERALLY, and others taken SCRIPTURALLY? Don't you have to consider to whom the scripture was written? And the cultural conditions prevailing there? How do you accurately differentiate what scriptures are to be taken literally and which spiritually?"

I then pointed out that in I Timothy 2:8-12 in consecutive verses, verse 8 isn't taken literally (men praying lifting up holy hands); verse 9 is taken literally (women not wearing jewelry); and verses 11-12 are taken to mean the exact opposite from what they say (2x2 women DO teach). There is absolutely NO consistency in interpretation here. WHY? How can you insist your interpretation is the only CORRECT one in these issues?

Long Hair: To look up a point we were discussing in I Corinthians 11 (the long-hair chapter), he got a different Bible version (I think it was American Standard or Amplified). I pointed out that you don't need other versions—you need to go back to the original Greek to get a true understanding of the meaning of the word when it was written, not to a translation of a translation. He ran his fingers through his hair—in body language, the sign of exasperation.

I Corinthians 11:16 "But if any man seem to be contentious, we have no such custom, neither the churches of God." Harry claims this verse simply means the friends have no custom of being contentious. I contend that being contentious cannot be classified as a custom—it's a behavior—and that this verse could not be referring to the act of being contentious because the word the verse begins with: "but," sums up all the discussion that went before this verse. It means after considering all the previous points, if anyone disagrees, we have no such custom of ___. My point was that everything under discussion pertained to custom, and was not doctrine, and certainly not to being contentious. His version left out the "but" altogether. He thinks it means we have no custom of being contentious— period, paragraph, end of book. He refused to consider the very nature of the word "but." It is similar to a "therefore," which sums up the previous dialogue.

When I backed him into a corner on another issue pertaining to women, he said "Well, we're not going to be able to agree on this, so we'll have to go onto something else." However, I ignored this request, and continued on with whatever I was interested in. Another time "This is the way I see it." Another time " I can't do anything about that."

Harry says he believes women would look the same as they do now, if they were not in this way.

I said "I can't agree with you at all in that; then why don't all the newcomers to the way already have buns on their heads? However, he meant by his statement that those who were sloppy in their grooming, would still have an unkept look, which may be true.

Cherie: "We let Krista get her ears pierced because I believed with certainty that it would result in her having a bitter spirit against Jesus (in particular, this way) if we hadn't. I could not give her one good reason why she couldn't. I read all the verses to her, and she didn't buy them. I couldn't buy them either. She was the only child in her class who didn't have her ears pierced, and it meant a great deal to her to have it done NOW."

Harry, shaking his head: "I sure wouldn't have done it if it had been my child, but you are the parent, and you must do what you think best, etc. for your child, and you know your child best."

Cherie: "I consider guarding her spirit against bitterness much more important than two holes in her ears. I've had to deal with the bitterness of not being able to do what others could do, without any reasons...it's a hard thing to overcome. What reasons would you have given her?"

Harry: "I would have told her she could do whatever she wanted when she grew up, but while she was in my house, etc. etc."

Cherie: "That is robbing her of something that means something to her NOW—It's now that she is the only man out. NOW that her spirit will be hardened against Jesus. At 18, she can choose to pierce them THEN, but that will not help how she feels NOW. You can't replace this time in her life at 18."

Cherie: "From I Corinthians 11, why are women to have long hair?"

Harry: "It is a token of submission."

Cherie: "So it is a symbol of something else?"

Harry: "Yes, you might say so."

Cherie: "Submission to whom?"

Harry: "To her husband. Another reason is it is a glory to the woman."

Cherie: "Define 'glory' please."

Harry: "Glory is beauty; like your child is your glory or pride and joy."

Cherie: "Glory to whom? God or the woman?"

Harry: "To the woman."

Cherie: "If it is a symbol of submission, then in those days long hair had the same meaning for a woman as this wedding band does on my finger today. The wedding band has taken the place of the long hair in our culture, as a symbol of marriage."

Harry didn't agree with that; he feels the ring does not replace the need to have long hair.

Since he had never acknowledged receipt of my letter, I asked him point blank if he received my letter. He had. Even though we asked that he not bring a companion when he came to visit us, he brought one anyway. We didn't mention that. The companion hardly said two words the whole visit. It is just his first or second year in the work, and he wasn't raised in the 2x2 way.

When Harry came to Oklahoma he told all the friends that they would come for 2-day visits, so they could really get to know the family, etc. We were expecting him to stay for a 2-3 day visit, since he had only come for short lunches before that. They had supper, spent one evening when we had 2 hours solid conversation; then the next morning (Saturday) we had 2 more solid hours discussion. They stayed til 11:00 a.m. when they just HAD to leave. I never received my requested verse by verse discussion of I Corinthians I, nor did he reply to anything in my letter unless I specifically asked the question. It was like I had not written the letter. I really think if I had brought up every detail in my letter, that he would have said he hadn't looked into that, because he was satisfied the way they saw it was the right way. Because I wrote about some words that have other meanings than that stated in our KJV, he has it in his head that I think the Bible was translated wrong, which is a preposterous idea to him. He verbally scorned those who claimed that the Bible was TRANSLATED erroneously in the LAST gospel meeting I attended.

The tone of the conversation was always good natured, peaceful, respectful, and we agreed to disagree. Harry said "If there is a gulf made between us, it will not be because I have pushed you away, Cherie, but because you have chosen to do so." The funny thing was Harry addressed all his remarks and replies to Dave, and hardly ever looked at me, even though I was doing all the questioning! It was like he was trying to convince Dave.

Cherie: "The friends here judged us by the appearance of my daughter and I the first day we walked into our first meeting in this city and state, and they refused to have anything to do with us—all BASED solely on our appearance. They certainly never knew us to base it on anything else. We have been asked over to 4 different homes of the friends for dinner in the 2-1/2 years we have lived in this city; two of them because they wanted some company visiting us, or because they invited everyone in the meeting over, and it wasn't particularly our company they desired. That's LOVE? No, that's judging. You don't follow my standards, so I'm not going to play with you."

Harry didn't agree that it was because of our appearance AT ALL, but couldn't tell me what it was. I proceeded to tell him of a friend of mine and her husband who came to visit with her family, whom Harry had met. I took them to gospel meeting. I nearly said before meeting to these friends, "Don't expect to meet anyone after the meeting. No one said a word to me the first time we came, other than two workers." Well, quite to my astonishment, practically the entire meeting went up to them, shook their hands, and introduced themselves. I had to knock people down at each gospel meeting to get to know who was who. I would target the folks I was GOING to meet this time, and set out to do so, introducing myself. They would appear friendly to me on the surface after that. The difference in this other couple and us was totally in appearance. The other woman and her daughter conform to the professing woman image, and my daughter and I do not toe the line. She wore her hair slick back in a bun on the back of her head, and not one dab of makeup. I wear very light makeup and the front of my daughter and my hair is cut short and curled. My daughter (11 years old then) usually wore hers down shoulder length. Whether or NOT Harry agrees, that was the reason. However, it's nothing new. It has been happening since Jesus day. James 2:2-4 gives a perfect example of it, terming it "having respect of persons."

When Harry went to leave, I told him I wasn't at all sure this way was the best way for me to serve God any longer; that it hampered my spirit, and did not help further my relationship with God. I didn't see that it could encourage my spiritual growth. I gave him copies of some letters from others he knew, setting out why they had left the group.

Chapter Thirty-One

Debbie Lerwick
Letter to the Friends

Dear Friends & Relatives:

I believe it's about time for me to write you to personally explain some of my recent decisions. If you believe you offended me, please put the thought completely out of your mind. No one has offended me. No one has preached to me and led me outside the "truth." It was totally my own decision made independently, based on my own study and observations, and no one is to blame. Don't be put off because I don't meet with you, or as you do. I have many dear friends in the "truth" whom I love, respect and want to keep.

For those who have asked and wondered, yes, I continue to read my Bible and pray. I feel a great need to serve God. I have always wanted to be a Christian, and I haven't changed in that regard. In fact I can honestly say that my desire is much stronger today than it was this time a year ago. The Word of God is my guiding rule, and to be a glory to God is my purpose.

You may have thought that I left this way because of the scandals that took place in the ministry in Alaska. Sexual misconduct of Bob Ingram and Truitt Oyler resulted in their removal from the work. I understand that numerous incidents of this nature took place over a number of years. However, these things were kept quiet by everyone involved—both the innocent and the guilty (even though if they had been found guilty under the law of the Old Testament, they would have been stoned to death; and in America justice would have resulted in imprisonment). When these workers were confronted face to face with their sins, they denied everything and did not repent. Naturally, this disturbs me since I professed through Bob Ingram and Truitt Oyler. For the sake of appearances, it appears that the people in this way are encouraged to cover up the crimes of the ministers, to the detriment of the innocent involved. Even though this is all very upsetting, this was not why I stopped going to meetings. I realize there are scandals in every church because people are not perfect. However, there DOES seem to be more sins of sexual misconduct in the religions that enforce a celibate ministry, such as Catholics and the "truth." In my studies, I never found where the scripture required celibacy. In fact in I Timothy 4:3 Paul seems to recommend the opposite.

However, it was partly the scandal that caused me to question the source from which we hear the gospel. How do we know who is right, and who is wrong? How could these men be planting the seeds of the kingdom when they were in unrepentant sin? Their outward appearance and spirit appeared to be right on the surface. Obviously, the fact that they are a part of a homeless ministry and the church that meets in the home didn't make them "right." In spite of their problems, I do feel that I was led to Jesus through them. However, I believe I could just as well have heard the gospel from what is often referred to in this way as "false prophets." After all, Jesus said in Matthew 23:3 regarding the Scribes and Pharisees: "All therefore whatsoever they bid you observe, that observe and do; but do not ye after their works: for they say and do not."

Several years ago I received a letter from a sister worker that mentioned "Jesus brought to the world a faith that can stand testing. and a doctrine that can stand investigation." However. the "truth" was not able to stand up when I closely examined it. I encountered many differing stories and some outright falsehoods concerning the origin of this way.

For one thing, it was quite a surprise for me to find the "truth" has a founder and is not of apostolic succession as I had been told. My experience and reaction could be compared to a child discovering there was no Santa Claus. I have in my own notes "we know this is the right way because it has no founder." But I find this is not true—there is a founder. His name was William Irvine. I first heard about him a few years ago when all the Lerwicks were at the farm in Wyoming for our nephew's funeral. Paul's sister in the work, Lorraine Lerwick mentioned that William Irvine started the "truth" as we know it today, but that shouldn't bother us because it is founded on the same foundation as Christ, and that's all that matters.

Recently I read a book concerning the history of the "truth" named *The Secret Sect*. If you are afraid to read this book, let me say that many of the friends and workers HAVE read it and have not left this way. Kenneth Lerwick said that it helped him to understand what the early workers went through; Geneva Durkee said that it increased her faith and Tom Layman liked reading it, but said that it was negative and did not describe the good things in the fellowship. Another brother worker read the book and based on information from George Walker and Andrew Abernathy, stated the book was historically accurate except for a few minor details.

Many details found in the book are gathered from articles that were carried in a newspaper called the Impartial Reporter of No. Ireland. It tells, among other things, about the life of William Irvine. For a few years he was a missionary in the Faith Mission in Ireland. Disagreeing with some of the customs of the Faith Mission, he decided one day in 1899, after reading Matthew 10, the ministers were supposed to go and preach just like Jesus sent his disciples. The result was the ministry and church, which we know today as the "truth." Some others left the Faith Mission to preach with him, and others joined them. All nine of the first workers had been led to Jesus prior to this time in other religions. William Irvine claimed he was saved through Rev. John McNeil, a Presbyterian Minister. The "truth" is actually a spin-off of the Faith Mission, and started just like many other denominations—with a man's idea.

Originally the workers preached that the only way to be saved was to sell everything you had and "go preach," and earned the nickname "Go-Preachers." There were no friends in those early years, just workers! No meetings were held in the home until 1908. However, it soon became obvious that everyone could not go into the work, and that is where the friends entered the picture. The doctrine that the "truth" is God's only true way to salvation was added in 1904. There were several years where they didn't take the emblems—to the surprise of other churches—and when they did, it was at convention. Conventions in the truth are exact duplicates of those that were conducted in Keswick in England. The notion to send women into the ministry came directly from the Faith Mission. Many other things were copied from the Faith Mission, including terminology like "professing," "workers," "special meetings," "testimonies." etc. They used a two-by-two ministry of men. as well as women, in spite of criticism against women preaching.

One big difference I could find between the Faith Mission and the "truth" was stated on page 41 of *Spirit of Revival* by I. R. Govan:

"The mission does not seek to advance its own interests, to draw away members from existing organizations, or run down others sects. Its aim is to build up THE KINGDOM, and for this purpose to have fellowship with all God's people."

Whereas, in the "truth" they try to convert people from other Christian fellowships and run down other churches in order to gain followers for the workers.

Some people who have read the book and realize there was no remnant of what we know as "truth" passed down from Jesus' day, believe that William Irvine was a prophet God raised up to "restore" the truth. I have serious doubts, or I wouldn't be writing this. How can God be the source of a prophet whose prophecies didn't come true—Deuteromony 18:22? Did any of the prophets God raised up ever fail so miserably or go as far off-base? He claimed publicly that he was one of the two Witnesses in Revelation 11 who would lay dead in the streets of Jerusalem 3 1/2 days and be raised to life again. All the time Wm. Irvine was in the work he supported his illegitimate son Archie until he was grown. Isn't that surprising that William Irvine never shared the "truth" with Archie, since it was supposedly the "only way to heaven"? Archie not only never heard the message of the "truth" from his own father, but became an Anglican preacher.

The workers imply implicitly and explicitly that they are the same ministry that originated with the apostles in Matthew 10, and has continued without break since the time Jesus sent out his apostles. But, they aren't doing what he commanded in Matthew 10. The apostles and disciples were told to preach to the Jews only that the kingdom of God was AT HAND, and to heal the sick, raise the dead and cleanse the lepers. The mission of Matt. 10 was a limited one, specific in its direction (to the Jews only); specific in its object (to prepare for the coming of Jesus and announce the nearness of his kingdom) and specific in its nature (attended by miracles, which verified the disciples' credentials).

Obviously, the workers can do none of these things, are not preaching only to the Jews, and utterly fail in carrying out the commission of Matthew 10 that they claim to be unique in following. They take the Great Commission (Matthew 28:18-20, Mark 16:15-16, Luke 24:44-49) seriously, and add that to Matthew 10. It differed in message (faith in the resurrected Christ, repentance unto the remission of sins through the blood of Jesus); in scope of the preaching (into all the world, unto all nations, to every creature); in duration (until the end of the world). There were no restrictions as to taking money or other provisions when going out to preach. The workers also ignore Luke 22:35-36 where the commandments in Matt 10 were retracted. Jesus never really instructed the apostles to continue going like he sent them in Matthew 10.

Over the last several years I have had many questions for which I could not get any satisfactory answers. It is very frustrating that many of the workers actually discourage questions and preach against it. Recently, at Special Meeting, Carl Hamilton spoke about "those who have a love for unhealthy questioning." This attitude is not supported by scripture. Anyone should feel free to ask the workers questions. It seems to be difficult for the friends to distinguish the difference between questioning MEN and questioning God. I am questioning MEN, not God. I have no problem having faith in Jesus, and the Bible; but I do have a problem in having faith in *men's* theories, interpretations or applications for which there is no scriptural support. I've noticed the standard replies, when workers don't have any answers, follow along these lines (which are all evasions or distractions, and not really answers at all): "If you had the right spirit, you wouldn't question"; "You would be doing this or that if you had the right spirit"; "You shouldn't question—it shows that your faith is too weak"; "You just need to submit more fully"; "You just aren't willing enough." These replies do not answer questions—they attack the character of the person asking the question. No doubt, about 50 years ago, the women were told if they had the right spirit they would wear black stockings, without questioning.

I have been studying the act of questioning in the Bible. I find that to confirm what you have been told or taught at any time is considered wise, is never sinful, and is supported throughout the Bible. I Peter 3:15, "but be ready always to give an answer to every man that asketh you a reason of the hope that is in you with meekness and fear." God does not condemn anyone who seeks to prove things concerning Him. The writer of Acts commended the Bereans because they checked the Scriptures daily to see whether the things Paul was saying were in accordance with the truth. Acts 17:11. They didn't accept what Paul said just because he was the apostle to the Gentiles, but found out for themselves. He commands us to try the spirits in I John 4:1. "Beware lest any man spoil you through philosophy and vain deceit after the tradition of men, after the rudiments of the world, and not after Christ" Colossians 2:8. To "beware," one must be skeptical, doubt and ask questions! Hosea 4:6 "My people perish for lack of knowledge." Knowledge is acquired by being taught and asking questions. "If ye know these things, Happy are ye if ye do them." You first have to KNOW these things for yourself, before you can be happy doing them.

Some questions that have bothered me are: Where in the scriptures are directions to have conventions? Why have I heard from the platform that there are no rules in this faith, and yet there exist numerous unwritten hardfast rules that must be obeyed? Why is this the only true way, and what scripture indicates there is only ONE way in which to assemble to worship? The verses mentioning "one way" all refer to Jesus as the way, not a method of assembling. Why are some things taken literally in the Bible, and other things spiritually? What is the criteria for deciding that things like fasting, taking up collections for the poor, praying for the sick (James 5:14) are to be taken spiritually, and not naturally? Where does it say in the scriptures that there are to be women preachers? I read where some women gave themselves in service by following and ministering to the needs of the Apostles, but it is not recorded that he ever sent out any women two by two into the ministry.

The gospel (good news) was that Jesus died on the Cross for our salvation and rose triumphant from the grave. This action provided the WAY to the Father, as in "I am the Way, the Truth, and the Life—no man comes to the Father but by me." The friends believe Jesus' Way is one and the same way as the "truth," but the "truth is actually the way that William Irvine started. They are two completely different systems, ways or methods. The system or method of the workers going out in pairs, and holding fellowship meetings in the home, is not the same as the gospel and Jesus' WAY to Heaven. Irvine's way, or the "truth" is merely one method of fellowship for believers on earth. According to the Bible, Jesus is THE ONLY WAY, the TRUTH and the life. The TRUTH is a PERSON, not a WAY. If Jesus had not lived, died, and been resurrected, there would be no way for men to get to heaven. HE is the only way that gives mankind the hope of salvation. He is the strait gate mentioned in Matthew 7:13. I don't find scriptural evidence for any other way, nor for the necessity of being a part of a way to the WAY Jesus provided. There is no Biblical scripture tying this way Jesus provided through his life, death, and resurrection to any church, to the "truth" or to the way Irvine started. Neither is there any scripture indicating that you must be in Irvine's way or any other way or fellowship or church as a prerequisite to enter the way Jesus provided for men to get to heaven. *Jesus alone is the only way.* For their salvation, the people in this fellowship seem to depend largely on an imperfect way started by an imperfect man instead of depending on a perfect Savior. Christ alone saves men, not a church, or certain preachers, or the following of certain rules. Incidentally, Jesus only mentioned the word "church" twice.

I have concluded that there is no perfect way on this earth. God created salvation through Jesus, and man created religion. I have been re-evaluating the value and authenticity of the "truth" since I found out its foundation is based on falsehoods. Most other churches freely admit their origins and founders. I can think of no reason to justify it being necessary to hide William Irvine, and cover up his function in this way with the lie that this way is of apostolic succession.

Some think that since this way "works" that proves it is Jesus' way. However satanic cults "work," and probably have more members; Seventh Day Adventism "works"; Catholicism "works." etc. Because something "works" or because God has allowed it to continue in no way proves their leaders are led by God or that their way is Jesus' only way.

People often use experiences as signs that prove to them that the "truth" is the only true way of God. We have all heard testimonies about how workers showed up after someone prayed for truth. Although I would never discount the experience of anyone, I simply cannot base my own convictions on the experiences of others. I have heard and read of many similar experiences in other churches, such as Nazarene, Baptist, Mormon. etc. The stories are very similar and moving, but not something on which we can base our salvation nor do they prove anything right or wrong.

Women in the truth are burdened by dress and hair codes that do not appear to be scripturally sound. No one has been able to clearly explain to me any scriptures that actually support these issues. I prayed for a long time for convictions along these lines but I never got any. I complied, feeling it was better not to offend but with no belief that they were necessary. Why should God appreciate that? It was, and I believe is for most women today, mere form. I was following a mandatory requirement without understanding it in the least

Deuteromony 22:5 is interpreted by the workers to mean that women should not wear pants: "The woman shall not wear that which pertaineth unto a man. etc." But continue reading. "Thou shalt not sow thy vineyard with diverse seeds...thou shalt not wear a garment of diverse sorts of woolen and linen together...thou shalt make three fringes upon the four quarters of thy vesture." You can't just pull out one verse of the Old Law and use it as doctrine and throw the rest out. These verses must be read in their historical context. During this time pagans dressed up as the opposite sex as part of their worship to false gods. This is why God forbade his people to do this. Those, who believe this verse pertains to women wearing pants for warmth, modesty and convenience had better be sure they don't sow two kinds of seeds in their garden, and that they aren't wearing a garment made of a wool-linen blend and that they have their fringes sown on properly. Whether or not some of the friends and workers still consider pants an issue depends on what area of the country you live in.

At least long hair and jewelry are mentioned in the New Testament in reference to women, and are not obscurely hidden in the Old Testament law. There are two verses (I Timothy 2:9 and I Peter 3:3) that are used regarding jewelry. If these verses actually forbid jewelry, then they are contrary to all the rest of the Bible on this subject. If God is against the use of jewelry, why do we find many favorable references to jewelry in both the Old and New Testament?

Long hair is also a subject that needs to be addressed. Why make long hair a part of a woman's salvation when it is not? "For by grace are ye saved through faith, and not of yourselves; it is a gift of Cod, not of works" Ephesians 2:8-9. Growing hair is a "work." There is certainly nothing in the Bible that says it must be put up. The chapter used to enforce long hair for women is I Corinthians 11. Is that really the issue Paul is addressing in that chapter? How can we be certain Paul intended for his instructions to the Corinthian women concerning the hair styles they wore to be applied not only to them in their culture and day, but ALSO to women believers from that day forward? There is no other time any New Testament author gave like instructions. In other words, how do we know Paul intended for these things to transcend culture and become universal to believing women for all times? What is the underlying principle in this chapter? It would seem to be that in some women there was evidence of a lack of due submission to their husbands. This was evidenced by the removal of their head coverings, the nature of which is not specified. However. this action does not represent a lack of submission in the American culture. In fact it has no significance whatsoever to Americans. When someone sees a woman with her hair in a bun, do they automatically know that woman is in submission to her husband? Of course not! The only thing a woman's long hair put up in a bun signifies to anyone is her choice of religious profession, i.e. that she is either professing, or she is a Pentecostal. It is meaningless as far as submission is concerned! It was an instruction intended for the women of Corinth, and was never meant to apply literally in our day and time. I firmly believe it's one of those traditions Jesus scorned of the Pharisees, "teaching for doctrine the commandments of men" in Matthew 15. One of the reasons women follow these traditions is because of the very strong peer pressure put on women to fit in with the way everyone looks. It's worse than that found in the world and dangerously similar to that of the Pharisees. Of course, the underlying fear of excommunication from the "only way to be saved" plays a big part in bringing about "willingness" to comply without question or conviction.

Jewelry can be sinful if it's worn with excessive pride. However, in that case, it's the pride that is wrong, not the jewelry. We can take excessive pride in our home, cars, clothes, education, job, etc. It doesn't matter what it is. I'm afraid that I have fallen into the trap of refraining from wearing jewelry because I was taught it was worldly, but did other things that were just as worldly. Hair jewelry is very popular now, as well as wearing pins and pendants. But gold is gold, and pearls are pearls. Does it really matter how or where they're attached? In our country with our customs, it is not a shame for women to wear jewelry, make-up, etc. Nor is a woman mistaken for a prostitute, if her hair is cut or hanging down. A brother worker who thought I should wear my hair up gave me this vague reasoning once. Our righteousness is as filthy rags to God. Can we really think that what we can put on, keep off, or GROW means anything to God? Worship is done in the spirit or in the inner man. God looks on the heart, not on outward appearance. John 7:24 "Judge not according to the appearance, but judge righteous judgment.." Actually these prohibitions actually ENCOURAGE the sin of judging. They give us a yardstick (of rules) with which to judge others, causing the friends and workers to become Pharisees. In view of this, their bad fruit far outweighs their good.

My hope is that all the problems in the "truth" will be dealt with honestly by the head workers. That all problems pertaining to the history will be brought out and laid on the table. Also that legalism will be removed as an essential part of salvation (particularly women's) so that people are free to be led by the spirit of God, rather than by rules of conduct, dress codes and hair styles. I feel that to preach that this is God's only true way to heaven is a falsehood. Jesus is the only way, not a particular system or method that has a 2x2 ministry and meets for fellowship in the homes.

My heartfelt desire in writing this letter is that my friends and relatives will study into these things for themselves, and show me where I am wrong in my beliefs and decision; or else accept my decision without grieving for me. I don't relish people saying that I'm crazy; unwilling; have the wrong spirit; and that I just have my eyes on the world, etc. To adopt one of these viewpoints is attacking me, judging my motives, and does not come anywhere close to accurately describing the agony I have experienced in uncovering this deception.

I believe Jesus Christ is the WAY to heaven through belief and trust in Jesus, the Son of God, and in what He did for me, as He lived a sinless life, and being the atoning sacrifice on the cross. It isn't enough to just say we believe, but we must repent of our sins and have a living relationship with Him through the Holy Spirit. We are saved by faith through grace which is a gift of God, not by our appearance or works. The church is composed of everyone who believes and does that. It isn't a method or a system or a group of people who meet in a particular way. Everyone who believes in Jesus Christ as our God and Savior is my brother or sister in Christ and it is wrong not to love them.

Quite honestly, I can no longer be a part of a deceptive, legalistic fellowship that covers up its history, doctrine, scandals, and then preaches it's the only perfect way. For those of you that would like to talk with me, please feel free to do so. Above all, I want to know and believe what is true concerning God, and if you can show me where anything I now believe is in error, scripturally or historically, believe me, I want to hear from you. I feel a need to be in fellowship with people who also serve God. I have been visiting churches with other Christian friends, but I will not be making a hasty decision along these lines.

Love in Christ

Address:
Debbie Lerwick
3206 Mark Lane
Midland, TX 79707

Chapter Thirty-Two

Don and Kathy Lewis
A Letter to the Friends

Dear Friends,

Kathy and I want you to know why we're no longer attending meetings and why you may not have seen us at convention this year. This is a difficult subject to cover in a letter or even in a face-to-face conversation, but we will try to at least convey some of our thoughts and feelings so you may be able to understand our position.

In order to dispel possible rumors in advance, we would like to cover some of the reasons we do not have for leaving:

1. *We have not been offended. No one has done or said anything to personally offend us, hurt us, or drive us away.*
2. *We have not rejected God or Jesus or the Spirit of God, and we do not have the wrong spirit.*
3. *We have not lost our faith in the Lord.*
4. *We are not guided by Satan.*
5. *We are not unwilling for the standards.*
6. *We have not been converted to some other false way or doctrine.*
7. *We are not confused.*
8. *We are not dropping out for a while to find ourselves.*
9. *We are not wanting to be worldly.*

Several years ago, I started asking these questions in my mind, "Are we really the only ones saved" and "is this really the only way to Heaven?" As I associated with other Christians and saw Christ in them, I started answering these questions with "No, I don't think so." But if others outside our fellowship were saved, how many were there? And if they were brethren, are we not supposed to love them? And if we don't love them and treat them as our brethren, do we really love God? (I John 3).

In connection with this realization that there are other Christians out there, I started being sensitive to the mocking and derision we sometimes hear professing people use when referring to others. I didn't like to hear friends or workers putting down sincere Christians or pastors for doing things like saying "Praise the Lord." I also noticed that along with an obvious lack of love for these people, they considered them worse enemies than Satan himself, and seemed to despise and condemn them to a lost eternity. I also became aware of self-righteous attitudes in the people acting this way.

Another question that occurred to me was "Why are more people not saved (in our Way)?" I saw other churches being much more diligent and effective in helping and reaching souls for the Lord. I was moved to witness to lost souls but unable to do it within the framework I found myself in—in an exclusive group that self-righteously set and maintained certain standards and attitudes that turned away more people than it attracted.

Then I started learning about the *true Gospel*: Jesus Christ (God in the form of flesh) died for us to save us from our sins. He lived a completely righteous life that could be substituted for our sinful lives. And He lives now, interceding for us. The *good news* is that all we need to do is believe on Him and we shall be saved! We need no mediator between God and man, except Jesus Christ. We cannot "earn" our way into Heaven by doing good or being good; it's only because of God's grace that we can be saved. Anyone who thinks he will get into Heaven because he has done his best, gone faithfully to meetings, been accepted by the workers, etc., will not make it because the Bible says those who will be judged for their works will be cast into the lake of fire. I want to be trusting in Christ as my personal Savior so I will have my name in the Book of Life, not in the books of works.

We've noticed that in the gospel meetings we have been to, the consistent theme is the two-by-two ministry and meeting in homes, not the blood of Christ. This message is not the true Gospel, and has deceived many into thinking they must hear the gospel from certain people and be in a certain group to be saved. They conform through fear and try to do the things they're expected to, but they never feel worthy and they can never have the confidence they're saved. At best, they can only *hope* they're saved and that they're almost good enough for God to accept them. Our main concern now is for people who are not trusting in Christ for salvation, but are trusting in themselves or others or "a way."

We do feel we were deceived for a long time by the teaching that the way was from the New Testament times, etc. It was a shock to find out *when* it was started and *by whom* it was started.

We can look back on our lives and see that everything God has brought us through, including the adversity, has brought us closer to Him, and has helped to open our eyes to the true Gospel. We trust God more now. We love Him more each day. We want to serve Him more. We are enjoying more freedom and happiness in the Lord. All because of what He has done for us in Christ.

We asked ourselves "Where would we go if we didn't go to meetings?" We realized that Christ is the Way, the Truth, and the Life and the important thing is to trust in Him. However, we do plan to attend a community church with sound doctrine that we have found where we can praise and worship God with other believers.

Perhaps you have had some of the same questions and answers. We pray that the information we can share and the communications we can have will bring us all closer to each other and closer to God.

We hope and pray that you and all those you influence will be placing your trust in the only one who can give us eternal life, our Lord and Savior, Jesus Christ. If you can still treat us as friends and associate with us, we would like that. If you cannot, we understand.

Love,

Don and Kathy Lewis

September 10, 1988

Chapter Thirty-Three

Kathy Lewis
Free at Last

Have you ever started putting a puzzle together and found a piece of a puzzle from another box mixed with the pieces? That is how I felt growing up in the church which calls itself the Truth. The church was the disconnected puzzle and I was a piece that didn't fit. I thought that I was supposed to fit, but I didn't, and for many years I didn't know what the picture was supposed to look like. This peculiar situation made me uneasy, extremely curious, and constantly trying to fit into something that didn't make sense; constantly looking for approval but rarely finding it; constantly trying to figure out what the picture was supposed to look like and what role I was supposed to fill.

Without a doubt, I grew up with the most wonderful parents and sister and some of the nicest professing people one could expect to find. It was the Pacific Northwest, where there are more professing people per capita than most anywhere else. There were lots of children our age and in our fellowship meetings and Bible study evenings there were more children than adults. We lived in the country where we were quite protected from the "world." And protection is what my parents did best. Mom and Dad instilled in my sister and me a deep abiding love for God. From my earliest memories I can remember loving God, looking forward to heaven, not afraid of death, and fully trusting God's Word. Mom and Dad were, and are completely devoted to us, giving my sister and I unqualified, unconditional love...but not unconditional approval. The approval came ONLY if we followed the rules set forth by the workers. So, we learned early to follow the rules because approval was extremely important to us. Approval was relatively easy to receive from our parents, but approval from the workers and friends didn't seem to come as easily, which puzzled me a lot because both my sister and I professed at age 12 and had followed the rules since childhood.

As I grew older, I observed that there were other important things that mattered besides the appearance and behavior code: an open home, which meant hospitality, social skills, a nice home and furniture, lots of professing relatives, writing lots of letters (on onion skin paper), an immaculately clean house at all times were also essential and if you played the piano that was even a higher plus in the eyes of everyone. However, it was the 1950s, the decade after the war when the economy was difficult and our family was struggling with the process of building a house which we lived in during the construction. My Dad had been raised during the depression and thus being very conservative, had decided to build it without taking a loan, so it was constructed in a slow and painful process. It wasn't exactly the ideal open home. There weren't many inside walls for privacy and the interior and exterior were pretty primitive most of the time. Even though our house wasn't finished, the workers did choose my Dad as an elder and we had Sunday and Wednesday night meeting in our home for most of my life. Meetings were held there until they became too elderly and had to sell their home and move.

While I was a child the workers rarely visited us, maybe once a year and for only one night or so at a time, which was unusual at that time because they often stayed for weeks in some places. When they did come, our parents made sure that we recognized what a privilege it was for them to sleep in our bed. And I can truly say that we never resented their use of our bed but I sure can remember how awful it was to be so tense and quiet and to watch our manners, how loudly we laughed and giggled or how rowdy we played and what we said. It was unacceptable to use slang terms such as "gee," "gosh," "darn," "shoot," or "you guys." We walked on eggs while the workers were around because we feared the frowns or the unseeing eyes if we were offensive in any way. In those days, the workers were quick to point out anything that was disapproved of by them. We were told the reason we had to be so quiet was because the workers were supposed to be praying and reading their Bible all day. Even though the workers didn't stay with us very often, they ruled our house as if they lived there. And we saw them at least twice every week at Gospel Meeting, therefore, we felt the connection of their presence.

Meetings, meetings, meetings, Gospel Meetings, Bible Studies, funerals, Conventions, Special Meetings, Union Meetings, potlucks, sings, visits from workers, getting prepared for meeting, driving to meetings...miles and miles from home...hours of driving it seemed. All vacation periods were filled with some kind of church activity. These were the days of our lives. I hated meetings, they were boring and stressful. Punishment was expected at least once during a meeting if you were a young child. If you wriggled, scratched or whispered, eyes would notice, glare or stare at you. I hated Sundays and

Wednesdays because those were always meeting days, and usually many other days were, too. Most of our gospel meetings were in dilapidated Grange Halls, Oddfellows Halls or school houses.. Occasionally there were funeral parlors or Masonic Halls or Bingo and Square Dance places. It was embarrassing to be seen at those places. They were icky or spooky, many of them were dusty and creepy, sort of like a haunted house. To this day, every time I pass a Grange Hall, I almost expect to see professing people outside shaking hands.

As a child, I was extremely aware of how the people around me behaved. Any facial expressions or aggressive voices and tones that were out of the ordinary frightened me. In my mind I sometimes labeled people as being "soft" or "hard." "Soft ones" were the tender, easy-going ones I could trust, "hard ones" were the ones to beware of for unpredictable tempers. The friends in our area that I grew up with were mostly friendly and predictable, but at convention and special meeting time I noticed a lot of unusual behavior. It is still surprising to me as a grandmother now, that so many adults are oblivious to children as being almost like videotape recorders of their words and actions. I learned to dislike many workers and professing adults for the way they treated children or acted ugly, mean or strange in full view of us, while acting prim and proper around other adults.

We understood the body language of our parents, the workers and friends at an early age. I can remember talking to my Mom about Aunt Queenie's frown at age 4 or 5, asking her why she was frowning at me. I think the workers felt it was their duty to keep children in line and I remember being quite offended, wondering who she thought she was, telling me what to say or do. I also noticed that my parents were extremely tense while the workers were there and would scold each other for trifling things that they wouldn't have ordinarily thought about, like how the table was set, topics of conversation, who was to say grace at the table, etc.

My Mom must have noticed my attitude towards the workers because she went on a big campaign to encourage me to love and admire them. She told me how much they gave up in order to preach the gospel, they were the "messengers of God," sort of like angels, how much they had *loved* the workers when she was little. She told me all about her own mother and how and why she had believed the workers' message. It was plain that Mom idolized her own mother and believed the workers because of her respect for her "mama." Her campaign didn't change my perception of them, but it did teach me to keep my opinion about them to myself. I learned very early to NEVER criticize a worker, even in my mind. Later, as an adult, it surprised me to learn that other professing people were not so reticent to mock workers or tease them. I used to marvel at the contempt some friends had for certain workers even though they worshipped the idea of the "example ministry," and would treat them as if they idolized them while they were with them, even if they personally disliked them. Nothing that Mom said overruled what I saw for myself, but when I was 12 years old, Rosetha Newman, who had been a school teacher before becoming a worker, came to our field. Here was the first worker I met that treated me as a person rather than an insect or a bother. She won the hearts of all the children in our field, because I think that nearly every one of us professed through Rosetha. Rosetha had a wonderful way of making things real to her audience, not to mention her emotion-packed visual pictures.

Her sermons were a real change from the boring sermons we had been accustomed to hearing. She was more gentle with children than she was with adults...a big difference in my experience. The day I professed, she had given a heart wrenching description of the crucifixion of Christ. I can remember sobbing aloud for several minutes before and after professing because of my grief over what Jesus endured for me. I figured if He could go through all that pain for me, I would gladly give up anything for His sake. And I was willing for the professing life...with all its misery, appearance code, public prayers and testimonies, humiliation, constant self rejection, etc.

From that point on, I tried to copy Rosetha, during the years she was in our field. I don't know how I picked up the idea, but I had the impression that I would receive approval if I dressed like her. I was a blonde and Rosetha was a redhead. Our complexions weren't similar at all, but I began to wear the same colors that she wore, autumn browns, greens, etc. and the same kinds of nylon "old lady" blouses and types of clothing. My hair and complexion coloring really required pastels, reds, blues, etc. I even tried to copy her hairstyle but it just wouldn't work for me.

While I was a teenager, going through the process of learning to groom myself, I noticed with surprise that the days that I looked awful, were the days that the workers and professing relatives and friends all smiled at me and gave me positive comments. And the days that I looked pretty and felt confident with my appearance they would frown at me. So I learned the importance of dowdiness and worked at it, especially when I was going to be with professing people. But neatness was important, so I worked at that also. It was sort of a catch-22.

You had to be neat, but not too neat. I learned how to shop for clothes. Reading, shopping or sewing became my pastimes. I didn't have any money, but still I was always looking at clothes or sewing them. Shopping takes a lot of work because finding the right clothing is extremely difficult. There are so many factors to take into consideration. It has to be the right style, not too modern, not too fancy, just the right length, the right kind of sleeves, the colors can't be too bright, (even metal buttons and metal watch bands were frowned on by some people), the neck can't be too low in the front or the back, not too tight, shirt-waist flowered house dresses, nylon blouses, and dark colored suits or jumpers were good. I also noticed early in life that the clerks in the stores didn't pay much attention to me. My appearance didn't command much attention or respect from strangers. (Excuse the change in verb tenses. There are some things that are still considered rules, others that were rules in the past.)

Hair styles are even more complicated than shopping for clothes. As every woman knows, each head of hair is different—the texture, thickness, the brittleness, how straight or how curly, the weight of the hair, how long it is, how fast it dries when wet, the shape of the woman's face, how physically active the woman is, her personality, her type of body shape—all these things are factors in what style looks appropriate for every woman. But—for professing women—these things make NO difference. Hair had to be long and up in a bun. This was a problem for me. I was a bouncy girl who liked to run, play basketball and volleyball in Physical Education class, swing on the bag swing in our back yard. I never got used to swimming because my hair took so long to dry, that drying it after a swim session was an all day job. Hair dryers didn't work on my hair because it tangled so badly. I was a late bloomer...or in other words...I stayed a kid for quite awhile. Fortunately, Mom let us girls wear our hair in pony tails rather than buns for most of our school years. I did notice some frowns and a few comments about that, but I paid no attention. Buns don't stay up on bouncy heads...When I did start wearing a bun, I had the worst time with hair pins continually falling out because my hair was so soft and fine. I could follow my trail of hairpins on campus, just like Hansel and Gretel following the bread crumbs. Finally, I started wearing an enormous clip on top of my head to hold my waist-long, heavy hair in place to keep the bun from falling down in the middle of the day. This resulted in a bald spot where the hair was worn off from the tension of the clip which I even wore to bed at night for many years, just to keep the hair out of my face at night. People who have never had long hair, especially men, cannot understand or know the inconvenience of long hair. I had to wash it every three days because of the oiliness. And then on hair-wash days I had to wear it down while it dried, which took hours. Then I had to set the front in pins or curlers to soften the front of it and that took a long time. Hair wash days I couldn't do much else. I was always humiliated if someone from school came to see me on a hairwash day. I actually had very pretty light blond hair and was always complimented on it, but the way I had to wear it made me look like a frowsy headed mess. It was too soft to stay in place and had to constantly be combed up and I hated messing with it. It took hours of work every day and only looked presentable for about five minutes at a time. Hair spray didn't help my hair for any length of time at all. I had to use a hair net, which was embarrassing for a teenager. Another hair problem, I found, was that I became sick and tired of a hairstyle after one year, and also in one year the hair length and thickness had increased and it became necessary to find a new way of styling it. So it became a sort of ritual. Each birthday I sometimes spent hours in front of the mirror trying to find a new style that would be acceptable to the workers and yet would somehow or another look presentable to me. I can remember my arms aching from working so long. crying with frustration that my hair wouldn't cooperate and that I looked so horribly shabby and messy, no matter what I did. One year my Mom felt so sorry for me that she took me to a beautician and had some bangs cut. I was so surprised and excited and yet quite embarrassed because this was a total no-no and caused me to receive a lot of strange looks from the workers and other friends. However, bangs didn't really improve the situation much because, although it made the front look more civilized, the back didn't match it, so I still felt like a freak, no matter what. After a few years I let the bangs grow out, just because they were more trouble than they were worth.

I hated my hair...even though now I realize what a wonderful blessing it is. It is naturally curly (a fact I didn't know until I was forty five years old) and when it is cut right, it is the easiest and most enjoyable hair one could wish to have. However, no matter how terrible I felt my hair was, it didn't compare to what I saw a poor woman at convention trying to work with. I'll never forget it...she was about thirty five years old and her hair was so thin that you could see her scalp in places. If she had been allowed to have it cut short and loosely curled, one would never know that it was so thin and it would have been attractive...but since she had to wear it in a bun, you could really see how pitiful it was. I witnessed her for a whole hour several different times combing and re-combing her hair, sighing and almost crying during the process. She would take her hair completely down and redo it, constantly try to cover up the scalp which was peeking through her hair. I couldn't believe it! I felt like yelling, "Stop it!" I was frantic in my heart, feeling her pain and frustration. I wanted to whisper, "Just go get it cut and forget this mess!" It made me hate the people who forced her to wear her hair like that. (Frequently, we feel more pain for others than we do for ourselves.)

Another really frustrating problem was that we had to wear meeting clothes at home, just in case someone came to see us. We had to be ready for workers who rarely came, or to be a right example to outsiders. I hated wearing dresses all the time, it was a big pain and expensive, too. I can remember thinking it wasn't right that the workers dictated to us what we wore in the privacy of our own homes. I thought: "when I am at home, it is nobody's business what I wear...I should be able to be naked as a jaybird if I want." But, NO—it was skirts all the time. I had been allowed to wear pants until I professed and then it was skirts. My Dad said he would spank me if he caught me in pants after that. However, he did let us wear pants when we played in the snow and when we went fishing. But I was told that in some places the professing women had to wear skirts over their pants which shocked me so much that it made me almost thankful that at least I didn't have to do that! One day when I was a teenager, we drove to the ocean on a Sunday and our whole family walked on the beach with our meeting clothes on. It was the most peculiar sensation. I can remember the pain of the moment even now, seeing everyone in swim suits and shorts and bare feet and we looked like aliens from another planet. It gave me a nauseous feeling to be so inappropriately conspicuous. I noticed a lot of people staring at us and wished that the sand would just swallow us up. I wondered what possible good it did anyone for us to be dressed like that on the beach. None of those people would ever come up to us and ask us what church we went to. I'll never forget hearing a brother worker at convention really scold some family who had gone to the beach and who wore their beach clothes home in the car and the workers were waiting on their front porch when they got home. The workers were indignant that the people had not changed into "the standards of the Kingdom" before their trip home. He said, "They won't do that again very soon!" I was offended with his attitude but just put it out of my mind immediately and made a mental note to be very careful not to let the workers see me in anything except skirts and nylons.

In those days, the workers purposely would drop in unannounced in order to test people to see if they were obeying the standards. If they weren't, there was a sermon the next week on the subject. If people objected to the drop-in visits, they would get scolded for their attitude.

As I look back, I can see that from the moment I professed, my critical thinking skills shut down almost completely. I had begun listening closely to workers' sermons at about age seven and had mulled them over in my mind, sometimes agreeing with what was said and sometimes not. There were lots of sermons about sheep and goats, with the goats always on the losing side. At first I felt sorry for the goats. "Why were goats so bad?" I wondered. The use of allegory was confusing to me as a young child. The older brother workers often mocked people who said, "Yes, but." They said, "You can always recognize a goat, because he's always butting." This statement bothered me because I felt that, perhaps, I was a goat instead of a sheep. I didn't have the mental skill to realize that this pun was not biblical. It is obvious that the scripture shows that there are lots of lost sheep as well. The workers often pointed out that dumbness was good, and that thinking for ourselves was bad. Goats wouldn't follow the shepherd, they were independent. Sheep were dumb animals, therefore it was good to be dumb. Think about it...all animals are dumb, or I should say, unintelligent. One of the characteristics God blessed man with is the ability to think. That scripture that speaks of goats and sheep isn't a warning against thinking or speaking out. It is simply an illustration to a culture familiar with sheep that there will be a separation of people in eternity. Those with salvation from those without salvation.

As I reached my teenage years I was aware of disapproval in the eyes of workers, as well as disapproval in the eyes of my peers at school. I had been a very sociable, outgoing child in grade school but as I grew into the teenage years, the disapproval of other kids towards my style of hair and clothes became painful. I could see the sneer behind the eyes and it became difficult to look at people. I learned to look away or at the floor while I spoke to others. Sometimes people would make remarks to me, such as, "You would look so pretty if you cut your hair and wore lipstick." Or, "Why don't you wear your hair down?" etc. These remarks drove me into books as an escape mechanism or I would take naps after school in an effort to forget the stress of being different. My earlier habit of noticing everything that was said and done was destroyed and I became like a walking zombie, not seeing or hearing much of what was going on around me because it was too painful. Lots of my time was spent in depression, daydreaming and mental space out. As I look back I think of myself as something like Mr. Magoo, the cartoon character who was near sighted, oblivious to what was going on around him. I also learned to compensate for my depression by acting non-depressed. I would act giggly or talk nervously to cover my insecurity. I felt anxiety no matter where I was. I didn't feel accepted by the workers and I didn't feel accepted by the world either. I definitely was not doing anything that should have excluded me from worker approval except that I was a teenager and most teenagers just aren't very well appreciated by the workers for some odd reason. This disapproval made me feel unaccepted by God and was a huge burden and a lie.

Even though I felt like a misfit, surprisingly, my favorite place was school. I found approval there from my teachers and I had several real close girlfriends at school who accepted me for who I was. Home was often a tension filled place. Mom taught us the rules and Dad was the enforcer of the rules. He had a temper at times which frightened me. His real personality was loving and tenderhearted but his role as a professing father forced him to be strict and harsh at times. He was also a tremendous worrier and always expected the worst things to happen. I believe also that he began showing the symptoms of Alzheimers at an early age, but it wasn't until later in life that we realized what it was that made him so difficult to live with. He found it extremely difficult to make decisions and it was left to my Mom to fill that role. My parents' personalities were both formed by the workers and I feel it harmed their marriage in many ways. But I am thankful they gave my sister and I the best example of loyalty to God and family, besides protecting us from potentially emotionally harmful situations both from the world and from the church. Mom's sense of humor always insulated us from too much grief.

I was a sensitive and serious child, and books were my means of escape. I had a wonderful Christian sixth grade teacher who did a good job of teaching us to choose which topics to read. Therefore, as I grew older, I chose mainly nonfiction books, biographies, self-help, self-improvement, psychology and educational topics and rejected the fiction and romance novels that so many professing women get hooked on. I didn't have a very good memory for details so I learned that the best way for me to remember information was to look for the bottom line logic of a subject—if I could understand the logic behind the subject, I was better able to retain the information and assimilate it for future use. This habit that I picked up early was what helped me later in my study of the Bible and in understanding the workers' doctrine. However, my interest in books also led me into contact with ideas that I now consider dangerous to unwary people. Because I was a hearty, ignorant "professing" person I had no way to evaluate whether these ideas conflicted with scripture. Sometimes I would read things from eastern religion, New Age, occult, secular humanism and whatever else is out there and some of the ideas would make sense and seem plausible, while some obviously contradicted what scripture says, but I had no way of knowing up or down, left from right. They just went in my head and mixed in with all my other beliefs and ideas. I would sometimes meet people who understood the ramifications of those different concepts and I envied them, wondering how they understood why certain ideas were trustworthy and others were not. I had not been taught to examine the histories, purposes, points of origin or the details of those ideas. If I had only known how to look for the bottom line logic in them I would have been saved from a lot of confusion. But there was no help from the workers, "God's only true shepherds." They didn't explain anything...they just expected conformity in appearance and compliance in lifestyle without question.

My mother who was the main one to instill 2x2 behavior in me, let me know that reading and higher education had not been an acceptable pastime when she was a child, but since she had been a schoolteacher she was more lenient on that issue than some other people probably were. Two of her sisters had quit school at the brother workers' instruction, but Mom and one of her other sisters went on to teachers' college, in spite of the workers' advice. My Dad instilled curiosity in me (at an early age) and encouraged me to study and look for answers. He always told me that if I ever wanted to know something that I should go to the library...the answers to almost everything could be found in a book. Although, I can also remember that he said that "You can't always believe something just because it's in a book." Mom taught me the professing rules by telling me stories about other people, but not in a gossipy way. She rarely repeated gossip. That was forbidden and any negative information seemed to fly out of her head. If a bad subject came up, she changed the subject and forgot it immediately. She didn't use the scripture to say what was right or wrong. She just told me about someone she had known who had done this or that when she was a child and what the workers said or did about it. Sometimes she would tell me the professing rule, but then qualify it by saying that it wasn't really important or that she didn't see the need for it and she would let me decide how I felt about it. I never thought about how incongruent that was, I just accepted what she said and then did as I felt according to the situation...but always with an eye to what was expected, especially if a worker or professing person was around. I understand a little better how the system works now than I used to. Newly professing people usually get their instructions about "the standards" from the workers they profess through, or from those that follow, but people who are raised in the group usually get their instructions from their parents. Depending on the workers and the area, the newly professing people can have a fairly easy time of it, or an absolutely dreadful time. I know of some people who developed severe emotional problems due to the intrusive behavior of some manipulative and coercive workers. Some workers just move in and take over, others are more lenient and let some other worker do the dirty work. The parental instruction is much more subtle and over a longer period of time. It is imbibed slowly and without the child's conscious awareness. My Mom was from Kansas which had stricter workers than some of the western states. So the rules I grew up with were from that background. Dad was from Idaho which had a different head worker and slightly different rules. So I remember there were conflicts on several different issues, such as celebrating Christmas, 4th of July, attitudes towards County Fairs, what kind of things could be done for fun, etc. Mom didn't believe in spending money on fun or frills. Dad did.

So, that caused problems and some confusion and
disappointment for us girls at times. Dad wanted to
do recreational things as a family but Mom hated
doing anything recreational. She said it was a waste
of money, or the workers would disapprove, or it
wasn't necessary to do those things. I believe that
the parental influence is more effective in inculcat-
ing the lifestyle in the long run, than the workers'
influence.

I do remember my parents discussing certain
professing people's decisions and their results. They
made the remark that "it is just better NOT to ask a
worker for advice because workers always have to
give the strictest rule, even if they don't agree with
it because they are afraid God will punish them for
saying the wrong thing. It is better to pray about it
and read the Bible yourself than to ask a worker.
The workers don't always have the best advice."
They said they had known people who had more
trouble after asking the workers, than they did before. (Since then, I have found out that sometimes
workers pressured to give the head worker's ruling
on certain issues rather than their own discretionary
view of scripture because if they don't, they may
find themselves without a companion and field of
labor.

I understand better now than I ever did before
how the contradictory messages confuse people and
destroy their integrity. It is a form of situational ethics. Because some workers ignore or condone
certain things while other workers absolutely forbid
those things, the people and the workers alike are
caught in intellectual dishonesty. They will give lip
service to the idea that the workers are the mediators between God and man, that their messages
give life and true direction...yet, all the while they
will disagree with some of the legalism, or beliefs

and will appear to conform, yet in reality live two different lives, or maybe even multiple lives, depending on who they are with. If the workers and friends are around, they behave in one way and then in privacy will behave in another. Intellectual dishonesty can eventually lead to moral dishonesty...something that is obviously a problem for some of the workers, including head workers. This kind of belief and behavior is very harmful to young people as well. They know it is hypocrisy and despise it. While many workers and friends would agree with the fact that this is a bad thing, they dishonestly refuse to acknowledge that this is not only common, but they refuse to consider that it happens at all.

I have an inborn love of flowers. It is a passion that I can't even describe and it took me years to accept it comfortably, because it wasn't "spiritual," nor practical; it appealed to the lust of the eyes and was a waste of time and money. My Mom was not a gardener and I didn't have any childhood training in gardening. I can remember telling Mom, "Someday, I want to join a garden club so that I can learn more about flowers and flower arranging."

Mom said, "No, the friends don't do that."

"Why not?"

"Because that is what high society women do and the workers don't approve of it." It didn't occur to me to question that...I just accepted it with disappointment; another thing I couldn't do. There were lots of things that I couldn't do, that I haven't covered in this small amount of space.

I remember talking to a professing man in Oregon about 15 years ago. He told me that he and his wife owned a beautiful home in an expensive neighborhood and he had loved working in his yard. He spent all his spare time gardening and working on the lawn and it was a showplace. The workers came and asked him if he wouldn't move to another neighborhood that wasn't so expensive and if he would stop spending so much time on the yard. It just wasn't a productive use of his time. He should invest more time and energy in the Kingdom. So, he did what they asked, but he seemed to regret it, even though he also seemed proud of himself for obedience.

I know of other people who the workers criticized because of the color of their carpet. It was white. They thought that was awful because it wasn't practical for meeting. Many workers used to make comments on everything in people's homes, not just whether they had TV or radios. Some of that kind of thing has died out a bit, and you will even find professing people and workers who deny that that ever happened. But it did and THEY KNOW IT! Who do they think they are trying to kid? Lying about sermons that we heard and lectures we received on a regular basis!!

There were lots of things that had bothered me since I was a small child. First of all was the fact that there was so little charity towards anyone. I can remember wanting to help poor children at a very early age...about age five or six. We heard so much about the importance of love and that God's people were the only ones who truly knew how to love. So I was very surprised when I learned that acting upon that love was discouraged. I remember a brother worker's sermon about the word "charity." He said "charity" doesn't mean giving money or things to people, it means "love." I was only about 9 years old, but I can still remember thinking, "yes, but if we love someone who needs help we will want to help him, in whatever way that we can...including money, food or clothes." His reasoning didn't really make sense to me, but I accepted what he said because I had been taught to believe whatever the workers say is directly from God. Who was I to ask questions?

Perhaps the most troubling thing that I noticed very early was how many unhappy marriages there were in the fellowship. Women talk about their husbands in front of children, so I learned early that not many professing wives were happily married. This frightened me a lot, worried that my future might be as miserable. I certainly couldn't figure out just what made some women happy while others were absolutely disgusted with their husbands. Men were frightening creatures to me, big and scary. I didn't have any brothers, so boys were a mystery and extremely puzzling and different from myself. The one impression I formed early was that I would never be able to love someone unless I respected him and I sensed that this was also true the other way around—that love must be built on mutual respect. I spent the night with many different girlfriends over the course of my childhood and it seemed like my unprofessing friends' parents were more happily married than many professing couples were. They also seemed more happy in every way, which was a bit confusing because I constantly was taught that "God's people" are the only people with true joy.

I remember the terrible feeling of sadness that professing people were the only ones with salvation. Some people feel good about this—to me it was horrible. Any time I was in a place where I was the only professing person, I would look at all the other people and think that it was horrible that they were going to hell and there wasn't one thing I could do about it except be a "good example." I wondered if they were noticing this pitiful wretch in the corner with the funny hairdo and if they would look back in eternity and think "Oh, if only I had asked her what church she went to." I had the eeriest feeling of being alone, no matter how many people surrounded me. Sometimes I had the feeling that I should try to attract attention to myself in order to get people to notice me so they could see my "good example." But, if they did notice me, then I felt uncomfortable and wished that they would stop noticing me.

Because the workers never spoke about sin in specific terms, we were made to feel guilty for everything that they did not consider to be a "good example." Embarrassing moments, bad manners, laughing too loud, accidental incidents, listening to the radio, doing something fun on Saturday evening, not being prepared for meeting, asking too many questions, having fun, desiring pretty things, etc., everything that the workers frowned at brought us guilt!!! We were even made to feel guilty if someone else did something wrong, because maybe we could have been a better example, or more encouragement, or something...yet, what was it? One day someone at school happened to mention the Ten Commandments. I didn't know what they were talking about, but of course, I couldn't let anyone know that I didn't know something that was supposed to be in the Bible. So, I went home and asked Mom, "What are the Ten Commandments?" She told me that they aren't called the "Ten Commandments" in the Bible but that the term refers to the laws that God had given Moses on the stone tablets. She said I could find them in the Old Testament...probably in Deuteronomy. So, I looked them up and found out what God had given commandments against, the sins which He would punish His people for unless they offered sacrifices to atone for their sins and repented and turned from them to obey Him. All of a sudden, it dawned on me what it was that was defined as sin. I wondered why the workers didn't warn people against these things and I asked Mom about it. She said, "Oh, that was in the Old Testament. Those are just the basics." It occurred to me that the rule about wearing "men's clothing" was also in the Old Testament, but I don't think that I mentioned that to Mom. It was at this time that I developed a strong conscience regarding the Ten Commandments even more than other things that the workers did talk about. I was very idealistic and that kept me hooked to the workers, because I believed that they were idealistic, too. Even though I was idealistic, I was far from being a perfect professing person, or perfect Christian.

The workers had a troubling way of making me feel unaccepted. They either acted as if I didn't exist or as if I wasn't good enough in some way, but whatever the "good enough" was, I didn't know. As a middle aged adult, it finally dawned on me that very few professing people or workers ever feel "good enough" or accepted. It was just a feeling of not measuring up and it filled me with gloom. As a teenager, during the 1960s, the workers climbed all over us girls for skirt lengths and hairstyles, but I realized that those things weren't moral sins, only worker preferences. Still, I tried as much as possible to fit in, at least when the workers were around. As a child and teenager I pretty much avoided the workers because I saw them as "hard" people and they all looked alike to me. I could never remember their names...there were so many of them, all dressing alike, all frowning. I definitely didn't trust them and felt uneasy around them.

Mom tried to get us to remember workers' names. She had two sisters in the work and so did Dad. The fact that they had close relatives as workers really solidified their loyalty to the ministry. She took great pride in knowing what they were doing and where they were. Most of her spare time was spent in correspondence with workers and she would read their letters to us at the dinner table. The letters were all the same and boring. I couldn't ever get excited about a letter from a worker but correspondence with workers and professing people was just as important as giving testimonies. It was expected. I would actually feel sick if I got a letter from a worker because that meant that I had to write back. It would take me nearly a year to answer because I couldn't think of anything to write. I can remember just sitting and staring at empty paper for the longest time, trying to think of something to put on the letter. Nearly every New Year's resolution I made was that I was going to try to write more letters. Mom encouraged me to find someone new at every convention that I could correspond with.

Professing people and workers seemed so different from the characters of the Bible, yet the workers consistently referred to them as if they were professing people and workers. Jesus had seemed to be a "soft" person, tenderhearted, loving sinners and children, always ready to help someone in trouble. The Jews of the Bible were so vital, so courageous and powerful, but many professing people were so hard, so crabby and often short-tempered. Some were also namby-pamby, so ineffectual, uninteresting and bland. Once I asked my Mom, "Has a professing person ever been president of the United States?" She laughed and acted like that was a silly question but it made sense to me. My Dad was always complaining about the president and I thought that if God wanted a good president that the best one should be a professing president. She didn't agree with me and said something to the effect that "God's people" didn't want fame. I didn't see that the motive for being president was fame, but rather an effort to lead people in the right direction and to help people. If professing people were the wisest and the only ones who knew God's will, then they should be the leaders of the country.

I also remember the first time I heard the word "neurotic" and I asked Mom what it meant and she told me it was a word describing people who were nervous, depressed and who acted unpredictably or were emotionally disturbed. Immediately I thought that it described professing people and workers and I wondered why "God's people" were neurotic. It seemed to me that they should be the most un-neurotic people in the world. The more I observed, the more I felt that the people considered "hearty" and approved by the workers were the most depressed, tense and nervous ones that I knew.

The terms "God's People, Kingdom of Heaven, Family of God, Kingdom of God, Chosen Ones, Spiritual Israel," were always used to apply to ourselves and for that reason, I believe, I became fascinated by the Jewish race and during my high school and adult years I read all kinds of books on Jewish folk stories, literature, history and traditions, pogroms, the holocaust of the Second World War, etc. The more I learned, the more fascinated I became. I often thought how different the professing lifestyle was from Jewish customs and lifestyle, how different the attitudes, etc. It never occurred to me to challenge the idea that WE were the "chosen people." The only Jews we resembled were the

Pharisees. When I think of it now, it seems ludicrous to compare professing people, most of them Gentiles, to Jews. What an insult to Jews. Jewish people have a hilarious sense of humor, they are not afraid to discuss ideas or challenge even their own beliefs. Professing people have very little to laugh about, they are afraid to question anything that the workers say or explore and discuss what the Bible says. They certainly don't understand the meaning of the Old Testament law, nor the customs of Jewish people, nor the radical commitment to God and His Word that orthodox Jews have. Jews actually experienced persecution, real life torture and murder. Professing people's idea of persecution is if someone doesn't like you or talks bad about you—a far cry from persecution.

I can't remember how old I was, probably about 15 years old...but I remember the shock I felt the day I read John 8:32, "Ye shall know the truth and the truth shall set you free." I felt angry...I felt like the Bible was lying. I wasn't free, I had never been free and I knew I never would be free!!!! What on earth was it talking about? I placated myself with the idea that it was just a vague idea of freedom. Maybe it meant free from the world—I didn't know and just put it out of my mind, immediately. It really bothered me. There were many other scriptures that bothered me because they didn't fit the professing way of life, but I just figured that somehow I wasn't understanding the real meaning of them.

While I was young, I dreamed of having children of my own someday. There were things that I noticed professing parents do that I hated and I was determined that "I would never do that when I have kids!" I romanticized having children much more than I romanticized having a husband, probably because Mom loved children so much, but she didn't want us girls to get married. But I knew I had to be a Mom, I longed for children and my biggest fear was that I might not have any. My other fear was that God would require me to be a worker and we had been taught that if He wanted us to be a worker and we were unwilling, that our lives would be cursed forever. Being a worker was the worst thing I could imagine. Their lives seemed to be nothing but traveling misery from all that I could observe. I noticed that they often attempted to convince themselves that they were happy, by talking about how wonderful it was. Giving my testimony twice a week was awful enough. I couldn't imagine a lifetime of giving sermons several times a week, living in other people's homes, sleeping in a different bed all the time, having no personal privacy. I noticed that the younger companion was apparently not allowed to speak unless the older companion seemed to give permission. I had tried to talk to younger workers once and the older worker would butt in and answer. What a dreary existence! I could think of nothing worse unless it was prison.

I had carefully observed the professing women in my world and had picked out personal qualities in almost each one that I wanted to emulate. This is not a surprising thing in view of the fact that a professing person's life is supposed to be "an example." So—I used them as examples, desiring to copy or avoid certain mannerisms or traits. *(The professing principle of "example" isn't exactly a scriptural concept because it focuses too much emphasis on another human's personality and outward appearance and causes harmful comparisons among ourselves. It is more scriptural to let the Holy Spirit direct our lives and use our personalities and talents to glorify Him. We need not "force" our lives*

*into some prescribed example, but instead be our-
selves with God's guidance.)*

I can remember thinking several different times
that it was a good thing that our great grandparents
and grandparents had professed because I was positive that if I had been in another church before
hearing the workers that I wouldn't have been willing for "the Truth" because I couldn't see the
workers' reasoning in the Bible. I understood the
workers message but it didn't seem to me that the
Bible was saying the same thing.

The life of a professing person is rarely very interesting or satisfying but I believe the most
miserable period of life is during the teen years. I
was bored or depressed most of the time. As professing girls, we were expected to stay home and
not do much of anything except sew or write letters. Fortunately, I had a best friend who was my
age and professing. Between her and my sister, I
was able to keep my chin up and in fairly good
emotional condition. If it hadn't been for them and
for the busyness of school and homework, I don't
think I could have handled life. I realize better now
than ever before, just how badly confused and depressed I was. Someone looking on would never
have known how depressed I was, I loved to giggle
and laugh and spent as much time finding things to
giggle about as I could. When I was young, it was
not acceptable to act interested in boys, or to talk
to them in public. The workers did not want the
boys and girls pairing off at meetings, gospel meetings, or conventions. That happened anyway, but it
was supposed to be kept out of sight and unac-
knowledged. This may have changed somewhat in
the later years, but when I was young, it was still
definitely a rule. Mom told me that in some places,
the men and women were separated during conven-

tion, even married couples. Even though I had never personally seen that done, the mentality still seemed to exist among many people, especially the workers. I was so unattractive, I didn't have many people interested in me.

My first year of college I took the required course in World History and for the first time in my life, history came alive. I'll never forget the introduction that the professor gave. It went something like this. "People who hate history don't understand it. We can't understand the world we live in, if we don't understand the history behind it. History is not a bunch of dates one must memorize...it is a record of ideas and the way those ideas impacted human beings. Don't look at the names and dates and places as much as at the ideas that made those names and dates and places famous. We can't know who our friends or enemies are, if we don't know something about the motives, and the philosophy of the people around us." He was one of the most motivational teachers I had, and I learned more about the Catholic Church than I had ever heard in my entire life. My whole interest in history began with that teacher and I became fascinated with world events after that. The reason I tell that story is because about 22 years later I learned the history of my own church and my life was changed dramatically. I suddenly understood the reasons for my beliefs.

I was one of the fortunate ones, I met and married a professing boy, an emotionally stable one. What a miracle that was. At the time I could hardly believe it was true, and I couldn't see why he was even interested in me. I felt I was the most unattractive and uninteresting person I knew, and I was well aware of the huge difference in the amount of professing boys and girls.

About one week before our wedding, I was walking down the street in Seattle, Washington, when I noticed Bob Ingram (the head worker of Alaska) walking toward me on the sidewalk. I was so shocked and surprised to see someone I knew that I skipped up to him and greeted him warmly. I didn't expect him to know me because it had been several years since I had seen him, so I told him who I was. He frowned his intimidating frown and said, "Aren't you the girl who is getting married?!" He said it in such a derogatory tone he made it sound as if I were doing something horrible. I said, "Well, yes, I'm marrying Don Lewis from Kalama...he is a professing boy." He said, "Well, your parents aren't happy about it at all, are they?!" I was shocked. I said, "Well, Dad was upset because he wanted me to finish college, but they like Don real well and they aren't against it." Then he frowned at me like I was guilty of a great crime and I went on my way, with my heart pounding. I really got a lot of flack before we were married. I had about six or more different professing people try to talk me out of getting married and only one person encouraged me, who happened to be an unprofessing relative who was a strong Christian. She also gave me the best marital advice anyone ever gave me. She quoted the scripture that said to never let the sun go down on your wrath and told me that no matter what kind of disagreement we might have that we should always make up before we went to sleep at night or before he left for work, because if one of us died before the argument was settled, we would be miserable forever. This set the pattern for our married future. It seems that the best marital advice we ever received was from Christians who were not workers or professing people.

My husband, Don, is truly one of the most accepting, patient, easy going people I have ever met. I had prayed that God would give me a good-natured, godly husband who would be a good father. After we were married I realized that God had answered all my prayers when He gave me Don. Just about the only natural prayer I can actually remember having answered. It took me a while to settle into being a wife—I definitely didn't know anything at all about being married: green as a frog. At first I had the wrong attitude towards men. I don't know where I picked it up but I thought it was my job to boss him around and sort of treat him like a mother with her little boy. (Maybe I had done too much babysitting) Anyway, it took me several years to adapt to being a wife—but after I did so, I was downright shocked at how wonderful marriage could actually be.

We were lonely during all of our adult professing years. Don and I had both had lots of friends while we were in school. But after we married and in the places we lived there weren't many close friends who were our age. We did things with a few other married couples at first but then we moved to another area and got into the rut of family life. We never really found very many professing people whom we could really visit with about things we were interested in. Friendships in the fellowship are more hazardous than they are worth. We found that the people we thought were friends could easily become enemies. There is just too much tension and too many rules on which so many different people have opinions. Life was also terribly boring. The only thing that one could do for fun was have people over for dinner and that was expensive and a lot of work. It seemed like every day, month and every year was the same...not much to look forward to except convention. I remember several times as I went shopping, thinking, "The only places I ever go is to meetings or the grocery store!"

After having children of our own, I became very aware of how difficult it was to be the kind of mother I had set up as an image in my mind. I was quite disoriented and dismayed with my performance. Also, I began to realize that the worst part of being a parent was taking the babies and children to meeting. I enjoyed almost every day of parenthood except meeting days, which isn't surprising since I hadn't enjoyed meeting days at any time in my life. I felt that all eyes were on us and that some kind of perfection was expected in our wriggley offspring. I felt myself turning into the frowny, depressed, "hard" kind of adult that I had disliked so much as a child. Yes, I had become neurotic! I can remember grieving while the children were young that I couldn't just relax and let them be kids, but that I had to begin molding them right from the start to profess—I had to enforce the rules even when I didn't understand them or agree with them. I remember the moment our first daughter was born, the first thought that flashed into my mind was: "Hair! I'll have to fix her hair!" Even though I was elated to have a daughter, the thought of long hair for her was depressing. Surprisingly, our children turned out well, in spite of my hardness, and seemed to conform to the professing life in every respect. For several years I felt that things were going well and that raising children wasn't as hard as some people made it out to be. Then the teenage years hit me like a ton of bricks. It dawned on me that I was no longer in control of their lives and decisions.

Ever since I was a small child I had noticed and had heard grieving parents crying on the workers' shoulders about their wayward children or problem husbands and I had pitied them, and wondered what it was that the workers had to say to such people. A majority of the children I was raised with left "the Truth." Some of them had multiple marriages, or live-in situations, even before that was a common thing in society. Some had developed drinking problems or drug problems and were a big worry and disappointment to their parents. Since all the counseling sessions are done privately, very few ever knew just what it was that workers said to grieving parents. The workers let us all know that they alone had the words directly from the Lord that no one else on earth could understand and counsel as the workers could.

However, the day came when someone very close to me was going through difficult waters and I happened to be in on the conversation with her and four workers. I was wondering what the four workers, all of them well into middle age, would have as words of wisdom and comfort for this woman I loved so much. Imagine to my surprise that they didn't have ONE thing to say except, "Poor girl, Oh, you poor girl." They didn't lay hands on her and pray for her, they didn't have any marriage counsel or any practical suggestions for what she should do next. I was so outraged that I wanted to yell, "GET OUT!! Get out of here and leave us alone!!!"

I had already begun to have my doubts about the superlative wisdom of the workers a few years before this when it began to dawn on me that their sermons were exactly the same things I had heard all my life, over and over. Nothing helpful for everyday living and nothing instructive about how we could reach a perishing world for Christ, no specific counsel for the professing people or children in how to avoid moral problems and sin. I had thought that eventually I would learn more about the Bible as I grew older, but I was getting older and the workers had not taught me anything that I didn't already know from childhood. I decided it was up to me to ensure some scriptural understanding.

When my own Dad had been in his middle forties he must have come to the same conclusion because he decided to do a topical Bible study. He bought dozens of inexpensive Bibles and about 40 notebooks, three ring binder types and he went through the Bibles and cut out and pasted all the verses together in his notebooks that mentioned the words or topics that he was studying. This project took hours every day and cost quite a bit of money for all the materials. The most unusual thing about it all was the attitude that the workers and professing relatives took towards his activity. They sort of mocked him as a simpleton. I'm sorry to say that at the time, I didn't see much reason for all the trouble, mainly because I had never been taught how to do a word study or a topical study, because we were supposed to depend on the workers to tell us what the Bible meant and also because the only thing expected from a professing person, even if he was an elder, was to get up and either say how thankful he was for "the Way" and the Workers or how he wanted to be a better example in the coming week.

Don and I felt that we should do all we could to help others "profess" and it became a big effort to try to bring people to meeting and to talk to outsiders about our beliefs. After several failures to convince acquaintances to see things as we did, we began to analyze what it was that we were doing wrong. We discussed our conversations and the workers' sermons and it dawned on us that what we and the workers were doing was trying to convince people that the Way and the Workers were right rather than to convince them that God's Word was true and that Jesus was worth believing in. This bothered us but what could we do about it? This was all we had ever learned.

During the late 1970's, after the Vietnam war was over, there were lots of boat people immigrating to the United States. every newspaper and magazine had heart rending pictures of people needing help. I was very troubled by the situation and wanted desperately to help some of these people. We had even considered adopting a Vietnamese baby. One day I can remember praying that if there were any boat people who God had his hand on and who would profess, that he would bring them into our lives so that we could help them. I felt very badly that the friends weren't involved with charity of this sort, because many of our neighbors were involved with the church sponsorship of Cambodians, Laotians or Vietnamese people and I participated in their collection of necessary items. But, I felt envious of their ability to organize an effort that was so worthwhile. In less than a week after my prayer, I received a phone call from someone asking me if we would consider sponsoring a Laotian family with four little children who had just arrived. I was quite surprised to have that prayer answered and we immediately said "Yes." That began an eye opening experience for us. We thought that the friends and workers would become interested in the situation and help us, or at least show an interest in the family which we brought to gospel meetings every week for a whole year or more. The man even verbally accepted

Christ while riding home from gospel meeting one day. The meeting hadn't been tested or anything. He told us in halting English that he had been raised Buddhist, but that he wanted to be a Christian and that he wanted to follow Jesus. He opened his hymn book and read the words to a hymn that sings of following Jesus. He had actually been primed for Christianity by a Catholic priest, while he was in Thailand in one of the refugee camps. He was very moved by the words to that hymn and even though I am sure he understood nothing of what was said in gospel meeting, he did want to be a Christian. I believe that he did receive the Holy Spirit, because his life has been spent in kindness and mercy to everyone who comes in contact with him. He even went back to Laos after the war was over and literally gave away over a thousand dollars and food to starving people and told us about lecturing a man who was neglecting and starving his own son, while keeping and eating food for himself. Souvanh gave food to the child. Souvanh is a very strong character, a hard worker, and extremely loyal to his family and friends. We felt blessed to know this family. However, NO one at meeting was interested in them. A few people would shake hands with them and act nicely. The workers visited them once or twice. But we noticed a few people who acted strangely, as if they resented the presence of foreigners, and there were a few offhand remarks that offended us. I remember, at that time, wondering just how "Christian" this group really was. Thankfully, there are many charitable, nonracist professing people in the group. I knew that there were lots of them, but that aspect of their character is actually discouraged by the attitudes of the workers towards charity.

As our two older children became teenagers, I noticed that the moral climate both inside and outside "the Truth" was much more hostile to biblical morals (i.e., The Ten Commandments) than when I was a child and I was worried that our professing children could become lured into situations that we wouldn't have any control over. Sex, alcohol and drugs had crept into the fellowship. (I didn't learn until later that they had been in the fellowship all along, just more hidden.) It dawned on me that we had not "taught" our children "to think as Christians" but only "to behave as professing people." It was a coercive, manipulative parenting technique, not an approach to their minds and cognitive wills. I looked for help from the workers and even asked one of them if he would do a special teaching session with the professing teenagers in the area because there were lots of teens in the field and I knew that all the parents would be needing help in this regard. He had often done special studies on other subjects, so I didn't see that this was an unreasonable request. He told me in no uncertain terms that it wasn't necessary to teach the children, that the Holy Spirit did this job. He said that if children didn't obey their parents, they certainly wouldn't listen to the workers—which is true enough. I should have known better than to have asked him because he obviously did not enjoy children and had no patience with teenagers. Moreover, I believe the lack of interest in the Ten Commandments, the Biblical definition of sin, keeps the workers from being able to warn the young people of immorality. Their broader definition of sin with its emphasis on the outer appearance is what keeps them occupied. The workers spend too much energy watching hairstyles and hemlines and warning against TV and don't pay attention to dishonesty, and immorality. The workers somehow have the idea that ignorance and innocence are synonymous. They are NOT! Ignorance can lead to a loss of innocence. I asked several workers why they didn't do more preaching on moral sin and received several surprising answers: "It doesn't do any good. The workers tried that once in Seattle when several people were committing adultery and it didn't stop them, they just kept right on." "Oh! The workers aren't policeman. They can't do that!" "It isn't necessary, the Holy Spirit directs people who submit." Yet the workers find time to scold people for ridiculous things like hair, TVs, sports, etc.

Later this same worker came to the point of privately threatening me that I would "lose out" if I persisted in questioning the workers' authority. I couldn't understand his statement until later because I didn't see that I had questioned their authority at all. I had simply looked to them to do their job of protecting the sheep, teaching and warning the people against immorality and they had failed me. It dawned on me later that he had meant that I was supposed to believe that the workers received direct revelation from God and therefore, they were the authority I was NOT to question or make suggestions to. When he rejected my suggestion to teach the children about Christian morals I decided that my only other option was to look to Christian information for child raising suggestions. I had heard other Christian friends of mine suggest Dr. James Dobson's books and radio program for helpful, practical things that parents could do for encouraging their children in Christian moral and scriptural understanding. So, I felt very little guilt to go elsewhere for information. My first entry into a Christian bookstore was a shock. I stared in disbe-

lief at the shelves of books all containing information I had wondered about for years. One of the
first books I noticed was a *Topical Bible*, exactly
what my poor Dad had spent years working on in
his bedroom. I bought it for him and he was
amazed to have it. The books for children were
some of my favorites, although my first choices
were on child rearing, on moral and social issues
and what the Bible had to say about what was happening in the world today. I remembered a
conversation I had had with a sister worker when
our oldest two were ages two and four. I had
wanted some Christian books with pretty pictures
and words geared to the mind of a toddler. I had
asked her why we didn't have anything interesting
for young children and she said, "Oh, God doesn't
want us to appeal to the FLESH!" I had accepted her
statement without question but now I began to see
that it wasn't the flesh they were concerned about.
It was the MIND! The workers don't try to reach the
minds of the people, they bypass the mind and go
for the emotions and will instead. But the will can't
be thoroughly convinced without the activity of the
mind. I had been raised on the adage that "The
only book we need is the Bible." I realize now that
that statement is an intimidation device, saying in
effect, "Don't you dare read any books except the
Bible." The early workers like Jack Carroll and Willie Jameison didn't allow people to own or use
Bible dictionaries and it is no wonder that many of
the friends and workers are so ignorant of the message of the Bible. The Bible is all we need to direct
our lives and receive salvation, yes! But if someone
comes along and twists the scripture into nonsense
it takes some work to straighten it out again. Christian literature which helps us reason our way
through certain issues can shorten the length of

time to figure things out on our own. I praise God for the men and women through the ages who have committed their lives to studying the Bible in great depth.

The workers always mock educated Christians and compare them to the scribes and Pharisees and say that God despises the wise and the prudent. But the workers have twisted the meaning of that text. God warns us against those who say there is no God and who believe they are wiser than His Word. God doesn't reject those who search the scripture. He commends them and rewards those who diligently seek Him. Many workers avoid people who are well versed in the scripture.

While our two oldest were teenagers, the home school movement was just beginning to gain momentum in our area. Our youngest daughter was unhappy in school and went to school nearly every day in tears, begging to stay home even though she was doing well in school and had plenty of friends. I was even doing volunteer work at the school in order to bolster her enthusiasm for it, but instead she begged me to teach her at home. We hadn't been happy with the high school experiences our two older children had had. Our son's last two years of high school had been filled with values clarification, secular humanism, death desensitization, anti-American ideas, lifeboat situational ethics, globalism, etc. When I objected to some of the ideas which were being presented to the students, the principal and superintendent simply ignored me and patted me on the head as if I was nobody who mattered. I had read two books by Tim LaHaye entitled *Battle For the Mind* and *Battle For the Public Schools* and was aware of the anti-Christian, anti-capitalism, anti-American bias which is the logic behind the National Education Association's agenda. I learned the source of the logic which was being taught and was shocked to realize that I myself had previously held many secular thoughts and attitudes. It occurred to me that this was really what the Bible meant by the word "worldly." I was shocked to realize that "worldliness" was a belief system rather than a "look." Our middle daughter was having trouble in school with a few girls who threatened to beat her up every once in awhile. I strongly suspect that the fact that she looked different had something to do with their hostility. I made her wear skirts to school every day and it was the custom of everyone else to wear pants to school. School had become a hostile place...not the haven it had been for me as a child. So, we began to homeschool Jeanne. It hadn't occurred to me that the workers would disapprove. Instead I had expected them to be supportive in the decision because my real motives were moral ones due to the secular hostility towards Christian morals and beliefs.

Imagine our surprise when the workers began to preach at us in meeting, come to our home and make veiled comments that sounded slightly like threats or warnings. Also, it was apparent that they were talking behind our backs to the other friends because some people who had been our best friends started shunning us after meeting. They told people that I was trying to persuade everyone to homeschool. This wasn't true and they knew it, because I told them I didn't think homeschooling was good for everyone. I myself had loved school and would have been very unhappy if I couldn't have attended. I just believed that every parent should know what was being taught in school that was undermining the moral principles of their children, so that they could counteract the logic which was being presented. We had been in good standing, had meeting in our home and Don was an elder. This kind of treatment was a new thing to us. It was frightening and disconcerting as well. At first we thought it would blow over, but it continued for months and the workers would only come and talk to me alone. They never would talk to Don and I together unless it was during meeting when they would preach at us, even in gospel meetings. It became almost funny because we would sit there and listen to them, knowing full well that every thing they were saying was directed at us and that anyone else listening to the sermons would wonder what on earth they were talking about. The main subject that they spent weeks trying to get across was that "knowledge was bad, but that wisdom was good." They were definitely objecting to the fact that we had gotten a conviction about understanding what we believed. We had been revealing too much of our understanding in our testimonies apparently. They didn't like our sudden interest in finding out what the scripture meant and making up our own mind about the meaning. We were supposed to accept the workers' meaning of what the scripture said. Their messages made very little sense...they would get up and make some kind of statement that was like a premise and then look for a verse or two to support it and the verses they chose nearly always contradicted their premise but they didn't seem to realize it. The Bible clearly teaches that knowledge of God and His Word is good. This kind of treatment woke me up...I had lived for years in a tunnel-like existence, averting my eyes and ears to all the signals that gave me pain or questions. Now, every antenna was up...I was looking at everyone and everything in a new light. My mind had switched on again. I began researching every subject I could think of, I started recording things that occurred to me and talking to Christian friends that I had met through the homeschool movement. Later I began listening to Christian pastors on the radio and Christian talk shows nearly all day long. I sent away for tapes of sermons that I heard about which covered topics I hadn't known even existed. All this time I still considered myself a hearty professing person. I had no intention of leaving the church, nor did I see any reason for leaving it. I had just decided that I wanted to know more about God and His Word and I was going to do all that was in my power to learn everything I could, no matter what anyone, even the workers had to say to me or about me.

Some people have asked me why I think the workers objected to us homeschooling, since in the past they had disapproved of formal education. I have recently found out, since then, that some workers don't object to it. Some do. I can't say, for sure, just why they put this pressure on us. Perhaps they sensed that we were becoming too independent, forming convictions on our own and out from under the bondage of their authority and they resented it. One worker said something to the effect of, "Yes, I understand why you object to what is going on in the public schools but you don't need to go to such extreme lengths to stand up for what you believe." I couldn't believe my ears. Here was someone who had given up the prospect of husband, home and children or career to do what she believed was right and she was telling me not to stand up for my convictions. I had been raised to believe that we were supposed to die for what we believed was right. It became obvious that the only convictions they wanted us to stand up for were *their* convictions.

Don was just as thirsty for scriptural information as I was. He was very serious about his role as elder and spent a lot of time praying and reading his Bible, praying for the people in our meeting, serious about his testimonies. For years he got excruciating, blurry headaches every Wednesday and Sunday. At first he thought they were sinus headaches, later, he realized they were "meeting headaches," caused from the tension he felt before and during meetings. (After we quit going to meetings he never had those headaches again.) He was bothered by the fact that he would read something from the Bible and form an understanding of what it meant, only to have a worker come along and make some other meaning out of it. He didn't agree with the workers' method of jumping around in the Bible, linking certain ideas which obviously had no connection with each other. He also had met several Christians in the work place and had respected them and felt strongly that they were saved. I learned later that he had begun having doubts many years before I had, but had just kept quiet about them for the sake of keeping peace. He had avoided Convention and Special Meetings as often as possible without appearing obvious about it. Now our marriage relationship was being cemented in God's Word in a way never possible before. We would talk way into the early hours of the morning about everything we had recently read or heard about in the Bible. We tried to think of questions that had never occurred to us before. Our children were tired of hearing us talk about the Bible. At first they were worried that we were getting off on the wrong track, following false teachers, but when they heard the strange reasoning the workers were giving us, they began to agree with us and joined the conversations themselves. We began reaching out to para-Church seminars which are seminars for Christians of all denominations and specialize in certain subjects, such as marriage, parenting, grief counseling, creation research, etc. I had begun a huge collection of books and tapes and kept them hidden upstairs in my chest of drawers so that visiting friends and workers couldn't see that I was going elsewhere for biblical information. I knew that what we were doing was highly "illegal" in the workers' eyes.

The more Christian information I received, the more I became very convicted about certain social issues that I had never thought about before. I was learning the "other side of the story" which is rarely, if ever, presented in the secular media. I formed a conviction against abortion that I had not felt before. One day I took part in picketing an abortion clinic. I was still a hearty professing person and I was alone with dozens of Christians who were willing for real persecution. It was a strange sensation. It was obvious that they knew far more about what was going on in the world that I did, and they had much more conviction about scripture than I had ever seen a worker have. I was extremely uncomfortable and afraid. I wasn't afraid of the abortionists or the public opinion...I was afraid of the workers and friends. As I stood there with my sign, I cringed every time a car went past because there were lots of professing families in that neighborhood and I was afraid a professing person would see and recognize me there. I was already in trouble for homeschooling and asking workers about moral issues. I was afraid they would come to our house and scold me for getting "involved" with worldly concerns. As I stood there feeling afraid, it suddenly dawned on me that I must be affiliated with the wrong church, if I couldn't stand

up and be counted in an issue as important as murdering babies. That night I talked to Don about how
much I feared the workers coming and talking to
me about what I had done that day. I'll never forget
his thoughtful answer. He said, "Well, if they come
and scold you, you tell them that Jesus threw the
money changers out of the temple because they
were corrupting the house of prayer. If Jesus was
angry about that, what do you think He feels about
butchering babies? Our bodies are supposed to be
the temples of God!"

We also became involved in helping an acquaintance who was running for political office. We
were strongly opposed to the ethics of the man's
opponent and felt that we should support someone
whose ethics we could agree with. We KNEW full
well how the workers feel about politics. They had
made that point many times throughout our lives,
but suddenly we could see that if Christians fail to
stand up and be counted for their convictions and
values, that it was the same thing as not being light
and salt in the world. So, once again we defied the
workers' rules. I began to feel that we were living
two different lives. A professing life and a Christian
life. We preferred the Christian life, but we were
stuck with the professing life because of our families.

About this time some professing friends, the Luxons, moved into our town and we renewed our old
acquaintance with them. They had moved around
quite a bit and we hadn't seen them in years and in
our very first visit we noticed that they, too, had
lost that "shuttered look" that we had begun to recognize as a typical trait of most professing people.
Someone has described it as seeing *the eyes regis-
ter the snapping shut of the mind.* (I believe the
shuttered look is motivated by ignorance, and fear

of having that ignorance exposed.) Hesitantly at
first, we skirted a few issues to test the waters to
see if they were interested in outside information.
They were! And our friendship was solidly built on
our interest in learning more about what the scripture really had to say rather than the same old
subject of meeting in the home and the ministry
without a home. The first tapes we shared with
them was one that a Christian friend of ours had
shared with us—John MacArthur's tape series, *Is
The Bible Reliable?* When I recently listened to
those tapes again, I had to laugh to think about
how extraordinary it was for me, an ignorant professing person, to hear that information. It was
absolutely heart pounding for me. It occurred to us
that what we had heard all of our lives was why
the workers were reliable rather than why God's
Word and Promises were reliable. As in so many
other areas, the workers' words are subtly undermined by their attitudes and behavior. They claim
to preach God's Word, but the friends lose confidence in the scripture rather than believing it. They
claim to stand for strong marriages, but rather they
undermine marital harmony and family together-
ness. They claim to uphold women and femininity
because they believe in women preachers and long
hair and skirts, but women are treated chauvinisti-
cally. They claim to be a family unit, united by
love and close friendship, but instead the friends
are afraid of intimate relationships with each other
because of the betrayal of trust and lack of agreement on doctrine and legalism within the
fellowship. They claim to be happy but many are
actually depressed most of the time. They claim to
be the only ones who know the scripture but they
know very little about it and can't explain it even
to themselves without a worker to verify it.

For two years or more, the four of us would get together every week for fun and end up discussing what we had recently noticed, or had been studying in the scripture. We attended seminars together and began to compare what the workers said with what the Bible said. We were noticing discrepancies everywhere. The big differences were in the bottom line logic of what the workers said and what the Bible said. Still, we weren't planning to leave the group, we were just disenchanted with it. We thought the Way was okay but the workers were just a little ignorant.

The Luxons had acquired a copy of **The Secret Sect** several years before moving back into our area. This is the catalyst that had disturbed and alerted them to the fact that the workers had not been honest about the history of "The Truth" and the activity of several head workers had undermined their confidence in the wisdom of the workers. They had offered to let us read it, but at first we had refused, believing, as we had heard, that it had been written by some unwilling, bitter person. But after awhile we decided to look at it. After all, we were quite capable of making up our own mind about whether information was true or not. What a shock! I had heard enough information from family remarks and from elderly professing people to know that the information in the book was accurate. We realized now that our church was not the original New Testament Church, founded by Jesus Christ and His apostles. It was less than 100 years old and the brain storm of an ignorant, egotistical, immoral man who had rejected Christian beliefs and started his own group using ideas borrowed from other cult leaders contemporary of his era. We were angry and shocked but still confused about what to do with our new knowledge. We couldn't tell anyone else, not even our parents. The shock had put us in tremendous turmoil, we couldn't bear to put someone else in the same kind of misery.

One day I was listening, as usual, to the Christian radio station and I heard some old acquaintances of ours, Conrad and Sandra Sundholm, speaking on the radio about their experience as Mormons. We had known them when they were Mormons and our oldest son had been close friends with their son in school. I remembered that I had prayed for them that they would leave Mormonism and "profess" someday, because I had really admired their meek and gentle lives and had grieved because they were "lost." They had been raised as Christians but when they were a young married couple, two Mormon missionaries had come to their door and had begun planting Mormon ideas into their minds. They had both actually, physically heard a voice telling them that Joseph Smith was "the true prophet of God." They had been Mormons for about 14 years and then Conrad had been put in charge of the Mormon Children's Sunday School curriculum for the full 12 years of school and while he was studying the information he became suddenly aware that the emphasis was not on Jesus Christ but instead upon the "example" of Jesus and the importance of believing the Mormon leaders "without question," and the importance of "having a testimony that Joseph Smith was the true prophet of God." How could that be, he thought, that they were the Church of Jesus Christ of Latter Day Saints and there was so little emphasis on Jesus Christ? Immediately he became suspicious but he was so afraid that someone would find out that he was having doubts and studying to confirm those doubts, that for a few years he kept all his notes and studies under lock and key, fearing even to tell Sandra about his doubts.

I became acutely interested in their testimony because we were going through the same kind of fear, keeping all our Christian books and information hidden in the bedroom behind a closed door. I was so paranoid, I even kept the address and phone number of Booksellers, USA hidden and not in my regular address book. Why should I fear someone would find out that I was learning more about Jesus Christ and His Word? Anyway our friends, Conrad and Sandra Sundholm were giving seminars to explain the differences between Mormonism and Christianity and wanted to help people understand better how to go about helping their friends and relatives leave Mormonism and turn to Jesus Christ for salvation. Don and I decided to attend, and the next few weeks we attended evening sessions which explained Mormon beliefs. The classes were not attacking Mormons, in fact they told what wonderful people they are and described just what it is that Mormons believe and do. Sundholm's ministry is called Truth in Love Ministry and that is just what it is. Their ministry has helped hundreds of people come to know the truth about Jesus and His salvation. As we sat there listening to the grief and fear that they went through in leaving the Mormon church, we were struck by the many similar thoughts, feelings and situations that we were having. I made a list of the similarities between Mormon beliefs and the workers' beliefs. Some interesting similarities were that Joseph Smith and William Irvine had both declared that Christendom and its creeds was apostate, and that they alone had been raised up to restore true Christianity. The two by two, door to door missionaries who traveled on bicycles, the "holy" underwear required of all

Mormons were not much different from the customs of Two by Two (Pilgrims) workers on bicycles with brown underwear for men and the black stockings for women that was originally required for Go-Preachers. The big emphasis is on the "testimony" of each person regarding their trust in a human leader. And the fact that Mormons believe that Jesus was just a man who gave us an example life of how to become a god, and the requirement of no questioning of the leadership or the information given by the leadership. There were dozens of similarities, but that didn't compare to the list I later made with Jehovah Witnesses beliefs.

I remembered once when I was a young married woman, after having had some Mormon missionaries come to our door, that I had asked the sister worker in our field what it was Mormons believed that was wrong. I had thought that if I understood their beliefs, I could explain to them why they were in error and what the Bible really said about those things. But the worker had emphatically told me that I did not need to know what they believed to know it was wrong. She used the old cliche about the counterfeit dollar—"We don't need to understand error if we just understand truth." Baloney! If you don't know what defects are common in counterfeit money, you aren't going to recognize it either! Especially, if all you have ever seen is counterfeit! I know now why the workers don't want the friends to understand cultic doctrine. It is too similar to their own doctrine. I have since learned of other professing people who were set free after studying why Mormon doctrine was wrong. They could see all the holes in the workers' doctrine. Every time I hear that old cliche about counterfeit dollars, my blood pressure goes up. There is no comparison between counterfeit money and cults.

One is a physical, observable piece of material, the other is a complex group of ideas which is much more difficult to examine, especially if there has been no written documentation of it.

A few weeks after we attended the seminar explaining Mormon beliefs, the Christian radio talk show host interviewed John Warren, a pastor affiliated with a counter cult ministry known as Witness, Inc. It was founded by Duane Magnani who had been raised as a Jehovah Witness and who had gone through the painful discovery that the Watchtower organization was not the "truth teaching" source that he had been led to believe. Magnani developed his own method of reaching the minds of people controlled by the Watchtower brainwashing system. He says that since the Watchtower is the authority of Jehovah Witnesses rather than the Bible, that one must expose the false and contradictory teachings of the Watchtower, thus destroying its credibility as the medium between God and the Jehovah Witnesses. John was describing the differences between Jehovah Witnesses doctrine in comparison to Christian doctrines. Then I really became alarmed. Many of the main statements made by Jehovah Witnesses are almost verbatim to what the workers say. Of course, there are some differences but the similarities far outweigh the differences. For instance, JWs call their system, "The Truth." They go door to door in pairs of two, they mock Christian people and churches with the same rhetoric and cliches, yet want to be thought of as Christians, themselves. They say that Christianity is apostate and that Charles Russell restored the original New Testament Church. They discourage their young people from education, careers, or marrying and having children and encourage them, instead, to spend most of their time for the Kingdom. They don't worship Jesus, nor accept Him as God. They excommunicate anyone who asks too many questions or disagrees with the leadership. They are secretive about their origin and their head-quarters. They refer to themselves as workers in the harvest field. Now, he really had my attention. If those things were not right—and I definitely could believe they may not be right, I HAD to know what other Christians believed were right. I still wasn't aware of what DOCTRINE was. This was the missing link that I had NOT examined. I had been under the impression that the word "doctrine" was unbiblical. It had always been used by the workers in a de-rogatory sense. So, I looked it up in the concordance of my Bible and sure enough, it was there and it was used in a positive light. Then I had to look up the meaning of it, which is simply "teaching." It amuses me now to think that I was so ignorant of what doctrine was, but originally I had only been interested in Christian morals and in in-stilling Christian logic and behavior in myself and our children. I could see that the workers are like the Watchtower organization—they are the authori-ties of the Bible and the mediators between professing people and God. And William Irvine had the same kind of cultural and religious background as Charles Russell, so Irvine wasn't such an unusual prophet, he simply stole someone else's ideas and added a few of his own. One of the biggest differ-ences between the Watchtower and the Workers is that the Watchtower believes in publishing its ideas and the Workers forbid publishing theirs. The Watchtower is the biggest publishing company in the world. The Workers are the most invisible, non-teaching people in the world. That is one reason they have been able to confuse so many people be-cause they refuse to come right out and tell people what they believe. If someone tries to pin them down on something, they say, "Oh, you misunderstood what was said." But they rarely try to explain what they do mean unless they think they can convince you of their point of view.

John Warren gave his home telephone number on the radio and invited people to call and ask questions and he would help them with information or even go talk to their JW relatives himself. Out of curiosity, I decided to call him. I wasn't going to identify myself, I just wanted to ask a few more questions. At first he thought I was a Jehovah Witness by the questions I was asking and finally out of embarrassment I blurted out that I wasn't, but that I had been raised in a group that didn't have a name, etc. He said, "Is this by chance the group known as the Cooneyites or the Two-by-Twos?" I said, "Well, yes, some people call it by those names." He said, "I'd like to come visit you if I may. I know a man who had been a Jehovah Witness and I got him out of that, but then he turned right around and joined the Cooneyites. I want to learn some more about that group." It turned out that he lived only about 15 minutes from our house and he made arrangements to come the very next day and be there while Don was at home. He wanted to talk to both of us. I liked that. I didn't want to talk to someone alone. (The workers usually put me in spot by myself.)

He came and sat in our living room and asked us point blank a few direct questions about who and what the workers said about Jesus Christ and when we answered them, he said, "There is no doubt about it, that is a cult. You need to get out of it immediately. Write a letter and let them know you are leaving it and why." We were shocked—not that it was a cult, for we had suspected that—

but we were shocked that we had to leave it. Don was ready, but I wasn't. All I could think of was our precious parents. I didn't really care about anyone but them, by this point. I had seen that the people we had thought were our friends, weren't really friends at all. All it had taken was for us to do something a bit different, ask a few questions, and we were dropped like hot potatoes. We had only a few professing friends who would still love us no matter what we did. But our parents would be heartbroken and worried sick. They would think we were going to hell and that all their hard work of loving and protecting us had been wasted. They might even reject us or at least there would be a breach between us so that we could no longer talk about God and feel comfortable in their presence. I didn't care about the workers. I had lost all respect for the workers by this point. I only felt extreme pity for them—even the ones I genuinely liked, I felt weren't to be trusted.

So, we said, "No. We can't leave it. We know it is a cult, and the beliefs are wrong, but you don't understand. These are our friends and relatives. We can't leave them. Maybe we can help them understand what is right. We love our parents. We can't hurt them like that. You just don't understand. God knows what we believe...we believe that our salvation comes through trusting in the blood atonement of Jesus Christ and that Jesus is fully God and fully man. We know it isn't by self effort that we are saved. We know we have salvation...we have the joy of our salvation and are secure, but we just can't leave the fellowship." John said, "Well, you'll see...cults won't let true Christians stay in if they start verbalizing the truth about Jesus. They will either kick you out or you will get so sick of them you will have to leave."

Before he left that day, John asked me if I would record for him all the different doctrines that the workers teach. He said that the counter-cult ministries had not been able to effectively warn people about the Cooneyites/Two-by-Twos because their doctrine had never been accurately recorded anywhere for Christian ministers to analyze and refute. Sure, I could do that. In fact, I had already started doing that on my own and I had been thinking of nothing else for about three or four years. Thus began an obsession that kept me busy for two years until it was published as *The Church Without A Name*. (I chose a pen name to protect the relationship with our families. The name, David Stone was chosen because I felt like David, throwing rocks at Goliath. I wanted to use a man's name because I know their chauvinistic attitude towards women. They would accuse me of unwillingness for the appearance code, even though I was willing for it. They automatically reject anything a woman says with the accusation of unwillingness.)

John Warren also asked if we would take him to some meetings so we took him to the next Portland Special Meeting. He sat there listening, absolutely floored and outraged. His face turned beet red and in the middle of one sermon he nearly jumped to his feet and started shouting in protest. It scared Don and me to death. We thought we were going to have a scene on our hands! He told us later that he had never heard such drivel in his life. He said the Jehovah Witnesses can preach better than the workers can! But he said that our singing and our hymns really reminded him of Jehovah Witness hymns—dreary and depressing.

Well, John's advice about staying in or leaving the group was correct. We had already experienced the pressure they put on us when we had asked ex-

tremely simple questions. We had immediately
stopped asking questions and simply started looking
for answers on our own. We knew what would happen if we tried to tell them the answers to some
questions they had apparently never considered.
And he was right about how the cult affected us
from that point on. Every meeting was suffocating.
We dreaded every one and could hardly wait to get
out of the house. We stopped attending gospel
meeting for fear that our presence there might give
people the impression that we believed the ignorant
messages. We loved everyone in our fellowship
meetings and could hardly stand to think of not
having them as friends anymore but we almost fell
off our chairs at some of the things that they would
say. Why had we never noticed how shallow and
repetitive the testimonies were before? I began to
remember some of my own ignorant testimonies
and was ashamed of myself.

We had learned that the key doctrinal questions
that distinguish a cult are what is said about the
Father, Jesus Christ, the Holy Spirit and the gospel
of salvation by grace through the Blood of Jesus
Christ. There are other factors of course, but those
are the preliminary ones. The burning question that
haunted me for about a week or more, was "What
difference does it make, who Jesus is?" I just
couldn't figure that out. I couldn't see that this was
an issue in the Bible. But then it dawned on
me...The Jews had always made a big deal about
Who God was and who it was that they worshipped. They would risk death before they would
bow the knee to any human being or idol. Worship
was important and Who we worship is even more
important. So, did we worship Jesus Christ or not?
If we worship Him and He isn't God then we are in
big trouble and if He is God and we don't worship

Him, we are in big trouble. So, is He God or is He just a man, like the workers say he is? I realized after reading all the different pertinent scriptures that He is fully God and He is fully man. And we must worship Him in Spirit and in Truth. But what was worship? I didn't see any worship going on in the meetings, nothing like the kind of worship described in the Old Testament or even in the New Testament. And due to their deceitfulness, I didn't see much truth there either. God had been dethroned and made into something just a little higher than a human, but in some ways not even higher, just more ethereal or mystical.

As soon as I understood and believed that Jesus Christ was in fact fully God, as well as fully human, it seemed that I understood how sinful I was. Realizing how pure and holy Jesus was made me know how unholy and impure I was. I had been willing before to acknowledge that I was a sinner, but it was more words than anything else. I felt like a good person. I was an obedient professing person and somehow felt justified by that, even though I also felt guilty and unaccepted all the time. As I saw who Jesus was and understood better what he meant in the Sermon on the Mount, I felt totally humiliated by my own sinful nature—not just what I had done or thought or said in the past, but of what I knew I was capable of doing and being. I realized that I had no right to claim salvation at all, no matter what I did. At the same time that I realized that, I also was filled with the most euphoric feeling of cleansing. I felt saved for the first time in my life...also I understood scripture in a way that I had never understood it before. It seemed so clear and readable. Why had it seemed so mysterious and foggy before? Some people feel that they were saved while professing. Myself, I am not sure when

I became saved. All I know is that once I was blind and now I see. It seemed like a slow process. I do know that when I professed at age 12, I was totally sincere in my desire to serve God. Maybe He accepted me then, I have no idea. I do feel that God had His hand on me all my life because I can honestly say that I always loved Him and felt that He was directing me and protecting me all my life.

The Luxons had put us in touch with two other ministries, Threshing Floor Ministries, and Booksellers, USA. This began the wheels turning for accumulating more information about the historical and doctrinal background of what the workers teach. I learned far more from them than I had learned from **The Secret Sect.** Threshing Floor had been collecting information from all over the world for about 15 years at that time, collecting case histories, information regarding scandals which we had not known existed, statistical data, boxes of pictures, sermon notes, historical memorabilia, etc. Booksellers USA was the most helpful in showing how the workers, especially the senior workers, actually oppose the true gospel of the Bible and how hard they try to cover up the truth of their origin. Up until our conversation with them, I had been under the impression that the workers simply were scripturally ignorant. After hearing the testimony and the actual recorded words of the workers whom they had dealt with, it became obvious that the workers were engaged in a type of conspiracy to keep people in bondage. It was shocking. Why would the workers want to continue a system which actually harmed themselves more than it did other people? I don't have the answer to that, except that Satan is the greatest deceiver there is. His deception destroys people in the worst possible ways. The harm done towards professing families is generational, very subtle and often invisible because the workers and friends have deceived themselves more than anyone else. Leaving the church doesn't help someone until he knows the reasons for his misery because once you are raised professing, you stay professing unless you get saved. No matter how wild a person may get in order to distance himself from this trap, he is still trapped as long as he believes the workers' lies. The suicides, divorces, miserable marriages, child abuse, nervous breakdowns, destructive lifestyles, even a few murders which have resulted from the workers teaching must be exposed so that the workers will examine what they are actually saying and doing that is harming people. They aren't preaching like Jesus, they are preaching like William Irvine. It isn't a message of hope, life and salvation. It is a message of bondage, death and deception.

Don said, "Truth is simple, but not stupid. The workers' message can't be the truth because God's truth couldn't be that ignorant." We continued attending meeting for several more months but it was extremely difficult. We had moved to another field and another state, which made it easier to remain invisible because we no longer had meeting in our home. But, eventually, Don gave me an ultimatum. We are leaving soon! I was having nightmares continually. I would wake up in a sweat with my heart pounding because in my nightmares I was preaching to the workers or drowning or having other very symbolic dreams. I also dreamed about telling our parents and siblings. I was constantly remembering old sermons or conversations. I would record the workers' interpretation and logic and then look to see if that was really what the Bible said. Invariably the workers were wrong. I was shocked at the extent of errors. At first, I had assumed there would just be a few errors, later I came to the conclusion that just about everything they taught was wrong. There were a few right things but even some of the right things they said had a double or hidden meaning. They sometimes start saying the right thing and end up saying the wrong thing. Some workers were more scripturally accurate than others, but the general outcome of the entire system is error.

I was going through grieving common to those who go through divorces. I walked around in a daze, thinking and talking only about "The Subject": what the workers taught and what the Bible said. I was angry and I felt that my life had been blighted by strangers I had never met. I realized that if I had ever met William Irvine that I wouldn't have had anything to do with him. His personality and ideas were repugnant to me. I was even annoyed with my ancestors for believing him. However, I understand a little better now that it is often the most idealistic people who are caught up in radical movements. They cannot see the outcome of the ideas while the ideas are so new.

It was difficult to concentrate on anything else. I felt like I was going crazy from the stress of it. The thing that kept me from having a nervous breakdown was the fact that I was writing down almost everything that we had noticed and discussed. I was better able to comprehend the issues after I had recorded them. Don's interest in the subject, his understanding of scripture, his sense of humor and our friends, Gene and Grace Luxon, also kept me from going over the edge. I also had another great friend, who had been my best friend since childhood. She had actually come to many of the same conclusions herself years before, but had not been able to share her feelings with me because of fear that I wouldn't understand. And, she was right,

I wouldn't have understood. I wasn't ready then. I had been oblivious, living in a tunnel, not knowing what my own best friend was thinking. As I began to grow mentally and spiritually, she and I began to confide in each other just as we had when we were young girls. What a treasure a friend is!!! I needed people (who understood) with whom I could talk and sort things out.

Our middle daughter had left home in rebellion to our enforcement of the workers' rules and the meetings. So she was the first one to break away from the workers' system about three years before we did. When she had left home at age 17, it nearly killed us with worry because it happened before we had realized the full extent of the errors. Fortunately, she didn't come to any harm while she was on her own and she eventually moved back home again. God certainly answered our tearful prayers. Our son had married a wonderful professing girl. They had both come to the same conclusions on their own. We had not really talked a whole lot with them since their marriage. It was too upsetting to our daughter-in-law to even discuss it. Our daughters too, were weary of the subject. They just wanted to forget the whole issue and get on with life. Our son's opinions had pretty much been formed by his own observations and Bible reading. One night they came to us and he said, "We just wanted to let you know about our decision. This Sunday we are going to announce that we won't be coming to meeting anymore. My stomach can't take the stress any longer. It has just made me sick." It was obvious that he was sick. He was white and thin. My blood pressure rose about 50 points. "OH, NO!!!" This meant WE had to leave too. I was both excited and relieved and shocked out of my wits. What was I going to do?! What was I going to tell our parents?

My husband thrilled me. He took control. Unlike many professing men, he had become a strong Christian leader of the family. He said, "I'll write the letter. I know what I want to say." I was so relieved. Immediately I xeroxed a bunch of Impartial Reporter articles because that was the only proof I had that this group had a historical beginning, contrary to the workers' lies, and I bought two copies of the Secret Sect, one for Don's parents and one for my parents. Don's letter began with the statement that we "have not gone crazy." I loved his letter but said, "Honey why don't you leave out that statement that we have not gone crazy. It sounds sarcastic." (So he left it out and later we found out that one of his aunts told people that we "had gone crazy." I was sorry that I had made him take that sentence out. Others blamed the fact that we had been home schooling, and took that as proof that we had really lost touch with reality.) Anyway, we sent his letter and a few old Irish news articles for proof that the workers had lied about the origins. I was so sorry that I didn't have any tracts or books to send them that explained the doctrinal errors. It was 1988 and there weren't any available.

Later, we found out that a worker had immediately gone to one relative who had received the letter and news articles and said, "Can I have these? I have never heard of this before and I see that my uncle's name is in this article. I would like to ask him about this." So the relative gave her all the information before she even got a good chance to examine it. Then Jenith went directly to Don's parents and told his Mom, "This book (**The Secret Sect**) has five errors in the first paragraph. You don't want to read something that is full of lies and mistakes. I'll take this stuff and get rid of it for you." First she said she had never heard of this information before, and then she said the first paragraph contained errors. How could she know there were errors, if she had never heard of this before? She was definitely lying in both cases. So, the workers confiscated the material that we had bought and given to our family to help them understand that we were leaving the group because of our love for Jesus and not simply because we were unwilling to follow the workers anymore. Later, one of the relatives asked if Jenith had been able to ask her uncle about the news article and she said, "No, he is in a rest home and his mind is too far gone." And she never returned the materials. She lied to them and she stole from them and from us.

Someone asked my Mom why we had left and she said something to the effect that we had just not been willing anymore. What a blow! It was as if she hadn't even read what we had sent her. We had been willing. Far more willing than we wished we had been. Here we were, middle aged...what were we interested in now, that we hadn't been interested in before? It really aggravated me to think that my own mother could be so easily swayed by that old cliche. But, I was well aware of how stubbornly I used to defend the old ideas implanted in my mind by the workers, so I tried not to take it personally.

Some people think that the workers should be pitied and left alone because of their dedication and their willingness for self sacrifice. I pity the workers, but their lies and their intrusion into so many families and lives compels me to speak out against their teaching. They must be exposed for the doctrinal errors they teach and reminded of the moral responsibility they have to their followers to tell the truth about their history and beliefs. Those who have used their position of authority in sexual exploitation, need to be reported to the authorities. The cover-up of scandal which has been going on for so many years needs to be stopped. The alarming thing I have noticed is that the workers who try to preach truth really do as much damage as those who preach lies, because when people hear truth mixed in with lies, they become even more confused than ever. The nice workers are, in the long run, just as harmful as the harsh workers. They are the bait on the hook. As long as I have relatives in that group (and we have many, many) I will continue to expose and explain the doctrine and history of this group to as many people as will listen to me. It has been amazing to me to accidentally meet strangers who have professing friends and relatives whom they have tried to understand for years. They are sometimes as interested in finding out information as professing people are. Even our own neighbors have family connections in the group and have been negatively influenced against God from their professing relatives.

Furthermore, I have a responsibility as a Christian to testify of the gospel of Jesus Christ. It is my duty to tell others the truth about Jesus and His sacrifice. He isn't just an example man and way shower. He is God and He is the Way. If he is just a human example of how to serve God acceptably then he is no different than any other religious philosopher. No, He is the Savior and the Way because He died to atone for the sins of the world and ALL who believe in Him will live.

After we left the group I felt 20 years younger, and 100 pounds lighter. I was FREE. I finally understood and experienced John 8:32!!! It was like we had left communist Siberia and had come to America. I could breathe, I could think, I could play, I could say what I thought, I could worship God in Spirit and in Truth, I could praise God without someone trying to intimidate me. I could read anything I want and attend the church that fed my mind and soul instead of binding them. It took me about three years to get comfortable with my new freedom of appearance and mind. Changing one's life after age 40 is a slow process but it has been wonderful.

While we were professing, I only wanted to live in the country. I hated living near people. We had had to live in suburbia, near the city because of Don's work and I had hated it—rarely going outside and even though I love flowers, I never wanted to go out and work in the yard or garden because I felt so conspicuous in nylons, skirt and my bunhead. Now that we can live a normal life and I can look normal and comfortable. I love living in town, I have become acquainted with our neighbors, whereas before, I wouldn't have even recognized a neighbor if I had run into one. I love working in my flower beds and my personality has changed as much as my appearance.

It took us approximately five years from the time we first set our hearts and minds to the task of seeking God for ourselves to the time we actually set ourselves free from the bondage of religious abuse. We had almost no information available to us, until close to the end of the journey. However, it is my purpose to make it easier for those on the same road to get free sooner. Only through the use of information which is accessible in the public market, will people find enough courage to make an educated decision regarding their belief in God. As long as the workers control the flow of information to their followers, they will be able to control their minds.

I have been so thrilled with the way God has answered our prayers, first of all for our children and grandchildren. They are such strong Christians and understand doctrine and Christian morals and the important issues. Our two oldest grandchildren are only two years old, but their favorite books are their little Bibles, they can sing Christian children's songs and they love to watch the videos we have bought them which explain Jesus and His life on their level of understanding. Our grandson voluntarily asked to have Jesus come into his heart when he was only two years old, and our 16 year old daughter helped him pray the prayer. What a thrill! They don't see the Bible as boring, but exciting and interesting. Already their little hearts are turned to God. Another prayer that has been answered is that God would send us allies in Christ. I have so many more friends now than we ever had while we were professing. I get overwhelmed with the process of staying in contact with them all. And also, our prayers for responsible Christian leaders and a healthy church have been answered. We are so truly contented that I feel like pinching myself to make sure that I'm not dreaming. It has been said that an unexamined life is not worth living and the unexamined church is not worth joining. I believe that is true.

1993

Kathleen Munn Lewis
Milwaukie, Oregon

Chapter Thirty-Four

Sue MacDonald:
The Only Way Out Is Through

I grew up the youngest of four children. I was an unplanned child and my parents had wanted me to be a boy. My Father was an alcoholic for as long as I can remember. My Mom was a Christian but didn't attend church regularly. She did send me to Sunday School. Because my dad was an alcoholic, he was an angry person. My fear caused me to avoid him and to become invisible. During my childhood I was the victim of incest and molestation and was emotionally and physically abused. (The incest was not with my father or brother.) I felt in the way and unwanted as a child. My family was pretty much dysfunctional, although there were some good memories as well. My great Aunt Maude lived with us and instilled in me a great love for Bible stories. The best part of my childhood was to crawl into bed with Auntie Maude and listen to her Bible stories and funny stories and jokes. She is the one who taught me to pray and to think of others in prayer. She instilled in me a good value system. Girlfriends at school invited me to Job's Daughter's which is a Masonic affiliation, an introduction into the occult, although to me it was nothing more than a social club.

I met my future husband, Phil Macdonald while we were in high school. The first time I met his Mother and two of his sisters, their wholesome appearance attracted me to the family. The second month I knew him, I met a house full of "friends" and relatives, all professing. Compared to my troubled family, they seemed like an ideal group of people. Later, I was to find out the reality that Phil had been just as victimized in many ways by his family as I had been my mine. I went to my first meeting at Benson High School in Portland. It was a Special Meeting held on Easter Sunday, so I thought it was an Easter Service. (It was about four years later that I found out that they didn't celebrate Easter.) Willie Jameison spoke. I was immediately attracted to the physical appearance of the women, their smiling faces, their pretty hair. My mother forbid me to go to meeting again, without explanation.

My first Christmas with Phil's family was at his parent's home and there was no Christmas tree. Phil's brother-in-law dressed as Santa Claus and asked me to put his make-up on since I was the only one with any make-up. He had rented a Santa outfit and looked the part quite well. He came downstairs with a big bag of toys for the children. The little ones were so excited and I wondered then why there was no Christmas tree even though they were exchanging gifts. I was told later that they "don't celebrate Christmas." The statement left me in a state of confusion for many years because it was obvious that they did celebrate something at Christmas time.

Phil and I got married when I was just out of high school. Phil was not professing. He always told me that he knew that it was "the only way," that everyone else, all other churches were going to hell, BUT that he just wasn't willing for it and didn't want to be a hypocrite, pretending to believe something that he couldn't live. We had been married just a few weeks when Phil's mother invited us to gospel meetings. Phil said to get her off our backs,

for us to just go. We attended but did not profess.
Phil stopped attending meetings because he was
studying to be a dentist and didn't have time. But I
continued going just for something to do and to be
accepted by Phil's family. Howard Mooney was the
worker in our field. He made it clear that this was
the ONLY WAY and if we weren't in it we were lost.

I was 20 when I professed at Boring Convention.
Willis Propp was speaking about Jesus and the crucifixion. I was spellbound and of course, professed.
When I came home, Phil knew immediately that I
had professed. My first words were "Can we turn
off the TV, I have something to tell you." That was
the end of the TV and we got rid of it. Phil wasn't
willing to profess, but he might as well have because he had to live with me and therefore had to
abide by almost as many rules as if he had.

My father-in-law died suddenly when I was pregnant with the twins. He was the most wonderful
man, loving, affectionate and of course, professing.
He was 55. The night he died, he had gone to a
business meeting related to the radiator shop which
he owned, instead of attending Bible Study, as he
usually did. He came home, went to bed complaining of not feeling well, saying "I feel like I'm going
to pass out." And he died of a massive heart attack.
This death was hard on all of us and there were
some who doubted his salvation since he had
missed that meeting the night he died and because
he hadn't taken part in meeting in years.

When our first children, twins, were little, there
was some kind of scandal involving workers and a
conversation arose which my mother-in-law immediately hushed up by saying, "Oh let's not talk
about that now, Sue is just a babe and doesn't need
to know about those things." Her statement and the
problem went right over my head and I accepted

the comment without protest. That was the beginning of many other nuances and questionable situations that I learned to ignore. I couldn't wait for my hair to grow long so I could look more like his family.

I was so excited to go to Gospel Meetings and to be a part of the fellowship and be accepted by Phil's family. At first I wasn't aware of the many restrictions, but gradually began to notice the subtle unspoken rules that governed everyone's thoughts and lives. I took part in all the meetings and if I didn't' give my testimony in a meeting, I felt terrified and overwhelmed with guilt and afraid to die for fear that I would perish before the next meeting. So, most of the time I would read my Bible simply to find something to say for the next meeting. There were times when I would be in a meeting and have a prepared testimony yet someone else's testimony would touch me so deeply that I would testify to something totally different than what I had prepared. And those were times that emotionally affected me and my desire to please God. Some meetings were more special than others, when the friends would speak about "love" and unity" and "joy" and the feeling would be so real that I would think, "Yes! This is the way it should be, this is why I'm here! I'm going to really faithfully serve God and love the people more!" ... Be more professing! And I would purpose to really follow the rules! The feelings of spiritual highs were brief and replaced quickly with new fears and more guilt and depression.

For a time I felt accepted by the family, but then it seemed to be so difficult because Phil wasn't professing and we had what is termed a "divided home." We had less social acceptance because of Phil's non-professing status and among the friends we felt left out. Life was chaotic. I had twins, Phil was in school, studying constantly or working at the radiator shop. There was never time for fun. It was meetings, meetings, work, school and entertaining workers all the time. In those days, the workers would stay for about five days and it was my privilege to entertain and cook for them. It was always the highlight of my life to have the workers in our home. After the workers left, I would vow to do better now and be more spiritual in order to please them. I tried so hard to please the workers and the friends, but if I ever did please them I never felt like I had succeeded. The few times that I did succeed I felt pity for those who weren't as spiritual as I was at that moment. But the moments didn't seem to last long enough to suit me.

During my second pregnancy, I had an abscessed tooth and other health problems and after Brad was born I got a breast infection and I had the abscessed tooth worked on. During the root canal I went into shock from the injection they gave and spent the next several months in bed. Subsequently, I had a complete physical breakdown and my hair started falling out. My doctor advised me to cut my hair and to wear it down so that my scalp could breathe, so I had to cut it to shoulder length and attempted to hide the fact that it was shorter than before. I would look out the window if anyone came to the door so that I could scoop my hair into a bun real quick. My doctor also asked me about my religion at that time, wondering why I had protested cutting my hair. He suggested that I attend another church and the idea horrified me. I said, "I can't!"

Phil graduated from dental school and we moved to Arizona when the twins were 6 and Brad was 4. When Lorci was six, she wanted her hair cut and I allowed her to get a pixie cut, much to the criticism of workers and friends. At that young age, she developed a tremendous sense of guilt after the disapproval of the church and she couldn't wait for her hair to grow out to the same length as her twin sister's.

When the girls were nine, and the boys were ages seven and three, I stopped going to meeting out of desperation to be myself and normal. I had gotten sick and tired of looking dowdy. I was worn out with trying to please the workers and God. In fact, I turned away from God. I figured if I couldn't please Him even while I was attending meetings, there was no chance that I could please Him if I didn't go to meetings and follow all the professing rules. But, while I wasn't going to meetings I was so happy because for once I was honestly myself.

A Christian girlfriend of mine asked me to attend church with her one day. I said, "Absolutely not! It would be a waste of my time, I'm a sinner and I'm going to hell. I can only go to meeting. We believe that is the only right 'Way' and that all other churches are wrong." She said, "You mean to tell me, if you don't go to this meeting, that you can't go to any other church or you will go to hell? That isn't true, Sue. You can be saved, you can go to other churches." I wouldn't listen to her, but her reminder of God triggered a major guilt trip in me that I had to go back to meeting. Soon afterwards, my sister-in-law and mother-in-law came to visit and after a night-long conversation, I started attending meeting again and re-professed and our twin daughters professed at age 12. Brad professed two years later and our youngest son, Duane, professed at age 11. The boys later admitted that the reason they professed was for approval from myself and the workers.

Even though I had re-professed, I was still miserable. I was so repulsed by "the professing look" that I fought it inwardly all the time. The only time I put my hair in a bun was for meeting. When the children wanted to do something normal, like attend a movie or watch TV, we would fudge the rules and then tell the kids to keep it a secret. It was awful, living two lives. I felt detached from reality and from my own feelings. I couldn't admit aloud how I felt, not even to myself.

There came a day when I knew that I had to leave the group again. The feeling had been growing for years. There was like a voice in my head saying "This can't be right! How do you know that this is the ONLY WAY?" I didn't know that the way was WRONG, I only began to feel that maybe there were other people in the world who were saved. I have always been an outgoing "people person" and love the people that I meet. After I professed, the idea of believing that so many other people were going to hell and were of Satan depressed me tremendously. I felt cut off from others and alone. Life seemed so futile. I thought, "Now why would the Lord die on the cross only for the few of us (in whom I saw so many imperfections—and had in myself, too), when all these other people had been created with so many tremendous gifts and useful godly traits?"

Certain sermons which we heard often used to leave me feeling more frustrated and empty than ever. And it left me with a sense of hopelessness. We heard the workers say that "we are nothing but dust," or "worms," that "we need to be emptied of self." But I couldn't see how to do that. I didn't understand anything except that I wasn't good enough. They told us to "lay up treasure in heaven where rust or moth could not destroy." but what

did that mean? And THEN these WONDERFUL WORK-
ERS would get up there and say they were "nothing"
and "not worthy" and "barely going to make it." I
would think, "What's the use? What is the point in
going on? If they can barely make it, where does
that leave me?"

Conversations, the futility of social interaction
which went nowhere began to bother me. Friends
couldn't be honest with one another and admit how
they feel and think about spiritual things or natural
things. We weren't allowed to think for ourselves.
There was a mindset against thinking. Friends
couldn't talk about what they believe, because they
don't know what they believe. They didn't talk
about the Lord because there was nothing to talk
about. They only thought of Him in the "spiritual"
realm, so there was nothing to comment on His involvement in their daily lives. They didn't praise
Him and they didn't seem to know Him. The "spiritual talk" would be a brief comment on how great a
speaker or how spiritual the worker was and perhaps something about the workers' latest convert or
travel plans. The conversations in a group had to
be "safe," therefore health, recipes, babies, workers, weather, and sewing were the accepted topics.
Occasionally you could talk about furniture but you
had to be careful in case you might offend someone
who had less possessions than yourself. The one-
on-one conversations among "the friends" almost
always was gossip, putting people down, telling on
them, passing on juicy information about workers,
elders and others. Afterwards, I would feel sick and
guilty and determined never to gossip again, but it
was inevitable.

We lived two lives, one that the workers wanted
us to live and the other that was normal for us. I
can remember hating the relationships with the

other friends, hating the meetings, hating the way everyone looked. It was like watching life from the sidelines, not living it. There were times that I felt like that I wanted to throw up from the lack of sincerity in the testimonies. I began having major panic disorders. Many times I would stand out in the hall or go in the bathroom because I couldn't stand being in the meeting.

For a time I became unable to leave home. Dinner time became a living hell. I couldn't even sit at the table with my husband and four children. My panic was exploding in my head. It would attack me in a physical way, almost throwing me to the floor. My doctor said I was having the symptoms of a seizure without a seizure and it was all due to the panic. The walls in the grocery store and the lines of people would appear to trap me in. I even became afraid of my own bedroom. I lost 32 pounds at once. At times I felt I was dying. I was diagnosed as agoraphobic and I went to a group therapy for panic disorders. I really got help from the therapy and overcame many, many fears that I had. The name of the therapy course was Terrap. One of the books that I read that was so helpful was *Living In Hell, An Agoraphobic Experience*. Another book that helped me, that was recommended by a professing person, was, *How To Live 365 Days A Year*. Now I realize there are so many other books that are even better that can be found in Christian book stores.

My depression and the feeling that life was out of control or full of chaos that I couldn't understand, led me to seek out psychic counseling. I went to a man who told me all about my past and my future, and scared me to death. Then I consulted still another psychic woman who went into a sort of trance and read my aura. Then another woman read tarot cards for me and I got really involved in Louise Hays metaphysical books. Another woman did fragrance and color remedies that were supposed to help my depression and health. All this while I was still heartily professing. I never had a clue that these things were dangerous and of the devil. Several other professing women were interested in such things with me and they still are. Then I went to a Tibetan pulsator who had me sit in certain positions and hum things. People were supposed to be healed by these activities. Later Phil and I attended the Silva Mind Control seminars, still looking for answers. All of these things gave me a feeling of danger, yet without any understanding of them, I kept looking but finding no answers and went on to something else. I also went to a man who conducted re-birthing sessions in his home. I went to three different sessions and each time I felt an actual physical warning in my spirit that I ignored and reasoned away. During the third session, after he had put me in an altered state of consciousness, he raped me.

One of the biggest challenges that I faced while professing was when my daughter, Lorci, who was living in California (and I thought was going to meeting) called me and told me that she was going to have a baby. She had broken up with her boyfriend and she wanted to come home. We went to California to get her and brought her home to Arizona. The pain we were suffering was magnified by the attitude of the friends and workers. This experience taught me one of the ways in which Satan lies to us. He leads us to believe that our sin is our business, that it won't hurt anyone else but ourselves. But we all suffered the consequences. Our love for Lorci was as strong as ever, but her pain kept her from feeling it. The friends were shocked and understandably so, because Lorci had been considered "worker material." But no one knew how to cope with the situation. Some went into denial, others were sympathetic, some began to draw away, but nobody thought to pray about it, or for her. And not even me. It didn't occur to me to pray about it. This was a natural situation and how could we ask God for help? She decided to keep the baby and everyone was accepting of that, but when she decided to marry the un-professing boyfriend who was divorced, all hell broke loose.

Dale Bors and Robert Gustafson talked it over and decided that Lorci would not be allowed to even attend meeting. Robert Gustafson and his companion came to our home where Lorci lived with the baby. They sat in our living room while Lorci sat with her baby in her arms and they told her that she could no longer come to meeting. I will never forget the look on her face when they sat there and so calmly condemned her to hell. Quoting the scripture about being unequally yoked they said that she couldn't come back. I said, Well couldn't she go to Sunday morning meeting and just not take part?" And they said, "No, she has blatantly done wrong when she knew what was right, so she can't come to meeting anymore." Then I said, "Well, what about Gospel Meetings?" They said, "Gospel meeting is for the public and we couldn't keep her from it, but what's the point of her coming anyway?" With that, Lorci got up with her baby, walked down the hall crying with such anguish and I just sat there numb with pain and did nothing, while they sat there and literally tried to take God from her. (But Praise the Lord, it didn't work. In retrospect, I wish I had ordered them out of my house and never gone back to meeting again, myself. But, I didn't know I had that option. Lorci did marry the father two weeks later, but the marriage didn't last but a year and a half. Since becoming a Christian, I have asked forgiveness from my daughter for the way that I handled that and she too, has become a Christian and so has her little boy, before the age of five.)

It was about this time that our professing relatives introduced us to the Wings Seminar, in Eugene, Oregon. I went first by myself, and they asked the question, "What is your purpose in life? What is burning in your mind that you want more than anything else?" Instantly the answer came to me, "I want to be all of me." I wrote it on a 3x5 card. But I knew that I couldn't be. The hopelessness of the situation washed over me. What was the point in attending a seminar like this, with the burden of professing and trying to live up to someone else's ideas of perfection? Depression was my constant companion. The idea of pleasing a God who was looking over my shoulder, ready to pounce on me with anger because I couldn't follow the professing rules and lifestyle. I never felt saved or forgiven.

Wings brought up more questions than it solved. While I was attending Wings, God was growing out of the little box the workers and I had put Him in. While I was terrified of the thought of leaving meetings again, that seemed to be the only solution to the situation. The cry of my heart was, "Lord, I don't want to perish, help me!! I want to be all of me." I began going to another counselor because of my panic disorder and she talked to me about religion. I said, "I don't want to waste time and money talking about my religion, because that's not the issue." The issue I thought was important was the abuses of my past, the incest, the physical and emotional abuse and the recent rape. I failed to realize, however, that I was currently suffering from spiritual abuse. The counselor pointed out to me that my religion was another form of abuse. She said, "Look in the mirror my dear, you are dead inside. Look at how sad you look. Look at your face."

Later, I remember sitting in meeting thinking, "This doesn't work for me, anymore." I felt scared that I felt that way, but I knew this time that I wasn't going to leave God out the next time I left meeting. God had gotten bigger. Wings gave me the skills to communicate with others and my husband. It began my journey of becoming a survivor instead of a victim. It allowed me to admit to myself who I was and that I mattered and that I did have potential and the responsibility to use it. I learned a real strong sense of right and wrong, something new to me. I learned about real sin instead of phony sin. I received a strong conviction about such things as gossip, about how to be a friend instead of a back stabber. I learned to play and to have fun and to be playful. I learned the importance of balance and that it is okay to be real. I found a confidence that was new to me. Wings does a lot of mother-father issues, forgiveness exercises, etc. It all helped me to let go of the past and move on.

While we were attending Wings, one of the founders of the seminar asked us, "Are you a part of that religious group that has been coming to the seminars? We have had more people from your church attend Wings than any other group." He was trying to understand why so many professing people were all looking for the same kind of communication skills. Many others have wondered why so many professing people and even some workers have attended Wings. I believe it is because of the widespread depression that the friends are trying to alleviate. Wings is a secular counseling system that works with large groups of people. It is helpful insofar that it helps people understand themselves and others better. It isn't meant to be a replacement of God and shouldn't even be considered a religious organization or religious counseling. Many workers are quite worried about the friends attending Wings. Howard Mooney said he didn't approve of people trying to "get in touch with themselves."

Phil and I went to all of the Wings seminars. We were starved and eager to learn more about communication. It was helping our marriage and our understanding of ourselves. It was at one of the seminars that I realized that meeting just didn't' work for me anymore. I wasn't growing in the Lord, nor did I know how to grow in the Lord. I wasn't learning about scripture or what it meant, even though I attended meeting regularly. I was both afraid and excited because I was going to go home and get my ears pierced and my hair cut. It was to be my statement of independence. It wasn't about vanity, it was about taking back my womanhood, my femininity that I had never had since professing. It was about taking charge of my own life again. I was becoming all of me. I wasn't rejecting God, I was just rejecting the workers' control of my life.

When I got home I went to my elder and told him that I wasn't going to come to meeting anymore. I asked him the question, "Where is the love?" And he agreed and sympathized with me, but had nothing to say to convince me that my decision was wrong. From that day on I never heard from him or his wife. Dale Bors, the worker called while we were out of town and our son Duane told him we would be home in two days, but he never called back. A sister worker called and asked, "Was it anything that I said to discourage you?" When I said, "No," she said "Oh, good, well, I hope you won't stay away too long." As I hung up the phone, I thought, "What just happened?" I received such an empty feeling from her attitude, that if I had been a drinker I would have gone out and gotten drunk. That was the last contact I have ever had with a worker. I was relieved and yet let down.

At this point, Phil and I began to go hiking on Sundays and on Easter we went to the top of Squaw Peak in Phoenix. We started in the dark so that we could be up there when the sun came up and each of us were lost in our own thoughts. While I was watching the sun, I thought about all the other people who were in churches, all over the valley celebrating Easter. I didn't think of the friends at all. I said to the Lord, "God, I know there's more and I want it all."

An ex-professing man who had heard that I had quit going to meeting, loaned me all the available books on the history and doctrines of the Two by Twos. Phil and I began reading them immediately and would read portions aloud to one another. When I came to the information about William Irvine's "revelations," I realized how terribly victimized I had been. I said to Phil, "I have been wearing my hair in a bun for a —— lunatic all these years!!!" I was pacing the floor with rage. I thought of all the pain I had put my children through. Their childhood had been denied them; friendships in school had been denied them. The girls had buried themselves in books to ease their pain. They had been denied Christian friends and education. They were the most professing looking girls their age and looked like workers. The other professing kids hadn't accepted them because they were too "professing." The boys felt like outcasts because of the effect it had on their lives. They didn't know what was right or wrong, up or down, they only knew guilt. Phil said, "You have every right to be angry." He was and still is so supportive of every stage of healing, although he hasn't always understood every emotion that I've felt. Our marriage has grown solid through the process of shared grief and experiences.

A few weeks later a woman who had sold me some skin care products called me and in the course of the conversation I told her that I had quit going to meetings. She listened attentively and then suggested that I talk to her pastor, Mark Fuller. I was resistant to the idea and cynical and thought he wouldn't care or know anything at all about what I had been through. However, I did call him and when I told him that I couldn't read the Bible or even open it without a panic attack, or even pray, he prayed for me over the telephone and it was the first time anyone had ever prayed for me out loud, personally. I was so overwhelmed by the Holy Spirit's attention through this man whom I didn't even know and by the healing that began in that moment. He prayed the power of the Blood of Jesus over me, and the presence of the angels around me to protect me and to guard my mind and then he bound the power of Satan and his demons who were tormenting and keeping me from reading my Bible and then he told me to go and read Phillipians 4:6-7 and Psalms 25:4-5 and then, "I'll see you in my office tomorrow." I did as he told me and was amazed that I was able to not only read it and understand it, but it fed me through the evening as I continued to think about it. The passage in Psalms says, "Show me your ways O Lord, Teach me your paths, guide me in your truth and teach me, for you are God, My Savior and my hope is in you all day long." AMEN! When I saw him the next day, he handed me the book by David Seamands, *Healing For Damaged Emotions.* That book started me on my journey out, and into joy. That Sunday I attended that Nazarene Church all by myself and I sat in the back row, and people were so friendly even though I knew no one. The pastor greeted me with a friendly hug (instead of a cold handshake). The music was overwhelming. I loved it! I had never heard any of the songs before, but the spirit of praise and worship to the Lord was so awesome that it overwhelmed me. I had never experienced praise and worship to the Lord before in my life!

My walk with Jesus had finally begun. The next Sunday the pastor asked me if I would give my testimony in the next service telling about my experience of finding Jesus after having been in a religious cult for 30 years. He said, "There are so many others who have had similar experiences who can identify with your story." I said, "Yes." I felt immediately drawn to comply with his request because I felt God had placed the request on his heart and I have never wanted to say no to God. So, I did it that next Sunday and as I was leaving the church there were a half a dozen people who came up and said they were going to be praying for me. Their prayerful response was awesome to me. To know that people would actually tell me that they were going to pray for me was something I was totally unprepared for. My church is so dependent on prayer. I have learned to pray and praise God in all things. I feel that one of the things that has allowed me to grow in Christ so quickly is the ministry of prayer, deliverance, and intercession that my Christian friends and pastor believe in so strongly.

Very soon I became part of the worship team, and a woman's Bible study, and I sang in the choir.

I was on top of the world. Life was wonderful. Church was wonderful. Most of all, *God was wonderful!* I thought life was going to just keep getting better and that I could forget the past and just keep going. And then one day I walked out of choir practice with a major panic attack! The same thing happened the next day in a Bible study and a friend followed me out to my car and asked, "Are you all right?" I said "No, I'm not all right, I'm depressed and I don't know why. How could this happen to me now that I'm a born again Christian?"

I had been seeing a wonderful Christian counselor who specializes in helping women who have been abused. I had heard about her from listening to a Christian radio station. She recommended that I go to Rapha in Scottsdale, Arizona, which is a Christian unit in a secular hospital. It was so comforting to walk in and see Christian quotations on the walls and an inspirational atmosphere pervaded the entire unit. From the first session, I began to experience healing. I won't pretend that it was easy, but it was so worthwhile and I knew that God in His Sovereignty and unfailing grace had led me there for the healing that I wasn't getting anyplace else. It was like God had said, "Okay, Sue, you have grown a little, now let's finish the healing, so you can really grow in me." It was such a safe place to be. My counselor said, "Sue, the only way out is through." I didn't think I had the strength in me and I didn't, on my own, but God was with me. She gave me a verse from Jeremiah 29:11-12, "For I know the plans I have for you, declares the Lord, plans to prosper you and not to harm you, plans to give you hope and a future. Then you call upon me and come and pray to me and I will listen to you. You will seek me and find me when you seek me with all your heart."

While I was there I met a wonderful woman named Shirley who became a best friend. We were roommates and right from the start had a special relationship. There were 12 of us in the hospital at the same time. It turned out that counting myself there were five people who had a Two-by-Two connection and they were all wanting to know about the Two by Twos after I told my story to the group. It was more than coincidence that we were there together. I put information in their hands to help them and they were so grateful to understand why their professing relatives believed as they did. I was in the treatment center for a month and we went to group therapy twice a day and we had daily Bible studies. We had private therapy sessions each day and on weekends we attended a local church. While I was there I began remembering things from my past I hadn't known were there. I had many breakthroughs which could not have been handled any other way. When I was admitted, the diagnosis which was given me was "Major depression, panic disorder and co-dependency." During our group sessions we used several textbooks, one of which was *Search For Significance*.

I had been through secular counseling for years. The difference now was that God was brought into the healing process and they showed us how people have bought into false beliefs regarding life. The Christian counselors would help us examine our past and then they would point to the scripture and say, "What does God say about this?" Secular counseling had some benefits, but it only dug up the hurtful past without the healing process of the cross and left everything up to ourselves to change on our own. Only God can change us, and heal us.

Since coming out of Rapha the Lord has healed me even more. What Rapha did for me was to give me the tools to cooperate with the Holy Spirit in my healing process. What I have found is that Jesus is the Answer to all our problems. It isn't about religion, it is about a relationship with Jesus. I can't express the joy that freedom in the Lord has given me. I love every day. I love every person I meet. I get excited about every person I meet. God has given me such an excitement about people. Jesus died for everyone and I can love them all. I do a lot of flying and every time I get on an airplane I am excited about seeing who I will meet and sit beside. I marvel at the people God brings to me. There are no accidental meetings. I can see God's hands in everything. After all the years of discontent, I am finally in the place of contentment. I love being in large groups of people now and knowing that many of them are Christians gives me such a feeling of security and pleasure. I don't feel at all uncomfortable talking about God with strangers, like I did while I was professing. Writing my story and knowing that others will be reading it has not been easy for me, but it was something that I felt I wanted to do because I have received so much help from the Lord. For those who have left the Two by Twos, but are not seeking the Lord, I just want to encourage you to not be afraid of a relationship with our Heavenly Father. He isn't there to hurt or condemn you. He is there to save and help and heal you.

Chapter Thirty-Five

C. M. and S. O. McConnell (New Zealand): To Whom It May Concern

For many years we have been disturbed and have eventually become fully enlightened about:

1. That while the workers reiterate their ministry is the only right way and the truth, they keep the body of Christ completely hidden. The little publicity given to gospel meetings via cards in boxes and occasional small adverts is totally inadequate in view of the total lack of publicity/knowledge of the existence of the body backing up the gospel meetings. Our appropriation of the words "the truth" is very wrong.

2. Connected to this is the fact of our exclusiveness and members are cut off in large part from many realities and kept in deliberate ignorance of so many facts, an example being the large amount of successful evangelism done by other bodies in foreign lands (ours is mere token).

3. The superficial nature of the workers' relationship with us and their refusal/reluctance to discuss the scripture, doctrine, and be open and on a level with us.

4. The lack of clear doctrine especially in gospel meetings is bewildering. In fact we wonder if they understand what the true gospel of Jesus Christ IS— they far too often take verses out of context and weave a good-sounding message around it without any regard whatever for the whole context and what God is really saying. They say we do not need deep knowledge of the scripture, only to be willing

to do it, but how can you have the "spirit" of it or
do it if first you do not fully and correctly understand it?

5. It is becoming increasingly clear that the
workers are almost totally ineffective in bringing
souls to Christ. We get the strong message that they
are more concerned about keeping OUT any doubtful or potentially troublesome people (i.e. those
who are likely to ask questions and expect answers
thereto), than about bringing them to Christ.

6. A lot of mindless repetition of phrases and cliches, one example being: "I want to have more
faith"—without specifying: faith in THE BIBLE, faith
in the life and plan of Christ, faith in THE WORKERS,
faith in THE WAY or WHAT. Another is: "I want to be
a good example"—which really means "I WANT TO
BE WILLING TO *APPEAR* TO GO ALONG WITH THE STATUS
QUO."

7. The lack of real study/understanding of the Bible (young fully excused) is appalling BUT MORE SO
is the complacency and indifference about same.

We have tried to speak to the workers for some
years about our concerns in all above matters and
have become saddened by their evasion and lack of
honest attempts to talk. Instead, their implied condemnation that we would DARE TO QUESTION "God's
servants" and told we have a wrong spirit, etc., etc.
We know down the years many have tried to witness to the workers, but they remain impervious
(for obvious reasons) and will be held responsible
by God.

We are now FULLY AWARE that the workers themselves are victims of the WAY which WAS NEVER
RIGHT. It is just a man-made fellowship founded on
ignorance, maintained by deceit and controlled by
intimidation. God has given plenty of time to correct original errors, but succeeding generations of

workers have chosen to cover up. The doctrine is basically a gospel of contention against orthodox Christianity and is a mixture of truth and error.

Since God has gently and kindly led us along the path to this knowledge, we now have no option but to leave and to trust fully in Him for the future. We cannot do any longer what kind friends have suggested, i.e. we "go along" with SUPPORTING a false gospel.

Please feel free to talk with us at any time - truth can stand any investigation. We overlook being ostracised by some, they have done it in ignorance. We appreciate the love shown by others and hope it will continue. We want no whisper campaign, all is above board and open, you can ask us any questions, and we hope you will.

WE HAVE NOT BEEN INFLUENCED to go out by others—we arrived at our decision independently over a period of time, and only after much prayer and study.

Letter to Workers Dated March 1, 1993

Dear George and Norman,

As there is no value put on openness, reasoning, honesty, there is obviously plenty to hide. It is a sad fact that many errors could have been put right down the years by above. The Bible *is* inerrant, but the workers or 'the Way' are not infallible.

By your non-negotiation you force people to be reluctant hypocrites i.e. "going along" with what they don't really believe, not daring to ask questions, etc.—questions that should be able to be answered. They are forced into either "going along" with it outwardly but inwardly all the while having doubts. Others simply go their own way, but attend meetings and appear to be in total agreement with you. Only the few honest ones are forced to a decision to leave. And it is a very difficult decision to make, we can assure you.

It is quite clear to us that the workers would much rather have a DISHONEST ADHERENT than an HONEST DISSIDENT. We just have to move on from this no-win situation.

We want to make it absolutely plain that we have nothing personal against you or any other worker, only great sorrow that you should be a part of a great deception, and unable to be open about it all.

Neither have we got a bad spirit and an unbelief in God or his salvation and the need to live righteous lives. Going "out" does not mean going out from the presence of God. Rather the opposite.

We feel we have tried to witness to you and to make it plain just what is unscriptural. Even in recent gospel meetings you have not shown that the sacrifice and righteous life of Jesus as our propitiation is the CENTRAL ISSUE OF THE GOSPEL. God knows better than we do ourselves our inability to meet the righteous standard He requires and to pay the price of salvation. So He planned it accordingly.

We feel today there is no use in us saying any more. We don't doubt you will turn it all around and just say we are unwilling.

Yours, sincerely,
C. M. McConnell
S. O. McConnell

Excerpt from a Letter to Don and Kathy
Lewis Dated March 11, 1993

Life in my childhood was simple, nearly everyone was poor, no outside entertainments (esp. for
country folk), no cars for the greatest majority and
the jet engine never heard of! So in some sense our
lives were the same as outsiders. My mother was
very particular to never talk anything seamy about
friends/workers in front of us children and when I
was older she deplored that other parents said all
sorts in front of their kids, but she had to add that
it seemed to have done no harm. I think actually it
helped the young ones to take the whole thing
more naturally, while we were conditioned to look
upon it as some sort of a sacred mystery. The workers in those days were more interested in the kids.
Times were real hard (the great depression). I actually remember being hungry once or twice and
waiting for Dad to get some money to buy the next
bread. I am very glad my parents did send us (5
girls, one boy) to high school (which was at that
time frowned upon by workers). At least we got a
reasonable education and were able to obtain good
jobs (mainly secretarial)—we saw plenty friend's
children otherwise. There was a stage when we got
called "Cooneyites" at school, but our parents refuted and comforted us about it. The Gospel
preached by the workers at that time must have
been as confusing as at present because even
though my intelligence is normal I could not make
head and tail of what for instance the Ark had to do
with professing. They did not make it clear that it
was a type of Christ's saving power—just filled me
with a lot of fear. I can remember many times actually shaking with fear in gospel meetings and on
Sunday a.m. It was not a fear of God or a fear of

death, but definitely a fear of the platform and of displeasing my parents.

I did have a very real experience at age 16 which has stood to me all these years. I was a fairly serious introspective child and one day went for a long walk along a deserted beach. Anyway, I felt heaven opened to me and God was drawing me to Himself, and it was a powerful love He was manifesting to me, not the gospel message of the workers that drew me, so now it has come full circle and it is still the love and redeeming grace of God that counts.

Among the friends in my childhood, there was a closeness not known today. The annual picnic of the friends was the red letter day, also an occasional evening where we met in someone's home and just chatted and sang hymns. We loved such simple things as to see our fathers playing games with us, running, and listening to the adults talking, and more or less treating us as equals.

In my childhood, one worker, Ned Manning (Irish descent), used to state often and definitely in gospel meetings that this way started in Galilee (and in my young way I said to myself "Uncle Ned, that is not right.") Yet as I expressed in my earlier letter, I was not distressed about it—along with most Irish, I have always known about the "early days"— but not the significance of it that we understand now. Strangely that you felt the workers from other countries were more appealing and sacred than your own—that's exactly as we always thought about USA workers. I do really believe they had more appealing open personalities and a better grip of the Bible than ours. We tend, of course, to be more English-fied. As we have shifted many times in our progress to our own farm, I am afraid I constantly cleaned up old notes, etc.

You mentioned the emotional troubles—sure we have them here—two ladies (one old, one young) in hospital most of last year, and the older one not recovering, still in hospital. I know it's exactly as you say—caused by repression. The husband told me recently the doctors have given up on prying out of his wife what is the real trouble—she won't talk. I dared to tell him that it is caused by repression to which he agreed, and listened to me when I told him what kind of repression it was—and to talk very openly with her, and get her to come out and say just what it is that is worrying her so badly. He said I had given him good advice and that he was going to try, as he is quite desperate. She is the typical submissive (to workers) type, he more amenable to open criticism, etc. I see it on all hands—this awful unreality—people saying one thing and thinking another. You can imagine the black marks I have got from my tendency to be open about things—I know the workers have got me "marked." I feel their spirit towards me (despite their outward politeness). However all that is now behind us and we feel so free, so unembarrassed about our salvation (which is such a change).

Now more about the womenfolk. About 8-10 years ago for reasons then unknown to me, Walter Franks (an older worker) sort of opened up a campaign about women in the way. He spoke out of the blue, you might say, at convention of the need for women to submit to husbands but not a word about the other side. It was all apropos of nothing. I went up to him on the convention grounds and told him he was misinterpreting the scriptures and being one-sided and it was the women who made the greatest sacrifice, who were 99 per cent of the time the stronger spiritually, and very largely responsible for the fact of the young ones professing.

He agreed to all and I asked him if my husband tried, for instance, to discourage me from attending meetings (which had happened in fact) would I "submit" to him or not. He got in a real panic and said "no, that would mean your eternal death, etc." For some years thereafter we women "got it" about one thing or another. I have since been told by others in different parts that I did not imagine this. Always one sided—that's what got me. One convention I went around asking any women that would speak to me what they thought about it—most couldn't care less. Some were angry, but not prepared to talk about it. Anyway, the thing culminated about 4 years ago when a youngish worker came home from working in Japan, had gospel meetings here in our city, and really went for us women in those meetings. (I don't think, at this stage, any outsider attending). I must say at this point that some of our elder men were by now exhibiting open signs of chauvinism and, of course, by using Paul's particular teachings, they seemed justified. Yet all along, no mention of their own responsibilities—it seemed to be assumed that men just always took their responsibilities!! Anyway this particular worker started into us about hair in particular—several had short hair (one for medical reasons), he apparently didn't care to check it out first. (Later I found that this particular woman's husband who is a secondary school headmaster spoke very definitely to the worker concerned). The worker used scripture in a cruel way, going back to Leviticus about "if she won't submit shave her, etc." He sounded awful. By this time I had lost forever my fear of workers. I complained a bit among the friends about the one-sidedness of it, got various responses, but all were afraid to say a word, so I wrote a strong letter to that worker. (Sorry, I got rid of it before leaving for an overseas trip to see family in Ireland.) Later he called with Bible in hand to teach me and to show me that women were indeed inferior (not quite his words). I showed him the other side of things. They could not get me to back down, so got up and left without a word of farewell. All this has been a real eye-opener to my husband who is anything but anti-women!! The then-overseer worker for New Zealand with one of the local workers called by appointment, just sat there making small talk, being so meek and mild. I was forced to open up and said, "you must have come for something."

He said, "Yes, to get you to submit to God."

I answered, "You mean to get me to submit to YOU." I would not have it that it was to GOD, that I *was* submitted to HIM.

They called me all sorts such as I was an unbroken, unsubmitted woman, etc.

I said, yes "I am unsubmitted to your half truths." The weird part was the other worker just sat there making noises as though he was backing up the older worker, but giving me the strong message, (he kept smiling at me) that he could not care less. I asked him if it was o.k. for me to attend his local gospel meetings.

He just said "sure." The funny part was when he next visited (by this time I had spoken to him and his young companion and told them no hard feelings), he *made such a fuss of me and almost ignored by poor husband!*

I told the overseer worker he could not put me out. I would just continue to be in fellowship at my good little meeting. He said, "You can't take the bread and wine then."

My husband said, "I will pass her the bread and wine!!" And he told him in no uncertain language that I did not have a bad spirit, but rather a jolly good one!!!

After all this I must sound like a really aggressive person. I am in fact a really shy person, but can get steamed up by any injustice and always have a strong desire to defend the underdog.

Would you believe this? Later I was told by some friends in Australia that Nathan, our real overseer (who was absent from New Zealand at the time above), agreed with me in principle, but that I had said too much!! (What is too much?!!) This had come from their son in Taurange, NZ where there is a big group of ex-workers and their wives/families living. Since then, to my knowledge no word has been said against women. I checked again with other parts and find this to be correct. What really amazes me about all this is how indifferent to what the workers say are most of the friends; it almost seems as though they couldn't care less, they just take what suits and ignore the rest. (I used to wish I could also do this.)

For the past 5 years, when visited I have told each succeeding pair of workers that I am concerned about our secretiveness and exclusiveness. At that stage I was not cheeky enough to tell them their preaching was confusing and contained no real doctrine. One sister worker did appear to listen to me and said she would speak to Nathan, but I am pretty sure she did not. Toward the end of the mission year (ends October 1992), I became guiltily concerned that I had not asked workers to stay and with the motive that I felt I must do my part to help my poor sisters who I knew by this time must have had them to stay several times, I invited them to come. No comment at the time. The older rang me and said, "We will come if you bring up no controversial subjects." I promised to do this and kept my promise, but what a farcical, un-enjoyable week!! As they left, I talked openly to them and told them I was increasingly unhappy about the matters I had already talked to them about. No helpful comments or advice or reassurance whatsoever.

I omitted to tell you that when I went around that convention talking to any woman about the anti-woman business, one lady told me that she knew why it was. Apparently in Australia there had been some trouble with a group of sister workers "taking over." Evidently, something went wrong, and the brothers got together and said they would never again let "the sisters take over." I know there must be some truth in this because that youngish worker that came to my house to correct me, said almost the same words. I did not question him, because I tried to stick to the relevant questions. I bet the real reason why the sister workers "took over" is because the men were neglecting their own responsibilities!!! That is all I really know, but believe that in principle it is right.

There are 8 of us in this city who exited the fellowship in the last 6 months. All arrived at their own conclusions without being influenced by anyone else, and all feel happy and free, and at present going around Churches and groups, waiting for God to direct us into a Christian fellowship. Already we have been shown kindness and love from so called "outsiders" and have enjoyed the Minister's sermons based upon scripture. At two Churches, one Brethren and one Baptist, we were approached by ex-neighbours/acquaintances giving us a big warm welcome, and hoping we would find what we were looking for with their Church. There are 2 young couples among us 8, and the poor young things hardly know WHAT it is wrong, they know SOMETHING is wrong, so we had a study together about what is the true gospel, and showing them from scripture how the workers add to the requirements, etc. We are, this Sunday, going to look into the Ministry. And us oldies, as we have studied it in readiness, have seen again how the workers ADDED to the requirements, and just ASSUMED.

New Zealand

Chapter Thirty-Six

Wendy McManus

In looking back on my experiences with the 2x2s and in leaving it, I am sure it is not totally unique—there will probably be similarities with others in some aspects, but God does help and deal with us in ways that match us individually.

I was not raised in the 2x2s, although I had an Aunt who was converted to it in the late 50's. I was an only child, very shy, not even on the "cute" side, friendly and active in school but not "popular," no dates, a hidden self-esteem. I went to a junior college, met a young man who paid attention to me (later to learn it was on a dare) and married for all the wrong reasons—even joining the 2x2s of which he was a member. I always believed in God, but was raised not to condemn other's beliefs—there is a total mixture of denominations in my family. I went to whatever church my cousins and aunts and uncles went to when I spent summers and other school breaks with them. In those days (the early 60's) you were still taught to take your husband's faith just to keep peace in the family. So when I married in late 1963, I was baptized and became a member of 2x2s. But God was faithful to me—in that even though I was in an abusive marriage that was all wrong, and took massive notes at meetings and conventions—my basic beliefs were not shattered too badly. But I noticed a lot of inconsistencies—lots of unhappiness under the surface. But, somewhat like Mary, I kept it all in my heart and gave my time and energy totally to raising my three children (protecting them from as much abuse as I could), and the various jobs I had to work at. The 2x2s put a lot of fear and guilt on to people, especially those of us who are quiet and sincere and want to do what is right with, hopefully, pure intentions and be pleasing to God.

After many years of seeing hypocrisy in action and knowing in my heart that I had to leave the marriage for safety sake, I tried twice to get a divorce. But even though my in-laws were sympathetic (they had converted to 2x2s in the late 1940's or very early 1950's) they and the workers said no, no, no. The only counseling being God hates divorce—it will go very badly for me, I will be condemned to hell, it would be a sin for me to sign the papers. I literally "cried unto God" on my knees begging for a clear cut word of why I had to go through all of this. I know with all that is in me that God put a signpost in front of me: "divorce him and I will bless you and take care of you and your children."

About that time, a college came to the area we were living in (three hours from the nearest city of size) and I was able to get my BA degree and then even my Masters. I finally gritted my teeth and signed the divorce papers. That ended up a dreadful battle—my husband accusing me of being unfaithful, a terrible mother, the kids unkept, etc; having to even take lie detector tests. We finally made it through all of that but the "friends" dropped me, the workers said I couldn't take part in meeting for awhile and left it at that. No counseling, no further conversation.

I got a job teaching school and I started on the trail of becoming the me that God intended. God put together a special group of people in the Masters classes that, even though we were from all different backgrounds, we cared that each and every one of us succeeded and got our degrees—in Guidance and Counseling!!! My co-workers were supportive of me in my slow evolvement. And God really took me on a slow journey so that I wouldn't get more frightened of the changes.

A year after the divorce, I asked the worker, at convention, if I could start taking part yet. He couldn't remember why I wasn't taking part, nor that he had said that I couldn't!!! "Oh, well, I wasn't meant to be an example to the others!!!" I went to meeting a few more times and then I began to go to a church for the first half hour to listen to the great praising music then go to meeting for the testimony part. I only remember the very last testimony I gave—which was that the people of the "truth" had lost their first love and needed to get back to worshiping God. (My ex-in-laws had left the 2x2s five years before-mainly because not one time during their illnesses nor even good health did the friends come visit them). The same had happened to me. All through the 2x2 years we had had lots of company, lots of "sings" at our house, lots of pot-lucks, but never invited to other's places!! The workers had stayed in our home. But I can honestly say, only one woman befriended me!! We still write to each other to this day, but unfortunately she is still in the 2x2 with an unfaithful husband.

God has truly blessed me with three beautiful Christian children who are now caring, responsible, Christian adults. We made it through! I was a single parent for 12 years. I kept my life squeaky clean—wouldn't even allow a repairman in the house unless others were around. I didn't even date. (My ex had made a lot of threats and being a revengeful person, he would have tried to carry them out. As it was, he left town after he dropped all kinds of rumors about me that took me several years to prove that they were false.)

Anyway, God slowly changed my outward appearance as He was cleansing the inside. I was in a church that praised the Lord, and taught the Bible. In some ways, I had to be taken back to before my marriage and start to grow from there. God erased a lot of the garbage from my memory both from my natural life and from the spiritual. My college classes gave me the "therapy" I might have had to go through to get my life back together. The "friends" tried to shun me—even to cross the street so as not to have to pass me. But I would just go up to them with a friendly hello and if they didn't speak that was their choice.

More recently, I have moved to a different area. I have remarried (a gentleman I had met 11 years ago at a camp ground he was managing). I had to quit teaching because of the move. But where I work now, when I see old familiar faces from the 2x2s, I get a little brave and go up to them and say "I remember you Mrs. _____, how are you," etc. Almost every time, for whatever reason, these people also hint that they too wish they could leave the 2x2s, that it is not honest, there is hypocrisy, lack of love, etc, but they are afraid they will be condemned to hell. I've tried to encourage, given the lack of time we have, but it seems so hard to say enough.

God took me on a path that was not the normal route. Yes, God hates divorce, but He loved me. He had to take me out of the marriage and out of the 2x2s. There comes a time when you know that you know you are doing the right thing, even if it doesn't fit the agenda of the world around you. God is a God of love and mercy and it is He we answer to and serve. God was my father and husband, Jesus died and arose again for me; God still loves me—told me to be strong and courageous and He would prosper and protect me. He kept His Word!! The very least I can do is honor Him and praise Him, and to show love and mercy to those of my past as well as to those I come in contact with now.

God Bless.

Address:
Wendy McManus
82 Hoquiam Wishkah Road
Hoquiam, WA 98550

Chapter Thirty-Seven

Rose Medich
A Letter to the Friends

Dear Family & Friends:

I am writing this letter so that you will have first hand from me the reasons why I left the fellowship commonly called the "truth."

As a little history, there were eight of us kids raised with professing parents in South Dakota. Only my mother and one brother still profess. We were not a well-to-do family. There was another professing family in the same town who had lots of relatives in the 2x2's and they could do no wrong. They were put on a pedestal on every occasion and why couldn't we be like them? We had no relatives in the 2x2's. I feel the real key in the different way we were treated is RELATIVES. They make a lot of difference in the eyes of the workers between being considered "a very hearty saint" and one that is just a "so-so saint."

It seemed to me that most people went to conventions for family reunions and to get boy friends. I did none of that. In fact, I couldn't stand most of the professing boys. They were arrogant, and had their pick of the girls because there were more girls than boys. I feel that God was overseeing my life because when I was 21, I married George who was 24 at the time. He was a Christian who had not been previously married, but all the friends noticed was that he was not a 2x2. He went to some gospel meetings and conventions, but he never professed. He never went to any church after we married, and to his credit, he never discouraged me from going to meetings. He has suspected all these years that the 2x2s were a cult, but he kept quiet because he couldn't prove it.

George is the nicest man, and he is so sweet. He has loved me for 26 years. Now, he even loves me more, if possible, since I left the 2x2s. It's like he has a new bride. I am now 47 years old, and I have professed since I was 14. Yet, very few people in the 2x2 fellowship really know me, and I have just come to understand why. It was because I married George, who never professed, which placed me in the "snubbed saint" category.

In the first Sunday morning meeting I attended after we married, I was interrupted while I was praying and cut off in mid sentence by a brother worker! I felt so ashamed! Nobody ever explained why—before or after. I was so young that I never asked why. I was not even to pray! It was three years before I was allowed to take part in meetings again—all for just loving and marrying a very good Christian man! That was the beginning of my being snubbed. I was so brainwashed, conditioned, and felt so unloved that I tried and tried to be accepted. I had no one to turn to. I could not get myself out of this mess. I didn't know the mess was such a mess!

After I left the 2x2s, a professing lady told me that all I had to do was repent and go back to meeting, like I did when I started to take part after I married George. Would you believe that after 23 years of taking part, I did not realize that my taking part signified that I had repented for marrying George? I had no idea!! I'm still shocked, and I've certainly never been sorry that I married George!

Nobody explained anything to me, and it's not something that is covered in the Bible. This is just a sample of the poor communication found in the 2x2s.

George could never understand how the workers could come and eat his food while disliking him so much. He never wanted the workers to spend the nights at our house. When I told Roy Dietzel, our head worker this, he said, "Have the workers over anyway." Although the workers would come and eat, they would never have a Bible study with me.

One special meeting there were a lot of workers at our house. When they left, I noticed one of them had taken down off the bathroom wall a little stuffed railroad mouse, a gift George once received when he was sick. Another time, five workers were here for dinner; afterwards they went into my bedroom, closed the door, and never came out until it was time for the evening special meeting. I had stayed home from work to be with them— snubbed again! At the time, I thought it was probably because we had a TV in our home. Roy Dietzel told me once as the workers were leaving my home that I had just been with some of God's angels.

Then one day in 1984, George happened to see an advertisement in our newspaper, which appeared for only one day. It was put in by Fred and Ruth Miller, Booksellers USA of Washington. I have thanked God over and over again for that! If you want to know about a church that meets in the home and has no name, the ad said to send for a book called *The Secret Sect*. George ordered the book and read it without my knowledge. Two weeks later, he told me he had read a book all about the "Truthers," his private term for the friends, but he was afraid to show it to me because he thought it might make me go crazy. I told him I wanted to read it. I read it, and I believed the facts it contained were true, but I didn't do anything about it because at that time I didn't see that the 2x2s were any worse than any other church.

However, I always thought something was wrong that the workers only dated back to early 1900. The pilgrims came to the USA for freedom of religion in the 1600's. If God was in control of the 2x2 way, surely there would have been a trace of the truth before 1900. I feel strongly that the friends have the right to know that the 2x2s were started by William Irvine in 1897 in Ireland, and this fellowship came to the USA in 1903. I have newspaper articles and letters to prove this. Why does this church not recognize its origin?? I think that the workers who know the truth about the beginning of the 2x2s owe all the friends a big apology for covering it up. It's all a big deception. Anything founded on a lie is not the truth.

It was fear, not the Holy Spirit, that controlled me and kept me in this fellowship: fear of asking questions; fear of reality and fear of the harsh answers I might receive; fear of finding out I had wasted my life; fear of hurting my parents; fear of rejection and losing my family and friends; fear of displeasing God; fear of excommunication and shunning; fear of displeasing the workers; fear of being wrong; fear of the grapevine's condemnation; fear of the friends' and workers' scorn; fear of appearing foolish; fear of people accusing me of forsaking God; fear of the accusation of wanting to be worldly; fear of being without a church; fear of the unknown and death; fear of lost security; fear of asking for help and prayers; fear of mental problems. I know now that God has given the Holy Spirit who dwells in believers the job of controlling, guiding and directing each believer, not fear nor the workers.

I don't think the workers realize the enormous effect they have on the lives of people with no-non-sense stuff (wearing dresses all the time, having long hair and wearing it up, no make-up, no white shoes, going to meeting all the time and countless other requirements that aren't supported by the Scripture). I remember when I was a teenager that my Dad told my sister and I that we had to wear dresses to the ball games in high school, or we couldn't go. We begged and begged—it was better to stay home most of the time. Some times we did wear jeans, but, oh my, the guilt feelings we had when we did! I no longer live in condemnation, Romans 14:22-23. I live by Ephesians 2:8-9. I don't have to be ashamed of the gospel of Christ—before I was. A man who is still in the 2x2s who was raised in the truth told me he would never ask anyone to the gospel meetings. I know what he meant because I have felt the same way.

Our meeting was full of people living together unmarried, behind the workers backs, of course. How could the workers not have known? We saw child abuse to the point that the law came to the door during meeting. This family was described by the workers as a very spiritual family. Of course, this was hushed up real fast. What a spiritual family! I could see people getting by with all kinds of sin; yet I was condemned and snubbed if I wore slacks while playing with my kids, or if I watched TV, or if I wore my hair down. I always tried to make it to meetings, but they didn't like it if I didn't call in each time I was unable to come. These things are not sin, but I was made to feel like they were. This list could go on and on.

I asked three sister workers how important was it to take the "wine" in meeting? I was not even given an answer, but was ignored, or snubbed again. In our meeting, there were people going to bars and who knows who some of the people were sleeping with? It seemed that every Monday, I was sick or coming down with a cold. I have lupus and my bugs are enough for me to fight. Since I wasn't sure of the lifestyle of these other people, I thought I would be better off not taking the wine, so I quit. Every Sunday, the elder made a big deal out of offering it to me, but he never asked me why I didn't take it. My colds got better, and I never regretted not taking it.

George never went to meetings, and was not interested in being with the friends. However, in our church, there weren't any couples our age to do things with, if he had wanted to. By this time though, there were two 2x2 ladies whose friendship I really valued, Betty, whose husband does not profess, and Iola—an elderly lady I looked upon as my grandmother. The three of us had our coffees together, and ate out and did our own thing.

In the years after I read *The Secret Sect*, I showed the book to four different ones of the friends, but no one had the same response to it that I had. However, one day I talked to a lady who came to town who had already read the book, and she helped me more than I can ever express. She believed the facts the book contained were true, as I did. It was so exciting to finally be able to talk and compare notes with someone who thought on my same wave length. I remember feeling such joy and peace. I realize now that reading the book was not enough for me—I needed to see and talk to someone who had responded to it the same as I did, which confirmed to me that my response was not off track.

One day in November 1990, I asked my friend Iola if she would read *The Secret Sect* and give me her opinion. As soon as she read it, she called me and exclaimed, "I feel like a fool—how could I have been that stupid?! Was I ever dumb and deceived! I should have known better! How foolish I was to allow myself to be brainwashed for seven years!" She felt she could not be a part of this deceptive group another day. She had been told that this fellowship continued down from Jesus' apostles. I never was one to fence sit either. Once it was clearly revealed to Iola and me, we had to act on it—it had to be one way or the other.

Since it was November near Special Meeting time, I told Iola maybe we should wait until after the Special Meetings were over before we left the group. Iola didn't agree. She thought we should quit "cold turkey" like some smokers who quit smoking. I said, "OK." I found out later that neither Iola nor George thought I would go through with it!

After Iola had missed two Sunday meetings, and I had missed one, we decided to discuss with our friend Betty the reasons for our decision. We invited her over and told her everything. She was shocked, and of course, she went right back and told the workers, who were knocking at our door within six days. They tried to see us separately, but God was with us, and we were together when they came to Iola's door. My daughter, Barb, had just left with her car, so they were quite surprised to see me there also. Iola was afraid to say much, but to my surprise, I was able to open up and tell them my whole story, and I didn't even cry! I had strength I never knew I had. I actually felt free to talk about how I felt to the workers for the first time in my life. When we asked Bonita Kleeb and Elouise Snow, sister workers, if the book was true, they said the book was only one man's opinion. Bonita told us she had read parts of *The Secret Sect,* and that she knows people who read the book and then professed in gospel meeting.

Iola and I feel God was helping us that day. When the workers left, they were crying. Iola went in the bedroom, and I thought she was probably crying too; however, when she came out, she had on a big smile, and so did I! We were so happy and relieved. Both of us would have cried if we felt condemned by what we did, but we didn't. We were free for the first time! I love John 8:36, "If Jesus has set you free, you are free indeed."

Together on November 18, 1991, Iola and I cheerfully celebrated our one-year anniversary—the date we set ourselves free of the bondage of the 2x2 fellowship! Iola said disgustedly, "Why did I ever get in it, anyway?" I feel God spared Iola so she could help me out of the 2x2s. I loved her very much. She died on December 16, 1991, just barely over a year after we left the fellowship. Over and over that year, she told me, "This is the best year of my life!" and "I know my Jesus." She was ready to meet the Lord. After she passed away, I saw the elder of the local meeting we had both attended, in a store, and I asked him if he knew Iola had passed away. He said, "Yes, and I'll tell you what I think. It's just one less of THEM—that sends out all that propaganda." I said, "Believe what you want to believe" and walked away.

Before Iola's funeral, while I was visiting with our friend Betty her husband and professing daughter concerning Iola's death, the daughter spoke up and said, "Too bad she wasn't ready." Betty and her husband pointed out, "We really don't know that." The daughter said, "That's debatable," and walked out, slamming the door—proving to me, more than ever, that we made the right choice in separating ourselves from such a judgmental unloving group. I feel sure Iola would have chuckled at their comments.

I have always loved the truth of God, but not always the "truthers" or this 2x2 way of fellowship Irvine started. So far, I haven't mentioned Jesus, love, God's grace, salvation and all the things I now enjoy studying because they aren't discussed much in the 2x2 way. They talk a lot about what the friends are doing, news, funeral, births and who attended whose meetings. A friend said, "People who talk about people are little people; people who talk about the saving grace of Jesus are big people." It's so nice to know that I'm not saved by my works (Ephesians 2:8-9), but by the death (grace/unmerited favor) of Jesus, who died for my sins, so I can live. I could not save myself, and self-denial cannot save any one. That's not God's plan. Faith saves and our love for his gift shows its appreciation in our works toward one another.

Works are not how I look, or what I wear, but rather works are helping the poor and the widowed, etc. Salvation is not earned by doing works; it is a gift of God to His children. Titus 3:5-7 says, "be careful to maintain good works." They are good and profitable, but cannot earn salvation. When my younger sister was in the first grade, my mother cut her some bangs, and Bertha Schmidt, a sister worker, scolded my mom. I never ever felt my hair was beautiful. As long as I can remember, I have always felt like an ugly duckling, which gave me very low self-esteem, and also made me think I was dumb. I know now that I am neither. I thank God for this. I have always felt that sports were out for me, because I was clumsy; now I found I'm not that either. I looked up everything, going back to the original Greek words about the women having long hair and discovered growing hair is a "work." Long hair is not my salvation. God would be insulted to think I could save myself by growing long hair! My purpose in recently cutting my hair, was to show that I am no longer identified with those who thought this a necessary mark for salvation—NOT so I could be worldly.

II Timothy 1:9, "who hath saved us and called us with an holy calling, not according to our works, but according to his own purpose and grace which was given to us in Christ Jesus before the world began." We are saved by believing in Jesus sacrifice—not by any sacrifices on our part, nor by the sacrifice of the workers.

I have now learned that the Father, Son and the Holy Ghost are three eternal persons within the nature of God; that Jesus was fully man and fully God. 1 Timothy 3:16 says that "God was manifest in the flesh" which is saying that Jesus is God the Son. He was our savior, not just our example. The 2x2s don't believe that Jesus is God. They see the fellowship Irvine started as the savior. 2 Timothy 2:19 says the foundation will stand because it has the seal and that "The Lord knoweth them that are his." We can read The Secret Sect and then test the foundation. The Bible says "try the spirits." "Let everyone that nameth the name of Christ depart from iniquity," 1 John 4:1.

Matthew 10 was canceled in Luke 22:35-36. Jesus never instructed the apostles to continue in the future to go like he sent them in Matthew 10 to preach only to the Jews. He told them specifically NOT to go among the Gentiles or the Samaritans, who were a people who were held in contempt by the Jews. The gospel was preached to the Gentiles, that is all of us who are non-Jews, in: Acts 10:44-48; 11:1-18; 13:46-49; 15:7-9, 11, 20, 24-25; 16:26-34; 17:32-34; 18:5-8; 20:18-21; 26:16-18; 28:25-28; Romans 9:24-26; 10:11-12; 11:12-20; 15:8-12. Galatians 1:15-17; Ephesians 3:1-11 "past mysteries are now made known"; 1 Timothy 3:16 "mysteries of godliness." Jesus had to die before the dispensation of grace of God could be preached to the Gentiles, Ephesians 3:2-6. This is the gospel or the "good news" not the meeting in the home. What wonderful good news or gospel of God! It sets us free to serve him out of love. "The wages of sin is death," Romans 6:23; but grace is the un-merited favor of God. "For there is no difference for all have sinned and come short of the glory of God being justified freely by his grace through the redemption that is in Christ Jesus," Romans 3:24.

I have also enjoyed Luke 17:20-21, "the king-dom of God comes not with observation—lo here or lo there. For the kingdom of God is within us." What freedom! What joy! What love! What a plan of salvation!! I am so very glad to know that people in other churches are saved. That other women who cut their hair, wear slacks and jewelry are OK. I am free to believe the Bible for what it says, not for only what the workers say it says!

I feel comforted now and I never felt comforted before. Now I truly feel like a Child of God. Before I never was sure if I was saved; maybe, depending on my mood. Salvation by faith is NOT the easy way out even though the workers say it is. I have to believe that Christ took my place to live righteously and died as my substitute for my sins. I am happy because I don't have to condemn myself anymore. I don't doubt anymore. I KNOW I am saved, present tense. I believe that Jesus finished his work on earth. He took my place and His Blood pays for my sins. I could never enter heaven by my own works and effort. In Jesus, there is no failure. Thank God for His marvelous plan!

Yours in Christ Jesus,
    Rose Medich

1991

Address:
Rose Medich,
RR2, 102 Prairie Road
No. Platte, NE 69101

Chapter Thirty-Eight

Fred E. and Ruth D. Miller

Letter to Mr. Doug Parker Dated April 30, 1972

Dear Mr. Parker,

Earlier this month just the day before we found ourselves leaving what we once called the church (and now call "the C.C. group" in accordance with their officially registered name, "Christian Conventions"), we received your newspaper, "Spiritual Fraud Exposed," from Mr. Fred Hanewell in Germany. It was an astounding exposure of the group and clinched the issue for us most effectively. We are very grateful for your considerable efforts.

We are a forty year old couple who have been wholehearted in this group for twenty and fifteen years respectively. I was in good standing in the work for six years here in Washington prior to our marriage thirteen years ago and for the past seven years have been the elder in one of the local assemblies.

Whether we have "left" or been "put out" is academic. We could not stay and they would not allow us to remain. However, they have not wanted to be in a position where it could be definitely said that they had "put us out." Perhaps your exposure of many being put out has made them more cautious in the practice of their methods. Although we had unanswered questions about the origin and history of the movement and had long been puzzled over the evasive response to our questions on that score, we had tried to push that situation aside in our minds, not having seen concrete evidence of anything being wrong and having nothing substantial to go on.

However, three years ago we began to notice that there was but scant reference either in the preaching or testimonies to the blood of Christ— scant reference to Christ as our Saviour and none whatsoever to Him as our redeemer and Sin-Bearer; much attention to His earthly life and ministry, none to His atoning death - only a heavy emphasis on Him as our Example, especially as demonstrated to us by the workers, which emphasis we knew was not that of the N.T. Gospel. (If following an example of God's righteousness could save, then the law could have saved. Scripture says it didn't. Romans 3:20ff; Galatians 2:16,21) Also we noted a heavy emphasis on works and scant reference to faith, a heavy emphasis on effort and less on rejoicing. Whereupon we began to wonder whether we had long been reading our own evangelical beliefs into the preaching and perhaps those beliefs were not actually held by the workers, albeit not denied.

Tactful enquiries kindly made were turned aside and the workers became suspicious of us. We continued to study the Scripture and to compare it with what we heard in the meetings—it seemed almost certainly different. So nearly two years ago we began *carefully* to speak of these neglected crucial doctrines in our own testimonies each week, at first simply to test the reaction to it. Later we began to recognize it as an opportunity from God to try to speak as clearly as possible of trusting the saving work of Christ to these who were so unaware of such Good News even though they were so pitiably earnest toward what they believed to be the things of God. And the friends listened and some enjoyed it, but in time became puzzled.

The workers' response was different and we were put under immediate surveillance They resisted our testimonies and tried every way possible to counteract them without having to oppose Scripture openly. We found they refused to be pinned down as to just what *they* believed, much less as to just what the gospel consisted of. We could see they didn't agree with us at all, but would not openly admit it. At every encounter (and there were a number of them) they tried to sidestep the doctrinal issue, even though they tried to counteract it in their preaching. In conversation they would only accuse us with: "There is something there in your testimonies which is not 'of us,' not the 'same spirit.'" And they eventually resorted to branding us with a "bad spirit" (an easy dodge), although we had been *most* careful on that score and the charge was completely without foundation. The workers' clever control of the friends was incredible—a brief word or look was sufficient, always inferring, never proving. Although we had enjoyed the respect and confidence of the friends for years, it meant nothing. It became clear the friends had learned to uphold the workers without question, but had learned nothing of upholding the Gospel of the grace of God.

As we this winter gradually learned more and more of the history of the church by letter from Mr. Hannewell, we were not actually too surprised. We resolved to say nothing of these things at the time, however, for we knew many would simply put their heads in the sand and say, "Forget the past; enjoy what we have today." (Many must have long since taken that very course, for we now see that most of this information was liberally distributed to workers and elders here in the Northwest in the fifties. Although I was in the work at that time, my older companion prevented my reading the literature and told me nothing of it.) Anyway, it was our hope to demonstrate that they didn't have a saving gospel *today*, that they were trusting a church (the "Perfect Way"), a set of ministers, their own imperfect faithfulness, their own efforts and "willingness to follow" a set of vague, ill-spelled out conditions; that they were not trusting the Saviour, nor relying on His atonement to reconcile them to God. And having learned something of the subtle power of inference, we always kept a positive approach in our testimonies, simply assuming that of course they shared our faith and confidence in the reconciling work of Christ, our thankfulness that we did not need to depend on the feeble above-mentioned substitutes, our praise to Him for meeting our need for a saviour.

One of our aims was to make the workers openly admit and demonstrate their opposition to salvation by grace by putting us out on that ground alone. However, they did their best to remain slippery on that point, not wanting to tangle openly with any of the Scripture which we used. Finally in April the week before your newspaper arrived, the workers formally forbade us the emblems before eight called witnesses on the ground that we were reported to have mentioned privately a few days earlier church splits in Australia and the church's having taken a name.

Still trying to dodge the issue: On exactly what specific grounds does a man become reconciled to God; just exactly what *is* the Gospel. They really don't want to come right out and admit: "**We** will reconcile you to God. **We** are the good News." It just wouldn't sound good, but it's what they actually mean. They constantly infer such and then wait for the attending outsider to absorb it. When he does, he is said to be "seeing it" and has now become "one of us," "able to see the Way" and "willing to follow in the Way" "with us—the people of God." The Saviour as such doesn't come into it. Actually they don't talk about "trusting Christ as their Savior," but of "seeing (through their workers' preaching) that this is *the Way* and being willing to walk in it." It is the Way that is upheld, not the Saviour. It took us a long time to realize this, as it's very subtle.

Well, to continue: It is of interest that when we countered their charge by asking them whether they expected us to praise the church for splits and name-taking, they replied that they would not answer that question. When we used our opportunity to turn to the doctrinal issue, they retreated with some reference to revelation as opposed to a reasoned examination of the Scripture. Incidentally, they did not deny us freedom to attend or to speak in fellowship meetings (we feel they would rather not have that on their record), but we feel their ground work has been such that our usefulness in that capacity is at an end.

Four months earlier I was relieved of the eldership and offered a variety of back-handed insults by a committee of workers, led by the overseer of this state, Therald Sylvester. Since that time an older worker has attended our every meeting, weighing our words and paralyzing the friends. Quite torturous months they have been and, although we were grateful for our opportunity to speak, we're glad they are over. Opportunities are open to us now which we could not use earlier, and we hope to do all we can to get the facts into wider circulation.

And so, our foremost reason for contacting you just now: Do you have additional copies of your newspaper which we could obtain for distribution?

We would be happy to reimburse you for them. The one copy we received is too worn to try to duplicate and had been so trimmed to fit its envelope that a number of lines of the text are missing on both pages front and back. (Mr. Hanewell's sight is quite dim.) In spite of the workers' controlling taboo here, we feel certain that at least 15 of the 55 families here will read and attempt to fairly consider such a piece. And, of course, we feel the responsibility of many contacts in other cities and states developed over the years.

Also, have you ever put out a fuller report? We would be most interested. (Curiously enough, just a few months before receiving your newspaper, we had been wondering what a trip to Ireland might possibly uncover. But we didn't dream the extent of it. We had supposed that it began away from public view, since it operates that way today. Again, thank you so much for your efforts.) By the way, a visiting Australian reported to us this winter that someone whom she thought was from England had visited her Australian convention last season in order to take pictures and gather information for a book he was writing on the group. He was put off the grounds, but managed to retain his camera, which the workers would like to have confiscated. We wonder if you have knowledge of such an effort and we would surely wish to obtain a copy of any available or forthcoming publication.

We were interested to hear that you had returned to the Church of England, although we are not familiar enough with it to know just what that means. One of the evils of the C.C. group is that it closes the door to fellowship with other believers even after individuals have left it and are supposedly free of it. We fear that some who have left the group may simply aspire to be the makings of something similar and are in danger of limiting the grace of God to themselves, recognizing no fellowship with other evangelical Christian groups and seeing no common Christian heritage with them. While we know, of course, that much of present day Christendom has succumbed to liberalism on the one hand or sensationalism on the other, we know also that there are still some conservative, evangelical congregations—plagued by imperfections, of course, but nonetheless preaching the Scriptures.

We would appreciate as early a reply as possible, for we know it is important to contact folks before our blackened name has had opportunity to precede our efforts. We surely feel concerned about the plight of the people in this church. They are blind, putting their trust in the church and its methods instead of in Christ. And we feel for those who are under the "stress" of making a "choice" to go into the group. When my wife professed as a young woman, the stress was such that in a matter of weeks she lost ten pounds and her auburn hair turned dark brown.

Do you know anything of John Kelley? See the second name on the enclosed list. We suspect some here will try to say he was an older worker through whom W. Irvine professed.

Sincerely yours in His Name,
Fred. E. Miller
Ruth D. Miller

Excerpt From a Letter Written by the Millers to One of the Friends, Dated July 4, 1988

You asked why we left the fellowship and what we are now doing to serve God. This could take pages and pages to answer, of course, but will try as best I can to give you some idea.

We had a very serious reason for leaving, of course. Simply put, and perhaps shockingly put, we left the group because we came to see that it did not teach the truth about how to get to heaven. To miss the most basic and most important teaching of Scripture could only mean that it was not of God.

This was not a hasty conclusion. We were forced to face it quite sadly after several years of careful thought, of searching the scriptures, of much prayer, of carefully examining the workers' preaching, of many, many sessions of careful talking with various workers about what they believed and taught, as well as what they did not believe.

We had hoped it was simple inability on their part to speak the gospel clearly as it was in the Scripture, but when we saw at length that they demonstrated and admitted opposition to what we knew to be the gospel, we knew we would have to leave. This was a shock to us, of course, for we had been very earnest in the way for many years. Fred had been in the work in earlier years and had been a highly trust elder for a long time and still was. But getting eternal life, being received of God, is important above all else and is a matter of life and death. We could not allow misplaced loyalties of any kind to interfere with it.

It was all very confusing and stressful for a long time, but we wanted what was true. We knew that was all that God could accept. Finally in desperation we tried honestly and consciously to rid our minds of any personal preference as to whether we would stay in or get out, and simply asked God to show us the truth. In a few weeks time our eyes were opened and we had peace. We could be sure what the gospel really was and that the workers consistently oppose it.

So we rejoiced in the gospel of the Scripture, trusted it completely, but felt very burdened for all those we knew in the fellowship. For that reason we stayed in the group another two years or so, knowing that we would be getting out, trusting completely in the gospel, not in the workers, but using time and opportunity to share what we had learned with others on the inside. You would know, of course, that usually the friends learn very little from the Bible except through the workers—and the workers (in spite of what they think they are doing) are not telling people the truth about how to get to heaven. This Way was surely not what we had once thought it to be. So that is why we left.

I have just stopped and reread your letter and do appreciate your frankness. Interestingly enough, every one of the problems you mention (problems which others have also observed),
- the judging and condemning
- the coldness and scorn toward the world
- the lack of charity toward the needy
- the pretense that the Way has not changed
- the evasiveness and veil of secrecy which crops up constantly
- the belief in being the only ones saved
- the many restrictions—the do's and don'ts
- the fear that holds folks in this Way and keeps them there

Every one of these things is a natural result of the workers' misunderstanding the gospel and teaching something which is not the gospel.

How I wish I could talk with you about what the gospel is and about the freedom and the safeness and the love that it brings! It really is GOOD NEWS! Great news, in fact. And it doesn't produce any of the things on the above list. Those things come about when men distort the gospel. I hope that you will allow me to try to clarify things somewhat and that you will search the Scriptures also for yourself.

To begin with, the gospel is good news, not (as many suppose) good advice. The gospel itself (see the enclosed statement) doesn't tell me what to do or not to do, read or hear and have confidence in because it is from God.

It says that God has taken care of everything (as regards the need of my soul) and I can safely rely on it - as I could never rely on my own doing or anyone else's. Ephesians 2:8.

It says that, while God (being a holy God) requires absolute righteousness of me, He saw that I could not meet that standard and (because He is love and grace) sent One to live righteously in my place—a substitute, a proxy. So the needed righteousness is mine, lived out for me by Another, God's own Son, our Lord Jesus Christ. Romans 5:19.

It says that while God's righteous law requires that any who sin must die, God (again in love and grace) sent Another to take my place on the cross and bear God's wrath against sin in my stead. Romans 5:8, Hebrews 8:28.

So the required life has been lived and the death has been died. Everything is done. God has accepted it, Christ has been raised again to life, and we can be received into God's love and fellowship ("accepted in the Beloved" Ephesians 1:6).

It only remains for us to rely upon what Christ has done as ours. And we must do so, or it is not ours. God will not force us to accept His provision. We can rely on something else if we wish, we can try it some other way, but He cannot accept it. It will mean failure.

Maybe you've heard this old, old poem, sometimes sung, I think:

> *Upon a life I did not live,*
> *Upon a death I did not die*
> *Upon His life, upon His death,*
> *I stake my whole eternity.*

Many, many have echoed this resolve and rested in this truth with glad assurance down through the ages and with great thanksgiving. The Lord invites us to do so each one. It is His own provision for us.

It is this news, of course, that gives us real cause for thanksgiving, real cause to love God who first loved us, real cause to want to please God who has been so thoughtful of our need, real cause for love overflowing to those about us. We have gratitude that God has loved us and provided for us so freely when we have not earned it, could never have earned it, and it makes it much easier to love others. We have received a gift above all other gifts, ("the gift of righteousness" Romans 5:17, 18, "the gift of God is eternal life" Romans 6:23, "Thanks be unto God for his unspeakable gift." 1 Corinthians), and we have cause to be generous to others. we have received a gift without strings, and we have no cause to want others to qualify for everything they get from us. We have no cause to condemn others, because we ourselves have not qualified for what we have received.

But sadly there are many others who have not rested on God's provision of a Substitute, who have relied on something else in the hope that God will accept them—the work of their own hands, something they "do" or "don't do," or some "way" that they identify themselves with, or some human mediators they rely upon. If all these ways do not rely first and foremost on the God-provided Substitute (as a substitute, not primarily as an example), they will be no more successful than the tower of Babel was. These are self-efforts and not only are they ineffective, but they tend to produce the list of problems you speak of.

Look at the list again and think about it. It is when we think we have had to work and pay a costly price for God's favor that we are tempted to judge and condemn others who we feel have not paid such a price. We can get a coldness and scorn of those who we believe have not denied themselves as we have. We put ourselves in a bondage which can make us envious of outsiders who may have more freedom than we. The scripture tells us that we are free, but we don't feel free, because we have bound ourselves over to something in an effort to secure God's favor. We restrict ourselves and our families more and more beyond reason in an effort to be righteous, but we become self-righteous and feel cut off from life. And it has not even brought us safety.

And then (check the list again), we have to protect the "way" we are depending upon, so that it will continue to appear trustworthy. Hence the evasiveness and secrecy and finally the actual lying to cover for its shortcomings. The workers, especially, must find this a terrible dilemma. Sometimes the friends will say that they are not trusting the way, but are trusting Jesus. If this is so, why do they feel so terribly threatened when the way is questioned? And, of course, trusting Jesus as an Example to show me how to do it is not at all the same as trusting in His perfect doing and dying in my place.

We can't trust our efforts to follow a perfect example, but we can trust His perfect doing. He isn't a
way-shower. He IS the Way. John 14:6.

And perhaps worst of all is the fear that holds
us, all the while we say that we are held by love.
True, there is a certain brotherly love there which
drew and held us, but I expect in most cases the
fear had the stronger holding power.

Now, the objection that you will hear brought
against the good news that God has done this for us
and given us a gift to trust in is that we will then
live bad lives, because we don't have to pay for
salvation by living a good life. There are several
things completely wrong with this objection:

1. It misses the point entirely. The point we're
talking about is not how to live a good life, but
how to get to heaven, how to get salvation. So this
objection is actually a clever changing of the subject.

2. We can't pay for it by living a good life, anyway. Our very best effort isn't good enough. It falls
short of God's perfect standard which He can't
bend for us. Only Christ Jesus could meet such a
price.

3. Above all, things just don't work out the way
the objection says they will. Trusting Christ as our
substitute does NOT make us live worse lives. For
this reason: receiving this gift makes it possible for
God to accept us. He then gives us a new nature
which desires righteousness. If we had only our old
nature, no doubt we might live worse if we could
get away with it (unless subtle, wicked pride made
us want to polish our image), but the person who
trusts the gospel has both natures, and the new one
finds sinfulness repulsive and wars with the old one
and moves us to please God. Paul didn't say "I con-
strain myself," but "the love of Christ constrains

me." Incidentally, after Paul had explained the gospel in Romans chapters 3, 4, and 5, he foresaw the objection mentioned above, and met it in Romans 6.

No, this news does not (as the devil constantly declares) cause us to have a lower regard for righteous living. After all, Christ's righteous life is a big part of the gift. How can we take lightly something we value highly and are so thankful for! Instead, our regard for righteousness rises. The way it actually works out when we rely completely on this news & the gift it speaks of, is that our desire to please God increases many times over, but with this important difference: we have been set free. No longer is there the striving and the pressure. We can express our gratitude individually as we freely choose. No arbitrary list of do's and don'ts handed to us by someone else. We simply have a desire to please God. We look to His Word for direction. Our efforts are imperfect, of course. But we have no fear that God will not accept us. We have already been accepted. The whole thing was God's own plan. We have been "accepted in the Beloved" and we are thankful.

I hope I haven't made the gospel seem involved. I don't usually go to such length. It's really very simple. *Look again at the enclosed summary.* The first statement says the whole thing. You'll see quickly enough that the workers spurn Christ's work as a gift and treat it as a reward. They have folks working, walking, following, hanging on, etc. in order to get salvation. Their gospel is simply offering folks a chance to "try out" for salvation, to see if they can make it.

But they are trying for something which they can never earn. The Lord, of course, has rewards for His own, but salvation itself doesn't come in that category. It's too costly. The price in solid right-eousness is too high. We have to take it the only way it's offered, the only way it is possible, as a gift, completely paid for by Another. Romans 6:23, Ephesians 2:8,9.

We pray earnestly that there are those in the group who are relying on Christ's work in spite of all the emphasis around them to the contrary. And we do believe there are some, some who may be privately trusting in the doing and dying of Christ in their stead and are blind to the fact that the workers do not. That was my own exact case, of course. And it's a pretty tricky blindness.

As to your other question: what we now do to serve God. Well, we do more than we ever did before, but it is not because we are "trying harder," and it has not been of our own arranging actually. Perhaps God has been working that out, too. We do more personal Bible study than ever, of course, and we hold a regular Bible study in our home for others. Also, the Lord has introduced us to some very needy widows and orphans we can be some help to in practical ways. We didn't even know any before, much less think we should personally do anything about it. I don't know what else I can say. We are very grateful to God, it is our pleasure to share what we have received from Him with others. Such situations seem to come along regularly.

About going to another church. One has to be very cautious, of course. Some teach the gospel and some don't. But there are Christians out there, ones who know and trust the gospel. And then there are plenty who are simply religious. But salvation doesn't depend on a church, of course. It is the Lord's to give. But a church may help us to find some Christian fellowship, especially if the gospel is trusted and kept foremost.

The charity efforts you speak of are wholesome as an expression of our gratitude to God. But if ever we use them instead as an effort to win God's favor, we're back in the old trap of trying to save ourselves instead of trusting God's provision. Some have fallen into this.

Using another Bible translation as you are doing will probably be a help to you, if only that it can give you a fresh look at the Scripture and help you to avoid old rabbit tracks. Helps you to think about what you are reading.

But trust God. He will show you. You are not alone. You may feel helpless, but God is not. Seeing these things clearly can be a slow process; but if that is the case, it is because God knows that is the best way. He is an excellent teacher. And He loves us. Remember, only Christ stands between us and God, not a church or a minister. He alone is our mediator. 1 Timothy 2:5. And He stands as a bridge to God, having loved us and given Himself for us.

We shall very much appreciate hearing from you further. We shall be praying for you and for your family, knowing that God will be helping you toward joy and peace in the gospel. Be assured that your sister and her husband, are welcome to contact us in any way they choose.

Perhaps I can enclose some other portions of letters which may be helpful to you.

"May the God of hope fill you with all joy and peace in believing." Romans 15:13.

In Christian Love,
Fred & Ruth Miller

P.S. It's interesting how many times professing mothers have begun to open their eyes when they have listened closely to hear what their children were being given in the meetings.

Notes Dated November 10, 1981

Just some notes I wrote with you in mind:

In the fellowship (I cannot call it the truth or the way) they believe their church to be different from any other on earth.

However, their basic error, their most serious error, is common to that of many other groups, even to the public at large. And this is not surprising because it is surely one the of devil's most important lies. It is simply this: *They believe that God will accept their best.*

This is not true. He *cannot* do so. *He is holy.* He requires perfection, heaven's wonderful standard. We can't meet that demand. (God knows that better than we do.) Even a perfect example can't help us. We need a substitute, a proxy. And that's just what a gracious God has given us when He sent Jesus *to live and to die* in our stead. Sure is good news! *We call it the doing and dying of Christ;* the Gospel (see Romans 5:18-19 and Isaiah 53:5-6). He *lived in our stead* with perfect righteousness as we could never do, and He died to pay the debt for our failure. Thanks be unto God for His unspeakable gift! 2 Corinthians 9:15. And it *is* a Gift (Romans 6:23). The only condition being that we accept it, rely upon it instead of anything else.

The sister worker told us she didn't want a cheap salvation. She wanted one that cost something and she was willing for any price. But oh my, we pray for her. She has no idea that the price is *so high;* it's way beyond her reach. So high that only

Christ could meet it. Perfect righteousness. And we're so very grateful that He met it for us.

Yes, the fellowship *misunderstood the purpose of His life*, and they largely ignore the value of His death. They *say* they believe in His death, but they don't *rely* on it to be saved. Why should they? Or rather, how can they? *The false premise that God will accept their best* denies their desperate need for a saviour. It makes the wonderful Good News (the Gospel) that God has freely given us a Saviour quite unnecessary. It's no wonder the devil has used this falsehood so widely to try to undermine the Gospel. We have to watch out for it on every hand, not just in the fellowship. It's deadly wherever it is. This thought that God will accept our best appeals to our human nature, to our desire for approval and for recognition of our dedication and sacrifices. It is a falsehood that is a subtle bid to our pride, encouraging us to take satisfaction in our own efforts to walk faithfully. It can give us a fine sense of purpose and determination, but with the wrong focus, a self-oriented focus. It causes us to turn our eyes inward to see if we are doing our best, rather than looking outward and rejoicing thankfully in what Christ has done *for* us.

They think trusting in a gift and not trying to pay a price will lead to careless living. Actually it's just the opposite. When we see how high the price is, how high a value God puts on righteousness, and see that He has written it down to our account because Christ accomplished it for us when He lived and died here long ago, it surely can't lead to lessening the value of righteousness in our eyes. We just don't have to "try to make it," "try to be faithful," etc. We just look in thankfulness to what Christ has done and forget about looking inward and rejoice. And God will take care of the rest. After all, the fruit of the Spirit is the fruit of the *Holy Spirit*, not our fruit—at least not the fruit of our nature. God will give us whatever we need, including a proper regard for righteousness. Romans 8:32 is just great!

The trouble with people setting standards of righteousness is that we don't understand righteousness well enough. Everybody has a different idea of what is right. And they generally wind up dwelling on a lot of superficial items. How come a simple little necklace (neither good nor bad in itself) gets so much attention and a subtle spirit of competition slips by with scarcely a challenge. It sure is a relief to leave all that behind.

And it's a relief to know that we are completely *safe* because we are relying on Christ's sure and certain work. Folks who are still in the fellowship talk about the Way and the fact that they are walking in it. We talk only about Christ (He *is* the Way.) God has accepted His work for us and it is unchangeable, and completely reliable. He finished it long ago and we can't add to it.

We say with John Bunyan: "Our righteousness is at the right hand of God (Christ Himself) where our good works can't add to it and our failures can't detract from it." And God's love for us is the same kind of thing. It's perfect. *Nothing* we can do can cause Him to love us more, nor can it cause Him to love us less. His love for us was expressed most deeply when He gave His Son to be our substitute, both in life and in death. John 3:16.

Folk in the fellowship speak of their death—"dying daily," a "deeper death," etc. We speak of our Saviour's death. 1 Corinthians 2:2, 1 Corinthians 1:23. We rejoice that He has given us life eternal. In a way, I suppose, that "deeper death" idea in the 2x2 caused us to separate ourselves from life, to hi-

bernate and mark time from one meeting to another. It sure is a relief to live again, to feel free
and easy, to be able to make choices freely. This
freedom is God-given and surely doesn't give a believer a desire to sin.

Interesting that while we owe everything that we
have to God, He holds us under no obligation. He
has given us a *Gift*, many gifts, and He is not even
suggesting a payment for it. It is a *real* gift. He gave
freely. We accept freely with no danger that we
will take advantage of His generosity because one
of the gifts He gives us is a desire to please Him, to
be in harmony with Him. But don't let anyone else
spell out to you what being in harmony with God
means and begin dictating your steps. You are
God's child and He will teach you and help you
Himself and make you free. No doubt He's taught
you that already.

I really must stop now. If there are any questions we can help you with or problems that come
along, don't hesitate to let us know. I can't write at
length, but more briefly at times, and of course
we've always a bunch of old letters we've written
to others in the years when we could handle more
which might help out some. In any case, we would
love to hear from you. Love in our Saviour's name.
Ruth & Fred Miller

Address:
Fred. E. Miller
Ruth D. Miller
6120 W. Umatilla St.
Kennewick, Wash. 99336

Chapter Thirty-Nine

Jane Morissette
Letter to the Friends Dated January 1, 1993

Dear Friends (for indeed you are my friends),

This is the most difficult letter I have ever written. Let me say at the outset that the decisions written in this letter represent YEARS of prayer, thought, soul-searching and Bible study. Also, please be assured that no one has offended me nor do I have anything less than a complete love and appreciation for all of you. I trust that you will read what I have to say and, if possible, that you will still consider yourselves my friends. I suppose I have put off this decision primarily because I value your friendships and I don't want to hurt anyone.

Although I value much of what I have heard in meetings, I can no longer honestly fellowship in them. I have become aware that some of what is heard in meetings is inconsistent with, and contradicts Scripture. My concerns have been growing for the past eight years. However, it wasn't until I started listening with the untrained ears of my children that my concerns forced me to confront the issues. I'm sure some of you have been concerned that Kirsten and Mary have not yet "professed." When I talked with them about it, I realized that they did not have the same understanding of the Gospel that I did. Since I was brought up in a home where Salvation through the Blood of Jesus was taught, I assumed that they had heard the same Gospel (the Gospel message that God sent His Son,

Jesus, to die on the cross for my sins). What I have heard and learned during the past 18 years were good lessons on living a life pleasing to God. But what I did not realize was that there had been no teaching on the saving power of Christ's substitutionary death on Calvary.

I believe that my salvation is dependent SOLELY on my belief in and acceptance of Jesus Christ's *complete* work on the cross (Hebrews 10:12). Jesus Christ, God's ONLY begotten Son is my Savior. It is His death on the cross that has redeemed me. I have been bought with a price (the life's blood of Jesus Christ) and no man (not even myself) can separate me from the Love of God. (Luke 19:9, 10; John 3:16; Romans 10:9-13)

Jesus said, "I am the way, the Truth and the LIFE. No man cometh unto the Father but by ME." (John 14:6). I do not need any other mediator (not a worker or a priest or any other person) other than Christ Jesus, my Lord, to reach my Heavenly Father. The Life of Christ is very important to every true Christian; but were it not for His substitutionary death and resurrection, He would have been just another good man.

Jesus said, "Ye shall know the TRUTH and the TRUTH shall make you free." I am not in bondage to any particular form or rules and regulations—only the law of Christ's Love. My salvation is not based on the form and method of a particular church. Ephesians 2:8-10 tells me that I am saved by GRACE, through FAITH, not of works (neither the "good works" of some denominations nor the works of dress, hairstyle and meeting format.) I want to please God, and I can only be pleasing through Christ's blood.

In Colossians 2, Paul reminds us that we are complete in Christ (vs. 10), the law has been abolished (vs. 14 & Matthew 5:17) and that outward expressions of humility do not really honor God but rather satisfy the flesh (vs. 23).

I don't have space to write all of my concerns and discoveries. However I would like to share what I have found with anyone who is interested. I love you and do not want to lose your friendship, but I would not be honest before God nor you if I continued to participate in the meetings. In thinking back on things that I have spoken in meetings, I have been honest. My greatest desire is to serve the Lord with a wholehearted service. But I no longer believe that this is the only true church. Christ's Church is comprised of ALL who have accepted the free Gift of Christ's SACRIFICE.

It is often spoken that "by their fruits ye shall know them." I have seen true fruits in the lives of other Christians who are not part of the "Friends." When Jesus' disciples questioned Him, He said, "He that is not against us is for us." (Mark 9:40 and Luke 9:49, 50) As part of a larger body of Christian Believers, we can have a greater influence in our community and in the lives of those around us.

I know that this letter may be as hard for you to read and accept as it has been for me to write it. As we encounter each other in the days to come, I trust that we can treat each other in true Christ-like love without judging one another. (Matthew 7:1 and Romans 14:1-13).

In Christian Love,
Janie

Concerns

I feel I must leave:
- To have a larger group of believers with whom to fellowship

- To get more "in-depth" Bible teaching (more than just the King James Version). I need more solid Bible teaching on how to apply God's Word to specific events in my life.
- To have a place of service.
- Because I feel stifled. I feel that I have gifts of service that are not being used.
- Because I cannot believe that this is the ONLY TRUE CHURCH. I believe that there are many false churches, but I don't believe that *every* other church is false.
- I believe that CHRIST is the head of the Church.
- my children need a larger Christian family in which they can build Christian relationships.
- I see great problems in our community which are not addressed at meetings: alcoholism, child abuse, apathy of youth, spread of Mormonism.
- I feel a need to reach out to those who know nothing of Jesus' love.

Inconsistencies and Legalistic tendencies

- Women wear long hair, but they are allowed to speak in meeting.
- Why no "adornment" but we do wear clothes!!
- Where is the grace and freedom Paul talks about in Galatians? "All things are lawful..."
- It often sounds as though people are trying to earn their salvation by "keeping faithful and enduring to the end."
- If we are following the design of the early church, why is there no speaking in tongues?
- Why is it wrong for me to remarry, but it's O.K. to divorce, live with someone, come back to meeting and be welcomed with open arms.

- Jesus and the apostles preached in the temple. Why, then, must meetings always be in homes rather than church buildings? Meetings traditionally have been held in homes as a safer alternative to public meetings in areas of Christian persecution. But does this mean that God only sanctions those churches that meet in homes?

Address:
Jane Morissette
710 W. Third St.
Hardin, MT 59034

Chapter Forty

Name Withheld

I truly believe that the Lord had his hand on my life from the very beginning, as you shall see by the time you finish reading this letter. I just thank my Lord Jesus every day that I did not "profess" into that "church." By the total grace of our Lord, I was saved from that fate. Let me tell you why.

From the time I was seven years old, I knew that something was "wrong" with that "church" and its teachings. Because of an incident that occurred in a Sunday morning meeting, I was turned off totally from God, Jesus, or anything which had to do with religion. I have never told anyone what I am about to tell you, other than my husband, Jim, and my closest friend, another Christian. One Sunday, in meeting, as they passed around the communion, I decided I wanted to be like the "big people," so when the bread went by, I took a piece. It was totally an innocent thing. No one ever explained to me what it was all about. I surely didn't mean anything bad by it. It was like the devil himself suddenly appeared in the room! Every eye in that room stared at me, I was horrified. I was suddenly filled with an incredible fear. My mother yelled at me for over an hour, (She never did tell me what communion was) among other things, she told me I'd be lucky if God did not suddenly strike me dead with a bolt of lightning! From that day on, I became deathly afraid of God. For years, I walked around, wondering when God was going to strike me dead.

Something was revealed to me that day, I couldn't
figure out why God, who was supposed to be so
loving and kind, as the "workers" preached, would
want to kill me. The overwhelming fear I felt did
not go along with the loving God they preached,
and what little I knew of what the Bible said. From
that day on, I hated that "church." Then when I
was about eleven years old, at one of the "gospel"
meetings, which were being held by one of the elderly "sister workers," I made up my mind that I was
going to give my life to that "church," (profess). I
never did look at it as going to give my life to God,
or to Jesus, but to the "church." I was going to do
this, mostly for my mother, to gain her love. Then
the "workers" proceeded to tell the story of a
young couple (no names were given) who were
members of the "truth," but they had stayed away
from the "fold," and were "lost." This couple were
engaged to be married. Then, about a week before
their wedding, they returned to the "fold" (the
"truth") and were "saved," then on their wedding
night, they were involved in a terrible auto accident, and both were killed instantly, but wasn't
God loving and kind to see that they were "saved,"
and not forever "lost"? I can remember this "sermon" very vividly. I was horrified! The whole story
was designed to play on the listener's emotions—
what I call "scare tactics." I never found out if the
story was true, or not. Well, play it did! When they
gave the invitation to "profess" again, I was filled
with an overwhelming fear, so intense, it paralyzed.
I couldn't move! I sat on my hands, and wrapped
my feet around the bottom rung of my chair, to
keep them from shaking. I became physically ill. I
almost fainted. I never again entertained thoughts
of "professing." As irrational as it sounds now, I believed that if I gave my life to that "church," I

would die. So, I just bided my time, waiting until I was old enough to say: "No! No more!" I eventually, gradually weaned myself away from that "church" over a period of years. Then, I went my own way, and did my own "thing." Unfortunately, by then, I had no self esteem, absolutely no opinion of myself, I didn't care what happened to me. I became involved in smoking "pot," and drinking alcohol, quite heavily. I got so I could not function normally, without a drink. I stayed "half-lit" twenty-four hours a day. Incredibly, I was able to entirely hide this life style from my family. I literally lived two different lives altogether.

Then I met my first husband, and when he asked me to marry him, (after knowing him three days) I thought it was incredible that anyone would want me, so I jumped at the chance to get married. I married him for many reasons, but none of them right. The biggest reason was to get out of my mother's house. I wanted to escape my brother, who was allowed to beat on me viciously from the time we were very young. I believe my mother thought my brother would "out-grow" this behavior, so she did nothing to stop it. Then by the time we were older, it was too late. He beat me so bad, I would be a mass of lumps and black and blue bruises. I had to wear clothes that would hide this all the time. These clothes fit right in with what the "workers" expected us to wear, so no one suspected a thing. He beat on my father this way too. Strange thing was, he never laid a finger on my mother, she was able to control him like a puppet. I soon discovered that as long as I had a boy friend around, he wouldn't touch me, so I jumped at the chance to get married. Unfortunately, I ran from one abuser, to another. My husband not only abused me physically, but mentally, emotionally,

and sexually. When I discovered that I was pregnant, I gave up the "pot" and alcohol literally
overnight. Two months into the marriage, I filed for
a divorce. By this time, I was nearly a "basket
case." I couldn't stay in the marriage, and I
couldn't get out. I was trapped by my own belief
that I would go to hell if I got a divorce. So, I made
up my mind that I was going to commit suicide. I
figured that if I was going to do this, I was going to
make positively sure I would not fail. Again, by the
total grace of God, I was saved. Just as I was about
to take my life, a woman came along and asked me
what on earth I was doing. I told her, as if I were
talking about the weather. She asked me "why?"
We ended up talking. I don't remember too much
of what she said, but she gave me hope, something
I had not experienced in a long, long while.

After this, I made up my mind that I would take
my chances with God. I went through with the divorce. That was the turning point in my life. Shortly
thereafter, I was shopping at a local mall with a
friend. I sat down on a bench to wait for her, when
a man came up and sat next to me. He pulled a
Bible out of his back pocket. My first thought was:
"Oh no! A Jesus freak! Maybe if I'm lucky he'll
leave me alone." No such luck! He didn't leave me
alone. He told me his name was Jerry, and he
asked me if I knew the Lord Jesus Christ. I had to
think about that one. I told him: "I know *of* the
Lord, but I can not honestly say I **KNOW** the Lord."
At this point he read to me John 3:16, but the Bible
he was reading from wasn't a King James. For the
first time in my life, what he read, and what he
said, actually made sense to me.

He asked: "Do you know Jesus loves **YOU**? Do
you know Jesus died on the cross for **YOU**?" He
pointed these things out to me in his Bible, in

black and white. I could hardly believe what he
was saying, I'd never heard any of this on a personal basis. I didn't even know there were other
Bibles other than the King James. I was fascinated! I
didn't quite believe it either. It seemed too good to
be true. Then Jerry asked me for my phone number.
I don't make a habit of giving my phone number
out to total strangers, and had no intentions of doing so, but for some reason, I felt compelled to do
so. He told me that the charismatic church he attended was showing Christian movies for the teens
and younger members of the congregation. I'd
never heard of such a thing. I was taught that movies were some sort of ultimate sin. What
charismatic meant, I had absolutely no idea.

Jerry called me faithfully, every Friday, for
weeks, he read the Bible to me over the phone, and
"witnessed" to me. Well, to be honest, I thought he
was a little on the crazy side, a "false witness," of
the kind I had been warned to stay away from all of
my life. But, what he said began to "sink in." I
wanted this guy "off my back," and not wanting to
be rude, I struck up a "deal" with him. I told him:
"I'll go to your church, if you go to mine.! I had it
figured he would back out. I was wrong. I wanted a
friend with me for moral support." The friend I
brought was my father. Well Jerry kept his end of
the deal, and attended one of the "truth's" gospel
meetings, along with his wife. It was the last one I
ever attended. I thought he'd be real impressed;
that he'd see the real truth, and be "converted"
from his "false ways." Again, I was wrong. Afterwards, when I asked him what he thought of the
service, he looked sick. His only reply was: "These
people are dead! I've been to happier, more joyful
funerals." He'd compared the service to a funeral! I

was insulted. I figured he was "blinded to the truth," by Satan himself.

However, I too, kept my end of the deal, and attended one of his church's Friday night movies and worship services. My Dad came with me. I was scared to death; terrified to set foot in the door of what I was taught, and considered a "false" church. I was so full of fear, my knees were shaking. I needn't have been. Had I not made a promise, I'd have turned around and ran! I didn't have a chance, I was so caught up in what I saw, heard and felt, I was amazed! These people danced in the aisles! They clapped and shouted and sang in praise to the Lord. There was a band, and they played beautifully! I was entranced! I also thought they were all crazy. But the people were all so wonderfully kind and accepting, and so full of *genuine* love for my Dad and I, even though we were total strangers to them. They hugged us, and said they loved us with the love of Jesus. Neither one of us felt in any way uncomfortable with this. They welcomed us right into their group. I felt like I belonged, as if I'd known these people all of my life. For the first time in my life, I belonged somewhere. They accepted me, and loved me with "no strings attached." I became one of them almost immediately. It was wonderful, just plain fun! I'd never heard of a church being fun. I'd never associated church and fun in the same aspect. Church to me was frightening, confusing and boring.

At that service, I ran into an old friend of mine, someone I used to "party" with. She was so changed by the love of Jesus, I didn't recognize her, she had to tell me who she was. Again I was amazed. Very impressed. There was so much love and acceptance, I just had to come back for more!

My Dad assured me that they were "on the level." He had left the "truth" several years before.

In the meantime, Jerry kept right on witnessing to me; he never gave up. He made arrangements for me to talk to his preacher. I have to admit, I was nervous. I expected to see a stuffy old man. My mistake—he was only a few years older than I was. He didn't "preach" to me. He told me about his life, his family, the miracles God had done in his life, and how he got "saved." Most of all, he listened to me. He was there for me. He could answer any question I had concerning the Bible. If I had doubts, he could show me in the Bible just what Jesus had to say about them. I could no longer dispute the Word of God in black and white. He talked to me for hours, on many occasions. The time he gave to me was his own time. Time he could have spent with his wife and family, but instead, chose to give it to me, a total stranger. Such was his faith in Jesus that he wanted me to have the peace and joy that he had in the Lord. The love won me over. Four months later, I gave my life to Jesus. *It was wonderful!* I did not know what these so-called "false" Christians had, but whatever it was, I wanted it too. I found out the moment I gave my life to Him (Jesus).

The amazing thing was that this wonderful gift was free to anyone who wanted it, just for the asking! By the grace of God, through His Son, Jesus Christ, my whole life was changed. By the power of the blood of Jesus, I was saved! All my past sins were forgiven. I was given a clean "slate"; a new life in Him! My whole outlook on life, and for that matter, death was changed. That was over twelve years ago now, and my Lord Jesus is still with me. The Bible says: "He will never leave nor forsake you." He is true and faithful to His word. It hasn't been easy at times, there were many fears and doubts in the beginning. I turned away from the Lord for a while, but He never turned away from me. He's been right there for me always. I truly feel that had I been raised in a true Christian environment, I never would have been exposed to the adverse situations that came into my life. I would have had the ability to take a stand against these things. I would have had a fighting chance. Perhaps if those in "the truth" had shown even a small portion of the love that was extended to me by these "false Christians" I may have stood half a chance with them. But it just wasn't there.

After I got saved, I threw my energies, heart and mind into studying my Bible. The very first thing I did was find a good, legitimate translation of the Bible; one I felt comfortable with, and could understand. I, incidentally, bought a Living Bible. It was such a joy to read a Bible that actually made sense to me. For the first time in my life, I could understand what I read. The Word of God suddenly became so clear to me. I felt like invisible blinders had been lifted from my eyes, mind and heart. I was starved for the Word of God. I was enraptured. I just simply could not get enough. I read, and read, and read. I wanted to dispute every lie and half truth I was ever told. My mother told one of my Christian friends that she couldn't figure out what was "wrong" with me, why I seemed so different, she said she had noticed an incredible change in me. My friend simply told her it was Jesus in me; she found Jesus. My mother refused to accept this. She would hear nothing more of it, period. Shortly after I received the Lord into my heart, I made a decision to be baptized. A group of close friends, and several others who wanted to be baptized, all got together at a little pond where the ceremony was performed by two good friends of mine. I was baptized by total immersion. It was one of the most exhilarating experiences in my life. It was perfectly wonderful. I have never felt closer to the Lord than I did at that time. I was totally and completely enveloped in His love. An incredible peace descended upon me. That was eleven years ago and to this day most of that peace is still with me, in my spirit. From that experience, I received an incredible freedom. I felt as if I were one with the Lord. It was beautiful.

About one year after I was saved, I met my husband. He too, is a "Born Again Christian." He is truly a gift from the Lord. Two years after we were married, he legally adopted my two children from my former marriage. We have now been married ten years. We have what I consider a real good marriage. We both work hard at it, and give the Lord His proper place in our marriage.

One of the first things I did when I broke away from the two by twos, was to start "finding myself"—who I was in the Lord, according to His Word, and to start letting my true personality to come forth. I got my hair cut very short. I did this gradually, each time I went in I got it shorter than the time before. This way, my family got used to seeing me like this on a gradual basis. I changed the way I dressed. I discovered jeans and flannel shirts. I bought the brightest colors I could find. It didn't take me long to realize that I detested dresses, from having to wear them every single day of my life. (To this day, my husband has only seen me in a dress once, and that was on our wedding day.)

I must admit, that all of this transition process took time and a lot of "victories" have not been easily won. I still struggle with doubts, fears, and "panic attacks." I found a Christian friend who has a real "deliverance" ministry through the power of prayer. Through her, Jesus has removed a great deal of my fear. This friend is someone I've known for most of my life, but was told to stay away from, because she was a "false" Christian and was in the same league as Satan. I had to overcome my fear of her before I could even allow her to pray for me. That in itself was a major victory, as I had a terrible fear of allowing anyone to lay hands on me and pray. Through this woman, my life has taken some major turns for the better. But, I had to learn to step past my fear and take the first step. I'm finding too that these people, who I was told were "false" Christians, are some of the most wonderfully kind, loving, caring, compassionate people you could ever hope to meet. Were it not for some of these "false" Christians, I cannot say for certain if I'd be here today, writing this. However, I truly must give the Lord all of the credit, because He brought these people into my life to bring me where I am today. I am confident that with the help of my Lord Jesus Christ, I shall overcome all of the problems associated with being raised in the two by two "church."

I have tried many times over the years to witness to my family, who remain in the "truth." It seems so hopeless. They act as if they do not hear a word I say. They act as if I am a little child who doesn't know any better, or an annoying "bug" that won't go away. I have pointed out different things in her own Bible, but she's an expert at twisting words and Scripture to say exactly what she wants it to say and she is very convincing. She wiggles right out from under me. They both refuse to look at reality in black and white, right before their very eyes! A few years ago, my brother told me he will never attend another "meeting," "as long as I live."

He calls them a bunch of hypocrites. If I say anything against the "truth," he becomes angry and is instantly on the defense. He doesn't accept them anymore, but neither does he accept any other beliefs. I tried talking to him about the origin of the "truth." He said he didn't know how all of the rumors got started, but that it is "all lies." So, this tells me that he has heard something from some other source besides myself. The "seeds" are being planted; they do have their doubts. That's a start.

One thing I find immensely helpful during the time I was "breaking away," and even to this day, is that I bought myself a small pocket Bible (also one I am comfortable with). *I never go anywhere without this Bible!* I also keep one in the glove compartment of my car. Whenever doubts or fears assail me I get out my Bible and flood my mind and spirit with the Word of God. Satan has no power against the Word of God and the blood of Jesus! I rarely listen to any music other than Christian praise music. Music is a wonderful balm for uplifting the soul and spirit. It has also helped me immensely to be able to talk to others who have gone through this process. I feel it is a great help to find someone to talk to that you can trust. Don't be afraid to share what you are going through.

This part of my story is not easy to share, but if I can help someone by sharing this, glory to Jesus. Even though I left the "truth" over twenty years ago (when I was eighteen years old), I didn't find Jesus until I was twenty seven years old (twelve years ago). I floundered around, not knowing which way to turn, having no one to talk to, because anyone I talked to and tried to explain just what sort of "church" I came from had never heard of it. I was in total darkness to the truth about the "truth" up until three years ago when I obtained some of the books that are being written exposing the "truth." My eyes were suddenly opened like never before! I went through an intense period of grief. I went through a "breaking" period, where the Lord allowed me to "get it out of my system." I locked myself in my bathroom (for privacy, being it is the only room with a lock on it) and I got down on my knees and gave it all to the Lord. I wept for hours. This went on for weeks, not every day though, and the days became farther and farther apart. I went through a period of "numbness," anger, anger at God, intense feeling of loss. I allowed myself to feel what the Lord wanted me to feel. I learned that if you can't express yourself to the Lord, who knows everything about you and still loves you beyond comprehension, you cannot express yourself to anyone. I went through this totally alone. This was excruciatingly painful. I may have been alone, without human companionship, but the Lord never once failed to show me His intense love for me. He never failed me. He always let me know He was there. I do not know how I knew this, other than I sensed it in my spirit. Even though it was very painful, it also felt good just to be able to "let go." When I finally made it out the other side, it was as though a great burden was lifted off my back. I felt light and free. It felt so wonderful. I did not even share this with my husband, until I knew I made it, for fear he'd think I suddenly lost my sanity. This is a grieving process, when you lose the only lifestyle you ever knew, and possibly all your friends. It is a sort of "death." It is good to allow yourself to grieve for these lost things. Jesus knows what you are going through. He went through it too! He was betrayed by one of His disciples, and deserted by all twelve of them. They were His closest friends! I urge anyone who is going through this type of experience to "cast all your cares upon Jesus, He cares for you." Not all of this has been a painful experience, some of it I found to be down right hilarious. Finding out just how ridiculous the "truth's" beliefs are, compared to the real truth of the bible, you wonder how so many people could be so deceived for so many years! It's mind boggling, it really is. When I say things were hilarious, I am more or less laughing at myself for being so blind. I do not mean to criticize anyone in any way, but there were times when I had to laugh too. There were times, when I didn't know whether to laugh or cry, but the Lord pulled me through. There are occasions when I still "go through the fire," but through all of this, I have learned a lot, and now have the strength to stand against these Satanic attacks, for that is what they are. When I can't stand alone, I call someone in my church to pray for me, and this works every time. I have my husband pray for me every night before I go to sleep, and most every morning, before he leaves for work. This works wonders.

My husband and I attend a large charismatic church. This church has grown from thirty members to nearly fifteen hundred members in three years! They have programs for the teens, a food and clothing ministry for the poor and homeless, a drug and alcohol recovery program, a ministry to visit the elderly and sick, a counseling ministry for marriage and for un-wed mothers, and a financial ministry for those in need of temporary financial help for whatever reason. This is the way a church should be run. We feel very blessed to be a part of this congregation. I suggest to anyone who is considering trying a church to ask a friend to go with you. Don't be afraid to take that first step. It's a big one, but it can be done. Once you see how loving these people can be, you will wonder whatever kept you away. Ask questions and see if the answers coincide with the Bible. Most of all, remember, Jesus is on your side. He loves you so much, with a love we cannot begin to comprehend here on earth! When you come to Jesus, He does not look at your past, or your sins, he sees your spirit and your heart. He sees the "real" you. Your past he remembers no more. To me, this is the most wonderful gift anyone can ever receive. They say "you can't take it with you," but there is one thing you can take with you, and that is all the friends you can lead to Jesus. I truly believe this with all my heart.

Now that I am nearly to the end of my story, I realize that I haven't said a whole lot of my experience within the "truth." I wrote this as an inspiration to anyone who is leaving the group, or contemplating doing so. I want people to know that there is life after the "truth." I did not have a whole lot of memorable experiences. As a small child, we had Sunday morning "meeting" in our home until it was discovered that my Dad smoked—then they took it away. When I got into my teens, I hated the way we had to dress. I was totally fed up with having to wear dresses every day of my life while my peers at school all wore jeans. That was the beginning of what the "workers" referred to as "rebellion" in my life. I just outright refused to wear dresses any longer. The "workers" tried to talk to me about my "rebellious streak," but most of what they said went in one ear and out the other. I know they talked to my mother about it. I refused to wear my hair in a "bun," and be criticized at school. I hated being "different" from the rest of my peers. The "workers" never had too much of a hold on me, because I never "professed." Finally, after several years of harassment by a pair of "sister workers," I point blank told them: "I'm not a professing member of this group, and you cannot force your opinions on me, because what you're doing is only pushing me further and further away. I do not have to do what you say." I had a few "run ins" with the "workers," but most all of it came from one "sister worker," who seemed to "have it in for me." For what reason, I never knew, maybe I was a challenge for her. I could spend a lot of time criticizing the "workers," but it would serve no purpose. I truly do not hold any ill will towards them. I'm sure they only said and did these things because they were concerned about my salvation. I have long ago forgiven them. There is much power in forgiveness. It in itself is the pathway to healing old wounds, a good start any way. The "workers" stayed at our home at least once a month while I was growing up. I always felt real special if they took the time to talk to me. I remember almost worshiping them, and the ground they walked on. I wanted so much to hear just one word of praise from them. Had they been more loving toward me, I may have "professed." Then, as I got older, it was too late. There was too much "water over the bridge." They must have realized they were never going to convert me to their ways, so they just gave up on me.

As I have mentioned, I pray that this story will be an inspiration to someone out there. I know that the few things I have read of others "testimonies" have been a great inspiration to me.

Always remember: *Jesus loves YOU!*

Wednesday: June 30th, 1993
Printed by permission of the author.

Chapter Forty-One

Name Withheld

Dear Friends in Christ Jesus,

I first began going to meetings of the fellowship in 1989. At that time sometimes I also still attended Mass at the Catholic church. The worker even recommended that I go to the Catholic church in the morning and go to Gospel Meeting in the afternoon. During part of that early time, I was working from 1 to 4 p.m. on Sundays. Gospel meetings changed from 4 p.m. to 7 p.m. This silent accommodation to me showed amazing care. The workers kind and seemingly far and open minded attitude seemed to me amazingly good—compared particularly with various pastors of churches I had attended for significant periods of time and also compared to Catholic priests. I went to meetings with a friend. I had been very lonely. One time, I believe it was in the summer of 1989, we went to an early evening Gospel meeting with my friends relatives, a very kind, older couple. It was quite a drive. Meeting was in the deep downstairs of someone's home—a huge big, beautiful house way out in the country. Both workers spoke eloquently, it seemed to me. They spoke about the "Gospel," "eternal salvation," close relationships with God. It seemed so sincere. It seemed to be what I had always been searching for!! The downstairs was packed with people. There were other "new" people like me, it seemed—lots of people. (If every meeting had been like this one, I never would have ever considered leaving.)

I have, it seems, a rather orthodox belief about the nature of Christ. But I did so enjoy the way devotion to Christ (apparently) resulted in a practical, definite improvement—a holy life, a minimum of hypocrisy, or so it all seemed to me at that time.

Also, gradually, the fellowship of going to meetings came to mean a lot to me. I superimposed my own beliefs about Christ (and the Holy Spirit) onto the meetings and the talks of the workers, not realizing a difference in concepts of grace, redemption, Christ.

It is becoming now a bit difficult for me to write about all of this. I have many valid thoughts, even though I am feeling upset inwardly about what was done to me—and the deception—so many things are relevant to say and to write. Such a confused mixture—such anguished confusion as I have gone through I would not wish on any soul. So many things to relate—both major issues and small minor ones. Perhaps it was the small issues and the small observations which led me to try very hard to examine the beliefs of the fellowship I had grown to love. But in trying to find out what these beliefs were—apart from the special paired "itinerant" ministry and meetings in the home—was just about impossible. I looked in libraries, with volumes about American denominations—did searches—I could find nothing out about the group at all. It was not even mentioned in anthologies or in dictionaries of religion!

It was small things, as I have indicated, that pointed the way. For example, having the elders wife and her two boys, my friend and her elderly relative over for tea—it seemed so enjoyable—I was so happy to have them! (I really loved these peo-

ple.) The elders wife seemed different suddenly—
shockingly different. The graciousness and warmth
were gone. She suddenly became very imperious
and icy with me and sat aloof from the rest of us. I
thought perhaps she was just having a bit of a bad
day, as we all sometimes do. Later she commented,
when we were discussing the nature of Jesus Christ
(I was probably asking questions), that they did not
believe Jesus was a man with a halo glowing
around His head as shown in the pictures I had in
my house—they believed it was wrong to try to pic-
torially represent Jesus. The reason I thought this
was odd—was that there was such a picture in my
youngest son's room which she could not have
known about or seen. Her sons, who were all over
the house, must have told her. Also, I have a real
orthodox icon of Christ in my bedroom, an original
painted by a Greek friend icon painter. (I don't
worship it—it is my constant outward symbolic reminder.) But she was not in those rooms. Her
school age sons were, so they told her about these.
How odd for young children to report such a small
thing. And yet, in discussing the nature of our Savior, the somewhat sarcastic, critical concentration
on these trifles was absurd! No doubt other things
were said - I know later we talked about the nature
of Christ in more depth, yet unfortunately by that
time our relationship had disintegrated. I believe I
did not handle the whole thing well! Not at all!

First of all, I was not tactful enough, careful
enough, discreet enough—in my confused anguish
eventually I was like a dog with a bone—I "worried" it constantly—I would not leave it alone. Yet I
didn't keep it to myself! I spoke with many others.

Probably, I was not even considered to be really
a part of the group thoroughly. Or if so, perhaps
briefly for a few months late in 1990. In a person's

prayer and testimony, I recoiled at being referred to as "this new babe in the word." That was another small thing that made me uncomfortable. (I felt I had been in the Word and in God's hand all of my life. I felt—perhaps unreasonably—that I was no more a babe than the others.)

The elder's wife had been incredibly kind and good to me, particularly through a terrible illness and operation I went through. She meant so much to me! I now believe she did not like me or enjoy my company at all—it was simply her duty. It makes me feel utterly sad and humiliated even now, because I loved and admired her so much, as a new dear, dear friend. So, there were two things (at least) going on - there was a growing confusion over the relationship with the elder's wife and the elder—particularly that it seemed it was expected of me to please them more—in that sometimes there were actual scoldings, which made me uncomfortable. (Although they never said anything about all our TV sets in our house! Or our outdoor lights at Christmas time, for which I felt very guilty for about three Christmases. They did ask me a lot about my husband's reactions and thoughts about a potluck luncheon around Special Meeting time—the day before—that my husband and children attended in which several workers did speak.) The scoldings were more about my feelings about things, my attitudes, my confidences, etc., which were apparently unacceptable. (I never heard anyone scold the elder's wife about some of her "bad attitudes" about her oldest child—it was o.k. for her to be cutting and sarcastic in the extreme about him—she was just being genuine.) My genuine concerns and attitudes (concerning struggles with my life—issues, but not sarcastic or cutting at all) were not acceptable. I guess I needed to polish up my "public persona," or it just seemed I was going to have to "put a lid" on absolutely everything. And yet in 1990 we were going through a lot of struggles in our family. It was a crisis year—my husband's job, my health, two truculent, very difficult teenagers. I lacked a buoyant attitude; I lacked everything I needed. The worst part of it was that I was so open! I do so regret that. Also, I must have been a real trial to the elder and his wife—particularly to her. Even now it saddens, embarrasses and humiliates me!!

All these things made me feel more determined to try to find out more about what the fellowship taught definitely—like about grace, and about sin, and about the Savior, and about healing! A friend who is southern baptist wrote (on her own) to her churches home mission board and obtained a few paragraphs about the fellowship and the name of the book *The Secret Sect*. I even showed this paper to the workers who were here at that time. I just did not comprehend at all that there should be secret, hidden things and it really didn't occur to me at that point that anyone could get angry and offended at my honest probing and my earnest and honest confusion (which was growing). I was so thick! That did not help! I prayed to God for help and guidance—that is what the workers advised. I believe God led me through, sustained me, and did help me—I had been on a road where I was struggling because I wasn't pleasing the elder's wife and elder, though those two said they liked my testimonies. Other's were colder to me after my testimonies and seemed displeased. God made me to be me and He gave me a mind to think, to reason and to be in closer unison with Him. These thoughts helped me—particularly helped me to define the bondage I had been recently living under.

If God created me to be me, then why should I try to be more like the elder's wife (she having said she was an example for the women in the group).

The Baptist friend suggested I ask at the Christian bookstore for the book *The Secret Sect*. I asked there and they said they couldn't get it, but the man who worked there knew a man who had it and gave me his name and phone number. I called him—and he had already been called by the bookstore man. He asked me if I would like other information—more than even mentioned in *The Secret Sect*. I was puzzled, but said yes.

The book *Church With No Name* and many papers were sent to me. I spoke with Mary Ann Schoeff. I was overwhelmed, utterly shattered, shocked, devastated!! Then for a long time I vacillated greatly. Though I stopped going three and four times a week to meetings, I still went sometimes, but I suffered constantly—wanting, yet not wanting to go to meetings. Initially when I was devastated, I told the elder's wife I could not sort out the book by David Stone; I asked her to help me—I really was so upset and confused—in utter mental anguish. She admonished me, then told me to toss the poison away, and refused to look at the information with me saying, I'd asked questions and I knew what they were about, etc. She was cross with me for begging her to go over different points in the book or in the papers with me.

It seems quite clear to me that the little odd things pointed the way to me about bigger belief system error. I am so thankful for God's help and care. Now, over two years later, I am thankful I never really lost my sanity in all the anguish! I feel strongly that any group and belief system that has a major element of confusing people—pleasing as its strong emphasis, and also has a wary, resentful, unloving, angry response to probing by an honest, open, earnest, Christ loving believer—is of THE DARKNESS OF EVIL, perhaps of THE EVIL ONE. There is no end to the havoc such a group can wreak and the hurt and destruction such a group can cause. Manipulation, bondage, hypocrisy, hatred, are words that come to mind.

There is much I have left unsaid—about the ministry, testimonies, special meeting, conventions, some beliefs. I simply can't write more now.

To sum up, though there is a sort of wistful nostalgia when I remember going to early meetings in the beginning and the peace, structure and friendship this brought into my life, I also feel there is something seriously wrong with a group that claims to be the only group of people who are saved—or who will know eternal salvation. The walk with God is not of love and devotion then, but of fear and legalism, resentment, bondage and eventual hatred and bigotry, perhaps with no access to healing grace.

August 20, 1993

Name Withheld
Printed with permission of the author.

Chapter Forty-Two

Name Withheld

I began going to "this way" meetings in January 1991, and stopped going in January 1992. In March, 1992, I moved to Montana knowing virtually nobody there. Not the easiest way to recover from the strange Two by Two world. Several months before that, after a couple of visits and hours of riffling through the two-volume *Encyclopedia of American Religions* in the public library in New Hampshire, (and still going to the "meetings" regularly), I finally came across a note quite closely describing the practices of my "church." It was listed as "Two by Twos." Through the interlibrary loan, I obtained some publications mentioned in the reference notes, W. E. Paul's and W. M. Rule's pamphlets and *Spirit of Revival* by I. R. Govan. I also picked out Willa Appel's book on cults. (It was just there, I still wasn't sure if it was the right path of research.) After I had read the first few chapters of the book I knew that I "had been had." However, the world of the Two by Twos was so unusual, the publications I had on them outdated and imprecise, the books on cults I had picked never referring to my particular experience, that I still couldn't figure out what it was exactly that I had been through and why it didn't want to go away!

The breakthrough came suddenly. There was a day in June this year that I just couldn't hold it any longer, I had to talk to somebody and it was my landlady I chose: a good-hearted, churchgoing, charging-the-lowest-rent possible woman, bless her heart. She subscribed to *Catholic Digest* and remembered that there was an article on cults there. Soon after we had finished talking, she knocked on my door with this particular issue. I was too distraught that day to deal with the cults anymore. I read it the next morning. At the end of the article there was an address, a telephone number and a short note on activities and goals of the Cult Awareness Network, a tax-exempt, public supported organization with headquarters in Chicago, Illinois. I called them straight away. Only four staff people work there, I learned later.

However, one of them remembered that in one of the recent issues of *Christianity Today* there was an article by Ronald Enroth in which the author made a mention of the Two-by-Two church. I was given the author's telephone number. (There were no reservations about that, just a lot of good will.) Dr. Enroth is a professor of sociology at Westmont College, California. His most recent book is the brilliant and highly recommended *Churches That Abuse*. He told me that he was approached by Threshing Floor Ministries, by the person who had devoted twenty years of her life to collecting information and helping the victims of this unfortunate, heartbreaking "religion." That was how he became aware of the existence of this enormously big and withdrawn church. I was given the addresses of Threshing Floor Ministry and Mrs. Mary Ann Schoeff. I wrote them. Within a week I received the hottest reading stuff I had ever laid my hands on. (Even going through the forbidden George Orwell's, *1984* didn't turn me on that much.) And more than that, I was assisted in contacting my first ex-Two by Two. It was then when the spell got broken really. And when I spoke on the phone with this person in

Montana, just a two-hour drive from my town, who with her husband had left "this way" about eight years ago (both of them born and raised in it), I felt like I was a Robinson Crusoe meeting again with a fellow human. The experience was profound and unlike any other. It was then, I may say with certainty, when my getting out process truly began.

Name Withheld
Printed by permission of the author.

Chapter Forty-Three

Someone Who Knows and Has Been There

Thank you for your invitation to submit a story regarding my experiences in the 2X2 religion. I do not relish this task, but if it will help just one person, I feel I must do it. If I were to relate all my experiences in the religion, my excommunication out of it, and the way it affected my life up to the present time, I would have several books in print.

I was born into this cult and taken to my first meeting when I was 10 days old. My grandparents on my mother's side, came to a small town in Eastern Canada in 1910, from England. Shortly after that (I believe in 1914, but my dates might not be accurate), two sister workers came and held meetings and my grandparents on both sides of my family professed, as well as several other relatives and people in the town. My mother was six years old when she came from England. The workers were Maude Slater and Lizzy Jackson and were among the first workers in Canada. By the time I came on the scene, in 1934 the 2X2s were well established in that particular town and surrounding area.

It is very hard for me to relate my story because it is like talking about a person that I no longer know. My life, attitudes, and understanding are so different that it is hard for me to put into words the agony of those years. Every time I receive a copy of *Forward Press* with all the letters regarding experiences, I feel I can relate to every single story.

I believe that fate sealed my life when I was three and a half years old and my father died. My mother was pregnant with my brother at the time. They had a store in a small town of twenty people and because of the depression my mother was in a sorry state. I had been the apple of my dad's eye and of course have no idea what my life would have been like had he lived, but I can only surmise that it may have been better. I have several very vivid memories of him although I was very young. My mother married my dad's brother about 14 months after my fathers death and he had an entirely different nature than my father. He was a no nonsense type of person, very rigid and controlling. My father, on the other hand, was very easy going and compassionate. My uncle thought I was very spoiled.

There are conflicting stories regarding why my mother married her brother-in-law. I was told by her, that he had offered for the work, but the workers advised him when my father died that his place was to look after his brother's widow. A friend of the families told me in later years that my mother chased him to death and that was how they got together. Whatever the facts, the one thing I know for sure, is that he resented me and my brother that was born four months after my fathers death, and we were always told among other things how lucky we were that he had married my mother or we would have been orphans.

My father's parents and my mother's parents never got along and my mother detested her mother-in-law even though everyone professed. To be fair to my mother there was a lot of mental illness on my father's side of the family and my grandmother and aunt were in and out of mental institutes many times. Combine that, with the legalistic bondage they were all in and it is not surprising there were conflicts. At one point my mother refused to have my grandmother and aunt in her home. There was also a lot of jealousy because my mother and father were fairly well off in later years and that did not sit well with the poorer relations. Anyone that had anything was considered to be very proud in those days. A sign of "poverty" was apparently a sign of "righteousness." The family feud continued for as long as I can remember and even today the ones remaining although professing, are far from "friends."

Years later, about ten years into my marriage, my mother left my father and came to live with me. He did not know she did not intend to come back when she left to visit me. She got a job, but after numerous phone calls and letters, a guilt trip was laid on us all in such proportions that she went back to him. It was all covered up of course and no one ever knew that my mother had tried to escape. He was also very mentally unbalanced and even more so when he returned from the war.

When my father died I was old enough to know that something was very wrong and I missed him very much. I deeply resented my uncle taking over my life, bossing me around and in general disciplining me and straightening me out. I refused to call him "dad" and this was not being obedient. When I was six we moved to Vancouver for a year. We stayed with my great aunt who was very English and correct. She had done much better than my grandmother and had married money. They were very prim and proper and one thing that did not sit well, was that I called my uncle, "uncle." She was embarrassed by the situation. The one thing I wanted most in this world was an Eaton Beauty doll. They were the rage at the time and it was all I wanted in this world. One day I was called into the den of my aunt's home and there on the sofa sat an Eaton Beauty doll. I was overjoyed and ran to pick it up. I was told that I could have the doll, but it was on the condition that I call my uncle, "dad." How well I remember the struggle of my little heart. I wanted the doll more than anything, but to me, I felt that I was betraying my real dad and also giving into another form of power and control. I can remember my hackles rising and the power struggle that was going on within me. Previous to this devious plan I had been corrected every time I said uncle, but I had persisted in doing it. The pattern of power and control was to be a ruling factor for nearly half a century. I really believe that subconsciously I probably knew that, and it affected my resistance. I took the doll and I never did like it. I was always reminded every time I played with it that I had replaced my father with that doll and I grew to hate it.

My dad (I will now be referring to my uncle as dad for the rest of this letter) was the Elder of the church in our home. Our home was a model saint's home and he was the power and control behind the scenes. My mother and him fought like cat and dog. Mom was always in the middle, but did not dare stick up for us kids or the war would be on. My mother mourned the loss of her first husband all her life and knew also that she had made a mistake. When my stepfather died years later, although it was nothing but a relief to my mother she acted out the sorrowing widow and as a matter of fact still does it. As far as marrying him in the first place, as far as I am concerned she had very little choice. It was a way out for her, or so she thought. She of course would have to marry inside the "way."

My dad was like a policeman, and I hated it when he was around, which was all the time except when he was at work. I never ever got any affection from him. I was NEVER hugged or kissed or sat on his knee. Never was there a reward for good behaviour. A constant nagging and put down were the order of every day. My hair, dress and behaviour had to be exactly what the workers would approve of. I was labeled the "ugly duckling" at school. Long brown stockings, dresses about 4 inches longer than any other kid wore, my hair pulled straight back in braids and I could not participate in any school activities. The workers stayed at our place most of the time and if dad was not on my case, they were. I was told the place of a child, was to be seen and not heard and they were all out to enforce that rule. One time when I was sixteen I was reprimanded severely for having on a pair of black pumps. The head worker that took me to task, told me I was the world's best flirt. I said, "even better than Marilyn Monroe?" How I knew about Marilyn Monroe is beyond me now, but at least I figured I was good at something. That answer did nothing to enhance my popularity. Oxfords were the name of the game but by the time I was sixteen I was so rebellious and such a hypocrite that I can hardly believe now that I wasn't put in a reform school. I believe the only thing that saved me from that concept is that it would not have been right for an elder to admit that he could not control his children. As I think back now a reform school may have gotten me away from the cult influence. How different my life would have been if I had of had approval, acceptance and love; three things that were totally missing from so many peoples' lives. When I see some of the professing teenagers today,

I wonder what would have happened to me, had I decided to dress and act like some of them do now.

I learned very early in life to be a liar and very deceitful. It was my only form of survival. Dad joined the army when I was twelve and was overseas for two years. The workers made good and sure that they took over the discipline in our home and they were always there. I never could figure out how they knew so much about children and marriage when they had never had either. When my dad returned from war, my mother got pregnant with my half-brother and I became maid and baby-sitter. They always had a huge home and took in boarders and I was very handy to have around. Of course I was reminded when I dared to complain that I owed my life to my "dad," so complaining did me no good. I remember one time in particular when it was a Saturday and the circus was in town. We had to wash the storm windows and there were a lot of them in a thirteen room house. Dad said that we could go to the circus when we were finished. We worked like little beavers and when we were finished he gave us each a dime and told us that was all we were worth!! We went crying to our mother and she gave us each a dollar and got into trouble for it, but we got to go to the circus which was a red letter day for us. Why it was alright to go to a circus and not alright to participate in sports etc; at school, I have no idea. If it had not have been for our mother we would never have survived. By the time I was fourteen I had severe bowel ulcers, psoriasis and was an emotional wreck.

My mother today has no problem telling a lie. She absolutely thinks nothing of it. Considering the years of practise she had, it is not surprising.

We moved for a year to a place further East. It was a business deal involving other 2X2s and it did not work out. We returned after a year to our original home. When we arrived in this new place and went to Sunday morning meeting, every one sat to give their testimony. My mother, father and I stood up. We were used to kneeling in prayer, they bowed their heads. There was a huge dissension because of this. There was a really big uproar, the workers were called in and a lot of hard feelings were established because of it. I can remember getting a huge kick out of this charade. It did not matter to me if I sat or stood. I would have been quite happy to not take part at all, but I did enjoy the focus being taken off me for a change and watching the conflict of control. There was one woman there who was a real tyrant. She was even worse than my father, if that was possible. Her poor kids were in constant trouble. She was a firm believer in spare the rod and spoil the child. One of the kids was always getting beaten and there was real fear in their eyes. She was in very good favour with the workers and my mother despised her. Her husband was a little mouse of a man and I can tell you he did not control her. The workers approved of her because she ruled her children with an iron hand. Most of the people in that place that were professing were related too. There was a lot of conflict in that family and among the friends there as well.

My brother left home at the age of sixteen and joined the Navy. He never did get sucked into the system. Most of my father's wrath was directed at me, but my brother took his fair share too. He hated dad and made no bones about it. He ran away once when he was twelve. His destination was my grandmother's place two hundred miles away. The police picked him up and brought him home. There was a big issue over it, but no one but our family knew about it. He was more subtle and never got caught in misdemeanors as often as I did. My dad always rode his bike to work as he was as tight as the bark on a tree and for instance, we would be severely chastised for leaving a room and not turning out the lights. My brother used to take the car out of the garage at night, as my dad worked afternoon shift, and he would go for joy rides. My dad never found out. My brother would have been locked up if he had been caught. I was a nervous wreck just thinking about it and used to beg my brother not to do it.

All the friends and workers just idolized my father and he looked after the widows and visited the sick and hated us kids. His greatest joy was to put us down in front of other people and make us look like fools. I was always told I was stupid and would never amount to anything. To defend myself was out of the question. If the quotation "brain-dead" had of been in vogue in those days that would have been my pet name. Meal times were a testing ground. We were not allowed to talk, or participate in conversation. Sit up straight, eat and shut up. I lived for the day when I could escape.

I had turned into quite a beauty just like the story of the ugly duckling and was becoming very aware of the opposite sex and their attraction to me. I was a walking accident looking for a place to happen because I craved affection and approval. I had to have my hair cut short because of psoriasis on my scalp, but that was not even a good enough reason although a doctor recommended it. I was outcast and put down for it. I had to stop taking the bread and wine and could not take part in meetings three or four times because of something I said or did. Of course every one looks at you and you feel like a speck of dirt. As long as we lived at home,

we HAD to go to meeting. My dad's greatest joy was
to see me squirm.

All I ever really understood about religion was
the threat of hell. I never could understand the concept, that if God created or made us with our
human tendencies and nature, why he demanded
that we become perfect, when he could have done
that in the first place. I was a hundred percent sure
that I was going to be struck by lightening, because
I knew I was not "good." No one that even thinks
or wishes that their Dad would die, could possibly
get to Heaven, but that was my secret wish. I kept
waiting for the axe to fall. By this time however I
was paying pretty close attention to the workers because I had enough brains to recognize the enemy.
I even managed to fool some of them. I even remember reasoning that if I could pull the wool over
on the workers then possibly God was as easy to
fool. That seemed my only hope. The workers were
more real than God and it kept me busy fooling
them and trying to survive. I thought very little
about God, but tried my best to put on a hypocritical front for the workers. I was terrified of death
and we had a couple of deaths in our family and I
had nightmares for months after each one. I was
not in love with this man God who had taken my
Dad away and put me in this terrible situation and I
can remember thinking in one of my more rebellious moods that if Heaven was anything like the
mess I was in now, then I did not want any part of
it. The only alternative was hell however and I did
not relish burning for ever. I did not want to spend
Eternity with anyone I knew at the present time so I
was in between a rock and a hard spot.

I had a couple of girl friends that were in the
2x2s and their lives were quite different than mine.
In both cases the dad did not profess and they had

a lot more freedom. The workers never stayed in their homes and in fact visited them very little. I was allowed to spend time with them as long as I behaved, but of course when I did not, separation from them was part of my punishment. I was very careful to never reveal any of our sins, like listening to the radio. In our home the radio was kept under my father's bed and only taken out when the workers were not around. They managed to do this when we were not around, but when I walked in unexpectedly one day, the explanation was that something was coming over the air that affected my father's job. Of course I was warned not to tell. I remember one time in particular when my father bought a new car. It had a radio in it and of course that was forbidden, but he had not got around to taking it out yet. Joe Lewis was the star of the day and he was under great discussion at school. All the kids were talking about him and making bets on the outcome of the next game. I sneaked into our garage and listened to it on the radio. I wanted to be able to participate in the talk at school. I ran the battery down, got caught and will never forget that episode.

I was very intrigued with the Royal Family. I collected and hid pictures of Queen Elizabeth who is only nine years older than I am. She was my fantasy and I wondered so often why I could not have been born a Princess. Her beautiful clothes were just a dream to me and she was so pretty and everyone loved her and clapped when they saw her. I could not even imagine what I had done to be so unloved and unwanted. My mother who had a soft heart decided she was going to take me to see the Coronation of Queen Elizabeth at a movie theatre, Mom was also very English and I am sure wanted to see the movie as much for herself as me. She programmed me for hours on how important it was that I never, never tell anyone. I was in a dream world. I did not even know what a show was, much less ever hoped to be able to be going to one. We got up on a Saturday and took the street car to the far end of the City from where we lived. When we stood in the line up my mother put a newspaper up to her face and pretended she was shading herself from the sun. I was directed to do likewise. She kept glancing behind her to make sure we were not recognized. I was beside myself with excitement and kept whispering to her. I cannot even imagine now, what the people around us must have thought or what would have happened if we had of been recognized. We obviously looked suspicious and in this day and age I am sure someone would think I was being molested and call the cops.

I was absolutely entranced with the theater. We watched the show twice. Mom threatened me with my life if I ever told one single person and promised she would take me to another show, if I would only be good. I was so good for the next while that I am positive everyone thought I was sick. Mom finally repeated the performance and we went and saw Barbara Anne Scott LIVE. Barbara Anne Scott was the figure skating champion of that day and another idol of mine and to see the live performance was something indeed. It is amazing to me that I repeated the same performance with my own children years later and smuggled them into a theatre to see *Pinocchio*. They were also under dire threats not to tell a soul. My mother went with us.

About that time, and the events related here are not necessarily in order, I had my bedroom moved to the basement. I could not figure out why my father came down every night and went into the furnace room. I decided to investigate and hid behind the hot water tank. Every night he wedged a piece of paper into the gas meter so that the meter was off during the night. If I had of got caught I shudder to think what would have happened to me. I can remember sitting in meetings listening to his testimony and wondering if cheating the gas company was sinning.

We always had a very nice home and we never lacked for physical needs. At that time Christmas was still celebrated and we always got nice presents. I can remember one of the workers playing Santa Claus and handing out presents that were under the tree. We were also allowed to participate in the Christmas concert at school. Several years later all Christmas celebrations were cancelled in our home. When I had children I was determined that my kids would have Christmas. My husband was very opposed and every Christmas there was a power struggle between us.

Compared to what you hear now, regarding child abuse etc: I guess our lives were not that bad. Emotional abuse was really the order of our day, but we did not suffer any extreme violence etc. I can remember in later years talking to a friend of mine who was a counselor for mental health and he asked me if I realized that I had been emotionally abused all my life. That stunned me and I said "no," realizing that I had accepted it as normal!!

My escape was reading and I got into a lot of trouble for it. I read everything I could get my hands on which was fairly limited. Nancy Drew mysteries, The dog of Flanders, *Little Women*, *Heidi* etc; were my cop out. By getting involved in fiction I could escape my real world. I was taken to task many times by my father and the workers for this "bad habit," but managed to hide books, read under the porch and in bed under the covers. My Dad checked every night to make sure my light was out. I was allowed to baby sit occasionally and used the money to buy batteries. I am sure the people at the store where I bought them wondered what I did with all the batteries.

Between the ages of fourteen to seventeen I had a lot of advances made towards me from professing married men and workers. I was a flirt, having discovered that power, and was prepared to do anything for attention. I had a very good professing friend that was a widow, who got pregnant by a worker and had an abortion. In one case regarding the advances of a married man, he lost all need for caution regarding his undying love for me and it was brought to the attention of my parents. I had not allowed any physical contact but this guy acted like a love sick puppy and of course it was all my fault. Again no one but the family knew of this. It was all covered up and smoothed over. What I went through with that ordeal would fill a chapter in a book. For one thing this man had a camp, out in the bush. His daughter was the same age as I was and he arranged that we would go with him to the camp for the weekend. There was only one bed. We all slept in it and I spent both nights trying to fight him off. He kept forcing me to touch him and would push himself up against me. I did not dare go to sleep or make any noise. His daughter was in the same bed. Again I was more upset by the presence of his daughter than in what was going on. I went to baby sit in another town for a month. He followed me there and brought flowers, records and lingerie. The name of one of the records was "The West A Nest And You Dear." The people where I was staying had a record player and he would come in and play it over and over to me. He would not take no for an answer. I was sixteen.

At home when I baby sat and was coming home he would pop out from behind a tree. This man was a lot older than I was. I was flattered by the attention, but scared stiff. That one experience alone was enough to drive anyone crazy.

When I was seventeen a head worker started making advances towards me. He finally told me that God had told him that I had been chosen to keep him in the work. That put an entirely different perspective on the situation. If a worker was telling me this, then I did not have to be afraid. This man was very respected and a great preacher. The relationship soon developed into an affair that lasted for a year. He stayed at our house whenever possible and being the head worker that was not hard to instigate. I slipped into his room when everyone was asleep and got a great kick out of getting even with my father. Finally I was loved and accepted. I was very proud of my achievements, and the compliments and love that I received from this man. He told me I was beautiful and he taught me how to walk and stand and took the only interest in me that any one ever had. I fell like a ton of bricks. He was very jealous of me and if I talked to any other male, he would lecture me. I used to sit in gospel meetings and wonder what everyone would have said and done if they knew I was sleeping with him. He was worshipped by nearly everyone, etc. and it felt so good to know that I was the most important person in his life or so I thought. He was twenty five years older than I was and was in fact the father I had been looking for. I would have done anything for this man. I lived in a dream world of love and acceptance. The secrecy and deceit only added to the excitement.

I had the privilege of looking after his mail. I noticed that about once a week there was a letter addressed to him and somehow the hand writing always intrigued me. It was like a haunting flicker every time one came and finally after a year I could not resist the temptation to open one and see what these letters were. They were letters from a sister worker who he was also having an affair with. The letters were very graphic in content and the reason the hand writing intrigued me was that he had sent her self addressed envelopes so no one would recognize HER handwriting. I cannot possibly relate my emotions at that time. To say I was angry, disillusioned, bitter, hurt, betrayed etc; are just words and they do not justify the extent of my emotions. This man was not in town when I opened that letter so I put the opened letter in an envelope and sent it to him and wrote, "thanks a lot." My mother knew that I was having an affair with him and was more scared to death my father would catch me than anything else. She was not about to go against a head worker's wishes. When he died years later I received a copy of his funeral notes. He was the most faithful servant of the Lord that you can imagine!!! He had left home and family and sacrificed himself for the work of the Lord. No one except a very select few ever knew of that affair and I am sure there were more people involved in his life besides one sister worker and myself.

It was out of the question that I could tell anyone. A young man that had recently professed and moved to our City had been making advances towards me. I accepted his advances and married him sixty days after that. I did this out of spite and if you ever wanted to see a more mismatched pair you should have seen us. I was so totally messed up and he was an alcoholic that had just professed. I was only married a very short time when I realized the mistake I had made. My husband hated my parents which was alright as far as I was concerned regarding my father, but I did not like him to treat my mother badly, so that created a lot of hostility in our relationship. Of course we were very poor and my father thought this man was an idiot. It took one to know one. We had gone North to his parents and got married on three days notice so my family were not at the wedding. My husband's parents, a young couple that stood up with us and two brother workers were the only people present. It is ironic to me that the one worker who gave us a talk on marriage, eventually got caught for molesting the friends' children and had been doing it for twenty years.

I am finding this very difficult to write. I have been accused in later years of telling my story to get even in a vindictive way. I can assure anyone that thinks that way, that I would be quite happy to never even think of these events again as long as I live.

The ONLY reason that I am doing this is to try and expose the deceit, lies and corruption that lies within this cult. That fact is true of a lot of religions, but THE COVER UP AND DECEIT IS THE WORST PART. Most of the people involved are as innocent as I was. By being around these people you become totally dysfunctional and your mind is completely taken over. Every single thing that happens to you, you blame yourself for. It was the greatest shock of my life and believe me I have had plenty, to discover years later, and read, *The Secret Sect*. I thought I was the one that was out of whack. I was too bad to live it. I blamed myself for everything and was packing around such a load of guilt that it was like a ton weight. Not until I read *The Secret Sect* did it ever even dawn on me that "the way," was wrong. By that time I had been "out" for nearly ten years and was over fifty years old.

My oldest son was born a year and a half after I was married. In the meantime we had moved out of the province and taken a job looking after one of the "friends" farms and working for him. This man made my dad look like a saint. He was very rich and powerful and we were his slaves. He hated me on sight. I refused to be controlled and he was a controller. When I say jump, say, how high?, was his motive. In order to get spending money his wife had to pick up bottles from the ditches. He owned ten sections of land. They stayed in a trailer in the yard and we had the house. He marched in every day and criticized my house keeping and just about every thing else I did. My husband, concerned that we would lose our job, sided with him. I was very angry and defensive.

Two brother workers came and stayed with us and had gospel meetings in the district. The older worker sided with me, admired my spunk which is a nicer word than rebellion and we became confidants. Soon we were madly in love with each other. He never criticized me and offered me the love and caring that I so desperately craved. For some reason that is hard to figure out, I was very committed to my marriage even though I knew that it was a mistake. We talked over our predicament and decided that nothing concrete could come out of a relationship. The brother worker in question was from a very rich family but the thought of scandal, divorce or whatever was more than either of us could stomach so to make a long story short, to this day we never even held hands. In desperation he went to one of the older workers, confessed his love for me and asked to be sent to another country. He told this worker that he would kill my husband if he stayed in the country. His request was granted on the condition he never see me again. They do not know that he came to see me before he left for foreign parts. He came in the morning just after my husband went to work. We had moved in the meantime and my husband had a job. We spent the day together and the agony was more than any human being should ever have to go through. When we parted he said he would wait for me for twenty years, I started praying the same prayer for my husband that I had prayed for my father. I prayed that he would die and release me from this terrible predicament. I have no idea how many workers knew about this, but I have a feeling there were several and my popularity did not increase. No one knew about my previous affair but I did not have a good reputation. Of course all the blame for this latest episode was placed squarely on my shoulders. I decided to make a clean breast of the situation and be honest for once in my life and told my husband that I had made a mistake in marrying him, that I was in love with this other man, but I had married him for better or worse so I was going to try and make our marriage work. In this case honesty was not the best policy. He never did believe that there had been nothing physical between us and when I got pregnant with our second child accused me that this man was the father. I just found out last year that my husband had told my son that he was not his father when my boy was fifteen. My son had lived with that thought until we spoke. The fact that he looks exactly like my husband's side of the family apparently holds no water. EXACTLY twenty years later this man left the work and got married.

I developed a martyr complex. Because of my great belief in God I had been willing to sacrifice my one big chance at love and stay with my husband. What I did not know at the time was that my husband was a schizophrenic. All I knew was that he had terrible mood swings and it was like living with a time bomb. I was very self righteous. My hair was properly "up," my skirts the right length and I developed the sanctimonious look of a "saint." Anyone that has ever seen the movie "The Thornbirds," could get an accurate description of my life. I raised my children the way I had been raised and the situation was much the same. My husband and I did not get along and I was very strict. I developed a work syndrome, took in foster children, raised large gardens and at different stages of my life either worked outside the home or milked cows, raised chickens and did whatever was necessary to keep my mind occupied. Inside I was a raging inferno. My husband told me he married me for a baby machine, and if I did not like my life, to take the road. He had many violent eruptions and has threatened me many times. I concentrated on having a testimony on Sunday morning and listened for the familiar tch of approval or amen. In later years we had the Wednesday night meetings in our home but never managed to meet the approval of the Sunday morning meeting. Our home was an open home and I entertained visiting friends for years that avoided hotel bills. Strangers we met at convention who wanted to visit the area where we lived would show up and stay for two weeks. I believe I was a professional actress and most certainly should have got an Oscar. When my husband and I broke up after nearly twenty two years of hell even my family was shocked. I certainly never had any intentions of letting my father know I had made a mistake. By now we were quite well off and had one of the better homes.

For some reason that I still do not understand, my kids never managed to become as brainwashed as I was. They have suffered however very much from the frustration and conflict, Anyone that had a mother that was as screwed up as I was and a generation of dysfunction behind them could not have been otherwise. By the time each of them left home, and some were around sixteen, none of them ever had anything to do with the religion. I figured that was my punishment for different things I had done and it only added to my guilt.

In the meantime the elder of the church we attended, a married ex-worker made it very obvious to me that he would like nothing better than to have sex with me. I lived with this knowledge for about three years. One day in a fit of temper my husband told me, I had committed adultery with him ever since a year after my marriage to him, because of my love for this other man. THE ONE THING I HAD HUNG ONTO WAS THE KNOWLEDGE THAT I HAD NOT HAD AN AFFAIR WITH THIS MAN AND I HAD NOT BROKEN UP MY MARRIAGE BECAUSE OF MY LOVE FOR HIM. All the pain, agony, self-righteousness and everything else that was boiling inside came gushing out. I said "if it is adultery you want, then adultery you will get." I telephoned this Elder that had made advances to me, arranged a meeting and quite frankly, and coldly committed adultery. He was more than willing to oblige. This particular man told me that when he was in the work he had sex with animals!! I was SYMPATHETIC. This man's wife was the coldest fish I had ever known and was the cause of a lot of dissension in the church. I can tell you that now she played the poor betrayed wife to the hilt, and as far as I know is still making her husband's life hell.

When that episode was over and I made no bones about my motive, I went home and told my husband what I had done. I do not believe the hydrogen bomb had as lasting an effect. The war was on and I asked that the meetings be taken out of the home and told a few people off that I had been wanting to smack for years. Some of the events that followed are still a blur. Several months later a very dear friend of mine died. This man was not professing and he and his wife were alcoholics. He had been raised in a professing home. He was a real good friend to me and sympathized with me. It was the first man that I had got close to that did not try and take advantage of me. I was devastated when he was killed suddenly. After the funeral three workers, his wife and my husband cornered me and said that the reason I was so upset was because I had been having an affair with him. No amount of talking on my part did any good, and the only person that knew the situation was dead. All the friends were told not to have anything to do with me and we soon moved to a remote island.

I was given an ultimatum by my husband that I either smarten up or divorce him. That was an easy decision and I divorced him in 1977. By smartening up he meant profess again which I had tried once and had no intention of trying again.

I cannot accurately describe the last couple of years before I left my husband. In the course of events, he kicked me out six times but I always went back. He would force me out one day and the next beg me to come back. I still entertained the workers with their cold hard stares of disapproval and tried to hold my family together. I had professed again once, but found out the workers had told the elder of the church where we went to meetings, not to believe anything I said, because I was a liar!! That was the last meeting I ever attended. I was coldly excommunicated over a period of about two years. Never was I asked to not attend meetings, but when I walked into a room an ice cube would have been more welcome. My husband treated me with cold hostility. At one point he asked me if the workers could come and hold a Sunday morning meeting in our home. We had moved to an isolated area and they had followed us. My husband and this other lady whose husband did not profess were the only people professing in that area, so they did not have much choice if they wanted a meeting. I said, "yes." The night before my husband and I attended a Christmas party that was put on where he was employed. He started to drink wine and got very drunk. We were living in a little cabin at that time and it did not have any running water or electricity. I had a hard time getting him home in the pitch black and we had to cross a creek. When we went to bed he sat up and threw up all over me. Of course my hair was very long and I had to get up in the cold and go and wash my hair in the creek. I also had to clean up all the mess he made. I had not had anything to drink and do not drink. The next morning I got up to get ready for the meeting. My husband could not get out of bed he was so sick. The whole place which was very small reeked of booze. The workers came and the other lady who professed. Of course I did not take part and lied and told them my husband had the flu. That was the last time the workers were ever in our home. Shortly after that I was kicked out for the fourth or fifth time and when I returned my husband wanted sex. After the act he apologised for "stooping so low" as to have anything to do with me. He said he just had a moment of weakness.

The second last discussion I had ever had with the workers, I started to ask questions again. The older worker spoke up and said we are not going to answer any more of your questions. I stood up and said "the reason you are not going to answer my questions is because you don't know the answers" and I got up and walked out. Although that statement was made in frustration and rebellion, I realized in later years just how true it was. I would welcome a debate now I can tell you, but none of them will talk to me much less get into a discussion!! When I made it clear that I did not want to be a part of their group, all my friends were threatened to not have anything to do with me. One lady in particular and I had been close friends for ten years. She was far from happy too. The way she heard about the truth in the first place was by having an affair with a professing married man!!! He told her about the "truth" and she went to meetings and professed. She also had a great deal of fear of hell and to this day is still struggling on and although I have told her she still insists it is my "wrong spirit" that is responsible for me being where I am today. Another friend of mine that has now become an ex-2X2 has a mother that lives in our area. I made up my mind to befriend her. I have put myself out many times for her. She is still a 2X2 and told her daughter one day that I am a very evil person. They have been very good friends of my husband down through the years. She does not mind me doing things for her though.

My last discussion with a worker was years later. I had met some people who were looking for religion. I was living in the North at the time and was anything but professing, I told them a minister was in town and they should go and see him. (I still believed that if there was a right way the 2X2s were it.) They asked me to go and talk to the worker who was there and have him come and call on them. This worker was very cold towards me and ended the conversation by telling me that God often uses people, but does not bless them!!! I do not know if he ever called on the people or not, or what they did about it, because I left that area soon after.

Shortly after my final breakup from my husband (he was still in town) my father was dying of cancer. My mother called and asked me to come home and help her nurse him. My husband was very opposed to this and said I was the biggest hypocrite that had ever been born. I did not feel my mother who was a lot older than my father should be alone, so I went. It was ironic that no one could do anything for my father, but me. He asked for me around the clock and I was his constant companion. One day shortly before he died he asked me if I could ever forgive him. I assured him that if I could not forgive him, I would not be there. You would have had to have a heart of stone to not feel compassion for him the way he suffered. He told me that day that he did not feel he had a reward to go on to. He said that he felt he had missed the mark. He was a very, bitter, morbid man and I could not understand at that time why he felt that way and had no joy or peace. His whole life had been spent in the 2X2s. I thought that all that was required for salvation was to keep plodding on in the religion even though you were pretty sure you would never make it!! Of course at that time I had absolutely no knowledge of anything else and did not understand his position. Every one I knew in the 2X2s were dull, morbid, sad and I had never

ever seen any joy expressed. A grim determination was a much more suitable description, so it never crossed my mind that a person could have joy or peace. There were over four hundred people at the funeral. We had to get a police escort. The workers were very sure of his salvation and preached him right into Heaven. I could not help but think that he should have asked them about his doubts and they could have reassured him!! It was not until years later that I started to question my father's uncertainty regarding where he was going to end up. He gave a lot of money to the work which probably had some bearing on being preached into Heaven.

When I finally got rid of my husband, I was very bitter and angry. I went on a ten year self-destruct course and did everything that I thought that God would hate, if in fact he did exist. I did not believe there was a God, but if there was and there was a hell I was at least going to deserve for once what I got. I was nothing but an unpaid prostitute, partied and swore and went nuts if anyone mentioned God or religion. I had two common-in-law relationships during that time and many more that were not for any duration.

My children were scattered to the four winds with the exception of my youngest who I had with me. Can you imagine what they went through? Here was their mother who was doing every single thing she had always preached against, making a complete idiot of herself and even I did not understand my deep bitterness and anger. Never once in this whole time did I ever question the "WAY." I could not understand why I had to go to a lost Eternity just because I could not go to meetings. I knew that they would never let me back in even if I wanted to and I would have sooner faced hell than go back any way. Being forgiven and saved by

Grace was something I had never even heard of. If they do preach that, like they claim they do, I do not know where I was, because I attended meetings and Conventions for over forty years. When I first heard about the Trinity I thought the people were mad. All I ever knew was you had to be in THAT way and follow the WORKER'S example and I do not remember hearing much about Jesus Christ. It was the WORKER'S sacrifice that I heard all about, and if that is not a crock, I do not know what is. They stayed in the best homes, drove the best cars, ate the best food, wore the best clothes, never had or paid any bills and lived like Queens and Kings including the worship aspect.

Somewhere along the line, in fact it was 1981, my only Grandson died of crib death at the age of six months. My daughter was not married to the man who was the baby's father and so my husband had refused to go to their home or see the baby. The first time he saw him was in his coffin. I totally idolized this child and spent a great deal of time with him. When he died I flipped out and came very close to going over the edge. I was really mad at God now and tried my best to assure my family that it did not matter what you did because God did not exist. I was also sure on the other hand that he was punishing me for leaving the truth. There were some workers and friends at the funeral and most of them stared at me like I had two heads. I hated anyone that even resembled a two by two.

The events that took place during this time led to my first commmon-in-law relationship being over and I soon was in another relationship.

In the meantime, about five years into my destructional mode, my brother got "Born Again." Maybe you do not think I was in a panic then. He was an atheist and alcoholic and the only difference between us was that I had tried to be religious for over forty years. The one thing that I knew for sure was that if he was stupid enough to be religious at least he had to be in the RIGHT WAY and I made it my business to save him from another disaster, like walking from the frying pan into the fire. My Brother never really did know anything about what the Bible said according to the 2X2s, but I can tell you he did know what it said according to God. I, of course, was an authority on the scriptures and you should have heard us. After blasting him initially and trying to straighten him out, I refused to discuss it with him at all. About three years after he was converted, I was in his City and he asked me to Church on Sunday morning. I was in my glory that I finally had a chance to knock some sense into his head and I agreed to go. When I walked into that place and heard all those people worshipping and praising God I could not believe my ears. Can you imagine doing THAT in a 2X2 meeting? Everyone was so open and free and it made an impression that I never forgot. After Church I argued again the legalistic versus the real truth and then did not see my brother again for another two years.

In the next conversation we had he asked me who Jesus was? I said that was the stupidest question I had ever been asked and proceeded to tell him my version. He was a man, I explained who was the son of God who died and rose again to prove that fact!!! When my brother pointed out that when Jesus died on the cross that He had taken our sins on Himself and we were saved by Grace I thought he had inherited his grandmother's mental imbalance!!! For anyone to accept me the way I was, forgive me unconditionally and forever, much less have it be Jesus Christ, was like trying to understand another language. I had never heard

anything so far out even in fairy tales much less reality. The concept that I didn't have to DO anything
was too ridiculous to even consider. I believe possibly that at that point the unrealistic fact that the
"way" might be wrong may have started to penetrate my sub-conscious. I do remember vaguely the
thought would penetrate my mind, but it was far
too painful to consider for any length of time. I also
can remember when I was on that train of thought
thinking, that if that was a possibility, then my own
father would have been wrong and he wouldn't
have been in anything that was not right so it was
immediately dismissed. IT JUST COULD NOT BE. For
years as a 2X2 I had called out to God and asked
him "where is the love." My brothers suggestion regarding the sacrifice and love of Jesus Christ was in
every aspect contrary to what I had been taught. I
simply could not comprehend that type of doctrine.

Around that time I was involved in my second
common-in-law relationship and we had purchased
a restaurant in another province. Some of our clien-
tele called themselves Christians. I used to sit and
watch these people and think, "if you are Christians
then I am a monkey's uncle!!" One of the women
in particular SMOKED and so did I, in fact I do so to
this day. How could anyone even think for one moment they were a Christian and SMOKE. As it
eventually turned out, this particular lady had a
great deal to do with bringing me to the Lord and
we are still friends today even though we are miles
apart. Because I have not been able to break this
filthy habit I have to think of Rahab, what she was
and how God used her, and to remember that she
is listed in Hebrews 11 as part of the faithful. I still
have a great deal of trouble believing that I am
saved. I accept 100% the concept, except when I
apply it to myself!!! My brother phoned that he was

coming for a visit. I told him he was welcome, but if he mentioned God then he would be out the door. He came, never said anything and that almost annoyed me as much as if he had of preached. I could not ignore the change in their lives and attitudes. I did a lot of watching that weekend, but said nothing. I could not get over the fact that they would visit me in my home when I was living with someone. One day about three years before this I was browsing through the paper and found an add for the book, *The Secret Sect*. I was very curious about it and cut the add out and put it in my wallet. It fell out of my wallet about four years after I put it there, but that is another story.

The Holy Spirit was working in my life. For some reason that I could not explain I started to feel a warmth instead of a cold fury when I thought about God. The seeds that my Brother had sown were starting to take root. My relationship was starting to fall apart and all of a sudden I was terribly unhappy. The conviction was not a stabbing pain but a gentle urging. I resisted for a long time. One night I was laying in bed and I very haltingly promised God that if he would get me out of the mess I was in, that I would never mess up again. He did what I asked, but I did not keep my promise. One night when things were particularly bad in my relationship, I was crying and fighting with my partner and the telephone rang. It was my brother and they were coming the next day. When they arrived I was ready for them. I wanted to know and understand EVERYTHING he knew about the Scriptures. The next day, I made the very shakiest commitment, packed full of doubts and fears, that I am sure anyone has ever made. Talk about a little child!! I was a new baby with the worst case of colic known to man. I cried, screamed, balked and rebelled against everything and everybody. I argued scripture until I was blue in the face. NO ONE EVER SAID, THIS IS ENOUGH QUESTIONS AND NO ONE CRITICIZED MY UNCHRISTIAN LIKE BEHAVIOUR. FINALLY I WAS LEARNING ABOUT LOVE.

My Mother has often told me that I cried the first year of my life. She said the doctor did not believe in feeding me any more than once every four hours. She said I was a terrible child and nearly drove them crazy. She realizes now that I was being starved to death. She would not have wanted to be around my rebirth either!!! All the bitterness, hate, anger and revenge were built up inside to enormous proportions. I still did not believe the 2X2s were wrong even though I was facing proof every day of my life. To walk into a FALSE church and listen to a FALSE preacher in a BUILDING, was the most difficult thing I have ever done. I thought, if you think God hated you before, you are really going to get it now. These people were so free and happy and that was a very foreign thing to me. How could you be HAPPY and have ANYTHING to do with God. My partner was an atheist and not at all happy with my decision. Our relationship ended shortly after and I moved back to the town where my daughter and three sons were living. My kids thought I had flipped my lid and most of them still do. I made and make so many mistakes every day of my life that it is no wonder they are confused. I want what I have, so much for them that I often use very little wisdom getting my point across. I do not blame them that they have very little respect for me and my efforts. What a joy to have a Father like we have that gently reaches down and puts us back on our feet. I really have a problem accepting His wondrous Grace and Mercy, and still cannot figure out why

He would want to be bothered with ME. Paul said he was the chief of sinners. That was hundreds of years before I was born!! I now can claim that title.

My ex-husband, the children's father who is still a 2X2 of sorts (they have disowned him in actual fact, but he does go to Gospel meetings some times) lives in the same town and will under no circumstances speak to me. This man hates me and lives with my son in the summer time and goes South in the winter. When he is here I am not allowed on my son's property. He considers himself a religious man and does these things in the name of Jesus. If there had of been nothing else on the face of this earth to convince me that the 2X2s are a cult, his behaviour and actions should have accomplished that certainty years ago. When my daughter got married two years ago he would not go to the wedding although he was in the same town. If I went he would not. I went and he didn't. It is very hard to explain these circumstances to my grandchildren.

Because of the events of the past six years being more recent I find them even harder to relate than the previous writing. Some of the pain of these recent years will NEVER go away.

When I returned to this town where I presently reside, although I was away from here for three years in the middle of all this, I started to attend church. The Pastor and his wife were wonderful people and I received a lot of help from fellow Christians. Some of the doctrine was far out to me, but in the condition I was in, I was so confused anyway that a lot of it went over my head. As I have mentioned, it was a big struggle for me to go to ANY Church and to try and explain to my children where I was at was almost impossible. The events of the next six years were to be the very worst time of my life and that was saying a mouthful. I am so thankful that our Father in His wisdom only asks us to trust Him for one day at a time.

Three months after I left my common-law husband my youngest son of twenty three years old was drowned. How I am going to describe the events of that tragedy I have no idea. Upon hearing the news the very first conscious thought I had was, how much family are you going to lose before you will understand that you are being punished for leaving the 2X2s? All I can say is that Jesus carried me when I could not walk, spoke for me when I could not speak, functioned for me when I could not function and slowly, gently let me try it on my own, off and on for the past six years. His body was not found till the following evening and I was going to say that was the worst part. There is no way to measure the worst parts, they were all a terrible painful tragedy. He was not a Christian.

I INSISTED that my Pastor take the funeral. I finally compromised to allow the workers to take the service at the graveyard. By that time they were so shook up that all they did was quote some psalm. My other kids were total basket cases. My one son and his wife had been with him when he drowned and she was pregnant. My oldest son and his wife are alcoholics, a trait that has captured them all. He threatened to commit suicide on a regular basis. We had a viewing and it was for family ONLY. The workers managed to come although they were not invited. The one worker sat in a chair next to the coffin, put his head between his hands and muttered what a waste, what a waste. Only my perception and control over my one son kept him from killing him. My ex-husband was there and of course if I came into a room he left. It was like watching some kind of a show on T.V. The kind where I cannot stand the agony of the moment and leave the room until a less emotionally charged part comes into play.

My son had been engaged at the time of his death. We were invited to her mother's place for lunch after the viewing. The workers also came and watched me as I puffed away on a cigarette. My husband was plastered and continued to drink wine. The one worker is no longer in the work and I really believe that funeral may have had something to do with it. I had my testimony printed up, to be handed out at the service. I chose Amazing Grace at the service and insisted on the hymn, "I've a Friend That Meets My Every Need," being sung at the grave side. At last I could mouth those words in perfect honesty. Many friends stayed over to visit and I got my eyes opened a little farther at the woebegone expressions and conversations. One girl came that was now married and who was a GREAT friend of my Husband. They used to go on picnics and be gone for hours at a time. They were very CLOSE. I suffered through that three hours of conversation. One professing lady said I do not understand you, you are not ACTING normal. I told her it was probably because it was the first time in her life she had ever seen me, when I was NOT "ACTING"!! One couple took two hours to tell me about the loss of their Son-in-law five years before. Their faces were so full of pain and anguish that I could not believe it. My former Sister-in-law attacked me verbally to find out what had really happened between her brother and me. She got her ears full that day. She did not of course believe one word I told her. My nephew by marriage asked me what I was trying to prove. I only know I got through those days by the Grace of Christ. Through them, but by no means over them!! For a long time I kept waiting to get over the loss and then one day I realized I never would, but would have to learn how to live with it. When my son died I felt I could not part with his hair, he had such a beautiful head of curly hair. I asked the funeral director to cut off a lock and give it to me. To this day I have been unable to look at it or touch it, the pain is still too unbearable.

Four months after this tragedy my Daughter-in-law had her baby. After the second day it was obvious that something was wrong. It was discovered that the mother had contacted salmonella and the baby got meningitis. For ten days he was in grave danger. I felt I just could not go through another death so soon. Thankfully they saved him and now he is a very healthy bright little five and a half year old. My girl friend was not so fortunate. Her daughter had a baby and she had the same thing as my daughter-in-law. Both the baby and the mother died. I could not go to the funeral. They are also ex-2X2s.

Just a short time after the mother and baby came home I was rushed to the hospital for major surgery. I got infection and internal bleeding and very nearly died. I was on morphine for a week and in the hospital for a month. I came home just in time to face the first Christmas without our boy. In the six months that followed Christmas, my grandchild got molested at school, my son had an accident on his bike and my grandchild got his heel severed with a broken bottle out in the yard. Another big blow came when it was found that my oldest son's wife had terminal cancer with a six month's prognosis. They are both alcoholics. I can not possibly describe the stress and tension at that time. Two other incidents happened about the same time. I found out (that is another story) that the church I

had been attending was teaching New Age. We
were in fact ALL little Gods etc; and etc. Imagine
my children's reaction when I told them I was
wrong again!!! One day I was cleaning out my
purse and the add for *The Secret Sect* fell out on
the table. I sent for the book. Two weeks later I got
a call from the bar from my second oldest son who
had been under heavy conviction since the death of
his brother. His dad had been putting the pressure
on for him to profess and telling him I was right
out to lunch. My son was crying and drunk. He
said, "Mom how do you know the 2X2s are
wrong?" I said I will come down there and you and
I will sit in the car and talk. I told him I did not
KNOW for sure about anything, but that we would
pray that God would show us once and for all, living proof of some kind that the 2X2s were wrong. I
did not know it at the time but that book was sitting in my mail box. When I got it and read it, I do
not think I have ever been so upset. I was devastated to learn that the whole religion had been
founded on a lie. Part of me was relieved by loads
of guilt and the other half angrier than I had ever
been. I telephoned my mother and when I found
out that she had not only heard of Irvine, but been
aware of the starting of the church, I was totally
devastated. I gave the book to my son to read and,
if possible he was more upset than I was. He gave
it to his father, who threw it on the floor and declared it a pack of lies. All my life I had been told
that the 2X2s had no earthly founder. They did not
take a name and it was the only true church passed
down from Jesus time. When I thought of what I
had suffered at the hands of these people and how
it had affected my whole life I was physically sick.
If William Irvine had not been dead I swore I
would have killed him.

At that time I had pretty well given up on religion. I only knew what was not right but had little idea of what was. I did feel however a closeness with Jesus and talked and prayed to Him all the time. We were all surrounded by such grief and pain and there seemed to be no end in sight. I moved in with my eldest son and his wife and tried to make some order in our shattered lives. My son threatened suicide every day and his wife was in no better shape. She started on chemo and was deathly sick. The children who had already been through so much because of their dysfunctional parents and grandparents were trying to cope with the thought of losing their mother. I prayed that the Lord would provide a means for escape as promised in the scripture. As it turned out it was the devil that provided the means, but I really believed at the time the Lord had a hand in it. A family friend who was not a Christian asked me to marry him and I accepted. He was from another province. My daughter-in-law's family also lived in the province where I was going. She was devastated at the thought of me leaving, so we managed through different channels to relocate them. We would still be several hundred miles apart, but at least we were closer than we would have been had they not moved.

I could write pages to try and explain the frame of mind I was in when I made the decision to marry my second husband. In the first place I did not trust any religious group or person. My emotions were shattered almost to the breaking point and I simply did not know where to turn. My children were in as bad a shape as I was, if not worse. I used this as a means of escape.

My husband was very good to me and I was happier than I had ever been in my life which does not say too much. I met a Christian lady who was a friend of my husband shortly after arriving at my new home. I had been married four months when my daughter-in-law phoned that she had to start radiation and she wanted me there. My husband encouraged me to go and be with her. I was away three weeks and very glad to get home. I did not make any attempt to go to church because I did not know where to go. I trusted no one. Shortly after I returned from helping my kids I attended a tupperware party. One of the ladies started talking about cults and said she had been raised in one. I asked her which one and she replied, "Oh, they do not take a name but some people call them 2X2s." I was flabbergasted and informed her that I also had been in the "truth" for over forty years. We became good friends and If I thought I was messed up I had nothing on her. Her life was a disaster and she was currently involved with the Mormons.

Through this lady I not only found out a great deal I did not know, but she put me in contact with Kathy Lewis in the States. I immediately wrote Kathy a very disjointed story of my life and although I have never met her, we became great friends. I started to become involved in correspondence with other ex-2X2s. Two other areas really interested me as well and that was spiritual warfare and the New Age Movement. I read everything I could get my hands on and studied the scriptures every time I had a chance.

I was very happy. My husband treated me well and we got along good. We made a couple of more trips to visit my children. So far my daughter-in-law seemed to be holding her own and at the time of this writing she has just had a clean bill of health. As far as I am concerned that was the direct results of hours of prayer.

I started finally to attend a church in our village. There were a lot of things going on there and conflicts with the Pastor. He did not believe the devil was a threat and by this time I was fairly certain he was and that he had been on my tail since birth. A lot of weird goings on confirmed my suspicions regarding the need for spiritual warfare. I was kept very busy with one thing and another. When I had been married three and one half years my friend came and told me she had been having an affair with my husband since four months after I was married. The affair had started when I went to help my daughter-in-law. The lady in question had been asking my husband to get a divorce and when he kept putting her off with broken promises she came and told me, hoping I would throw him out.

Up to this time in my life I thought I had experienced every emotion known to man. I was wrong. All the emotions in this world flooded over me and I was, to say the least, very upset. I was actually beside myself and could not function. I wandered around in a daze. I alternated between forgiving my husband and wanting to kill him. I did not trust myself to be anywhere near this woman because I was not sure what I would do. I received lots of conflicting help from Pastors and Christian friends. One Pastor said that if his wife ever did that he would never forgive her. Another one advised me to forgive him and stay with him and yet another said I must leave him because adultery was just cause.

I could not eat, sleep or read my Bible or even start to pray. I guess, in a way, I was praying—because all I could say over and over again was, "God help me." To make a very long agonizing, painful story short my husband said he loved me and wanted me to stay with him and I agreed to do so. Six months later I found out the affair was still going on and I finally got together enough funds to leave and returned to my present address. Somehow I believe that the pain would not have been so bad if this woman had not professed to be a Christian.

I SAID I would never divorce him and that when he straightened out he would know where to find me. I said that because I made a vow for better or for worse and until death do us part. It took me over a year to begin to recover from the emotional roller coaster I had again been on. My mind seemed to be working fairly rationally, but my body simply said, this is enough. I have not seen my husband since I left and have only spoken to him twice. I keep praying for his salvation and repentance, but so far nothing has happened. I have been informed by leaders that it was my own fault for marrying an unsaved man. I have been told it is my duty to divorce him. I have been told I could never marry again while he is alive and I have been told I could. I have been attending church again, off and on, since a month or two after I returned here. Very often I withdraw because I cannot stand the conflict.

I have been asked on several occasions what the difference is between the 2X2s and any church that rules with power and control, has legalistic tendencies and does not stick to the simple good news of the gospel. In ANY cult the teaching is that you MUST be in that way to get to Heaven. If you are not in THAT WAY you are automatically going to hell. Once you have made a personal relationship with Jesus Christ, I think it is the FREEDOM that makes all the difference. NO MAN can separate me from the love of God. When I found out the church I was attending was New Age, all I had to do was walk out and go to another church. It did not affect my salvation. I am absolutely positive if the 2X2s recognized salvation in any other organization there would only be a very small handful of people that would EVER go to another meeting. I also believe that the fear of being thrown out of the way is more real to most people than the reality of hell. ANY CHURCH that will not be accountable for finances, cannot tell you when and how they were founded and has an organization of rules, and power is not a true church. Many organizations that I know of are united in the bond of peace and love.

I still have many problems that are a direct result of the way I was raised, I recognize some of them at least and that is a step in the right direction. I am very distrustful and especially since my last experience. I have to be in control. Simply no one on the face of this earth has the power to control me. There are no shades of grey in my life. It has to be either black or white. I am very opinionated. I have very little patience with people that hurt or offend me. I am very sensitive and EASILY offended. I am like a porcupine that will throw it's quills at the slightest sign of danger. I ENJOY probably more than anything the freedom to voice my opinion even though my outspokenness is not often appreciated. I cannot handle being falsely accused. I recently got fired from a job. I was railroaded because of jealousy, and a great many accusations and lies were hurled at me. I was physically sick for a week. It simply knocked me off my feet. All the bitterness, resentment, and anger of a lifetime resurfaced during that time. My son said a short time ago that I still have a lot of legalism in me. I find it very hard to accept any type of criticism. With a great deal of control I tried to analyze his statement and found out it was more true than false. I find myself LABOURING to be perfect and carry around huge guilt for the things I cannot seem to change. It is very very hard for me to let go and let God.

We have all been stunned in recent weeks to hear about the Waco Texas cult. Does anyone recognize the similarities? Every worker thinks they are EQUAL with Jesus Christ. THEY ARE HIS EXAMPLE. The dictionary quotes the word "example" as follows: "a representative SAMPLE." No true pastor that I know even pretends to be a representative sample of Christ. Notice the cult member portrayed himself as Christ. Also take note for anyone that saw the cult movie that the leader TOLD the women and children that the LAMB had told him to have sex with them. In my case I had also been convinced it was the will of God, and God had told this worker that I had been chosen to keep him in the work. Immorality, child abuse, homosexuality, sodomy, adultery, molestation and every other conceivable thing is much more prevalent in the 2X2s than any one would really care to admit.

You must stay in the 2X2s "to be saved." The threat of hell is always hanging over your head. You must be separate from the world. Child discipline is very important. Women are treated like dirt in a lot of cases. "Obey the workers," is the number one rule. As far as I am concerned the similarities caused me to have goose bumps. Actually I believe this cult leader was more honest than workers. Everybody knew that he was having sex with a lot of people. WE may care to remember that in the Alaska scandal each sister worker thought they were the only ones. Just for the record I do not think that the leader of the Waco Texas cult is dead!!! He was much too smart and devious to let that happen to himself.

At the time of this writing I have been hit with two more rather major crisis in my life, but I will refrain from adding any more at this time. I wish to extend my heartfelt best wishes to anyone reading this and if I can be a help to anyone, that is my greatest desire. Please excuse all errors and omissions. There is much more I could relate, this is just really the tip of the iceberg. When I start writing about these things many more happenings come to mind, but as I have stated it would take several books to contain it all. The hardest thing to do when writing this was to be perfectly honest. To think about these experiences is one thing, but to tell the world is quite another. There was no point as far as I was concerned to attempt this without honesty. To any that finds this too graphic or offensive, I apologize. It is poorly written and jumps around a lot, but a few of my experiences are at least conveyed. One thing this has accomplished as I read it over and over is the realization that if Christ can love me, he can love ANYONE. I must also say in closing that any experience anyone has to go through to get out of this cult is well worth the pain. How very easily I could still be floundering around in it. I do not and cannot blame any individual. They are ALL victims of satan's lies and deceit. Does it not say the very elect are in danger of being deceived? If the elect are in danger where do you suppose that leaves these poor people? They have no concept of the gospel. We must forgive and love them. That was why it was so hard to write this letter in the past tense. My feelings then, towards those people are in no way relevant to my compassion now.

I am so happy that I made the Lord Jesus Christ my personal friend and Saviour. He has much yet to teach me and I have much to learn. It is the greatest joy of my life to be in His presence without condemnation. He is my only reason for living.

I have decided to not sign my name because at the time of this writing my mother is still alive and a 2X2. I am sure most people reading this, that know me, will have no difficulty identifying me. Anyone wishing to write me, I give them permission to get my name and address from the editors. Take heart, there is a forgiving Saviour and He is alive!!!

Someone who knows and has been there.

Name Withheld
Printed by permission of the author.

Chapter Forty-Four
Name Withheld

I grew up in a family of "Christian Non-Denominationalists." Both my mother and my father were raised in the Methodist and the Congregationalist churches. After their marriage, they moved to rural North Dakota and settled by neighbors who were instrumental in the conversion [to the 2x2 church]. And so, when I decided to marry a man outside of their church, they were somewhat supportive of me. They always have treated me as their daughter and my husband as their son and seldom, if ever, push us toward their beliefs. I believe this is due in part to their recognition of my membership and active participation in the Lutheran Church. It didn't take me long to become active after my marriage. One Sunday morning my husband got up and said he was going to church. I was welcome to go along with him if I wanted. There was a deep desire to make this marriage work and I knew a spiritual unity would certainly help. And so, I did begin to attend and I couldn't believe the difference. We smile and greet one another and sometimes laugh— OUT LOUD—in church. Sure tears are shed on occasion but normally it is a celebration, a time to be joyful. The Good Book tells us over and over again to worship the Lord with joy!!!!!!!!

Just a few weeks ago I was a guest of my relatives in another state and because I would have invited them to go with me to worship when they invited me to attend with them, of course, I accepted the invitation. I had forgotten how gloomy and sad their gatherings could be. I do believe they peeked at me and spied my pierced diamond earrings and my makeup that I usually wear, but most of the adults sat with their heads bent in perfect 90 degree angles. And again, many shed tears throughout the meeting. I listened keenly at their "testimonies." And again confirmed what I'd previously believed. They take one verse or even a portion of a verse and build an entire testimony on this. They wouldn't think of using another source to help themselves understand the true meaning or literal meaning of a book, chapter, verse, etc. A whole concept based on just a couple of words taken from the King James version, of course, can become a way of life for them and never to be questioned. Why, it took me 25 years to realize that I wouldn't go to hell for one sin. The Lord said to forgive 7 *times* 70. that's a lot of forgiving and sinning. My father threatened me as a little girl that he would cut off my fingers if they caused me to sin. I had used clear nail polish!!

And tell me why no one will repeat the Lord's Prayer? I can't understand why—a prayer that was written by the Lord Himself they wouldn't be caught uttering. I remember hearing some say that a prayer like that didn't come from the heart, because it was simply repeated and repeated over and over again. Well, let me tell you, my dear, dear mother has repeated the same prayer for over 50 years or more. But this appears to be acceptable among the "Saints or the Friends." They always exclude my family and me when they use these terms. But my feelings are by calling themselves these names appears to be a bit presumptuous, wouldn't you think?

I was never baptized either. In fact, no one even approached me about it. My memories of Baptism go back to viewing it as a child. A middle aged handicapped lady in the meeting was wheelchaired out into the murky waters of a leach infested river. She was absolutely frightened to death. They completely submerged her and I really thought she was going to die from the shock of it all. It was terrifying just watching. To this day, I have wondered what those workers said to convince her she had to allow the total submersion.

My sister, who has been out for 25 plus years also told me she chose to be baptized. And on the specified day everyone gathered and she was singled out, taken aside and threatened to refuse to baptize her because she had short bangs on her forehead. They did baptize her in the end, however. Don't they know that baptism is one of God's gifts to his children, all of his children.

Another practice I have so much trouble with is their choice to physically look the way they do. Most women will only wear their hair in a bun, no makeup, no earrings or necklaces, but they will wear ornaments in their hair and jewelry in the form of a pin. They will jump around trying to play volleyball and other games in a long skirt and an hour later don a skimpy swimsuit and go swimming. How can that be explained? I do believe I'm purged from the ambivalent feelings I used to have. It has taken many years though. But with a supportive and understanding family to help me through it, it can only get better.

Many times as a child I heard these people condemn other religions for passing an offering plate. You know the old adage that Jesus went out with nothing, receiving no wages, etc. But I know and recall vividly my father very discreetly handing these workers money on numerous occasions. Pray tell me...what is the difference? Even the Holy Bible talks of tithing and offerings.

I have asked some, when this church was started and I always get the answer that it began in Jesus Day. That's somewhat different from what the Book *The Secret Sect* says.

And finally, I recall conventions. When I was about 13 or so I wanted so badly to stay on the grounds. We lived about 15 miles away. But I was told by the workers that it wasn't a good idea because they had to make room for those who came from further distances. Which was alright, but everyone from the "better" families who lived within two miles were the first ones to stay. Funny how little things like this stay with you. Also I remember my job at convention. It would usually be waiting on tables during mealtime. Once I was delegated to the job of waiting on the worker's tables. Did you know they ate steak while the rest ate stew at noon and they ate eggs and bacon while the rest had gruel? Oh, and yes they had lovely angel food cakes while the rest had broken up oatmeal cookies. And as I grew up and became interested in the opposite sex, of course this was the perfect breeding ground. I remember visiting with a boy until close to 10 PM in a car when the workers tiptoed through the parking lot with their flashlights peeking into windows telling people to get into the buildings.

Oh, those scary Saturday nights. One of the Jardines (usually Walter) would arrange to speak last and he would go on and on for such a long time. Shouting, ranting and raving!! Until many were reduced to tears. It was very frightening. I believed there was no forgiveness for a sinner and that was it. I can still hear his voice after speaking for an hour or more, then he would in a very low softer tone, say "now when all heads are bowed and all eyes are closed" would those who wanted to seek eternal life stand during the last verse of hymn number?. Then everyone would cry and cry. Immediately afterwards my mother would be asking who this one or that one was who professed. Apparently she wasn't bowing her head with her eyes closed.

I could go on and on for pages. I feel I have rambled enough. Life has not been always easy with a background such as this. It's very difficult to think openly, but I'm trying and will continue to try.

Bless all of you who are in the same predicament and maybe together we can get on top of this.

August 31, 1993

Name Withheld
Rural North Dakota

Printed by permission of the author.

Chapter Forty-Five

Fred and Deanna Printz

Letter to the Friends Dated February, 1992

My Dear Friends,

I feel it laying heavy on my heart to write you and explain what is going on with us and why. I know that some of you may know part of the situation, but I would like to explain a little more fully. I pray that you will take the time to hear MY side of the story.

First, I want to tell you how much it has meant that some of you have continued to reach out to us in love and concern. We will always remember your special efforts. Others have not been so kind. For the most part, we have been ignored; others stay in touch, but keep their distance—maybe they are afraid to get too close. We realize now that the love in the "two-by-two" church is very conditional. It is there as long as one fits into the mold, but if one has questions or different opinions, and makes them known, the love seems to dim. Jesus taught that we were to love everyone, unconditionally, because we are all brothers and sisters.

For quite some time now, there have been things that I saw going on in this way that I felt were wrong. I have watched professing people (I include myself in this), living double lives, obviously not totally "committed" and "convicted" of all the legalism (rules) placed on us by the workers. I have always wondered how a person was to develop a conscience or have a relationship with God, when we simply follow a form laid out for us by the workers. For myself, I found it much more profitable to let the Lord lead me and learn from my mistakes, rather than to try to live in a totally protected environment where I never learn to think for myself or deal with things.

I watched the workers telling people they weren't worthy to take part in meeting or have a meeting in their home, because the workers didn't agree with something that person did or said, or something they had. Once the person breaks the *workers'* code of ethics, they're judged unworthy. What about all that the Bible teaches us about not judging our brethren? How is anyone, including the workers, capable of judging the heart of a person? Only that person and God know their heart. The Bible says, "Judge not that ye be not judged." That would pertain to all of us! I feel that we should have a *personal* relationship with God, and he will lead us individually. After all, we are all individuals with different personalities, desires, problems and strong points and to try to fit everyone into the same little cookie mold is not only unnatural, it simply won't work! We are each to use the gifts that God gave us.

The workers tell us that the only people to be saved are those who profess through the workers and go to meetings in the "two-by-two" fashion. This doctrine was confirmed by Barry in our home. I absolutely do not believe that!!! I have known many people outside the "two-by-two" way who truly loved God and exhibited the qualities required by God. They believed in Jesus and were truly thankful for his sacrifice. Some of those people exhibited more of the qualities than I have seen in some professing people. I am in no way implying that everyone at meeting is wrong—I merely believe that there are others who are also right in their hearts where it truly matters. *We are not to judge.*

You would remember Bruce Brush. I feel that he was a prime example. He loved the people at meeting, he loved the way, and wanted nothing more than to be able to come to meeting and have a part. However, the workers wouldn't let him unless he renounced all previous religious experiences and started over by professing. He didn't feel right about that since it would be denying the very dealings of God that he felt so strongly in his heart. I now fully enter into his feelings! I feel closer to God now than ever in my life. I read and study more and I truly love it! I know that most at meeting would feel that I am now "worldly" and just doing what I want to do, but that is not true. The spirit of God has set me free from "man's bondage." If anyone told me that I would have to deny God's dealing with my heart as I know he has for the past several months, I would also say, "No way!" and walk away shaking my head just as Bruce did. I wonder how many others have been turned away in the same way. Bruce was denied because the *workers judged him unworthy.*

I see disagreement among workers about how to handle different situations and differences of opinions about whether things are right or wrong, yet I am told to believe this is God's only true way. If it is God's way, and if workers are able to judge us worthy or not, doesn't it stand to reason that they will all have to be in total unity and harmony about everything? Since we are all afflicted with human nature (including workers) it is obvious why the Bible tells us not to judge and the *only* mediator between man and God is, Jesus Christ. (I Timothy 2:5)

A very good example of this happened this past summer in the Ft. Wayne area. The friends got together for a picnic and some volleyball. Several of the girls wore culottes, and the sister worker made quite an issue of it. She spent the next few weeks going to each of their homes telling them they shouldn't wear culotte, even in the privacy of their own homes. She told them that if the culottes were above the knee they were like shorts and below the knee they were like slacks. I should think that modesty was what those professing girls had been concerned with, and that is scripturally sound. The workers use Deuteromony 22:5 (also confirmed by Barry in our home) for not wearing slacks. If you will study that entire chapter, you will see that verse 5 is taken totally out of context of the rest of the chapter of OT laws. It would be ridiculous to use one law and disregard the rest, however, that is exactly what we have been taught to do. After studying about this verse, I found out that in OT days, wearing clothes of the opposite sex was done during *pagan* worship. *That* was why it was referred to as an abomination! Furthermore, in Bible days, men AND women *both* wore robes. The only way to tell men from women was by the decoration on the clothes and that men had long beards. If both sexes wore robes in the Bible days, why would it possibly be wrong for both to wear slacks in our day? Maybe men should still have their beards. Making doctrine about slacks is "teaching for doctrines the commandments of men." Saul wore a skirt as did other men in the Bible, but we know that was the custom of their day. We too, should dress according to the custom of our day and where we live, as long as it is respectable and modest. Slacks are comfortable, warm, and modest. In fact, now that I think about it, if women are made to feel they must wear dresses, then men are wrong for getting away from their skirts, as the Bible speaks of!!

Not only was the culotte issue in itself so serious, but that sister worker got so carried away with going house to house, that she ran out of time to visit a man dying of cancer before she had to leave for convention. I asked myself, "Just what are the real priorities here?" When other workers were told about what had happened, they couldn't understand the fuss over culottes. Granted, she is entitled to her opinion, but it is *just an opinion*. We are to work out our own salvation with fear and trembling. Making doctrine out of apparel is wrong, because aside from modesty, the Bible doesn't tell us how to dress. Different countries and localities have different dress codes, and we would look ridiculous wearing a sleeveless shirt in Alaska and a fur coat along the equator!! Godliness comes from within.

I found a wonderful book that I would recommend everyone read, men as well as women. It explains the customs of the Bible days and also cross references many things that I had read yet never connected with other verses. It is a real eye-opener. I realize now that many things that I had been taught were wrong, now I can see really weren't wrong. That is the real reason behind the change in my appearance that you now see. The book is called, *Women's Adornment—What Does The Bible Really Say?* It is written by Ralph Woodrow, and can be ordered for $3 from Ralph Woodrow, P.O. Box 124, Riverside, CA 92502.

Another situation I just recently heard of made my heart ache. A girl was to be baptized at convention, and she was refused because a sister worker had seen her somewhere in slacks!! I thought Jesus died on the cross, and then we were *personally* to go to God with our sins and our problems. I wonder how the workers justify taking such a stand. Maybe that girl had fallen to her knees in repentance over what she had done, and here they are holding it over her head *and* judging her. I remember a worker speaking about that very thing—not to hold someone's mistakes over their head; God will forgive them and so should we.

These are just a few of the things that have happened over the past few years that have made me stop and ponder it all. Then entered the book, *The Secret Sect.* I had heard of the book a year or so ago, but like the obedient professing person, I refused to read it, because to doubt is of the devil as I have heard so many times. Then we went through Herb and Sharon's interest in Mormon. WE WERE ENCOURAGED BY THE WORKERS TO GATHER ALL WE COULD ON MORMONISM to show Herb WHAT A FALLACY IT ALL WAS. I checked out everything that I could find at the library about the Mormons. We read it and shared it with Herb and Sharon. Of course, we chuckled about our findings with the workers. After a while, I just couldn't ignore *The Secret Sect* any longer. I felt that it was wrong for me to go out of my way to tear up Mormonism and not be willing to check into what I had been taught to be right all my life. Besides, "truth" will bear scrutiny, right? WRONG!!! What we found was totally shocking! In a matter of a few days, our world came crashing down. This way, which we had been taught was from the very beginning, has an earthly founder just like the other denominations. His name was William Irvine and it started in Ireland around 1899. He had been a part of the Faith Mission and at that time felt he got divine revelation as in Matthew 10. He traced his personal salvation back to a Presbyterian minister named, John McNeill. A few years

after he started this way, Irvine was excommunicated and so were friends who continued to support
him—so began the cover-up of the founder. Someone said that paper doesn't refuse ink, but we have
seen *plenty* of evidence *besides* this book to leave
us with absolutely no doubts!! The Faith Mission
has been contacted and a letter returned by them
verifying that William Irvine had once been a part
of their service, and had left to go out on his own.
A book about Faith Mission that we read contains
many of the same terms that we use; workers, meetings, professing, platform, convention, etc., and
even many of the sayings I have heard in our meetings are quoted in the book. *The Impartial Reporter*
of Northern Ireland was and still is in existence
there. At the time this all started, their custom was
to sit in the meetings and conventions and write
about what was happening and being said. Once
again, they have been contacted, and written verifi-
cation has been received that the articles are in
fact, legitimate! During the period of W.W.II, the
"two-by-two" church was listed with the U.S. government as Christian Conventions. In George
Walker's letter to the Selective Service he states
that *"During the closing years of the last century
and the first years of this century* a number of people in the British Isles and in America...became
fully convinced that there should be a return to the
methods and purpose taught and carried out by
Christ and his Disciples." His signature on this
document was compared to his signature in the
guest books of friends. I have seen recent newspaper articles interviewing workers in 1988 and 1991.
In 1988 a head worker admitted in an interview
that there was a founder; then in 1991 the same
worker denied the founder...WHY? I have seen other
workers' letters which show the same thing. Won-

der how "One True Way" could have discrepancies? It is also interesting to note that there are no hymns in our hymn book written by workers before 1900. One would think that if this way has been here from the beginning that there would be hundreds of hymns written throughout the ages.

Some people try to pass this all off by saying that Wm. Irvine could have been like Peter and others in the Bible who make mistakes, but were still used by God. However, the workers kill that theory with their own doctrine that one can only be saved by a worker. In that case, Wm. Irvine could not have been right in the first place. And to say that he could have been a prophet raised up leaves open the possibility that Joseph Smith (Mormon founder) could also have been a prophet! I personally don't believe that *either* were prophets.

This leads to another very important point! Using the theory that one can only be saved through a worker, would mean that there could have been NO HOPE of salvation in America until Wm. Irvine and fellow workers arrived in the United States in 1903. Think of the implications here! All of the people in America before the workers arrived are doomed to a lost eternity?? The Pilgrims arrived in Plymouth, Mass. in December 1620. *"If"* the "two-by-two" way were God's only true way on this earth, isn't it likely that God would have seen to it that workers would have been on the Mayflower? After all, those people were fleeing religious persecution in England! I wonder how many of you have ever thought about this. I know we hadn't until the past few months. George Walker was the first to come to Indiana—what about all the people who lived before his arrival here? God saw to it that the Bible has always been around, but not the workers.

We started doing some real studying into what the Bible really teaches and we feel we have been way off base. An extensive study of the Pharisees—what they were, what they believed, and how they conducted themselves, was a very scary realization of how close to them that we had become. When we talked to Barry about all of these things, we were shocked. There was evasiveness and I was personally attacked with the statements, "Deanna has a deeper problem" and "Maybe you missed something from the beginning." It hurt me to think that he would feel that way when I know how hard I tried to be right. I don't think those of you who know me would ever doubt my sincerity. Once again, we come back to judging.

It seems that every day we learn of something new that proves once again how deceived we have been. I know just how you will feel when you read this, it has torn us apart to learn that what we had put our heart and soul into is not what we had thought it was. I'm sure that the majority of the friends and workers are innocently believing, just as we always have. Things that never really added up before, we accepted because we thought this was God's only true way which had been here from the beginning. Now in finding the real truth about it all, we understand the double standards between the eastern and western U.S. We understand why there is far more emphasis placed on outward appearance rather than the real things the Bible tells us are sins. We understand the emphasis placed on submission to workers versus placing our trust in the blood of Jesus. In fact, when I asked Barry if we were saved by grace or works, he said grace and I was shocked! I had never heard that before. All the rules and bondage we live in certainly would not convey that to anyone. I could never figure what the point really was when all I ever heard at meeting was that our best would never be good enough. I never felt that I had a chance of Heaven and I was always feeling down because I forever felt like a failure. Does that sound familiar?

We have been taught that church buildings are wrong, but that's not what the Bible says. It says WE are the temple of God, meaning that He dwells IN US. Temples made with hands would include any man made building, including houses, schools, banks, meeting sheds, tents, churches, etc. The point isn't that it's a sin to worship in a building, but that we are to have the spirit of God *dwelling within us*.

Don't be put off by the statement that it's right because it works. Look at all the religions that have been working for centuries! Many continue to grow rapidly and are thriving much more than this way.

I really started studying what Jesus taught and do you know what I found? I found that the main thing was LOVE! He said, "Love the Lord your God with all your heart, soul, and mind and your neighbor as yourself, for on this hangs all the law and prophets." And He taught that we should BELIEVE in Him. Just as soon as a person believed, they were baptized—they didn't have to wait a year to see if they were willing to submit enough to be worthy!! The Bible tells us that we are saved by grace through faith, not of works lest any man should boast. Our only boasting is in the death and resurrection of Jesus for our sins. He paid the price that we would never be able to pay! We were born with a sinful nature and we will have it until the day we die. Because of our gratitude for all He has done for us, our attitudes will change and we will find ourselves truly more in touch with him.

I am so thankful for how I feel today. I no longer feel the burden of worshipping and obeying the workers. The workers did not save us, but the blood of Jesus did. I am so thankful for all that God has revealed to me. A hairdo, a certain attire, not watching TV, doesn't make us more Godly, but it is having *Christ within*. Jesus was the Way, the Truth and The Life—not a certain religious denomination. And above all, Jesus was Love. To be filled with unconditional love for everyone regardless of color, religious affiliation, or despite the mistakes that they have made in their life, they are still my brother and sister and I am to love them.

If we are filled with love, then our life will be guided by love. If we love our brother, then we won't do anything to hurt him. If we truly and un-conditionally love, we will be keeping God's commandments not because of a code written by the workers, or anyone else, but because the code of God's love is written within our hearts.

I do not write these things to hurt anyone, but to let you know the *real* reason I'm not going to meet-ing any longer. All of these findings have been quite a shock to me as I am sure they will be to you also. Please don't toss this aside without look-ing into these attachments. Don't just take my word for it, but check it out yourselves. It has been amazing to see how the scriptures have opened up to me in different ways when I read with an open mind and not influenced by all I had previously been taught. The book of Galatians has been espe-cially helpful.

You will be surprised to know that there are a whole network of ex "two-by-two's" out there who have discovered the "truth about the truth" and are living happy, productive lives spiritually. The real spirit of God's word has brought peace and joy beyond compare to them. The workers will try to frighten you with the quote, "In the last days there will be a great falling away," I Timothy 4 (that was the tactic used on us). But when you study this, you will discover that the real issue here is *false teachers*. It is up to us to prove for ourselves who the false teachers really are. We should *never* be made to feel guilty for questioning the workers. The Bereans were commended for proving whether Paul's teachings were right and we are told to "try the spirits" to see whether they are of God. The only way a person learns, is to study and ask questions. One should never be criticized for this. After all, when Jesus was questioned, he gladly answered. The truth *should* be able to stand regardless of questioning—in fact, the questioning *should prove* that it is truth!!

Most of all, know that I love all of you even though I no longer go to meeting with you. I feel I must tell you these things to make you aware of them. What you do will then be up to you. I am still the same person, but I am happier than ever and I am finally at peace with God.

With sincere love and care,
Deanna Printz

Letter Received from a Worker Dated June 1, 1992

Dear Fred and Deanna,

Just a note to let you know we think of you often and the offer to visit is still open.

We have no desire to quarrel with any but apparently from reading Deanna's letter, we must not have made our points very clear during our visit.

Possibly sometime in the future it may be important to you to understand what we were actually saying.

Trust all 3 are well.

Love as always.

Response to the Previous Letter
Dated July 28, 1992

Dear

We received your letter and appreciated your taking the time and interest to write us.

We are very happy these days and now feel a peace and joy that we never dreamed could be possible. God just keeps revealing and working in ways that make it all so clear as to what He wants us to do. I have prayed for the answers and they have come with a power and clearness that God only can give. We have prayed for tokens to let us know if what we were doing was His will; those have also come. We never dreamed that we could feel so close to God, but we are so very thankful for it.

We have found a wonderful body of believers to worship with and truly feel fed both spiritually and in the fellowship. No certain dress code is required; people wear what they feel comfortable with. The emphasis is on the purpose of the gathering, not how one looks when they gather. This results in unconditional love for one another, rather than a judgmental attitude toward them. People are loved for the person on the inside. I heard a minister on Christian radio speaking that Jesus was a walking, talking example of grace. How true! Jesus loved everyone with unconditional love. He loved the sinner, it was the sin he didn't like. I realize now that love is the very most important thing of all. We are to love EVERYONE because we are all a work of God. I truly feel that love for God and it has caused me to love others even though I may not always see eye to eye with them. I realize now that everything that Jesus taught in the Bible is based on that love. If love is flowing through us, our lives and hearts will be guided by God. Love is the key that opens the door to God in our hearts.

In our new church, we sing songs of praise to God. They are happy and thankful songs for what has been done on our behalf. Again, this is very scriptural—there is much in the Bible about the musical instruments and singing songs of praise and thankfulness. For the first time in our lives, we realize that Jesus' death on the cross for our sins was a wonderful GIFT. There is nothing about any of us that makes us worthy of His gift, but it is by his unconditional love and grace that we have received these blessings. Even in natural life, a gift given for no particular reason, but love and kindness seems to prompt a special thankfulness from the one who receives it. Perhaps that is why God planned it this way—He knew it would bring out the best in us. What we do now is motivated by love from within our hearts, not out of sense of duty. Again, things done purely out of the sense of duty aren't received with nearly as much enthusiasm.

We really enjoy the spontaneousness in the church services and the home fellowship meetings. When we sing, people sit or stand according to how the spirit moves them. Some may close their eyes or raise their hands in the air. Again, they are free to worship God in the way they feel moved in their hearts, without fear of rejection or criticism from others. It is all very orderly and edifying. The pastor is a wonderful teacher of the scriptures, but doesn't want us to treat him any differently than we treat each other. I haven't been to a service yet that I haven't cried because I feel so close to God and so thankful for what we have in Him. In prayer, I appreciate the fact that nothing is too big or too small to bring before God in prayer. He is our Heavenly Father, and he wants us to be open and honest before him in all things. Like a natural father, he wants us to feel free to talk to him personally about ANY problem we may have. This is a wonderful source of comfort, because we know there is nothing that we and our Heavenly Father together can't handle. We know that we will never be alone in anything.

We are never asked for money. There is a box in the corner where we can give freewill offerings as we feel moved to do so. There is faith that God will provide as needed, and He hasn't failed. The people work together in love and harmony, all results of the liberty that we have in Christ. I realize now that HE is the source from which the living waters flow! Once He is allowed to dwell within us, there is an inward work that totally changes us, but it isn't based on outward rules. He will guide us individually, from within our hearts.

The letter I wrote was not with the intention of hurting anyone, but I was merely pouring out my heart. For so long we had so many questions for which we could get no answers. No matter how hard we tried to live the life we were told was expected of us, the peace and understanding never came! WE were so busy trying to fit ourselves into "man's" ideas of what was acceptable, that we were losing touch with God and what *HE* really wanted! We realize now that when man makes the rules, God's spirit is smothered out and He can't deal with us in his own way and time! God is placed in a box to be heard from when we choose, rather than letting HIM choose!

We no longer feel that any one particular denomination or group merits God's favor any more than another. What brings God's favor is to be filled with unconditional love, to open one's heart and ask God to come and live inside of us. Once we do this, we open the door to a living relationship with God; one where it's just between Him and ourselves. He can guide and direct us each individually. That is what it means to be "born again."

None of us will ever be perfect. We will all fail many times in our lives. But like a natural father, our Heavenly Father loves us and understands us. If we are repentant, if we continue on in love and just admit that we are nothing without Him, He will never forsake us. And knowing all of these things is what brings the true peace and joy that God has promised us.

We hope you will share this letter with the other workers and friends alike so they will know from us and our own words, what our feelings really are.

We send kind greetings to all!

With love in Christ,
Fred and Deanna Printz

Address:
Fred & Deanna Printz
5271 N. St. Rd. 9
Greenfield, IN 46140

Chapter Forty-Six

Cheryl Rupp

My name is Cheryl Rupp and I am an ex-2x2 member, I'm writing to you because I need fellowship with people who can understand what I've been through and what I'm going through. In contacting ex-members I've found a great deal of support and encouragement that confirms I'm going in the right direction.

First I'll tell you a little bit about myself. I was raised in the "sect" as were both my parents. I professed twice, once when I was twelve and again when I was sixteen. In 1980, at the age of eighteen, I married a man who was adopted into the "sect." In 1982 I was baptized because I knew I was drifting out and I hoped this would, by some miracle, fix everything: including me. A couple of months later I felt like nothing had changed and I quit going to meeting. My husband had stopped going about a year before that. I found myself for years defending the church even though I couldn't live up to their standards. I guess in the back of my mind I thought that some day I would get it together and then God would still know me because he had heard me tell people about his church and know that I hadn't broken too many of the rules. See I still had my hair long, I wore no make-up, and when I would run into professing people I hoped I had fooled them.

In October of 1988 I started attending a Twelve-step recovery type meeting and in this meeting they talked about all kinds of addictions and one was religious abuse and addiction. The more they talked the more I denied. After a couple of months I wanted to find God because the steps ask for one to allow God to take over his/her life. Well I assumed that this meant I needed to go back to meeting, so I did—twice. It was the most upsetting time I think I have ever experienced in meeting. The workers were extremely negative and what I was hearing wasn't matching everything I had been learning in the Twelve-step meetings about how much God loves us all—and nothing even close to the love I had been experiencing. So I went to a Sunday morning meeting. I left depressed. Nothing had really changed at all. It was me who had changed and for once I was really seeing things with my eyes open. Well I thought maybe I just needed to talk to the workers and enlighten them with what I'd learned and ask some questions and inform them on where the church had gone too far. WRONG! Their response was that only the people in this church are doing God's will and therefore going to heaven and if I wanted to know more I had to come to meeting. Wow, were my eyes opened. Today, as a Christian, I know that if someone is interested in God's word and his will for them, they turn to Scriptures, read and pray. I also now know that the reason this church continues the way it does is because it's people don't really know what the Scriptures say. I bet most of them were like me and they only opened their Bibles in time to get something to speak on for Sunday. They have never really been taught. There is no true learning about what the Bible says because they take verses out and interpret those without taking the whole Bible into consideration. They lie and deceive people because they feel they can because they are God's only "chosen." This makes me very angry because they claim that other churches are false for the reasons of, for example,

- that other churches were started by men—so was theirs (by William Irvine).
- that other churches are organized—so is theirs, it is just not talked about. (Head workers, printed church letters, workers lists, bank accounts etc.)
- They say that without money those other churches couldn't survive (this church exists because of money; money to send the workers overseas, to pay for hall rentals and convention grounds and to use for who knows what because no one in the congregation ever asks where their money goes).
- They say other churches are false because of scandals (this church has plenty of scandals but they are covered up, like sexual molestation of children by workers, affairs, William Irvine etc.).

As you can tell, I am still a bit angry about the dishonesty and the pretenses of perfection by the leaders of this church. My mothers reply is always "Well you go out and find a perfect church and then let me know." And always my response to this is that I'm not looking for a perfect church because we all know that one does not exist, but I am looking for a church that is willing to *1)* admit they are not perfect but *2)* be willing to address their imperfections and work on them (not deny that they exist and that they need work like the "sect" has always done.) I want and will expect any leader in any church I attend to be held accountable to most degrees for keeping to the scripture and what it teaches.

What I am experiencing now with the new people I chose to meet with is an unbelievable joy and true happiness for the life that God has given them and how they enjoy sharing that same love and joy with others that others may also be able to enjoy it too. Most of the people of the "sect" don't have the joy or the love. They have the guilt and the shame of "Not being good enough!" And what is it with the workers who say at the end of every meeting "This may be your last opportunity!" To Do What? They use this as a fear and guilt tactic to get people to profess. Does this mean if I am killed on the way home from the meeting and I didn't stand to my feet in meeting to profess, that I am going to hell? Yes, I think they actually believe that. They are then saying in a way that God plays a very small part in your salvation compared to their part. In reading the Scripture I have found that God knows my heart and He, and only He, will decide whether I served him or not.

My Mom is still professing as well as many aunts, uncles and cousins. My father, step-mother and my sister however have just this year left the church after a great deal of abuse from the workers and the self-righteous people. Not all members are that cruel but I have found that the truly sincere one's are passive and don't like to rock the boat when it comes to something they don't like.

Well, enough of my opinion. If you would like to share your story with me I would love to hear it. I have found out in the last couple of years that in sharing my story there has been a great deal of healing. My ability to look at myself and my part in it all has also helped me to work on all my relationships. My husband and my kids have benefited from the changes I've made in my life. Ron and I were on our way to a divorce and I was driving my children nuts. Today things are a lot different and God continues to bless us.

If you would like, please feel free to write me any time. My address is:

Cheryl L. Rupp
3624 W. Victor
Visalia, CA 93277

November 13, 1990

Update: May 7th, 1993:
Many things have changed for me since this first letter; I'm no longer a practicing "Christian" and am currently not attending any church. I **do** however consider myself to be spiritual and continue to have a personal relationship with God. For me, I found that some belief systems still contained the elements of judgment, prejudice, self-righteousness and ignorance that can be found in the "sect." At this time I choose not to participate in anything that divides humans (God loves us ALL); my friendships now span across religions, races and cultures.

I'll never regret leaving the "sect" and continue to thank God everyday that I am "free" from the bondage I experienced there. I still have contact with ex-members and value their honesty and growth. For those still inside, if they are happy, I pray that they will continue to get what they need, but for the many who are not, I pray for their release from the church and for support from those of us who have been there. May God continue to Bless us ALL.

Chapter Forty-Seven

Janet Schmidt
An Open Letter to Unknown Friends

I have agreed to have my letter, written in 1989 regarding my desperate search to know God and my separation from "the truth," be printed. September 9, 1993

I have done much soul searching before agreeing to this and I have asked to have this letter also printed. My motives for writing this letter are that I know how alone I felt when I made my decision to leave "the truth," and how much the letters from others helped me. I also wanted to let others know that it doesn't necessarily mean the end of a marriage, if one partner leaves the church while the other remains.

It has been four and one-half years since I told my husband that I could no longer be a part of something I no longer believed in. I was so worried that our marriage wouldn't survive all the struggles we have been thru, and looking back, I believe it was that fear that kept me in the church so long. We still have conflicts regarding religion, but far less intense than in the beginning and much less frequent. We rarely discuss religion. We have both learned to compromise. Jerry goes to meetings almost every Sunday and Wednesday night. I don't complain. We do not have the workers come to our home anymore. Jerry doesn't complain. I take the children to church with me sometimes, when they go with Jerry, I get them ready.

Thinking back to the time I left, I have a few regrets. I wish I would have written letters to my closest friends in the truth to tell them how I had made my decision. Only two women from our church called me to express their concern. I tried to be as open and honest with them as I could, but the notion that Jesus, our Savior, asked only that we believe in Him to be saved, was so remote to them. They just kept saying "faith without works is dead." I feel that if I had personally told everyone closest to me it might have cut down on the rumors. There is no way I could have been prepared for the loneliness. Within a week I had lost almost all my friends. Jerry is no longer trusted with some information, because his wife has "lost out." This is a major point of irritation to him.

Many things seemed to help. Praying. Writing to others who have been thru or are going thru the process of leaving. Writing to or confronting the workers regarding some of these things. Going to other churches. Working thru the tremendous anger I had toward the workers. Learning about cults and how they affect their members lives. I also receive help from a very special pastor who took the time to read *The Secret Sect* and *The Church Without A Name* so he could better understand where I came from in order to help me.

Perhaps some of the things that helped me the most were written to me in a letter by Garry Scarf, who had been a former member of the People's Temple before their mass suicides. Garry is a member of the National Cult Awareness Network. He advised me to be patient with myself, submit to open and honest dialogue, and question, question, question the workers. He said we should all recognize we are special, unique, and created in God's image.

My attempts at dialogue also helped to confirm my feeling that the workers believed that they bring salvation to those who profess. A sister worker, whom I had known my entire life, wrote several letters to me—first calling me a doubter and later bringing up rebellion of my youth in an attempt to insult me and take the focus off my questions. Oddly, her response was so confusing, it just proved to me that even she is not sure of what she is preaching. I also realized that I was living according to the will of the workers and trying to fit into a mold they told us was right instead of developing my own special talents.

I have begun to love differences in people. I'm truly glad God didn't make us all carbon copies of each other. I love the freedom not judging other people's lives brings. I also love the freedom of choosing what is right for me!

My heart goes out to all who are searching their hearts and troubled by their life in "the truth." I pray they will know the peace I began to feel as I allowed God to direct my life. I pray they will feel the grateful heart of a person who knows the precious gift Jesus gave us cannot be bought by any actions regardless of how good they may be. I never could have guessed how much the focus of my life has changed and I thank God everyday because of it.

Sincerely,
Janet Schmidt
W3503 Ranch Rd.
Watertown, WI 53094

Quotes from April 1989 letter from a worker
(underscores are as in original)

I felt so sad when some one made mention you were no longer going to meetings. Is it true you read the book written by someone who turned against truth? Have you ever stopped and thought of comparing the Bible with that book? Surely faith in God would cause you to believe the Bible?? Unwillingness in one person could cause them to write much that would be contrary to God's word. Matthew 24:24 warns against those who would rise up and if it were possible they would deceive the very elect. A meeting in our field will study 2 Corinthians 2 next week. This A.M. I read it and noticed the 11 verse. Paul was warning them of satan lest he would take advantage of them. He is still very busy. We need to not be ignorant of his many devices. This week on Wed. night we studied Hebrews 3:1 says <u>Consider Jesus</u>. Hebrews 12:2 <u>Looking unto Jesus</u>. This chapter also deals with <u>unbelief</u>. V19, they could not enter in because of <u>unbelief</u>. Just becoming <u>doubtful</u>, also v12 <u>Take heed lest there be an evil heart of unbelief</u>. There are many, many more places in the Bible where we can see what is of God, and in the end if will be only the ones on his right hand who will enter into eternal life. Matthew 25. I write this because I love you and have a real concern for your soul. I would love to hear from you and know how you really feel.

I think back of when you were home with your mother and we were in your home. You seemed to love the meetings, your bible, and above all the Lord. You can be sure you are all in my heart & my prayers." Balance of letter was regarding her travels and meetings, the weather, memories of being at their house, and concern.

Reply Dated May 1989

I'm glad that you took the time to write to me recently. At the time I stopped going to the meetings I promised God and myself that I would answer as honestly as I could any questions that were put to me regarding that decision.

More than three years ago I saw an advertisement in the Watertown *Daily Times* for a book about the church with no name that meets in the home. At the time I saw the ad, Kathy Dooley & Sharon Carroll were staying at our home and they saw the ad also. I mentioned that I was going to order the book and Sharon said when I was done with the book she would like to read it. That evening the girls went over to Gary Hoffman's to have dinner with Harry Johnson. When they returned I felt Sharon was trying to discourage me from ordering the book. She told me that they had discussed the ad with Harry. He knew of the book and he believed that it was written by someone who had turned against truth. I sent for the book.

When the book came I read it and then gave it to Sharon as I had promised. I told her that the book had brought out some questions in my mind that I would like answers to. She told me that a worker from Canada wanted her to write down some things from the book so the workers could refute them. Months passed without Sharon returning the book and I again asked to have her return the book. At that time I told her that I felt the workers should openly address some of the questions the friends had about this book and the beginning of this church. The questions were never answered, so I began my own research.

The questions that I had were: "When did this religion actually begin?" "Was it with Jesus as we have always been told in Gospel Meetings, or by a man named William Irvine in 1897?" "Was salvation from Jesus only brought to people thru the workers, or was God's plan that we rely only on Jesus dying on the cross as hope for forgiveness of sins and hope for salvation?" I took these questions very seriously because there is nothing more serious than our salvation.

From your letter I do not believe that you could have read the book I have referred to earlier in this letter. Perhaps you are assuming what you think is in the book or are relying on rumors regarding the book's contents. The book entitled *The Secret Sect* by Doug & Helen Parker is without a doubt speaking about this religion. I do not believe that it was written by someone who has "turned against 'truth,'" but rather by someone who learned that this way was not from the beginning with Christ, but began with a man named William Irvine in 1897. I do not believe this book, or any other book, can or should be compared with the Bible. This book is not an instructional book regarding how God wants His people to live. As I see it, the book is a history of the beginning of this religion. The book documents how Mr. Irvine left a church he had been preaching in because he felt that he should follow more closely to the teachings of Matthew 10. It tells of how Mr. Irvine called the workers to go forth with him from the beginning in Ireland and moving to the United States, Canada and on to other countries.

For the last three years I have written to many sources and have obtained much documentation as to how and when this religion was truly founded. Once I had that settled in my mind, did knowing that there had been some deception about the origin actually make this way wrong? I don't believe it

does. Then I came to the question about people
getting to know Jesus and receiving hope for salvation only by professing thru the workers. I spent
many hours studying the books of the Bible dealing
with this (Romans 3,4,5,6, Galatians 3). I felt a
great responsibility to search this out through
Prayer, reading the Bible, talking with and writing
to people who profess and some who have left the
way including a former worker. I have obtained articles written by reporters in the United States and
articles published in newspapers from Ireland during the years when Mr. Irvine was starting the first
conventions. I have read instructions written by the
head worker of a state to other workers in his state.
I have learned that the Cult Awareness Network has
a file regarding this church.

What I learned was that I had not been truly believing that Jesus died in my stead, and that is the
only thing that brings salvation to within our reach.
Accepting His free gift is what sets us free, not trying to earn it. We can't walk worthy of salvation,
because we will never be worthy of it. Jesus' blood
on the cross is diminished, if we believe that it is
not enough to save us or that it is brought to us by
any other person. It is believing in that which has
given me a feeling of being renewed and increased
my love for a Father who would give His Son to
save the world, and a Son who died because His
Father knew we would all perish if there was not
forgiveness and cleansing for our sins. Accepting
this has made me want to do the things that I feel
will fulfill the special talents God has given me.

I have not become doubtful of Jesus, nor do I
have any unbelief regarding anything to do with the
Bible. The Bible shall continue to be my guide for
living.

I have enclosed a reprint from a published book which may enlighten you. I will continue to Pray that the workers will start preaching the true Gospel to those attending the Gospel Meetings.

Sincerely,

Quotes from the Worker's October 5, 1989 Reply

I'm going to type on a seperate paper what I have to say regarding your questions and the copy you sent. The copy of reprint from a Published book was to enlighten me. I must say as I read it my faith was only deepened in our faith and what I know to be right. My young companion last year who professed in recent years and went in the work in January 1987 said in reading it, she was made sure and her faith was only increased in what she has.

My heart was saddened as I read it, knowing they were writing about the Way of God as seen in Jesus and were making so many untrue statements. I feel I should point at least some of them out to you. I am doing so by drawing a circle and numbering them. On a seperate sheet I'll put my comments & scripture. I hope and pray you'll have an open mind regarding it. You have known me since you were a girl and I hope you'll believe me? I've been in the work since 1955 and I know for a fact untrue things are said. If you choose to not believe me, at least I have tried. All that is in print cannot be trusted.

*[Following are the sister worker's references quoted from **The Discerner** January-March 1985 edition, along with her written comments]*

1. "The Bible, according to the leaders is a dead book unless it is made to live through the mouth of one of their workers/preachers."

Worker's Comment: "We do not claim this. The revelation comes from God. 1 Cor 2:10, Gal. 1:11-16, Matt. 11:25-27."

2. "The originator of the movement was William Irvine."

Worker's Comment: "We believe Hebrews 12:2 'Looking unto Jesus the author and finisher of our faith.' I would like to give you some references, that mean a lot to me as we carry the gospel to people and point them to something that is from the beginning and not to something began by a man. These are the references. John 17:5. Jesus was praying to the Father and prayed of the glory which he had with the Father before the world was. John 1:1 'In the beginning was the Word, and the Word was with God and the Word was God.' Both these speak of Jesus being from the beginning. And Isaiah had revelations of the Christ. In Isaiah 9th ch. he wrote of the Christ that would be born into the world, and in Isaiah 28:16 he spoke of the foundation, the corner stone. And in Hebrews 13:8 we read 'Jesus Christ the same yesterday, and today, and forever.' So there is no date for the starting, as it was with the Heavenly Father before the world. Why would we want something started by a man when we have in the scripture something that is from the beginning and scripture backs up? Will only add we are sure our ministry is the same as Jesus lived and established."

3. "They [the Tramp Preachers] insisted that all others were going to hell and the only way to escape that end was to join their movement. Basically this belief has not changed and that is still what the 'workers,' those who have dedicated their lives to be preachers, proclaim in one way or another."

Worker's Comment: "We believe God is the judge of who goes to hell and who is in a saved eternity. We read of one of the malefactors that was also on the cross and Jesus said to the one 'Today shalt thou be with me in paradise.' Was the heart of this man that made it possible and not joining something. There is no such thing as joining this. People are born into it, being born of the Spirit and water (word) John 3:5."

4. "The friends are subject to the workers in all things."

Worker's Comment: "The workers try to be guided and moved by the Spirit of God to help those they are in fellowship with. But in no way do they lord it over them. Heb. 13:17 teaches people to obey those who watch for their soul. When people are submitted to God, they want to have some guidance."

5. "They feel that whatever the workers say is from God because they alone possess the Spirit of God."

Worker's Comment: "In no way do we feel the workers alone possess the Spirit of God. 1 John 3:24. 1 John 4:13, Romans 8:16."

6. "Because of this the workers exert a strong, however, subtle, control over all the friends in their jurisdiction. Actually, the people in the organization, the friends, have given up their own wills and submitted themselves totally to the workers, believing that this is the only true and perfect church and their only hope of salvation."

Worker's Comment: "I disagree with this statement. The workers encourage the people to submit to God, not to the workers."

7. "Salvation, incidentally, is not based on the finished work of Christ on the cross but by professing acceptance to the worker, the message proclaimed by him, and then walking in the 'Jesus Way.' The 'convert' must break all ties with any religion or faith of the past and must conform to 'the Way' and the expectations of the worker."

Worker's Comment: "Salvation is the Christ within. Romans 1:16 tells us the gospel is the power of God unto salvation. The statement the converts must break all ties with any religion, is not something the workers make them do. If they have truly received a revelation, they'll want to and do it on their own, they are not made to do things. And are not taught to conform to the expectations of the workers. It is the matter of putting off the old man and putting on the new man. Col. 3:9-10."

8. "The overseers expect from the workers exactly what the workers expect from the friends-total submission to their authority. As in any organization this leads to power plays and some measure of rebellion and, sometimes the expulsion of a worker or his voluntary departure. Whichever takes place, it results in the departed one being declared to be 'losing out.'"

Worker's Comment: "This is not true. We believe James 4:7 'Submit yourselves therefore unto God.' Hebrews 13:17 does say to 'obey those who have the rule over you and submit yourselves, for they watch for your soul, etc.' Maybe I should add what Paul said in 1 Cor. 11:1 'Be ye followers of me, even as I also am of Christ.'"

9. "A worker may become an overseer by strictly conforming to the demands of his overseer and being accepted into this 'hierarchy' by the approval of others who hold this position."

Worker's Comment: "There is no truth in that statement. When Murray Keene came to Wisconsin to be the overseer it was thru prayers of God fearing men. There were 3 or 4 older brother workers praying about it and when they got together they had gotten the answer it should be Murray come. Each one in private prayer got the answer. The positions are not given because of conforming to demands or desires of others, but by prayer."

10. "Those speaking do so without notes, because in Matthew 10 the disciples were told not to take any 'scrip,' which the workers misapply as meaning script or notes."

Worker's Comment: "The first time I heard that. We don't use notes or literature, as we depend on the Spirit of God to give the message. Notes and literature is pretty dead. Spirit of God gives life."

11. "Conventions are also used to convert and indoctrinate any new converts as well as to present any new decisions reached by the corporate body of overseers."

Worker's Comment: "Another false statement. Our conventions are to strengthen, warn, correct, reprove, encourage and reassure as God sees fit by His Spirit."

12. "The membership is more or less self-perpetuating for almost without exception the children follow on in the movement."

Worker's Comment: "I really don't know how you can believe this. There are many, many families whose children do not follow. This is sad. but like Ezekiel 15:20 says 'Tho Noah, Daniel and Job were in it, they could not deliver son, daughter, etc.' And in my own experience in the work we have met a number who had no professing relatives. We have seen them come to meeting and accept the gospel and it becomes their life."

13. "There are several reasons for classifying this group as a cult. They do not preach that one is saved by faith alone in the sacrifice of Christ on the cross. Their concept is that assurance of salvation is dependent on personal merit and following explicitly the dictates of the overseers and workers."

Worker's Comment: "It's hard for me to grasp you would believe this statement. We being classified as a cult. James 2 tells us clearly 'faith without works is dead.' Salvation depends on the Christ within Col. 1:27 'Christ in you the hope of glory.'"

14. "They do not believe that anyone can be 'saved' unless he hears the 'gospel' from the lips of a worker."

Worker's Comment: "I would not say the only way is by workers, but that is scripture. You would notice in Acts 8, when the people were all scattered except the apostles. Philip was preaching the word, and when the apostles heard about this they sent Peter and John. They were to confirm the work of the gospel because Jesus had established a true ministry. Our faithful friends do much today in helping and speaking to others. But then they are brought in touch with 'the true ministry' and fellowship with them. My own parents were in only 1 gospel meeting before they accepted this. My aunt talked to them and explained the scripture to them and they could see she had something. After they had started having part they attended gospel meetings. I feel we need more than to just rely on Jesus dying on the cross. He did what we cannot do, but we need to do what we can. In 1 John 1:7 we read 'But if we walk in the light as he is in the light, we have fellowship one with another, and the blood of Jesus Christ his Son cleanseth us from all sin.' Thus we must walk in the light to have cleansing. Many people like to feel Jesus did it all. It's true, eternal life is a gift, but we must do our part."

15. "They believe that one must 'keep faithful' and that involves personal sacrifice."

Worker's Comment: "Personal sacrifice has nothing what so ever to do with reward. The sacrifice all must give is presenting our bodies a living sacrifice. Romans 12:1."

16. "Anyone who disagrees with their concepts is excommunicated."

Worker's Comment: "Rather than excommunicating people, every means of help is given to people to try to help them follow Christ, the true Shepherd. I have never excommunicated anyone."

17. "Most of the friends are in the organization because they have not been taught the Word of God properly."

Worker's Comment: "First of all this is not an organization. This whole statement is untrue."

18. "If you are able to shake their confidence in their worker and his interpretation of the Word, and get them to think on spiritual matters apart from the worker's influence, half of the battle will be won."

Worker's Comment: "All I can say is what is recorded in this article 'Nameless Cult' must have been the result of someone who rebelled. I can read it in many statements, and when one is rebelling you do not have good and correct reasoning. You know for yourself in growing up days you had some rebellion. And would seem by your letter you were still refusing advice given. You were encouraged to not order the book, but you did. You mentioned in your letter the bible would continue to be your guide for living. I've wondered where you meet for worship and fellowship? Hebrews

10:25 tells us to not forsake the assembling of ourselves together. Also this article you sent was
written by Rev. Ewald Eisele. Psalm 111:9 tells us
'holy and reverend is his name.' Name only belonging to God.

"I could have commented on other things. But
perhaps this is enough. One can read too many
things written by man. One woman told us she had
read so much that she no longer believed Jesus was
the Christ. Sad, Sad. Destroys faith."

Chapter Forty-Eight

Margaret Erickson-Schader

The year I was 40 (I am now 74) was a big turning point in my life. That was when my parents and I removed ourselves from the 2x2's. I heard about the early days of the "truth" as they then called themselves from the cradle. My parents had both professed before they were married. They were both very devout Christians. I never saw my father leave the house to work without first taking time to read and pray—my mother too was very faithful. My parents' faith was evident every day, not just on Sunday. We three children saw more Christianity from our parents than the other members or from the workers. When the workers came to our home everything revolved around them, and they expected it to be so. Over the years, numerous incidents were responsible for my parents' loss of faith in the workers. It was a gradual process. I heard my parents discussing these things when they thought they were alone, so I always felt that God was with our family, but the workers were human, and the true spirit, as in the New Testament was not there. We grew up and first I professed, then my 2 brothers as they became of age. My brothers went off to WW II, neither being CO's (conscientious objectors): Bob joined the Navy and John said he could not refuse to go where he was sent, after taking the induction oath. God protected both of them from having to take a life.

The final break came when August Gustafson came to our home. (He was an old man from Swe-

den, who had once been a worker, but was put out
by a group of older workers some years before because he would not submit to the line of doctrine
agreed upon. I believe he and Eddie Cooney were
put out about the same time.) August had been visiting in California and Kay Arvig (now Downs)
encouraged us to invite him. James Jardine came to
our home and delivered an ultimatum: *if August
came to our home he must not be allowed to testify in the meetings.* My parents and I were polite
and did not argue with Jim and he left our home
that evening thinking he had brought us into line.
During the nite, God told me this was wrong, and I
purposed that I would move out if my parents submitted. (One of the St. Paul meetings was in our
home.) To my surprise, my parents had decided
during the nite they could not submit to Jim's ultimatum, since it was not according to the
commandments in the Bible: "quench not the
spirit." As we were agreed, we composed a letter
together, made copies and sent to all who came to
our home for meeting, and other interested parties,
with the original going to J.J. The news traveled fast
and the "saints" were informed this was the work
of the devil. We were ostracized—no one called us
to hear our side of the story. It was an abrupt
change, but out of the loneliness that followed, the
Lord sent us a comforter in Jesus. My parents have
both been dead now many years—when they came
to the end neither had any regrets. Both were glad.

Although we were very lonely after August left
(he stayed a few months), it was sweet release to be
free of all the 2x2's rules. When my parents died
there was no one to conduct a funeral, so they
were both buried without ceremony. Relatives were
notified after the burial was over, according to both
parents' wishes. I think of the rich man and the

poor man who lay at his gate. When they died the rich man was buried, but the poor man was carried into Abraham's bosom, and the wide gulf was fixed. The three Jardine brothers died and were buried with large funerals, people coming from far and near to the funerals.

The Lord has been very good to me; He has plucked me "as a brand from the burning" many times. When one stands for truth it is a lonely experience, but God is there to pick us up and help us onward. I have no regrets! The years in the 2x2's were a great learning experience, and the years since have been lonely, but rich. I'm still learning and I have a lot more to learn.

Address:
Margaret Erickson-Schader
1181 Edgcumbe Rd., #1401
St. Paul, MN 55105

Summer:
Box 128
Grand Marais, MN 55604

Letter from the Erickson Family to James Jardine
Dated July 13, 1958

Dear Brother Jim:

After you left our home Wednesday evening, July 9, 1958, we talked things over and decided we couldn't conscientiously agree with the conditions you laid down for continued fellowship with the Christian Convention group. Before you came that evening, we had all three purposed not to argue with you on any line, but to let you have your say and talk it over by ourselves later and decide afterward what was best to do.

Now we have had sufficient time to seriously and prayerfully consider the matter and we believe God has revealed to us what He expects and we are afraid to do otherwise than follow as He directs, lest He should remove our candlestick (Rev. 2:5) and cease to strive with us forever.

For at least a dozen years we believe God has been preparing us for this final step. We have gradually become aware of a departure from the teachings of the Scripture on the part of those who have been in authority among us. It has been apparent that there has been a gradual drifting away from the pattern and what was taught us in the early years. We have gradually come to realize, as a result of experience we have passed through, that there are man-made rules which cannot be justified in the Bible and are set down by those in authority as the only way to obtain eternal salvation. We have also been grieved to notice that a greater stress is placed by the workers on the attendance at the gospel meetings than on attending the Sunday morning fellowship meeting.

We have also become greatly concerned as to how to explain to others why the platform speakers have stressed the fact that buildings are wrong and yet is has been known that some have taken 2 or 3 months off from preaching the gospel in the summer in order to repair existing buildings or build new ones on the convention grounds, which are put there for the sole purpose of worship. The fact that these buildings are referred to as "machine sheds" is misleading and outright deception. We have found it impossible to justify by scripture either the buildings or the time taken to build them by those who have given their lives to preach the gospel and serve souls.

We have found it almost impossible to take "outsiders" to the gospel meetings during the past number of years, because we felt that we could not honestly tell them that these men really are homeless (as they preach from the platform) when they continue to stay in the same places year after year and refuse to accept invitations to other homes.

We don't begin to say what you and others are responsible for, and this letter is only for the purpose of telling you what God has been revealing to us. We are all individuals before God and as such we will be judged by the Lamb who Himself was "without spot and blemish" (I Pet. 1:19 and Rev. 27:11 and 12). And as individuals we have come to realize that if God's spirit is going to continue to lead us, we must be in bondage to no man and to no rules of doctrine. Rom. 8:15 (Moffatt) says it makes you lapse into fear, and we believe that is just where we have been, and we do not want to continue in that condition.

Therefore, we are now prepared to stand alone in this matter of serving God. Joshua 24:15, Rom. 8:31 to end of chapter, and II Cor. 6:17 all explain much better than we can our position in this respect. Consequently, *we are hereby notifying you that as of this date, we are severing all connections with the Christian convention sect and we are asking that you immediately make arrangements to remove the meeting from our home.*

This does not mean that we are forsaking the assembling of ourselves together, we intend to continue to meet according to the pattern that is given us in the Bible and we are looking only to God for guidance in this. "To walk by faith means to live for things eternal; consider Him who trod the path alone." Anyone who comes to our home in the name of Jesus and is willing to give Him the glory and the preeminence will be given the right hand of fellowship by us.

We have been accused of joining ourselves with some so-called "out-casts" on the West coast. We have not joined ourselves with any other group nor do we ever intend to again become affiliated with any other form of organized religion.

In regard to the impending visit of August Gustafson, our home is open for any discussion that is mutually agreed upon between both parties concerned.

Respectfully,
Frank & Edith Erickson
Margaret E. Erickson

Chapter Forty-Nine

Testimony of Iola Shirlaw of North Platte, Nebraska

I was born February 25, 1905, and taught piano for over 40 years, before I retired. I became a born again Christian as a young girl, and went to the Christian Church where we believed, relied upon, and trusted in the blood of Jesus for our salvation, rather than trusting in a particular "way" or certain type ministry and fellowship to save. Later I married a Catholic and went to that church for 28 years. My first husband passed away in 1962. I remarried in 1963, but we did not attend any church.

I was invited to a meeting here in March of 1983. My husband, Ray, was in a nursing home 22 miles west of here. I had just been told that he would never stand again, and would always be there. I was truly depressed, wondering how I could ever meet all those bills. A piano student of mine, who was also a 2x2 invited me. She knew just when to invite me—when I was vulnerable. I was impressed by the friendly people. The workers called and invited me to meetings. I went. Ray came home May 1, in a wheelchair, but home.

In October, I was due for eye surgery and needed help caring for myself and Ray. It was arranged for two sister workers, Elinor Kleeb and Cocha Smith, to come into my home for one month, and take care of us. Having three gospel meetings a week, they made good use of my big living room and corner lot, where there is ample parking space. At the end, I asked what I owed them, and was told, "Nothing, you do not buy love." However, they took the money I offered them.

I professed November 18, 1983. Ray did not. He always said, "They are a bunch of moochers." I went to my first convention at Antioch, NE in June, 1984, and was baptized September, 1984, at York, NE. Ray passed away July 8, 1985. Then the workers took over my home and my life. They had meetings in my basement two to three times a week, as well as special meetings, seating 50-60 people. I was cooking for a lot of them. Often I took the workers out to eat, because sometimes I was not able to stand and cook.

Counting myself, there were about 16 friends in our meeting, plus children; out of which, two unmarried women live with men, and one unmarried man lives with a woman. However, all prayed and gave "flowery" testimonies in meetings. We watched child abuse at every meeting, even to the point the neighbors complained and a policeman came to the door during a Bible Study! We talked to the workers about it, but nothing was done, other than to hush it all up. The elders wife once said to me that it seemed to her better to just live with someone than to marry them if they don't' profess, because then they could continue to take part. There is a young man in our meeting who is trying to make a living in the plant nursery business. He was raised in the Truth, is divorced and remarried. He has two children and she has two. On their own, they have been coming to meetings for seven years—very faithfully, but not taking part. At the 1991 York convention, they were both baptized, and now are allowed to take part. When my evergreen shrubs died, I mentioned to Roy Dietzel that I needed to have my yard re-landscaped. Roy told me to contact one of the friends who lives 50 miles away. I hired the man who went to our meeting.

I was in and out of the hospital for the last few years—blood clots, heart problems, etc. Once while I was in the hospital, I decided to leave some money in my will to the church. I called one of the friends and asked him how to go about it. He told me to buy a Certificate of Deposit jointly in my name and his name, and to put on it that he is a member of the Christian Convention Church. "That is the name we use for things like this," he said. I did. That was the first anyone here had heard of that name. Some members of 50 years couldn't believe it!

Once I had to lay with my leg elevated on a pillow, due to a blood clot. My friend Rose brought me a pair of jogging pants which she knew would be better for me than wearing my pajamas to keep my leg warm. This made Bonita Kleeb, a sister worker, so mad that she went into the bedroom and slammed the door so hard the whole house shook.

When I professed, I owned a $750.00 television. On the last day of York convention in 1985 Roy Dietzel, the head worker at the time said, "Iola, we have waited three years for you to get rid of that TV—now we are telling you." I sold it for $150.00. He even asked me what I got for it! I also got rid of all my jewelry and my beautiful expensive slack suits. Mildred Schrimer, who has the meeting in her home here, said, "Iola, bring your slacks down to me, and I will make you skirts out of them, and you will have some nice suits. I did—never have seen them since. I have thin hair, and have worn a wig for over 25 years. Often I was told I should buy one with long hair. However long-hair wigs do not come in grey. I was often told I was taking God's name in vain, when I said "gee" and "golly."

One day, my good friend, Rose Medich, asked me if I would read a book called *The Secret Sect* by Doug & Helen Parker, and give her my opinion. I read it, and called Rose and said, "I feel like a fool. How stupid I have been!" When I joined the 2x2s, I did not know what they believed. I asked Roy Dietzel about their doctrine and his answer was for me to "come to the meetings and learn." I didn't have any idea they didn't believe in the triune nature of God, nor in God's saving grace, and that the workers were necessary as mediators between man and God. However, later, I could see these were clearly their beliefs. I was told it had started when Jesus was on earth. When I would ask questions, all I was ever told was "Just come to the meetings—we learn by hearing." In the meetings, I have never heard about the blood of Christ. Was I ever foolish, dumb and deceived! I should have known better! Not only was I deceived, but I feel used. How foolish I was to be so brainwashed for seven years! I felt I could not be a part of this deceptive group another day. I had been told that this fellowship continued down from Jesus' apostles. Rose agreed with me that we must leave this deceptive group.

Since it was November, near Special Meeting time, Rose suggested we should wait until after the Special Meetings were over before we left the group, but I didn't agree. I thought we should quit "cold turkey, and Rose went along with me. Rose and I left November 18, 1990, just before Special Meetings, exactly seven years after I first professed. After I missed two meetings and Rose missed one, the workers came over. We felt God was with us, telling us what to say.

We asked about their doctrine and their beliefs. They said "All we need is the Bible," which proved to us they don't really know what they believe. We explained some of the things that led to our making our decision to separate from the 2x2 group. That we had learned that the fellowship was started in 1897 by William Irvine; that the foundation of truth was very important to us; that we did not want to be used or condemned any longer; that we saw no point in following numerous man-made rules which had nothing to do with the dispensation of Grace, and had no Biblical support.

We asked Bonita Kleeb if she had read *The Secret Sect*, and if it was true. She said she had read parts of it, and that the book is only one man's opinion. Also that she knew people who read the book, and then went on to profess in gospel meetings. They said they loved us and they left crying. They asked me if I wanted them to drop by and visit. I replied, "No, if I need you, I know how and where to find you." However, Rose and I were far from crying. We smiled happily at each other—we were so happy and relieved. We were finally free indeed! "If Jesus has set you free, you are free indeed," John 8:36. I wanted to leave this group long before I did and I thank God every day that I am free of it now. Poor souls, all I can feel for them is pity. It has been easy for me.

The workers told one of our friends to stay away from us, and to read Romans 16:16-18. However, Betty told them she could not do that as we had been friends for several years. Betty still calls and comes over to my house, but we do not see the other friends. Every Thursday evening, we have a Bible study with several former 2x2s. Joe Grubbs leads us. He is the youth pastor of the Berean church and was raised in a 2x2 home but left years ago because he could not please the workers. Rose and I also get together on Sunday to study the Bible where we are presently studying three different Bible courses. I have come out of the 2x2s with a strong determination to learn more of God's Word so that I KNOW for myself what His will is according to the Scripture, so that I will never be deceived again. Trying to make up for lost time, I am cramming all the time I can possibly find into studying the Scriptures.

This past year has been the best year of my life. Together on November 18, 1991, Rose and I happily celebrated our one-year anniversary—the date we set ourselves free of the bondage of the 2x2 fellowship! I said disgustedly, "Why did I ever get in it, anyway?" Rose feels God has spared me this long (I am 86) so I could help her out of the 2x2s. Rose is like a daughter to me. I love her very much.

I am just bursting to show Him my love and appreciation for His Love and grace towards me. I love the verses in Ephesians 2:8-9; Luke 17:21; 1 Corinthians 13. I pray every day for guidance and understanding. I can truly say "I know my Jesus!"

**Dictated by Iola Shirlaw,
October, 1991**

Iola Shirlaw died December 16, 1991, from acute myelomonocytic leukemia, just barely over a year after she and Rose left the 2x2 fellowship. Rev. Joe Grubbs officiated at her funeral service. She is buried in Floral Lawns Memorial Gardens in North Platte, Nebraska.

Chapter Fifty

Letter Written by Mr. A. Singleton, Ex-elder of the Two-by-Two Church

Dear sir,

Just a few lines in answer to your last in regard to your experience with the Christian Convention Sect. It is all very typical of the procedure that started with William Irvine in 1899. He was one of the worst characters that any respectable person could come in contact with and become a victim of his influence. Although he has long passed away, the same procedure continues and has been the means of blighting the lives of thousands of honest people and continues up to date to do so.

We do feel very sorry for many of the people who have not taken time to go into detail in regards to the origination of this vicious hostile sect, registered and documented in Washington, D.C. It was hard to take or believe on account of what we had heard in the beginning, about the year 1914 and 15 from Willie Jameison and his companion, Henry Hanson. My wife and I accepted what Jameison preached without any reservation. On the face, it looked like what was right and we did as best we knew how to be faithful and to bring our then young family up in fellowship with that way.

Once in a conversation with Jameison I asked him about the origination of his ministry. He told me about William Irvine, what a wonderful preacher he was and how through him he had accepted the gospel and went to preach because he wanted to be able to preach like him. I told Jameison I would like very much to meet William Irvine. He told me it was not possible because he was recuperating from over-work and not in good health.

I found out later this was a made up lie by him and others of his brethren to keep people from knowing the truth. William Irvine was excommunicated out of the ministry and fellowship by Jack Carroll and others and had taken up his abode in Jerusalem as he claimed to be the second witness spoken of in Revelations. Jameison continued to resurrect this man and brings him to the platform with him at conventions and many other places. He ought to be ashamed of any remembrance of Irvine. But the old saying is true: "Birds of a feather flock together."

A few years ago, Jameison came to our home and stayed overnight. He seemed badly disturbed about many things that were taking place. I asked him where these things originated and he said in the ministry. So I told him it was better to settle it with the ministry and not bring it into the churches. I was then an elder and the church had been in our home from the time we professed, almost forty years at that time. After relating to us all these wrongs in the lives of others, before he retired, he went to his grip and produced a bottle of whiskey, helped himself to a large quantity of it and told me if his friends knew he imbibed in such stuff they would not have any faith in him. So dear friends, this is not hearsay. It is personal experience. So you see it is a pure case of the blind leading the blind.

We could no longer go along with the inconsistencies. Jameison removed the meeting from our home and expected us to go to another home. We said no, if we were not worthy of meeting in our home we would not be worthy to go to someone else's home. So friends, that has been the end of our fellowship with the Christian Convention group and will continue to be so. I know from past experiences, if you will stay out of the Christian Convention group you will enjoy more of the presence of God and His Christ in your lives. Jameison has proven to us that he and many of his associates have never gotten any victory over the flesh.

Because we were friendly to Ron Campbell he asked me to renounce Ron and I told him I would not do that to anybody who had never done me any harm. Since then I have learned he was asking me to renounce the wrong man. It has all turned out to be a blessing from God to be free from bondage to such a source.

He thought that because we were his converts, we would not expose him and we were living in fear of being taken out of fellowship. He found out he was very badly mistaken. I exposed him plenty, but he denied it all and made some of his friends believe it. Some people are so much in bondage and fear they believe anything that is told them by a worker regardless.

In the 5th of Jeremiah verse 30 and 31 ("A wonderful and horrible thing is committed in the land; the prophets prophesy falsely, and the priests bear rule by their means; and my people love to have it so; and what will ye do in the end thereof?")

This is the very condition that existed between them and many of their friends; lies, falsehoods, alibis, covering up their faults and failures, blind leaders of the blind, blind to what they are going to have to face in the end.

I could keep on writing many pages of my past experiences but we were never discouraged, just disappointed in men. The promises of God are sure to those that learn to love and honor His Son and no power on earth can separate us from it.

Christ, and He only, is the author and finisher of our faith. As Paul says, "I planted and Apollos watered, but God gave the increase. Neither he that planted or he that watered are anything."

Some years ago a friend of ours who professed in same meetings we did, decided to get more details in regards to both sides. So we wrote to William Irvine in Jerusalem and got an answer to our letter which my friend still has in his possession. Irvine at that time still believed in an exaggerated form of the old opinion of an inner illumination and regarded the Bible as simply a dead book. He wrote and preached that God made him the Head of the Church, ignoring the scripture that Christ was the one and only Head.

So evidently at the close of Irvine's life, he realized he had left a dirty trail across the European and American continents and was convicted in his conscience. He stated in his letters it was all just an experiment when he claimed to be the second witness spoken of in Revelations and that he belonged in Jerusalem. Jack Carroll and others encouraged him to do so. He realized these fellows did it to get his mantle and for no other good reason as their lives were no exception to his. Or in other words, were doing the same things he himself was guilty of. He admitted his own faults and failures and that is more than they ever did, only behind closed doors. So we can see now, and have for a number of years that they were never based upon the foundation of the apostles and prophets and have never complied with the commission given to the twelve apostles or the seventy.

These men know that they have not the faith that would enable them to exist to do so. That is the reason Irvine and Cooney adopted the system of conventions and they got the idea from the Faith Mission. Irvine said, we must look to Keswick. It will get our people together and we will get finance to continue on and that is just what it has materialized into today—the financial life line.

You and I can plainly see that what they claim to have is from their own beginning and has absolutely no marks of that which was planned of God through His well beloved son in his beginning. There is a transformation—Satan is also transformed into an angel of light and his ministers as the ministers of righteousness.

So dear friends, it is not with any hatred or rebellion in our hearts that I write these things as our experiences in the past has been a blessing. And it helps us to see how easily many people can be deceived to think that they are walking in the light of Christ and are not.

Will close for now and hope this answer to you will not make you weary.

Greeting, Your friends in His name and Way and no other,

A. and H. Singleton and family

September 30, 1962

Chapter Fifty-One

Laura Singleton
Issues

Children: not addressing their needs

1. Lack of knowledge of Bible:
   a. No stories of Bible heroes
   b. Historical continuity of Jewish and Christian faith----many New Testament Scriptures are related to Old Testament.
   c. Parents lack knowledge - you can't teach what you don't know yourself.

2. Home training:
   a. worker worship
   b. no knowledge or devotional time on their level.
   c. Parents lack knowledge of basic principles of "Christ as personal Saviour", etc. No personal commitment, just conformity to rules of the group.
   d. Multiple "guilt trips" hung by workers and others with their own agenda. My daughter reports feeling shame and pressure because of failure to perform (give testimony every Sunday) and conform to rules. Always a feeling of not "measuring up".
   e. Invasion of privacy of the home by multiple "live-in" guests (workers and drop-ins).

3. "Overseers" are not accountable.
   a. Money received and spent is dispensed according to whim and status of workers.
   b. World-wide travel by workers----at the

expense of family needs----children go without shoes or proper food while workers travel.
c. Nothing provided for medical and physical needs of those people in missionary fields who are starving.

4. "Cover up" is a way of life.
    a. Denial of sexual misconduct on part of workers.
    b. If you are a VIP in the group----what you do is "swept under the rug."
    c. If you are not in line with the workers, you are brutally judged and your misconduct is exaggerated by gossip and malignment.

Those who continue in the group report that "things are changing." Why change if you were the "only way to heaven" to start with. I sincerely feel that no amount of relaxation of rules will change the foundation of the group which is man worship and secrecy.

Address:
Laura Singleton
1670 N.W. 143 Avenue
Portland, OR 97229

Chapter Fifty-Two

Fern Strouse

Dear friends,

The Two-by-Two church seemed to be the answer to a great need in my life at age sixteen. My brother had been killed in World War II. The church gave me faith in God and the fellowship gave me family warmth that I lacked. My mother was Jehovah Witness and my father not religious.

At age 27, I saw a great need in the church and gave my life in the work for thirty years. I labored in North Dakota, Minnesota, Idaho, Montana, and Oregon. I don't regret having given my strength, years, and natural inheritances. I began asking those raised in the church how it was growing up with the rules, etc. Some told their story with bitter tears. I wish they would share it with all. While in Oregon two of my brothers died within three years apart—alcohol suicide. My professing doctor suggested I see a family counselor to cope with the pain. I also went to AA and Alanon and my overseer and companions knew what I was doing. Soon I was sent to Idaho, and next to Montana, farther and farther away from my doctor and source of help. It never dawned on me that there was serious objection going on behind my back. Next I was dumped on my home state, North Dakota. The overseer there kindly gave me a place in the work, however, there were spies on the job!! I couldn't continue as I lost faith in the operation of the system. I bailed out at age 59—got a live-in job right away (in Oregon). I also clean houses, so I'm doing great—hoping to have 40 credits for Social Security and Medicare by age 70. This means I work while others are in church. This does not mean I have turned my back on those who kindly supported me in the work. I haven't written an exit letter to the church. I didn't sign in to an earthly group, so why should I sign out?? If I can help, give me a call.

Love and care,
Fern Strouse

March 3, 1993

Address:
Fern Strouse
9725 S.W. Melnore
Portland, Oregon 97225

Chapter Fifty-Three

Kirby and Isabel Ward
A letter sent to a number of churches across Alberta.

If you aren't too concerned about the kind of Gospel that is preached or if you have little concern for results, then you probably won't want to read this letter or this book.

The Body of Christ is not a human organization arranged and supported by worldly powers. It is not sustained and nourished by secular influences. The true Church of the Lord Jesus Christ is the total company of *true* Christians of *all* churches, with the Lord Jesus as head!

The New Testament is not written to bring about unity, it is written to bring about truth. (Read II Timothy 4:3-4) God knows that when *we* get truth that is where the unity is, not the other way around. Preachers are not called to preach unity at any cost but "to preach the WORD." —II Timothy 4:2

It is impossible to always be positive while contending for the truth. Jude said we must earnestly contend for the faith. The faith means the whole body of revealed truth, and to contend for all of God's truth necessitates some negative teaching. Any error or any mixture of truth and error calls for definite exposure and repudiation. To condone such is to be unfaithful to God and His word, and treacherous to souls for whom CHRIST died. When a false doctrine of any stripe is transplanted into the kingdom, it must be stripped of its camouflage. *The TWO-BY-TWO DOCTRINE* is a FALSE ONE.

I sincerely believe in the coming day we are going to see clearly the distinction in that which man in his puny effort is trying to establish and that which is being built by the Holy Spirit. If anyone tries to accomplish His (the Lord's) work without fully realizing it is not I but *HE* who can accomplish this task, it will NOT work. Only those ministries whose work is totally consumed by the enabling power of God will stand after the shakings that all true ministries will go through.

I ask you who say, "OH YOU MUST LOVE THEM." What is Love? What is truth? If the two by two's don't find out the truth they are destined for HELL! Are we demonstrating love if we shelter people from truth?

"Am I therefore become your enemy because I tell you the truth?" Galatians 4:16. We may disagree on the non-essentials (such as the rapture, the evidence of the Holy Spirit and a host of doctrinal differences, *but* we must NEVER disagree on how to be saved. BY CHRIST ALONE. If you think you can be saved by works or denomination or any other way, like a combination of Christ and works, then JESUS CHRIST died in vain! I am forever thankful that Christ is my savior. He poured out HIS atoning blood on the cross for me and rose again the third day and is now at the right hand of the father interceding for me. PRAISE GOD! The Word tells us that the Holy Spirit will lead us into all truth and I trust HIM! And I trust the Word! The life is in the Word. OH YES HE IS!

I would ask anyone who is reading this letter to pray that the Lord will give you the opportunity to reach one of these deceived two by two cult members with the true Gospel message and *don't be fooled by their cover.*

We have shared this information with you because three and one-half years ago our daughter got involved with a fellow who has been raised under this lie and the hate is very evident. I do not need to tell you all the details as God is in control and His timing is always perfect! I would ask that you pray for our daughter and our three unseen grandchildren's safety and for their freedom. God is faithful and HIS joy and Love are truly sufficient.

We called many places before we were finally led to a couple who had some information on this group and since then we have never stopped searching. **Two-by-Two** members told us no one but them are Christian and you must have human agency (GO-PREACHER) for salvation. They also told us they go all the way back to Peter! (genealogy)

If you know of anyone who has been involved and is looking for information on the **Two-by-Two CULT**, please share the information you have on them with them. Thank you for sharing the LOVE OF CHRIST with others.

Address:
Kirby & Isabel Ward
Box 27, Blackfalds, Alberta
T0M 0J0

Poem sent by the Ward's:
BROKEN DREAMS
As children bring
their broken toys
with tears for us to mend,
I brought my broken dreams to God
because He was my Friend.

But then instead of leaving Him
in peace to work alone,

I hung around and tried to help
with ways that were my own.

At last I snatched them back and cried,
"How can You be so slow"—
"My child," He said,
"What could I do? You never did let go."

—Author Unknown

Chapter Fifty-Four

Georgia Wiens

Dear Friends,

First of all thank you for sending me the book, *The Secret Sect.* I have already read it, and enjoyed it very much. It is Thanksgiving Day in Canada today and there is so much to be thankful for. I feel that God has visited me and some of my family and delivered us from a life of captivity and bondage, and now I feel like I am truly worshipping and thanking God as I should.

There is so much to say that one can hardly say it all in a letter. My name is Georgia Weins. I professed to serve God in the "Two-by-Two" religion twelve years ago with my infant daughter in my arms. My sister and niece professed one year previous to me. I put my heart and soul into this faith, not realizing what a poor understanding I had of the doctrine. I feel I was coerced into trusting in this religion basically by the ministry. The workers appear so wise, pure and unselfish. The workers and friends were so friendly and full of flattery. Once rooted with the fear of God in you, they could more easily manipulate you with their ideas and standards.

I started to wonder about certain things about two years ago, but never felt comfortable in approaching any workers or elders about my questions. They feel if the Spirit of God is in you, that you should know the answers.

Their usual answer to any problems is to get to all your meetings and you will receive the answers. Most of the time, the meetings created more questions. For instance, if there is so much love and joy in God's true way, how come the people look so unhappy and uncomfortable with one another? A few months ago, I questioned a worker about her method of authority. I think I shocked her. She had an answer, but it wasn't very satisfying. It wasn't long before I felt the full extent of the word "reproach" in my meetings, by the friends. I am so glad that God had created in me a quiet spirit, as I could continue doing my honest part in meetings and felt only concern for the friends.

By this time in my professing life, my infant daughter is now grown and professing as well. I am in a "divided home," as my husband does not profess or my two teenage sons. We have had many gospel meetings in our home, and workers stay in our home. My family has always been kind and courteous to them. Professing families have not always had the same consideration for them. My brothers, sister and niece are still professing as well, at this time.

It was the first week of July of this year that my sister received an anonymous letter (by way of MacGregor Ministries in Nelson, British Columbia, Canada) from a concerned friend stating that she should examine the religion that she is in—that it is a cult. My sister (twin) and I are quite close and have been concerned about many things for some time. Friends and workers have a unique way of destroying your emotional system and making you very dependent on them. This letter seemed to have all the answers to the questions we were wondering about, but were too afraid to ask. The timing of the letter was perfect.

One week before convention, Carla (my sister) got the letter in the mail, read it, and picked up my niece twenty miles away and then proceeded to my house another forty miles away. They traveled thirty miles per hour as they feared God would cause an accident before they got to me. I was frantic before they got here, because I feared the same thing. Imagine the fear!!

We sat down together and came to some hard decisions. *1)* We would not go back to meetings or convention until we had investigated everything and felt satisfied our questions were answered. *2)* We would let the workers and elders know that we are investigating the "Truth," as we have been informed it is a cult. (Now this information sent the workers scrambling, as my brother informed me that if I had gone to convention all my answers would be there. The workers spent a lot of time talking about cult teaching and their origin.) *3)* We would go to pastors of other churches and find out about their doctrine.

Well, as the weeks have gone by, I am totally convinced the "Truth" is wrong. My sister and niece are going to a Baptist Church. I am going to a Mennonite Brethren Church with my daughter, and my husband and sons are starting to come as well. It has not been easy in many ways, as I left workers and friends behind that will be angry at me forever, because when I left I declared that they are a "cult." It has been an embarrassment to my brother and his family and many of my relatives still in the Sect. I am enjoying going to church now and feel refreshed and alive. Prayer is my greatest source of strength, as through the power of prayer I can only hope that I can help those left behind.

I will close this letter off now. A person could go on, and I do in my mind. My thoughts are always on the "Truth" as I try to rationalize every-thing. It's nice to hear of others who had the strength to leave as well. Bless you all, and may God be with you.

Take care,
Georgia Wiens

October 11, 1993

Chapter Fifty-Five

Oriana Wesley

I just received your letter. It was forwarded to my new address. I would like to tell you a bit about my experience with the 2x2s and how hard it's been since I left in about 1989.

I was raised in the "truth," but lived in a divided home. My mother was a third generation 2x2, and it now runs through to five generations on her side. It was extremely difficult to be in a divided home. It's almost like being a half-breed—neither side wants you and I grew up feeling like I wasn't worth squat to the "friends" or the "world." It's a real no-man's land. Being told you *have* to belong to this particular faith to be saved, and yet feeling that you aren't really wanted. The workers visited our home once a year, if we were lucky and no friends ever visited or extended invitations to their homes either. My dad was a very friendly person, so I can't say our exclusion was because the friends weren't welcome. I know of several other divided homes in this Prince George area that were treated the same. Needless to say, none of those kids are professing now. Or not many of them anyway.

I began to seriously question the validity of the "truth" when I turned thirteen. I just couldn't believe that this way had no earthly founder, even though the workers sternly admonished me that this questioning was WRONG. Unfortunately for me I had a very intellectual mind and I continued to question. I searched the Bible for answers and nowhere could I find any scriptural backing for all the rules we had to follow. I was forever in trouble with the workers for all my "misdemeanors." But I also felt so guilty for the things I'd do that I'd immediately run to the workers and "confess." Thus would begin another period of repentance—I'd have to quit taking part for a specified amount of time until the workers decided I'd repented enough. Talk about control!

I spent a lot of time in psychiatric wards as a young adult. I was diagnosed as everything from a schizophrenic to a manic-depressive. I'm sure much of my problems came from the confusion and conflicts I dealt with in the "truth." I went in and out of the "truth" so many times, I can't even count. I felt like a total failure and I developed an extreme fear of death that still rules my life today.

After I married, I sort of went in and out of the "truth." My husband is not, nor ever was, a 2x2. I never felt free, even if I wasn't actively "professing."

Then in abut 1985-86 I connected with Kathy Lewis and got a hold of the book *The Secret Sect*. It confirmed all the suspicions I had about the real origins of this sect. In a way it was a liberating experience, but I had to give the workers a chance to respond, so I began a canvas of the workers asking about the book. I got a different response from each one. Gail MacMurray is the only one who admitted that the book was true. But the others all tried to refute it, even saying that Gail didn't know what she was saying. So in 1989 I wrote an "exit" letter and officially left.

My life has been very hard since. I feel so ignorant of any real Bible knowledge and I found myself mixed up in another cult—the Mormons. Without any real knowledge of the Bible, or God's real plan of salvation, it is easy to be dragged into other cults. My need for rules to live by is still quite strong. And I feel very uneasy if I don't have someone to "guide" me spiritually. I don't trust my own understanding or knowledge. I know I should trust God to guide me, but I just feel so uneasy without a lot of guidelines to follow. I'm scared I won't be doing all I should to be saved. I'm struggling to understand and trust Christ's finished work on the cross for my salvation. It all just seems too easy somehow.

I find that I suffer from a religious "addiction" almost. I can't seem to settle into a church or seem to settle my beliefs. I just keep hopping around in an utter state of confusion. When I left the "truth" the workers came and basically put a curse on me, saying they hoped I'd come to the "end of myself" and realize I'd made a big mistake. Maybe that's what's happening. I feel as if I'm demon-possessed. I feel as if I'll never have spiritual peace. I feel that being in the 2x2s has ruined my chances for spiritual happiness. My mother, sister, brother and most of her side of the family is still in the 2x2s, and I sure feel alone. I've often considered going back to it just to feel accepted again, but then I say NO— I've fought so hard to come this far.

Well, that's it basically. If you can connect me up with someone who has come out of the 2x2s and resolved their issues, I would sure welcome some help. I feel so very confused and hopeless right now. Any help would be most welcome.

Yours truly,
Oriana Wesley

May 20, 1993

Chapter Fifty-Six

Dale and Joyce Wesenberg
Letter to the Friends

Some of you probably wonder where we stand. We hope this letter helps you to understand our position.

At present, we are examining ourselves—2 Corinthians 13:5 "Examine yourselves, whether ye be in the faith; prove your ownselves..." We are searching the scriptures—Acts 17:11 "These...in that they received the word with all readiness of mind, and searched the scriptures daily, whether those things were so." We are trying the spirits—1 John 4: 1-3 "Beloved, believe not every spirit, but try the spirits whether they are of God; because many false prophets are gone out into the world..."

After many years of observing that we did not have the love, victory, etc., we started to examine our own hearts. We could come to only one conclusion—we did not have Jesus. Instead of seeking the approval of God, we sought the approval of man. Instead of trusting in Jesus Christ, we trusted in a "way of fellowship." The results of this misplaced trust were: guilt, fear, discouragement, depression and bondage; ever working but never experiencing God's promise of spiritual fruit—Galatians 5:22-24 "...love, joy, peace, longsuffering, gentleness, goodness, faith, meekness, temperance..." We were forced to admit that we were not born again. John 3:7 "Marvel not that I say unto thee, ye must be born again."

With much prayer we began to make a deep study of the word of God. There are many places in the scripture where we are encouraged to know God's word. One such place is in 2 Timothy 3:15-16 "And that from a child thou has known the holy scriptures, which are able to make thee wise unto salvation through faith which is in Christ Jesus. All scripture is given by inspiration of God, and is profitable for doctrine, for reproof, for correction, for instruction in righteousness." We are comparing what we see, hear, and experience with the word of God.

Now we can say of Jesus, as in John 20:28 "And Thomas answered and said unto him. My Lord and my God." And in Titus 2:13 "Looking for that blessed hope, and the glorious appearing of the great God and our Saviour Jesus Christ."

We finally understand now that Jesus Christ is our substitute in life and in death. Ephesians 2:8,9 "For by grace are ye saved through faith; and that not of ourselves; it is the gift of God; not of works, lest any man should boast." Ephesians 2:13 "But now in Christ Jesus ye who sometimes were far off are made nigh by the blood of Christ." Galatians 6:14.

There are those who do understand true doctrine and are putting their faith in Jesus Christ. However, we are concerned for others who may have missed it as we did. It would be so easy to miss salvation by putting our trust in man, form, and works. We plead with you to search your hearts with all honesty, examine your priorities and motivation, then study God's word for yourselves.

We now experience a portion of love and victory never experienced before. 1 John 5:3-5 "For this is the love of God that we keep his commandments and his commandments are not grievous. For whatsoever is born of God overcometh the world: and this is the victory that overcometh the world even our faith. Who is he that overcometh the world but he that believeth that Jesus is the Son of God."

Galatians 5:24 "And they that are Christs have crucified the flesh with the affections and lusts."

Psalm 119:140 "Thy word is very pure; therefore thy servant loveth it."

Thank you to those who have shown us love and concern. Your prayers and encouragement are appreciated.

Your letters continue to be welcome.

With love in Him,

Dale & Joyce Wesenberg

Address:
Dale and Joyce Wesenberg
Box 143
Niton Junction, Alberta
TOE 1SO Canada

September, 1992

Chapter Fifty-Seven

Cindy Whaley

I am writing in response to the note you sent regarding exit letters from the "TRUTH." I do not harbor any bad feelings for the people who continue to participate in this religion. I am not interested in "bad mouthing" anyone. I have the deepest personal respect for many people in Oregon and in Utah who choose, for whatever reason, to continue in this way. I left for strictly personal reasons.

I found that I felt more discouraged and negative after meetings. I would go to a fellowship meeting feeling quite upbeat and hopeful, hopeful that I would be able to feel the spirit of God and that my faith would be increased. My experience is that the positive affirmations and personal considerations that my family and I experienced at one home was absent at the next home that we were "assigned" to attend. We were transferred without any incident or obvious reason, and certainly without being consulted.

I am aware of others who feel betrayed because of the lies regarding the origins of the group, etc. I could have overlooked the lies if I had felt that I was assisted in my search for spirituality. I became aware that I was in fact being hindered by the negativity of the group in the home where we were assigned.

August 31, 1993

Address:
Cindy Whaley
551 E. Cobblestone Dr.
Midvale, UT 84047

Chapter Fifty-Eight

Paul and Debbie White
A Letter to Family and Friends

The purpose of this letter is not to tear anyone down but to advise you of where Paul and I stand in our service to God. Over the last five years we have been increasingly more troubled by "the truth" since initially researching the origins of this way.

While this research answered many of the questions I have had my entire life about the beginnings of this way, it was not inconceivable to me that God could send a man to go and preach as Jesus sent his disciples. I reasoned that this way was the closest thing I had seen to how Jesus sent out the disciples. What has continued to trouble me more and more is conflicting scripture, dogmatism in lieu of clear thinking and sole reliance on men (workers).

I frequently come into contact with people who claim Christ as their Savior and live a Christian life. It has become impossible for me to believe those people are going to Hell because they don't attend meetings and know the workers.

Allowing God to deal with me and gradually unprogram myself has been a tedious task. I now feel as though I was in a very dark room with just barely enough light to survive. I can now see so many things through Christ, the joy and love in my heart are inexpressible. I now love to read my Bible and hear about the Word of God. All the previous duty and labor of serving God is gone.

I have come to realize that I can't put limits on God. We cannot work for salvation, it is a gift from God. Titus 3:5 "Not by works of righteousness which we have done, but according to his mercy he saved us..." Ephesians 2:8-9 "For by grace ye are saved through faith; and not of yourselves; it is the gift of God. Not of works, lest any man should boast." I no longer believe that there is a singular group of people who claim exclusive rights to salvation, but that there are right people in various ways. Salvation doesn't come through a particular way but rather through a personal relationship with Jesus. John 3:16 "Whosoever believeth in him should not perish but have everlasting life."

Paul and I have mutually decided that we can no longer serve God within the spiritual limits of this way. I have spent my whole life hearing that the way is perfect even if the people are not. We have come to realize that this way teaches reliance on men (workers), human centered reasoning, fosters false pride in being "right" and "the only way." John 14:6 "Jesus saith unto him, I am the way, the truth and the life: No man cometh unto the father but by me."

While we have not lost our faith in God, we have lost our faith in this way. I believe Jesus Christ is the way to heaven through belief and trust in Him. There are no perfect people and there is no perfect organized church. However, we feel there are other churches where worshipping God is central to their faith.

My intention in writing this letter is not to condemn or imply you are in a wrong way. I understand your beliefs and realize you will probably feel that we have never had "a good understanding" and are "losing out." For this I am sorry. We feel that we have never had such a clear understanding or love of God until now. The love I have for the friends and the workers has not changed. It is my hope that although you may not agree with what we are doing, that you will pray and read with an open mind.

Address:
Paul and Debbie White
10982 Tioga
Boise, ID 83709

Resources

More information is available through libraries and from the following sources:

Booksellers, USA
P.O. Box 1612
Richland, WA 99352
U.S.A.

Threshing Floor Ministries
P.O. Box 9899
Spokane, WA 99209
U.S.A.

Chrisian Research Inst.
Calgary, Alberta
Canada
T2M 4L7

MacGregor Ministries
Box 73
Balfour, British Columbia
Canada

Breda Centre
Glencregagh Court
Belfast, N. Ireland
BT6 OPA

Religion Analysis Service
P.O. Box 806
Brainerd, MN 56401-0806
U.S.A.

Positive Action Centre
P.O. Box 99-758
Newmarket
Auckland
New Zealand

Written Materials Available Include:

The Secret Sect by Doug and Helen Parker. Accurate and well-documented history of this sect.

The Church Without a Name by David Stone. Explanation of major doctrines of the Two-by-Two church, and how they have affected the personal lives of friends and workers alike.

Reinventing the Truth by Kevin N. Daniel. A look at the historical claims and rationalizations put forward by notable Two-by-Twos to justify their origins, doctrines and apostolic form of ministry.

A Search for the Truth by Lloyd Fortt. A wide-ranging work, focusing chiefly on exposing the group's deceptive terminology and the doctrines behind it.

Impartial Reporter and Farmer's Journal. Eyewitness newspaper reports of the original doctrines and founding of this movement during the period of 1903-1917.

They Go About Two by Two by William E. Paul. A short booklet describing unique aspects of the group.

No Name Fellowship by Carol Woster. A short, overall description of the group.

The Encyclopedia of American Religions —Third or later editions. A very general description, interesting mainly due to the group's lack of recent coverage in relevant reference works.